PLAYING WITH NATURE

To my friend

PROFESSOR RANJAN CHAKRABARTI

who had introduced me to the
wonderful world of environment

Playing with Nature

HISTORY AND POLITICS OF ENVIRONMENT IN NORTH-EAST INDIA

Edited by
SAJAL NAG

Routledge
Taylor & Francis Group
LONDON AND NEW YORK

First published 2018
by Routledge
4 Park Square, Milton Park, Abingdon, Oxon OX14 4RN

and by Routledge
605 Third Avenue, New York, NY 10017

First issued in paperback 2023

Routledge is an imprint of the Taylor & Francis Group, an informa business

Publisher's Note
The publisher has gone to great lengths to ensure the quality of this reprint but points out that some imperfections in the original copies may be apparent.

Print edition not for sale in South Asia (India, Sri Lanka, Nepal, Bangladesh, Afghanistan, Pakistan or Bhutan).

British Library Cataloguing in Publication Data
A catalogue record for this book is available from the British Library

Library of Congress Cataloging in Publication Data
A catalog record for this book has been requested

ISBN 13: 978-1-138-28063-2 (hbk)
ISBN 13: 978-1-03-265247-4 (pbk)
ISBN 13: 978-1-315-27188-0 (ebk)

DOI: 10.4324/9781315271880

Typeset in ITC Galliard Std 10/12
by Manohar, New Delhi 110 002

MANOHAR

Contents

Preface

Until recently, the global concern over environment did not seem to have reached north-east India. There was a strange complacency about the deteriorating environmental conditions. Environmental history too was an almost unheard of discipline in the universities of the region. There were just three available works in the field. A.C. Sinha, *Beyond the Trees, Tigers and Tribes: Historical Sociology of the Eastern Himalayan Forests* (1993), Arupjyoti Saikia, *Jungle, Reserves and Wildlife: A History of Forests in Assam* (2005), Rajiv Handique, *British Forest Policy in Assam* (2004). All of them were on forest history. I had just published a work *Pied Pipers in North-East India: Bamboo Flowers, Rat Famine and Politics of Philanthropy 1881-2007* (2008).

The time coincided with my meeting with some renowned environmental historians of India which prompted me to understand the urgency of introducing this subject to my university in the Master's and Doctoral level. This was the background on which I organized an international seminar on Environmental History of North-East India in 2010 with financial assistance from Indian Council of Historical Research, New Delhi and Maulana Abul Kalam Azad Institute of Asian Studies, Calcutta. It was attended by environmental historians of repute from different parts of India and abroad. Not only the participants but the students seemed immensely impressed by the scope and coverage of environmental history. The acute need for reading material on the subject for north-east India was sought to be covered by the publication of the seminar proceedings. As such scholars were requested to revise their respective papers and send it back for publication. Not all the contributions in the seminar were on north-east India. Hence it was decided to publish two volumes instead. One dealing with north-east India and the other with rest of India. The papers in this volume are revised versions of essays on north-east India. The due process took long but the final result, it is hoped, will be worthwhile. It will provide the much needed reading material for environmental history of north-east India and encourage universities of the region to now introduce the subject in their curriculum.

Thanks are due to the two funding agencies as well as my colleagues in the Department of History, Assam University, Silchar and Diphu Campus, Dr. Eshwar Rao, Dr. Suryasikha Pathak, Dr. Jangkhomang Guite, Dr. Habibullah Mazumdar, Dr. Binayak Dutta, and my students Dr. Debojit De, Dr. Debasish Roy and Dr. Mahbubur Rahman Laskar who worked tirelessly to make the seminar successful. The Association for South Asian Environmental Historians was one of the co-organizers. My friend Prof. Ranjan Chakrabarti of Jadavpur University, Kolkata helped me in organizing the seminar in various ways. In the editorial and publication process I received utmost support from my publisher Ramesh Jain of Manohar. Siddharth Chowdhury saw it through to the press. My most sincere gratitude to all of them.

Silchar, 2016 SAJAL NAG

Introduction

SAJAL NAG

North-east India is called nature's gift to India. It is mountainous, thickly forested, nourished by abundant rainfall, massive rivers, has a diverse wildlife, inhabited by a number of forest dwellers called tribes who have through the ages cherished an environmentalist ethos. Yet environmental history in north-east India has yet to take off. The region has been experiencing environmental depletion which was a result of colonial policies, exploitation of its ecological and mineral resources, large-scale trans-border immigration and settlement of people, establishment of plantation industry through deforestation, dependence of dairy industry on grazing and so on. Yet people of the region did not realize the dangerous stage the state of its environment has reached. There was no environmental activism, state turned a deaf ear to the little protests that emerged and violating the traditional tribal ethics favouring environment certain individuals and cartels ruthlessly exploited and devastated the environment of the region. It took the Supreme Court verdict to halt the rampant destruction of whatever little was left of the woods and a National Green Tribunal intervention to halt the unscientific mining of coal which had not just polluted the air and water bodies of the Kopili Valley but spelt doom for the entire region.

OMINOUS SIGNS

The first ominous signs of the impact of global climatic change on north-east India were the long dry spells over the region even during monsoon period. The entire north-east, climatically, falls within the high rainfall zone. Drought has been virtually unknown to the region. Rather it was the devastating flood and inundation that was characteristic of the region. Ironically in the Copenhagen conference in 2009 it was Assam's flood that was discussed as part of the discussion of the impact of climate change over South Asia.[1] In fact, the year 2008 Assam was declared by the state as 'drought affected'. In the same year, however, there was flood surprisingly in the month of October when monsoon was already over. The irregularity and irrational behaviour of the monsoon was beginning to be evident. The city of Gauhati has been experiencing massive dust storms during March-April every year for the past about three years; the intensity of it was increasing every year. The dust storm was so severe that it brought life to a standstill. Massive dust covers made it difficult to see through within the range of few metres. It stopped pedestrians on the way; vehicular traffic came to a halt and air traffic was disrupted for almost a week. Schools were declared shut for days and life was halted periodically during such storms. Such dust storms were characteristic of only a desert area, not a hilly rainfall area. The people of Assam now began to expect it every year around March-April. Similarly, the highest rainfall spot of the world, Cherrapunji, was experiencing spells of dry seasons frequently. Climatologists had already been discussing and monitoring the rainfall. They observed that the average rainfall decline was not much, there were severe dry spells in some years. Deficit of rainfall coupled with massive shortage of potable water had become a problem for the people of Cherrapunji who were used to living in a high rainfall zone. The acuteness of the problem had been understood when Cherrapunji was declared to be no longer the recipient of highest rainfall and a nearby village Mawsyram was declared to be that spot. Soon even that shifted to a place in South America. Cherrapunji is now battling not only to come to terms with the lost glory but also manage its drinking water problem.[2]

Nearby Cherrapunji, there was another hill station called Jatinga which was known for strange bird behaviour. By the end of the monsoon, around October-November every year birds used to fly in massive numbers at night attracted by the flame of the torch that villagers used to light whereupon they used to be caught and killed by the villagers. Jatinga therefore came to be known as the place of suicidal birds which tourists visited to observe the phenomenon and ornithologist visited to study the phenomenon. It was believed that these birds were migratory who used to be confused by the lit torches as dawn and flew into the burning flames. But for the past several years despite the best effort of the government and people to attract the birds, birds had not been visiting Jatinga. It is believed due to the change in the climate the birds have changed their migratory routes. Similarly Lakes known as 'pats' in Manipur play a vital role in the socio-economic and cultural life of Manipur.[3] Wetlands cover nearly 2.37 per cent of Manipur's total geographical areas. There are about 155 wetlands of which 153 are located in the central valley of Manipur. Loktak the largest fresh water lake in north-eastern India, which includes 4 tiny wetlands like Sanapat, Laphupat, Thaunamchapat, Utrapat and Keibul Lamjao floating park covers an area of 24,672 ha during monsoon. Most of them are on the verge of extinction and fast disappearing. Meanwhile another threat has emerged in recent times. Hurricane like strong tropical winds which was presumed to have been originated from Arab countries have started to reach Manipur in between April-May every year from 2008. This has uprooted standing crops in hundreds of hectares besides destroying houses in the last three years. In contrast floods have become regular occurrence from the same year during October-November when the monsoon had long gone. It was a clear sign of climate change palpably observed by common people not just the experts and climatologists.

As a result of global warming and climate change, glaciers in the Himalayas are retreating at an average rate of 15 m per year which is found to be inconsistent with the rapid warming recorded at the Himalayan climate stations since the 1970s.[4] The famous Gangotri glacier, the head stream of river Ganga has been receding at a rate of 28 m per year. The impact of such receding of glaciers are manifold. Under a warming environment the Himalayan glaciers are expected to melt faster leading to increased summer flows and flooding initially for a few decades following by progressive reduction in flow as the river feeding glaciers recede and disappear from the headstreams. The scientific community already warned about the consequence as widespread water scarcity due to decrease of glacial contribution in the river basins like those of the Indus, the Ganga and the Brahmaputra river system (known as Yarlung Jhangbo in Tibet, China) and some its tributaries like the Subansiri and the Jia-Bharali are partly fed by snow melt run off. Such prediction further compounds our anxiety knowing the fact the summer monsoon rainfall is found to be decreasing significantly over the north-eastern region of the country during the last century at an approximate rate of 11 mm per decade. At this stage an effort to relate such predictions of the scientific community with some of the recent cyclic events of natural calamity in this region seems to be a meaningful exercise. The case of immense draught in Assam in the year 2005 and 2006 may be mentioned here as a reference point. It had created havoc in the life of agricultural community as more than 75 per cent of the 26 million people of the state of Assam are associated with agriculture for their livelihood.

The IPCC Report of 2007 also justified it as a signature of climatic change as rainfall in the region witnessed nearly 40 per cent below normal.[5] Other states of the region also received rainfall 30-40 per cent below their normal rainfall except for Mizoram. Apart from the incidence of draught the region also witnessed the incidence of devastating flash floods resulting from cloud bursts in recent times. As a point of reference it can be mentioned that in 2004 two devastating flash floods in Goalpara and Sonitpur district of Assam bordering Meghalaya and Arunachal Pradesh were caused by cloud bursts of unprecedented intensity. One in the western part of Meghalaya hill and the other in the western part of Arunachal Pradesh. This flood flash of 2004 caused scores of deaths in these districts of Assam. Again in 2008 Lakhimpur district of Assam suffered flash flood as rivers of Ranganadi, Singra, Dikrong and Kakoi overflowed and thus resulting in the death of about 20 people and inundating more than 50 villages leading to the displacement of 10,000 people. Of course the cause of the flood was sudden downpour in the hills of Arunachal Pradesh. In this context it is important to remind that the scientific community already predicted that with climatic change there could be formations of more glacial lakes in Nepal, Bhutan and Tibet Himalayas and thereby lead to increasing glacial outburst of floods. Similar to this the incident of landslides in the upland river courses in the Himalayan region may cause formation of landslide dams. There may be more frequent flash floods in the downstream with greater devastating power resulting from outburst of such dams in the days ahead.

Now it is a popular perception in the north-east of India that climatic cycles do not follow the earlier pattern, rather marked by irregular rainfall pattern with rainfall starting quite early and flash floods becoming more frequent and dry period becoming longer in different parts of this region. Understandably the impact of such climatic changes on agriculture are manifold as it adversely affects sowing and harvesting of crops thus thrashing the life of millions in a vulnerable situation in this region.

People in north-east India have been experiencing the impact of these changes. Here winters have shortened, there is decrease of rainfall, increase in heat waves, rise in temperatures and decrease of migratory birds. The deficit in rainfall and increasing temperature has been immensely noticeable in the region for past few years.

The maximum temperature in Guwahati was 2 to 6 °C above normal in June 2009, 2 to 5 °C above normal in July and 3 to 6 °C

TABLE 1: RAINFALL DEFICIT IN NORTH-EASTERN STATES IN 2009[6]

State	*Actual Rainfall (in mm)*	*Normal Rainfall*	*Percentage of Departure*
Nagaland	681.8	344.1	49
Meghalaya	3,148.0	5,585.7	44
Arunachal Pradesh	1,248.9	1,834.9	32
Manipur	615.9	839.3	27
Mizoram	1,086.6	1,345.1	19
Assam	1,180.3	1,434.1	18
Tripura	1,348.2	1,476.6	9

above normal in September. In August the maximum temperature was below normal. Similar pattern was observed throughout the past three years in the region.

Traditional subsistence economies and access and availability of water are directly impacted. Cherrapunji of Meghalaya, once the world's wettest place is increasingly facing water shortage. Umiam Lake is facing water shortage due to limited rainfall. The trend of floods in Assam and Meghalaya has become increasingly unpredictable and severe in impact. Climatologists have confirmed steady decrease in rainfall in the region. Mizoram witnessed increasing dry spells and many springs and streams are drying up with large scale landslides. Natural wetlands were shrinking in many parts of the region. Dipor Bil in Guwahati and Chatla Hawar in Cachar are glaring examples. In Manipur the year 2007 show two devastating floods, first one at the onset of spring and the second one at the end of summer both leading to crisis in food production. Interestingly the year 2009 is drought with rains coming almost at the end of the monsoon. Already floods had marred the state twice in the year 2010. One in June and the other in September-October. Salt water intrusions on fresh water supplies caused by higher water levels of Bay of Bengal and the contamination and reduction of ground water, extinction of endangered species of plants and animals will also be some of the impact on north-east.

DEFORESTATION AND CLIMATIC CHANGE: THE INTERRELATIONSHIP

Although climate change are a global phenomenon and has global reasons, Ozone layer depletion, are responsible for it, local reasons are no less important. For example, during the last three years, 2007-9, there have regular sand storms in Assam, mainly in Gauhati during February and March. It is strange that a city which has the mighty Brahmaputra running through it has dust storm of such intensity. In 2009 it was so bad that it was like a thick fog in the middle of the day and nothing was visible within a distance of 12 ft because of the dust. Flights had to be cancelled continuously for one full week. It was reported that the dust storm was generated from surrounding hills of Gauhati, mainly the Khasi hills, which were completely denuded of its green cover. Without the trees, the dry grass cover was further exposed to sunlight and forest fire. Jhumming practices made it worse

TABLE 2: DISTRIBUTION OF RECORDED FOREST AREA IN THE NER AS PER STATE FOREST REPORT 2003[7]

(area in sq km)

State	*Reserved Forest Cover*	*Protected Forest Cover*	*Unclassed Forest*	*Total Forest Areas*
Arunachal Pradesh	10,178	9,535	31,826	51,540
Assam	18,060	–	8,958	27,018
Manipur	1,467	4,171	11,780	17,418
Meghalaya	1,112	12	8,372	9,496
Mizoram	7,909	3,568	5,240	16,717
Nagaland	308	508	7,813	8,629
Tripura	5,452	389	–	5,841
All India	3,99,919	2,38,434	1,36,387	7,74,740

TABLE 3: LOSS OF FOREST COVER IN 2003 ASSESSMENT COMPARED TO 2001

(area in sq km)[8]

State	*Loss due to shifting cultivation*	*Loss due to Other reasons*	*Total*	*Gain due to natural Regeneration & other reasons*	*Net Change (loss or gain*
Arunachal Pradesh	925	256	1,181	155	-26
Assam	609	2,086	2,695	2,807	112
Manipur	855	108	963	1,256	293
Meghalaya	684	71	755	2,010	1,255
Mizoram	687	900	1,587	2,523	936
Nagaland	1,332	57	1,389	1,653	264
Sikkim	–	–	–	69	69
Tripura	384	1	385	1,413	1,028
All India	5,476	3,479	8,955	12,886	3,931

by burning the dry forests. As a result the dry soil cover of the hills were dustified and blown away by February winds which is strong in the region generating the dust storm. The north-east has a substantial part of India's remaining forests. According to some estimates somewhere around one-third of India's forest resources is to be found in the region. The official figures speak of forest cover of 80 per cent of the total geographical area. But there is an alarming rate of forest loss estimated to about 8 per cent annually. The Brundland Commission says worldwide we lose about 11 million acres yearly. The Indian north-east situation is of equal alarm.

The north-eastern region is not only undulating and a terrain trodden with a spread over of all types of rock from sedimentary to metamorphic, it also has objectionable land gradient at many places. Hence it is absolute necessary to preserve its top soil cover at any cost. The Cherrapunji region has already been termed as the wet desert. The hilly part of the region would in no way be able to protect or preserve its top soil under the impact of mega rainfall unless there is adequate green coverage in the concerned areas. Hence deforestation of the region would be synonymous with desertification as is evident from the table below:

TABLE 4: CHANGES IN FOREST COVER IN NORTH EAST INDIA DURING THE 1990S

(in sq km)[9]

States	*1990-1*	*1993-5*	*1995-7*	*1997-9*	*Net Gain (+)/ Loss (-)*
Arunachal Pradesh	-96	-40	-19	+245	+90
Assam	-243	-447	-237	-136	-1,063
Manipur	-64	-63	-140	-34	-301
Meghalaya	-106	-55	-57	-24	-242
Mizoram	-156	-121	-199	-437	-757
Nagaland	+27	-57	-70	-57	-157
Tripura	+3	0	+8	+199	+210
Total	-635	-783	-316	-278	-2,220

Source: Zahid Hussein (ed.), *Environmental Issues of North East India*, 2003, p. 199.

Hence arresting deforestation and spreading plantation and other agrarian activities in the possible deforested parts of the region are two most fundamental propositions to be realized in practice at all cost in the NER to save the region, particularly the hilly areas. The deforestation issue took a critical turn and the apex court of the country had to intervene.

TABLE 5: LAND COVER CHANGES AROUND SOHRA (CHERRAPUNJI) FROM 1910 TO 2002[10]

Land cover	*1910*		*1966*		*2002*		*Annual rates of change (%)*	
	sq km	*%*	*sq km*	*%*	*sq km*	*%*	*1910-66*	*1966-2002*
Forest	6.46	12.12	3.80	7.13	2.63	4.92	-0.09	-0.06
Grassland	45.49	85.37	46.94	88.08	45.53	85.44	0.05	-0.07
Agriculture	0.16	0.30	0.00	0.00	–	–	-0.01	–
Built up area	1.18	2.21	2.32	4.36	4.55	8.54	0.04	0.12
Quarry	–	–	0.23	0.43	0.58	1.10	–	0.02

In Nagaland out of the total land areas of 16,57,900 ha, forest occupied an area of approximately 8,62,930 acres. The forest cover as per forest survey of India for the year 2003, was 82.09 per cent. In 1998 it was 85.43 per cent. In five years there was a decrease of 3 per cent of dense forest.[11] Both Nagaland and Meghalaya administration could do nothing about the decreasing forest cover as more than 90 per cent land was not under its jurisdiction. Because of scheduled area provisions Meghalaya state has control only over 4 per cent of its forest land and Nagaland only 11 per cent. At the same time to improve the situation the forest cover needed to be increased to over 60 per cent which seemed an impossibility. The receding forest cover in the north-east as was recorded in 2003 is as follows:[12]

TABLE 6: FOREST AREA IN THE NORTH-EASTERN STATES

States	*Geographic Area*	*Recorded Forest Area*	*Percentage of Forest Area*	*Forest Cover*	*Percentage of Forest Cover*
Arunachal Pradesh	83,743	51,540	61.55	68,019	81.22
Assam	78,438	27,018	34.45	27,826	35.48
Manipur	22,327	17,418	78.01	27,826	77.12
Meghalaya	22,429	9,496	42.34	16,839	75.08
Mizoram	21,081	16,717	79.30	18,430	87.42
Nagaland	16,579	8,629	52.05	13,609	82.09
Sikkim	7,096	5,841	82.31	3,262	45.97
Tripura	10,486	6,293	60.01	8,093	77.18
All India	32,87,263	7,74,740	23.57	6,78,333	20.64

The Supreme Court of India issued an interim order on 12 December 1996. The judicial intervention surely helped in conserving the bio-diversity and forest cover in the region. Ultimately the Supreme Court disposed off the writ petition by passing an order on 15 January 1998. The judgement clearly states that the felling of trees will be controlled by the government and local requirements will be met through conservation and maintenance of environment and ecology. But this is not enough. More accountability of Forest and Enviroment Department is essential. There is the consistent threat to forest from the *jhum* (swidden cultivation) or shifting cultivation which is widely practised all over north-east India. Despite efforts from the respective state governments, *jhum* is still the most prevalent agricultural practice in the region. The effect of this practice in depletion of forests is all but visible. Miles after miles of hills look barren, dry and bereft of any vegetation at all.

TABLE 7: SHIFTING CULTIVATION IN NE REGION[13]

States	*Annual area under shifting cultivation in sq km*	*Fallow period in years*	*Minimum area under shifting cultivation One time or the other in sq km*	*No. of families practising shifting cultivation*
Arunachal Pradesh	700	3-10	2,100	54,000
Assam	696	2-10	1,392	58,000
Manipur	900	4-7	3,600	70,000
Meghalaya	530	5-7	2,650	52,290
Mizoram	630	3-4	1,890	50,000
Nagaland	190	5-8	1,913	1,16,046
Tripura	223	5-9	1,115	43,000

According to an expert committee recommendation,

> All the states in NER should raise forest protection force for conservation of forests. The demand and supply gap of forest produce has to be narrowed down through alternative sources of non-conventional energy as a substitute of fuel wood ... the shifting cultivation has to be checked though terracing and semi-tangua system ... local people have to be conceived to grow bamboo which grows very quickly and can be used by handicraft artisans similar to China.

In fact, 61 out of the 127 species of bamboo are available in India and most of them are indigenous to the north-east. According to experts, the world has identified bamboo as the material for the future. Germany is doing research to find ways to extract fuel from bamboo while China and Japan are trying to utilize bamboo as a source of charcoal. The reduction in soil erosion through aforestation/ plantation/vegetation, in turn, would reduce siltation in the rivers down below in the valley areas there by diminishing this disastrous impact of flood in the region in sustained manner.

CLIMATE CHANGE AND FOOD SECURITY

Climate change has slowly begun to tell on us. It has attacked our food security. Unseasonal rains with great wind speeds especially at a time of ripening of rice and other crops followed by long spells of dry weather when it should be raining has devastated farmers. They can no longer depend on weather. Sensing the change in climate and in an attempt to adapt to this changing climate the farmers have stopped growing traditional indigenous crops because they do not yield as much as they used to. So under the auspices of Agricultural department they have now begun growing more exotic crops in controlled conditions. But whether this coping mechanism affects bio-diversity is a study not yet conducted. In most areas the cropping patterns were of rice cultivation twice in a year. Sali, a variety of rice was sown in the monsoon while Boro, the other variety was sown in winter after harvesting the former.

In Meghalaya for instance strawberries have become the horticulture crop of choice because they have a ready market and grow well in some of the warmer areas of the state. Another favourite crop is Jatropa – the bio diesel crop which is supposed to augment fuel needs of the country. Using fertile lands for this crop could seriously imperil the state's food security. But this shift from food crops to horticultural crops also means that the state now has to depend on neighbouring states even for the normal vegetables that it used to produce for its own use and even for export in the past. Meghalaya grew potato, cabbage, cauliflower, beans and peas beside other vegetables. Now farmers in large parts of the state complained that the pea plantation has been badly hit by sudden thunder storms which came at a time when the plant was flowering and required a month of sunny weather with light rains. Strong gales destroyed the flowers and there was very little crop. In the plains of Meghalaya farmers have shifted to tomato cultivation beside many other hybrid vegetables. However, thankfully they continue to grow the traditional crop of ginger and turmeric and it is hoped they would not shift from this yet. However, everything is not honky dory with the farmers. North-east supports 63 per cent of the country's green cover. But it is slowly depleting because of mining and other commercial activities. All minerals are located under virgin forests. But the Ministry of Environment and Forests continue to clear mining licenses without setting guidelines for the miners. So the rivers of Jaintia hills have been poisoned from effluents such as sulpheric acid draining out of coal mines reducing the ph content of water to 3 and 3.7 per cent making it highly acidic for human consumption. Traces of arsenic have also been already found in the water of the area. The shift to alternative crops leading to large-scale depletion of forests has another dimension. The state sponsores support towards cash crop production. The Rashtriya Krishi Vigyan Yojana (RKVY) excludes forestry, wildlife and plantation when particularly the two forestry and plantation are not only very important for NER but the exclusion of the two a huge area as well as a very very important agro industry like tea, coffee, rubber and bamboo would go out of its provision. So the inclusion of plantation with the RKVY as a special incentive to the region would increase the area coverage under agriculture and that in turn would only be a direct boost to the NER states for enhancement of plantation but would also increase the overall allocation of RKVY for the NER states:

TABLE 8: AREA UNDER PLANTATION IN NORTH-EASTERN REGION IN HECTARES[14]

States	*Area under tea in 2002*	*Area under rubber in 2002-3*	*Area under coffee in 2003-4*	*Total areas*
Arunachal Pradesh	2,250	372	1,009.00	3,631.00
Assam	2,70,163	13,208	2,093.70	2,85,464.70
Manipur	950	1,708	102.00	2,760.00
Meghalaya	370	4,586	2,053.50	7,009.50
Nagaland	1,270	2,087	3,418.00	6,775.00
Tripura	6,700	28,853	1,267.85	36,820.85
Mizoram	400	696	1,006.50	2,102.50
Sikkim	300	–	–	300.00
Total Area	2,82,403	51,510	10,950.55	3,44,863.55

No doubt that large-scale deforestation of north-east started in the colonial period itself. The major reasons of such deforestation were reported to be wasteland settlement for increase of agricultural lands/revenue purposes, immigration and clearing of new forest land for their settlement, wasteland grant and clearing of jungles for tea plantation, large-scale export of timber to Europe and America by the colonial state, clearing of forests for creating grazing reserves, cash crop production, introduction of railways and to meet its increasing demands for laying of tracks, use of timber for packaging of tea leaves, slash and burn cultivation by the indigenous population. Surprising, a re-look at the above discussion would show that, most of the same reasons are at work even now to cause deforestation in the region and the consequent havoc in climatic cycles.

Mining of coal, limestone and petroleum in north-east India started with the British. No one would believe that there was once petroleum mining in Cherrapunji but the colonial extraction has taken the last drop of it from these hills. Little bit of coal is still available which is going to be exhausted soon through systematic rat hole mining. As coal in cherrapunji was getting exhausted, people discovered coal in Jaintia hills and part of Garo hills. Since the area is under the jurisdiction of Sixth Schedule of the Indian Constitution, outsiders could not mine here. The local landowners were thrilled at the discovery of black gold mine under their land. Thus started a spell of coal extraction through unscientific rat hole mining. While a number of these non-descript hills soon became stinking rich through the sale of coal, the hills were soon denuded of their forests. The green hills soon turned black as if it were black washed. Water bodies and rivers turned poisonous. Bodies of millions of dead fishes began to surface till the rivers were denuded of all its life forms. Soon the rivers like Myntodu and Leshka too dried up and rivers turned into long dry canals – dumping ground of garbage. These were declared dead rivers. It was at this point, at the complaints of Dimasa organizations, All Dimasa Student Association, the National Green Tribunal intervened and stopped the coal mining. The mine owners were aghast as to how dare the NGT do such a thing in an area which is under Sixth Schedule and how dare the Dimasas – tribe of Assam, not even inhabitants of the state of Meghalaya, complain against coal mining in another state? The answers being that the NGT being a Super State Environment regulating body did have the power to impose a ban on mining which affected the environment. As far as Dimasa were concerned, though they were a tribe living in the neighbouring state of Assam, they do live along the valley of Kopili river. The Dimasa inhabiting these villages earned their livelihood from the river and the pollution of the river had not only affected their livelihood, even potable water had become scarce due to massive poisoning of the river. Gradually the Dimasa began to leave the Kopili Valley and deserted their villages. It was due to such environment related displacement resulting from pollution upstream due to coal mining that the Dimasa bodies took the cause with the NGT. Even some Jaintian villages are Borkhat, Natbor, Kwator, Dem Lakang, Pdeng Wah Khynriam, Kharkhana, Pasadwar, Lumpyngngad, Kamsing, Jalia Khala, Sangkhat and Tongseng, Sakhri, Sunappyrdi, Shymplong, Lejri, Bosara, Kuliang suffered the same fate. For so long the villages which are precariously located on steep hills and very close to the rivers earn their livelihood from betel nuts and betel (*pan*) leaf plantation and fishing. But for people downstream of Lukha, their worst nightmare began in February 2007 when the river turned blue and killed every living being in the water. And the people downstream of the river Myntdu still remember with great sorrow the summer of 1984 when the water from uphill laced with poison killed hundreds and thousands of fishes of all shapes and sizes. If one visits the area one can even see the telltale signs of the Acid Mine Drainage (AMD) on the banks of these rivers as the rocks, sands and pebbles on the entire stretch of the rivers has a rusty colour. Even if one takes a handful of sand from the river one can see tiny coal particles mixed with sand when one opens one's palm. Pollution of the river is due to coal mining and evidences that can be seen even to naked eyes are all over the place. The people in these villages used to have a very close relationship with the rivers; they fish, they bathe, and wash in the rivers and they know all the fishes by their names. For them Myntdu, Lukha and Kupli are not just rivers, they are part of their lives but that's all gone now. They have not only lost their livelihoods to mining; in the process part of their culture has also gradually faded away with the dead rivers. Such phenomenon are quite common in north-east India which is not reported either in the media or environmental reporting. There is a necessity that such phenomenon are historicized and put in historical perspective so that it attracts intervention from the state or activists. There is an urgency that the historical process that led to the environmental degradation is investigated so that measures could be taken to prevent further devastation of the environment of the region. This collection of papers cover some of the themes related to the environment of north-east India that need in-depth understanding, comprehension and intervention.

The collection opens with a paper by Rila Mukherjee. In her paper entitled 'India's North-East: An Enigmatic Absence in History and Cartography' points out that the term 'North-east India' is a relatively recent one. This paper is basically an introduction to the geography and climatic history of the region which subsequently came to be known as north-east India. Her study is on the basis of six cartographic maps, prepared by the classical European geographers and scholars, who were eager to a locate both India and China, the two lands of the Orient with which the Roman world had developed a flourishing trade relationship. The paper contended that the earliest foreign texts referred to this region in diverse terms and perceptions. While the first perception of the area was in terms of limits. In this context reference was made of the perception of this region by Eratosthenes between 276 BC-195 BC, where he referred to a region 'Thina' which was the easternmost limit of the known earth, the second perception was built in terms of geographic location. Reference was made of Strabo who wrote about the area in term of distances; it was clear that the area was not familiar to him. The other scholar was Pliny who too talked of Thina. For him, this region was China, from where silk was procured for the Roman Empire. The next scholar, referred to was Arrian, who in 140 CE spoke of Sinae or Thinae as the 'people on the remotest part of Asia'. The notion of the north-eastern region as a limit of the known world was also re-emphasized in the writings of Ptolemy, the greatest geographer of the early world, who asserted Eratosthenes notion of Thina being the last known eastern most limit. Reference was also made to this region, in classical works of this region, in terms of the people inhabiting this region. In this context, the presentation made a reference to the *Periplus*, which referred to the region through the term 'Thinae' which, contrary to popular perception was just not China, but the entire area between India, north Burma and south-west China, a reference which has led some historians to interpret Thinae as the ancient kingdom of Kamarupa or Pragjyotisha which, according to the *Periplus* was the home of the Kirradoi (which has been claimed to indicate the Bodos). The presentation concluded with a final reference to the 'notion of the limit' which was the most powerful concept associated with this region, as a land sandwiched between the two expansive powers – India and China.

The article 'Marsh, Rice, Religion: Aspects of Environmental and Religious Changes in the Early Medieval Surma Valley' is by Birendra Nath Prasad. Commencing his presentation with a critique of Richard

Eaton's work on the 'Rise of Islam in the Eastern Frontier', Prasad argues that it is a singularly significant work in shaping academic perceptions about the region and its social and natural environment. He argues that for centuries, one of the major dynamics of Indian History has been the concrete attempt of the population of the 'areas of attraction' to expand agrarian frontiers into 'areas of relative isolation' and areas of isolation. With reference to significant epigraphic records he deals with the expansion of agrarian frontiers into this region of Barak-Surma Valleys. Forward movement of agrarian frontiers was, according to Prasad, accompanied by significant environmental, socio-economic and cultural changes, in this area under study. In his words, the extension of *janapada* had an adverse impact on the jungle. The paper deals at length on the various grants made to temples and the impact of the agency of temples on the transformation of forest land. In an analysis that traverses through a detailed reading of five copper-plate inscriptions, the presentation concludes with an analysis of the impact of this expansion of *janapadas* and settlement of population into forest areas on the relationship between the settlers and the tribals.

The paper entitled 'Man, Nature and State in Pre-Colonial Kachar' by Bazlur Rahman Khan. The article studies the intimate relationship between man and nature, and Kachar presented no exception. The presentation traced the history of the period between 1752 and 1832, i.e. period which marks the arrival of the Dimasa Kachari ruling family to the plains of the Kachar district to the period of its 'annihilation', by the British. The author highlighted that till the shifting of the capital of the Kachari kingdom to Khaspur, Kachar was a land of forests and swamps and a hotbed of disease. It was this hostile environment that made human settlement in this area sparse and made the natural world unexplored. The paper attempts to establish the factum of the balanced relationship between man and nature in the period under study. Making an overview of the geographical diversity of Kachar, the paper examines the impact of geography on man in this area. Rahman also highlights the impact of natural elements on the development of human settlement, its expansion into new, till then uninhabited areas and the impact of nature on the pattern of human settlements and the various customs and practices that developed in Kachar, with regard to conservation of nature. The final section of the paper is devoted to the examination of the role played by the state and society as institutions for the preservation of forests and rights of the forest dwellers. A unique element of the presentation is its valuable reference to folk literature to develop an insight into the man-nature relationship in this area.

Kaushik Roy, in his paper 'Environment and War: Small Wars in North-East India, 1845-1913' argued that colonial military invasions had an adverse impact on the ecology of the region. Making a comparative analysis with the pre-colonial situation in the initial part of the paper, he pointed out that the tribes of this region had an involved relationship with their ecology. The people were shaped by their ecology. He pointed out that colonial interventions in this region after the Anglo-Burmese war, brought them into a close contact with the tribes. He observed that contrary to the colonial perceptions about the Bengalis who they perceived to be effeminate, colonial perceptions about the tribes was that they were irrational, adventurous and martial. On the tribal situation, Roy argues, that there was elaborate discourse between the civilian and military officials, and as a result of such an interaction emerged the colonial response to the tribes and fashioned colonial military interventions into the tribal situations of north-east India. The colonial power adopted different methods to control the tribes which were reflected in their military strategy. Roy argues that the colonial army was horrified with the prospect of moving into the jungles and hence inducted the local tribes into their forces. He also discussed the colonial administration belief that the colonial state would have to engage the tribes into colonial economic system, grant them same benefits which would win them over and bring about some attachment between them and the colonial state. Roy, in this connection pointed out that only military exploitation was not enough to subjugate the frontier tribes on the eastern frontier. Reference to the colonial interventions in the system of cultivation and undertaking road project which provided jobs to the local tribesmen were made to refer to a few methods adopted by the colonial state to control the north-eastern frontier. As a final point, Roy also refers to the steps taken by the colonial army to stop random cutting of trees by the indigenous people of the region as also some measures adopted by the colonial state, such as conservation of forests which were elephant habitats, as indirect initiatives of colonial conservation of wildlife and ecology in north-east India.

Srijani Bhattacharjee in her paper 'The Coming of British Forestry in Assam in the Nineteenth and Early Twentieth Century: Initiatives and Problems' argues that it is now established that British forest policies and exercises re/shaped and altered the natural environments of the countries colonized by them. In India the British forest policy had two perspectives. On one hand, it emphasized on the preservation of trees having commercial relevance for colonial use while on the other it enacted laws to curb the indigenous rights of the rural communities to hunt, graze livestock, farm and resource use in the woodlands under conservation programmes. By the end of the last decades of the nineteenth century, forests in most parts of India were under the authority of the British Forest Department which implemented various laws of conservation and exploitation with the underlying principle of generation of revenue. The author established this in the context of the British province of Assam in India.

The next paper is by Rajib Handique who also deals with colonial interventions in forests of Assam in his paper, 'The Ecology and Social Watershed: Colonial Intervention and Forest Use in Assam'. Ecology as a relationship between organisms and their environment, is, an unavoidable element of understanding the traditional society in any region. In this context Assam is no exception. He dealt at length about the diverse social fabric of Assam which was a home to as many as 240 societies. Delving into varied texts, including epics and mythologies, the presentation argues that though in the Ahom rule, forest resources were used and exploited, there was no destruction of forests. Colonialism as an attempt to integrate the forest resources to the World Capitalist system was more destructive for the forests. For the first time the forest products came within the ambit of taxation, e.g. taxes being levied for the use of reeds. Another aspect of colonial exploitative policy was wasteland grants. The main contention of the presentation was to present an overview of the colonial forest policy and through that history, prove the disruption of the sympathetic relationship that existed between the forest and the people of Assam.

Suryasikha Pathak in her paper entitled, 'Forests, Fields and Pasture: Environmental and Revenue Debates of Land Usage in Colonial Assam in 1910-1920', investigates issues of environment vis-à-vis the grazing land in Assam. She argued that the interface of agrarian and environmental histories is essential in understanding the relationship of people and the environment. The colonial period has been understood as a very transformative period, and recent environmental historians have accounted for many changes that have affected post-colonial India in this colonial watershed. The overwhelming thrust of environmental studies is to understand forest and its relation with communities and the state's role in defining that relationship. But the colonial state's revenue, forest and agrarian policies were also intertwined and therefore to differentiate between the 'forest and the field' in an opposing dichotomy is misleading. This paper is an attempt to address such a history. The tea gardens, forestry, and extension of agricultural boundaries due to immigration changed Assam from a land surplus region in the beginning of the nineteenth century to a province with unequal land-men ratio. Pressure on land kept on increasing for various purposes and as a result of that pastureland suffered. Decreasing pastureland, immigrant professional grazers and taxation levied on grazing all affected the indigenous grazer and cultivator and influenced the policies of the government. This paper seeks to look into the various land usage by the colonial government in Assam and in the process how pastureland diminished in the face of expanding tea gardens, wasteland settlement rules, forestry, immigration and how the colonial state exercised political power to control the resources to maximize its revenue earnings. It also focuses on the changing British policies regarding patterns of land usage since their occupation of the province from 1826 and how it changed the landscape of the province. Stringent land management by the colonial government in the interest of the tea gardens also adversely affected the grazers and the agriculturists. The land problem was compounded by immigration of ex-coolie labourers who settled down for agriculture, the Nepali graziers and the east Bengal peasantry.

The paper by S. Victor Babu is entitled 'Colonialism and Deforestation in Naga Hills'. The paper attempts to tell ecological history of Naga Hills, from pre-colonial period to and through the colonial rule over Naga Hills. The highlight of the paper however is the intimate relationship that the 'Nagas' share with their forests, in Victor Babu's words, 'Forests are a part of Naga life'. Though the information about the hills through history, in the ancient and medieval period, is scanty and fragmentary, reference may be had about periodic incursions of the Nagas into the plains, as can be gleaned through Ahom chronicles, called Buranjis. Colonial intrusion changed Naga life. The autonomy that the Nagas enjoyed in the pre-colonial period with regard to their forests and its resources was taken away. Colonial intervention ensured colonial control over forests in the form of reserve and protected areas. The taking over of the right to grant permission for the use of their forests, by the colonial state disrupted Naga life. The paper also highlighted the role played by colonial laws in increasing colonial stranglehold over Naga forest resources which prompted the Nagas to organize rebellions, which took many white lives. The significance of the paper lies in its success in establishing the relationship between colonial control over forests and exploitation of its resources in Naga Hills and repeated occurrences of anti-colonial rebellions organized by the Nagas. The presentation also deals with exploitation of forest resources for the raising of colonial revenue and its contribution to the colonial war effort in the world wars. The paper is a successful attempt at painting of a comprehensive picture of the ecologically devastating role of colonial control of Naga Hills.

Debojyoti Das in his paper 'State-Science, Hegemony and Shifting the Cultivator: Contesting the "Anti-modernity" Discourse on Shifting Cultivation in South Asia', intervened in the debate emerging in the environmental history of South Asia on shifting cultivation and tried to locate the 'anti-modernity' and anti-technology discourse on shifting cultivation that has evolved with the colonial foresters' forest management programme that finds its place to this day in the post-colonial forest policy of South Asian nation states. The author says, 'thus my take is not to romance the *jhumias* past through Standard Environment Narratives (SEN). Rather he tried to engage the readers to the violence and rhetoric of modernization and agricultural improvement that has often meant the withdrawal of the *jhumias* from their livelihood and integration to hybrids that break their social obligations, reciprocal exchanges and land relations and tenure.

The paper by Bashabi Gupta, the title of the paper being 'Land Use/Land Cover Change and its Impact on Climate in the Barak Valley, Assam'. The author began with a brief historical background of the Barak Valley and outlining its geographical specifications. The paper contended that today more and more water is being withdrawn from the river which has contributed to siltation of the river. Gupta contends that while rivers and pools have experienced a lot of siltation, cultivation has also undergone a lot of decrease. She points to the declining rainfall in this region and the rise of the average temperature, breaking down the argument into statistical terms. She argues that, while rainfall in Barak Valley was 1345 mm in 1975, in 2006 it was only 1000 mm. Lack of water and change in climate has had a degrading impact on the river. The nature of land use has also undergone a lot of change in Barak Valley between 1975 and 2006, the two limits of the paper's time frame. This paper tries to relate changes in global climate system to the climate changes experienced in the Barak Valley, to establish the general linkage between land use/land cover and climate.

The paper on Cherrapunji entitled, '*Rain, Rain, Come Again:* History of Rainfall, Deforestation and Water Scarcity in Cherrapunji, the Rainiest Spot in the Globe', by Sajal Nag dealt with Cherrapunji. At the beginning of the twentieth century a major chunk of scientists believed that climates of the world had been essentially constant over at least five thousand years. In the next eighty years the belief was demolished. But still very little is known about the possible effects of past climatic shifts on human activities. Historians have given scant regards to this aspect until in the 1950s and 1960s a number of historians notably Gustaf Utterstrom, Fernand Braudel and Emmanuel Le Roy Ladurie showed some willingness to pay serious attention to the possible effects of climatic change in historical situations. In a subsequent article on the 'History of Rain and Fine Weather', the *Annales* historian Le Roy Ladurie stated that, 'the aim of climatic history is not to explain human history nor to offer simplistic accounts of this or that remarkable episode not even when such episodes prompt us with good reason to reflect upon the great disasters of history ... (these are merely) spin off of the history of climate'. Ladurie was concerned only with producing a 'clear picture of the changing meteorological patterns of the past ages' in the spirit of 'cosmological history of nature'. Turning to Cherrapunji, known to be the rainiest spot of the world the author not only traces the history of rains in this zone but how climate had influenced the history of Cherrapunji, and indeed reflect upon the environmental catastrophe that the place came to symbolize. From the wettest spot how Cherrapunji has become a 'wet desert' – denuded of all forests, all mineral wealth and yearning for every drop of water is the thrust of investigation of this paper. The highlight of the paper is the investigation into the allegation that large-scale deforestation had caused the rains to disappear from this part of the world and the conclusion that the area was after all never so thickly forested historically.

The paper by Binayak Dutta entitled 'Challenging Times, Challenged Body: Decolonization, Displacement and Disease among East Pakistani Refugees in South Assam, 1947-1954' tries to establish a connectivity between improper and inadequate rehabilitation measures and human health and mortality on the one hand and evolve a critique of post-colonial relief and rehabilitation policy of the Government of India and Assam between 1947 and 1954, on the other. The paper had two major sections. The first part was devoted to narrating the history of decolonization and relating mass displacement of population from East Pakistan with it. The second part of the presentation was an attempt to relate displacement and rehabilitation of the dispatched refugees with the outbreak of disease and consequently high human mortality in this area of study.

The paper by Bipul Chaudhury entitled 'The Empire as a World of Sport: Aspects of Hunting in Colonial Assam, *c.* 1850-1900'. The paper begins by pointing out that colonial intervention with the forest of Assam marked an important milestone in the evolution of modern forest policy in Assam. It argues that until 1900, the colonial state had no concrete notion about the protection of nature and wildlife and rather it viewed them as sources of revenue and entertainment. The ethnographic accounts of the colonial officials in the nineteenth century reveals that nature and environment was viewed as unending reserves, even after wasteland settlement and immigration of people from East Bengal. Forests were viewed as obstacles to notions of Western progress and at the same time an arena for the British to display their masculinity to the natives, for which *shikar* or 'hunting' was used. The colonial forest policy, the author argued, was guided by notions of power and was instrumental in large-scale deforestation and killing of animals, which had a long-term impact on the ecology of the province. The presentation was designed to critically examine the notion of the 'jungle' as perceived by colonial officials, and as gleaned through the writings of nineteenth-century travellers with special reference to the Brahmaputra Valley.

Geetashri Singh in her article 'Colonizing the Wild: British Policies towards Wildlife in Assam, 1874-1947' discusses the encounter of the British with the wildlife of colonial Assam. Assam has a large number of animal sanctuaries which had been started by the British. But it is not widely known that they were first participants in the systematic destruction of wild animals. They innovated all kinds of methods and rewards to annihilate the last of the wildlife until the complete disappearance of some pre-historical animals loomed large. The paper provides a vivid historical account of such mass killing and its impact on the region.

Monishankar Misra, in his paper entitled, 'Encountering Floods: Colonial State and the Flood of 1916 in Surma-Barak Valley of Assam' points out that Assam was a flood prone area due to seismic and meteorological reasons and once the British came into this region as political masters, they also had to negotiate these difficult ecological challenges. He argues that the colonial policy with regard to flood was ad hoc and piecemeal. He draws attention to the flood of 1916, which generated a hue and cry from the nationalist leadership in India as well as among the colonial officials. It was this flood and reactions associated with it which is the main focus of his presentation. The paper which begins with a brief history of floods in this region makes a major point centring around the appointment of an official commission set up by the colonial state to enquire into the issue of floods in this region. This paper also relates the flood of 1916 to the construction of railways in the Surma Valley. Based on primary sources, this paper makes an important attempt to construct a narrative of the first major hydraulic intervention by the colonial state in Assam.

The other paper under this rubric is by Shyamananda Bhattacharjee, who tries to establish a relationship between violent seismic activity, topographical change and environment, with special reference to the great earthquakes of 1897 and 1950 in north-east India. In his paper entitled, 'Environmental Impact of the Great Earthquakes of 1897 and 1950 on North-East India', Bhattacharjee elaborates the various impact of these two earthquakes on the topography of north-east India and to various surface features such as water bodies, land mass, with special reference to the denudation of the top soil in large areas of land and its impact on the flora/fauna of the region. He points out the impact of these earthquakes on the desertification of areas, with special reference to Cherrapunji. The greatest adverse impact of this violent seismic activity was in large-scale destruction of vegetation and wildlife. Bhattacharjee makes a reference to the uprooting of as many as fifty thousand *sal* trees, which were an irreparable loss and the death of various species of mammals which were completely wiped out. The impact of the earthquake in white buffalos, gaurs, deer, was highlighted to emphasize the magnitude of the earthquake. The paper makes a special mention of the impact of these earthquakes on the flow of rivers and the process of siltation flooding and marine life within the rivers.

Kerry Little in her paper, 'Mythology as a Protest Narrative: A Lepcha Tale', does a remarkable job by exposing that a large number of hydro-electric power project by the construction of huge dams in the rivers of the state which are underway and how the indigenous Lepcha tribe is using their folklore to resist these constructions. The multi-modal protest narratives belonging to Lepcha activists in Sikkim incorporate ownership, tradition, culture, religion, and concern for the environment. These themes were the cornerstone messages which were repeated, modified and then codified as a narrative template for a protest movement against several hydro-electric projects slated for, and being built on, the Lepcha Reserve – Dzongu – in north Sikkim. The Lepchas draw heavily on their folklore and mythology to establish their position as protectors of a sacred place. They talk frequently about the environment, biodiversity, their culture, their traditions, and their 'sacred' relationship with their land. Kerry Little's work involves recording traditional and contemporary Lepcha stories and examining how modernity and globalization has impacted on Lepchas' connection to their traditions. The author records stories over two periods of time – the traditional narratives of the distant past, and was told by Lepcha elders, and contemporary narratives that relate to a Lepcha protest against mega hydro-electric projects which are at different stages of development in the Lepcha reserve – and motherland – Dzongu in north Sikkim.

NOTES

1. See report on the Copenhagen Conference, 2009.
2. For details, see Sajal Nag, '*Rain, Rain, Come Again*: History of Rainfall, Deforestation and Water Scarcity in Cherrapunji, the Rainiest Spot in the Globe', Guwahati: ICHR, 2008.
3. Sobhapati Samom, 'Dying Welands of Manipur', in *North East Sun*, 16-31 January 2011, pp. 8-11.
4. M.K. Chakma, 'Environmental Thwart Will Wreck North East', in *Look East*, October 2010, Kolkata, pp. 12-13.
5. Report on the Regional Consultation on Combating Climate Change in the North Eastern and Lower Himalayan Regions of India; reproduced in *Look East*, October 2010, pp. 16-18.
6. See *The Telegraph*, North-East Edition, Guwahati, 10 October 2009.
7. *Basic Statistic*, NEC, Shillong, 2008.
8. Ibid.
9. Zahid Hussain (ed.), *Environmental Issues of North East India*, New Delhi: Regency, 2003, p. 199.
10. H.J. Siemlieh, 'Environmental Conditions over the Southern Parts of Meghalaya Plateau', paper presented in a Seminar on Environmental History and Politics in North East India', 16-17 February 2010.

11. S. Victor Babu, 'Ecology, Nagas and Development', in Th Robert Tiba (ed.), *Scheduled Tribes of North East India and Development*, Delhi: B.R. Publications, 2010, pp. 123-9.
12. *Basic Statistic*, NEC, Shillong, 2008.
13. Ibid.
14. Ibid.

CHAPTER 1

India's North-East: An Enigmatic Absence in History and Cartography

RILA MUKHERJEE

THE NEGLECT OF THE UPLANDS

Anyone working on the north-east knows that this region is little studied, because it falls outside conventional area classification. This neglect is echoed in cartography. Van Schendel writes that 'anyone interested in finding fairly detailed modern maps showing the region covering Burma, north-east India, Bangladesh, and neighbouring parts of China knows that these do not exist. This is a region that is always a victim of cartographic surgery'.[1]

How is this surgery evident? Van Schendel writes:

> Over the past half-century, the scramble for the area has influenced mapmakers as much as the rest of us, and atlases commonly have maps with the captions 'Southeast Asia' and 'South Asia'. These apparently objective visualisations present regional heartlands as well as peripheries of parts of the world that always drop off the map, disappear into the folds of two-page spreads, or end up as insets. In this way, cartographic convenience reinforces a hierarchical spatial awareness, highlighting certain areas of the globe and pushing others into the shadows.[2]

All of us who have studied maps of this region know how true this is. Van Schendel notes that although in terms of physical space criterion this area shares language affinities (for example, Tibeto-Burman languages), religious commonalities (for example, community religions and, among the universalistic religions, Buddhism and Christianity), cultural traits (for example, kinship systems, ethnic scatter zones), ancient trade networks, and ecological conditions (for example, mountain agriculture),[3] it is now relegated to the margins of ten valley-dominated states with which it has antagonistic relationships, e.g. China, Vietnam, Laos, Cambodia, Thailand, Burma,

India, Bangladesh, Bhutan, and Nepal.[4] We have always neglected the uplands and this has been the fate of India's north-east in history, in academia and in cartography.

UPLANDS AS ZOMIA

A new approach to the study of this marginal area can be through the notion of Zomia, derived from the term 'zomi', used in Chin-Mizo-Kuki languages to denote uplanders.

This notion was initially formulated by Van Schendel in 2002 as

> a neglected – an invisible – transnational area, which overlapped segments of all four sub-regions (Central, South, Southeast and East Asia) without truly belonging to any of them. It is an area marked by a sparse population, historical isolation, political domination by powerful surrounding states, marginality of all kinds, and huge linguistic and religious diversity.[5]

William G. Clarence-Smith noted in his editorial note to the special issue on Zomia in the *Journal of Global History*:

> following Fernand Braudel's seminal writings on the Mediterranean, much research has teased out historical links between lands bordering great bodies of water. Similar zones of interaction around major 'wastelands' (such as mountains, forests, tundra, and deserts) have yet to attract the same degree of attention. Zomia is not only situated in one of the most stupendously elevated mountainous zones of the planet but it also crosses well-entrenched boundaries that Area Studies have created since the Second World War, between Southeast Asia, East Asia, Central (Inner) Asia, and South Asia.[6]

This new kind of spatial conception, overturning the geographic conception of area studies, helps tease out the history of this marginal space. Geographies of the state label these areas as wastelands, often, but not always, transforming into borderlands, where human agency and older ideologies prevail over statist policies.[7]

States did not emerge in these borderlands because, Fiskesjo says,

> the violence of state-making is easier to perpetrate on lowland farmers, and highlands offer an escape. But the dynamics of state–margin relations may be even more crucial. Insisting on the global context as directly consequential in the internal dynamic of these upland Southeast Asian polities, Friedman points to how pre-existing states may block the appropriation of resources and expansion that otherwise could fuel local aggrandization. Environmental

degradation, likewise inseparable from the regional context, also may preclude the mobilization of surpluses driving competitive spirals. Secondary states may emerge anyway, built on the control of trade routes or other resources, and evolve into large-scale 'predatory' states based on conquest and subjugation just like primary states, albeit often reliant on trade rather than on agriculture.[8]

The Shan states of upper Burma and the north-eastern states are prime examples of such secondary state forms.

Zomia as conceptual theme and geographic category is sometimes unstable,[9] nevertheless it is necessary to recover this space because

global processes cut across traditional spatial categories, causing many to question inherited geographical scales, including the post-war inspired division of eastern Eurasia into the regions and disciplines of Asian studies. The institutionalization of these regions has produced scholarship capable of investigating certain preconceived geographical scales, including civilizations (East or South Asia), nations or empires (China, India), or regions (mainland Southeast Asia). But if geographical scales – the spatial configurations of power, culture, and economy – are not fixed, and are instead produced through historical processes, then the inherited scholarly traditions and institutions are 'ill suited to deal with human activities spilling over' the boundaries of civilization, state, and region.[10]

COLONIALISM, AREA STUDIES AND ZOMIA

I suggest that the sad fate of zomia is linked not only to the scramble for area studies after the Second World War but from the onset of colonialism itself. As zomia was thinly populated, the European notion of empty spaces/wastelands was applied to the area in the course of the nineteenth century. Large parts of zomia were non-state spaces and this factor, too, added to the disdain of the colonists. We shall see further on how this disqualified zomia from being mapped, historically and geographically.

It is clear by now that this paper is looking at India's north-east region as zomia. If manpower, and not mere territorial aggrandizement, was the logic of the pre-modern Southeast Asian paddy state, as Scott argues, then clearly zomia lost out in the hierarchy of states in this part of the world.[11]Although partly colonized, the north-east was left out of the ambit of the grand developmental projects of the colonial state. Missionaries and not merchants held sway here. The region was held as frontier, and not as an integral part of the colonial governance. It was never integrated to mainstream India, nor to its economic heartland.

THE NORTH-EAST AS ZOMIA

But this approach, the conventional one, looks at the north-east as *part* of India. If I look at the north-east as an integral part of Zomia there is a perceptible shift in my viewfinder. My lens size increases and now my vision of Zomia is somewhat different. This is a greater Zomia linking parts of south-west China, northern Burma and the north-east with the sea, more specifically, the northern Bay of Bengal, thereby connecting Zomia with the littoral. This is a region with its own economic dynamism.

Van Schendel's Zomia concerns itself with links *within* the region stretching from the uplands of Southeast Asia into South Asia, but here I propose linking the space of Zomia and its silk roads and wool routes with the littoral, more specifically, the south-eastern Bengal delta, today centred on Dhaka in Bangladesh, without privileging either space. This is not a spatial exaggeration. The south-eastern delta contained many land routes combining a mix of land and river crossings and the existence of some of the earliest travel in this region is attested to from the first century of the Christian era.[12]

One example of Zomia connecting with the lowlands would be that of Yunnan through, one, its supplies of silver and gold which the Bengal deltas accessed, two, its need for *cauris* which the Bengal deltas supplied from the Maldives, and three, its strategic position on the Silk Route between China and Persia,[13] a route that connected it with the south-eastern delta. Yet other examples would be medieval Tibet and Kuch Behar that supplied Bengal with horses and silver. A third would be some ancient divisions of Central Asia – such as Parthia – which had considerable economic and political connections with the deltas. A fourth would be certain parts of the north-east that granted Bengal access to the silver regions of northern Burma-Mizoram for example.

The autonomy of the north-east is not imagined; it is also recorded in its history, as evidenced in the medieval state chronicles of the Tripuris, Manipuris and Ahoms.[14] But this history is seen as a 'little' history and falls outside the grand narratives that make up the history of the nation. But Zomia has always been important to Bengal and Burma as social entity, economic being and political unit.

A GREATER ZOMIA: FROM THE MOUNTAINS TO THE SEAS

For my part, I envision this greater Zomia by documenting routes and networks of discovery, travel, trade and conquest. This visioning is two-pronged, one, I will look at sources from the east regarding this region and two, I will study sources from the West regarding the area. I hope to show, thereby, that this was not such a neglected world in the pre-colonial period. Moreover, I will show that although we tend to privilege Western sources, these are quite unsatisfactory as regards the north-east.

The Eastern End

The section of Zomia that concerns us here is the borderlands that Giersch writes about: the present transnational area between China (Yunnan, southern Sichuan, Guizhou and western Guangxi), north Burma and Siam and India's states of Arunachal Pradesh, Mizoram and Nagaland,[15] the last three an area without recorded history.

There are many references to Zomia in the ancient world. Chinese annals noted the lucrative trade India conducted with Ta-ts'in (Roman Orient or Syria, with the chief port at Petra[16]) and An-hsi (Parthia or Persia) but noted that An-hsi blocked a direct Syria-China trade.[17] Thus did An-hsi seek to keep its locational advantage, and this was successful until 166 CE when the Ta-ts'in sent an embassy to China through Annam.[18] Thereafter the Chinese trade to the Red Sea went via Annam to Sri Lanka or the Malabar ports.[19]

From the second century BC once China discovered Bactria, the Chinese attempted to open trade with western India (Sindh) and ambassadorial expeditions were sent from China overland through the north-east and Central Asia.[20] This suggests that the sea route from China to India was unknown at the time. The Chinese gradually knew the sea only from the first century CE. The account of *Wei-lio* (written before 429 CE) suggests that the Chinese first encountered the Indian Ocean from the Persian Gulf.[21]

The Chinese expansion into Yunnan and Bengal, soon after, shattered An-hsi's position as intermediary in the trade of the east and west. By the third century CE the Tsang-ko route through Szechuan, Yung-ch'ang and Tibet was the shortest route to India.[22] The Chinese noted soon after that the Huang-chih region, identified tentatively with *vanga* or Gange, exported pearls and opaque glass and imported gold and silk.[23]

Wang Gungwu writes that although trade with the Shan kingdoms was by land in the first century CE, there was a Shan mission that came by sea to China in 132 CE. Two missions came by sea from T'ien-chu in 159 and in 161 CE.[24]

What was the geography of the maritime route? It seems it was a mix of sea, land and river crossings. Schoff writes that

> the route (of a Shan mission recorded in Chinese annals in 120 CE) is, however, clear; the embassy came by sea to the southwest of the Shan country, that is, the Gulf of Martaban, the shores immediately east of the modern Rangoon, and proceeded inland up one of the river valleys. The modern rail route leaving Rangoon follows the valley of the Sittaung river to Mandalay, thence up the Irawadi. At Bhamo, the head of navigation on that river, the overland route to Yun-Nan began crossing the parallel gorges of the other rivers by suspension bridges. The earlier route probably ascended the Salwin passing the Shan capital Theinni and crossing the other rivers a little lower down, both routes having as their destination Yun-nan-fu, Cheng-tu-fu, and finally Singan-fu. Another Chinese record informs us that in AD 166 the king of Ta-Tsin, 'An-tun', who may of course be identified with Marcus Aurelius, 'sent an embassy with tribute from the frontier of Jih-Nan', and that 'merchants of this country frequently visit Fu-Nan, Jih-Nan, and Kiao-Tsi', but that 'few of the inhabitants of those southern frontier states ever went to Ta-Tsin.'. . . Another record dating from the fourth century gives us the route from the Chinese capital to its Tong-King seaport, and the routes down the other rivers as follows: 'southeast you come to Kiao-Tsi; there is also connection by water [in fact by both river and ocean routes] with the principalities of Yun-Nan and Yung-Chang [near Bhamo; that is, through Burma].' Chinese interest in distant lands is reflected in this same record. . . .[25]

So we see that while the Central Asian route was known earlier, now the maritime route became more prominent.[26] The importance of the maritime route was further underlined when, from the late third century, China broke into two halves: the north being torn by incessant warfare between small, short-lived dynasties and the south having no access to Central Asia. It was only after 494 CE that embassies from north-west India visited the Wei court.[27]

Between the third and sixth centuries the maritime route reigned supreme. The Ta-ts'in trade went through Pegu, up the Salween or Irrawady, through the Shan states into Yunnan and thence into China.[28] Between the fourth and sixth centuries Sassanid Persia was brought into contact with After Wei China.[29] It is at this time that the Bengal ports became linked with the Persia-China trade, as evidenced in coin hoards found in Bengal. This trade took off when the T'angs appeared in China, and land routes revived.

Various land routes connecting Sassanian Persia and T'ang China with eastern India traversed this space now by way of Central Asia[30]and the north-east. The sea route into eastern India starting from the Gulf of Tongkin, was popular and much used. Many of the Chinese pilgrim-scholars who came through this route then moved on to north India and from there into Central Asia. They returned from Central Asia to China by the land route through the extreme northern part of the north-east. Sometimes they came to Central Asia first, by way of the north-east, then came down to India and returned to China by the land or sea routes. We see that from around the fifth century the land and sea routes operated *in tandem*, no longer in isolation, and thereby the north-east was brought into the ambit of the littoral.

Later, even more new routes came into being. These routes, combinations of land and riverine pathways and sea-lanes, were much used. Moore writes that at the end of the eighth century a route is described from Yung-ch'ang to the Pyu capital, then going up the Chindwin and on to Manipur.[31]

But it seems that by the eighth century the direct route through Burma and Kamarupa became more popular as it was shorter.[32] This was once again the land-riverine route and it lay in the area that concerns us here.

From the end of the seventh century, Central Asian and Chinese Buddhists knew of the south-eastern Bengal delta, of a place called Ganga Dwara, signifying, literally, the portal of the Ganga. This was the entry from the sea into Bengal, the south-eastern deltaic area of Harikela and of the state of Kamarupa, which by way of the Karatoya and the Brahmaputra rivers linked deltaic Bengal with the land routes fanning into Tibet and Yunnan.[33]

I Tsing noted in the seventh century that one of the Gupta kings (possibly Srigupta at the end of the third century CE) had a temple called Temple of the Cinas erected at the end of the third century in honour of the visit of twenty Chinese pilgrim scholars using the land route from Yunnan and Burma to visit his kingdom.[34] Roadways were fairly well developed: Bhattacharyya writes that land grant documents of ancient and early medieval Bengal speak of an infrastructure which had developed out of link roads, that a network of communication existed in Bengal and that this connected with southern India as seen from the Chola and Western Chalukya invasions of Gaur and Kamarupa.[35] Despite the evidence of the maritime route, Stargardt assumes that the land routes spanning India, Burma and China were more important than sea routes before the Song period: 'the Pyu embassy (of 802) must have taken the land route to the imperial court and, in fact, there is no record of a Burmese embassy travelling to China by sea before the Sung dynasty'.[36]

This is partly because Chinese ship-building technology before the Song period was unable to construct ships that could make the long voyage from China to India. Srivijaya in Southeast Asia on the maritime route was thus a significant intermediary in the trade between South Asia, Southeast Asia and China. Likewise the north-east remained an intermediate staging stop in the long land route between China and India.

From the eleventh century longer sea voyages became more frequent along the Bay as many states accessed this technology: see the exploits of the Cholas, the Songs, the Mons and those of Pagan. Dars writes that the great Chinese junks were only constructed from the twelfth century[37]and Lombard and Salmon write about thirteenth century ships.[38] Whether the importance of the north-east declined because of this shift is not known.

However, the northern uplands from Bengal remained a significant geographical area for these routes that transformed into networks over areas such as Tibet, Bhutan and Nepal in the early medieval period.

Western Routes

Schoff writes 'overland caravan routes (from the Roman side), became exceedingly active between the first and third centuries of the Christian era through the discovery of the periodicity of the trade winds and the opening of active maritime traffic.'[39] The Ta-ch'in or Ta-tsin (eastern Roman Empire) sent a mission to China in 166 CE.

The *Periplus of the Erythræan Sea* is of course the most important Western source for this time, but other sources speak of the north-east region, although not by name. Classical writers such as Eratosthenes (*c.* 276 BC-*c.* 195 BC), Strabo (*c.* 30 BCE-*c.* 23 CE), Pliny (23/24-79 CE) and Arrian (*c.* 86 CE-after 146 CE) wrote about Thina or Thinae as the easternmost *limit* of the known earth, as an easternmost people, and as the place from whence silk came to the West. Strabo wrote of the area in terms of *distances*; it is clear that the area was not familiar to him: 'From the Indus to the mouth of the Ganges 13.500 stadia, from thence to Thinae 2,500 stadia'. Ptolemy (second century CE), possibly the greatest geographer of the early world, asserted Eratosthenes' notion that Thina was the last known easternmost *limit*.

Thina or Thinae was not just China but the entire area between India, north Burma and south-west China. This has led some historians to claim that the ancient kingdom of Pragjyotisha in Assam was the Thinae of the *Periplus*.[40] Schoff suggested that Thinae, the eastern metropolis, may be the same in name as Theinni, the Shan capital.[41] So Thinae may be China, Pragjyotisha or Thenwi (Shan). The *Periplus* reported that the Kirradoi, taken to be the Bodos, peopled this region. Lotika Varadarajan claimed that the Bodos made the earliest silk and this is referred to as the Kirradoi in the *Periplus*.[42]

Marcian of Heraclea, generally considered a mere compiler out of Ptolemy, gives further details of the far eastern voyage. The unknown land east of the Sinae, and the unknown land south of the sea called Prasodes (this name being identical with the Green Sea of the Arab geographers and the Erythraean or Red Sea of the Greeks, although apparently derived from the Sanskrit *prasada*, 'pacific') came together, making 'a sort of angle near the Gulf of the Sinae'. Above the Sinae, he said, was the region of the Seri and their metropolis; the unknown eastern land was dotted with 'stagnant lakes, in which great reeds grow, so closely crowded together that men cross over the lakes by walking upon them' – which may readily refer to the lakes of Yunnan and the bamboos used for bridges there. He mentions Thinae, the metropolis of the Sinae, as 'the border between the known and the unknown land'.[43]

There is apparent confusion here between the overland Turkestan route to north China and the combined sea and land route to south China, vindicating our stand that the north-east had not yet come into its own in outsider perception from the west. The *Periplus* mentions Chryse as 'an island opposite the Ganges and under the rising sun' and tells us that beyond Chryse the sea comes to an end, and that to the north was 'a land called This with an inland city called Thinae from which silk was brought overland through Bactria to the Gulf of Cambay and by way of the Ganges to the ports of Damirica', that is, Tamil Land, the Tamilakam of their poets.[44]

Schoff writes:

Richthofen (*China*, 1.10) and others followed the whole route between the Pamirs and Sera metropolis, which may quite surely be identified with the ancient Chinese capital Singan-fu. This was the great trade route of the silk merchants, and that trade was already of importance in the second century before the Christian era. The sea route was opened first to the west coast of India and Ceylon, where contact was made with another sea route leading further east known to the natives of India as the 'golden route', and its eastern termini as the 'golden and silver islands' – whence silk was also obtained. Inland from these islands (or shores, either interpretation being possible), was a metropolis Sina Sinorum, known to the Roman world by hearsay only, and assumed to be identical with the earlier known Sera metropolis, so that both caravan and maritime routes were supposed to have reached the same trade centers.[45]

The Roman world, therefore, was aware of the region, but in a much more indistinct fashion than Chinese and Southeast Asian travellers.

BARRIERS, PASSES AND RIVERS

Early European geographers had no actual knowledge of the north-east region between the third century BC and the second century CE For over five hundred years, they merely emphasized the region as *limit*. It was a blurred zone. The region of which we speak was seen as sandwiched between two expansive powers: China and India. It was truly Zomia – a non-state space, seen as a space without history. This ambivalence was reflected in maps and the cartographic confusion continued until James Rennell mapped the lower Brahmaputra Valley and Sven Hedin explored Central Asia, particularly Tibet. Therefore the region only took cartographic shape between the late eighteenth and the early twentieth centuries.

The north-east was known to be mountainous, penetrable through hostile passes and traversable only through the large rivers of the region that linked it to the delta. Consequently, the cartographic depiction of the region contained a lot of detail on mountains and rivers. However, due to inadequate knowledge of the area, the depiction of rivers and mountains in the north-east were confused. Without knowing their geographical extent, they were also collapsed in terms of projection. There was no notion of the Himalaya Mountains, much less of the eastern Himalayas. Prevailing names for them were the Imaus or Emodes Mountains, the Taurus Mountains, the Tartarian Mountains and the Caucasian Mountains. These would not be dispersed until a century of European travels in Central Asia discovered discrete mountain ranges and plateaus.

All eighteenth-century geographers agreed that rivers in the region issued from the eastern uplands, but their sources were not mapped at this time. As early as in 1596-7 Giovanni Antonio Magini showed the Meghna as the third Ptolemaic mouth of the Ganga, so at least one river of the lower north-east had already penetrated European geographical consciousness.[46] But a century later geographic notions had made no progress. Duval (1679) showed a mythical and unnamed river in *India Extra Gangem* reconciling China, Tibet, Annam and Burma, derived from Ptolemaic notions, and reinforcing the notion of rivers as commons.[47]

This was seen to be not accurate enough, as travellers and geographers gradually penetrated the area. Therefore, a mysterious river called Caor made its appearance for over two hundred years in European maps as the chief river of the north-east, and sometimes the Lakhiya or Laquia, in Delisle (1740) and Bellin (1747-61) for example, was mentioned as the chief river of the north-east, both of which connected with the southeastern delta.[48] The Laquia fed into the Brahmaputra in Bellin's map, but in the same map there was also depicted a very large river called Lecki which ran parallel to the Brahmaputra before emptying into the Bay near Dhaka. There were therefore, in Bellin's map, two Lakhiya rivers.

What is the significance of depicting the Caor and Lakhiya as the chief rivers of the north-east? The Caor and the Lakhiya were surrogates for the Brahmaputra, and both the Karatoya (Caor) and the Lakhiya existed, although the Karatoya has now dried up. What is interesting is that names such as Meghna, Caor and Lakhiya were finding their way onto maps while the Brahmaputra took cartographic shape much later.

CONCLUSION

There is a fundamental disconnect between the sea of history and the sea of cartography, as regards the north-east. We see this in our enumeration and analysis of the sources regarding the north-east. Moreover, in the absence of written sources, which we always tend to assume emanates from the West, Chinese records such as the *Ming Shi Lu* which provide much data on this region, need to be accessed and utilized if we are to write a history of Zomia in the north-east. This paper also shows that not just 'cartographic surgery' but also cartographic blunders dominate the mapping of the north-east.

The links between perception, cognition and representation, as well as the lag between them in the cartography of the north-east need to be recognized. Not only was the mapping of the north-east inadequate and erroneous, the cartographic depiction of the north-east contained also cognitive practices from an earlier past-witness the persistence of the Emoda, the Caucasian, the Taurus and the Tartarian Mountains, of Kamrup – a state which had ceased to exist by the time mapping started, of Caor as river, fortress and city – all as nodes in an earlier cognitive network, denoting sites of earlier exchanges and travel. This proves that, contrary to what is assumed, Zomia was a much travelled space.

Finally, in attempting a history of the north-east, the historian would be well advised to adopt a broader lens. Only then would a true, and honest, history of this region be written, as Zomia, and this needs to be rescued from oblivion.

NOTES

1. Willem van Schendel, 'Geographies of Knowing, Geographies of Ignorance: Jumping Scale in Southeast Asia', *Environment and Planning: Society and Space* (New Haven, 20, 6, 2002), pp. 647-68, see p. 652.
2. Ibid., pp. 651-2.
3. Ibid., pp. 653-4.
4. Ibid., p. 654, fn. 15.
5. Jean Michaud, 'Editorial – Zomia and Beyond', in *Journal of Global History* (2010) 5, pp. 187-214, see pp. 187-8 (henceforth *JGH*). See too van Schendel 2002.
6. William G. Clarence-Smith, Editorial Note – 'Zomia and Beyond', *JGH* (2010) 5, pp. 185-6, see p. 185.
7. Sarah Turner, 'Borderlands and Border Narratives: A Longitudinal Study of Challenges and Opportunities for Local Traders Shaped by the Sino-Vietnamese Border', *JGH* (2010) 5, pp. 265-87; Magnus Fiskesjö, 'Mining, History, and the Anti-state Wa: The Politics of Autonomy Between Burma and China', *JGH* (2010) 5, pp. 241-64.
8. Fiskesjö 2010, p. 261.
9. For a critique of Zomia see Michaud, 2010; Sara Shneiderman,'Are the Central Himalayas in Zomia? Some Scholarly and Political Considerations Across Time and Space', *JGH* (2010) 5, pp. 289-312; Bernard Formoso, 'Zomian or Zombies? What Future Exists for the Peoples of the Southeast Asian Massif?', *JGH* (2010) 5, pp. 313-32.

10. C. Patterson Giersch 'Across Zomia with Merchants, Monks, and Musk: Process Geographies, Trade Networks, and the Inner-East–Southeast Asian Borderlands', *JGH* (2010) 5, pp. 215-39, see p. 217.
11. James C. Scott, *The Art of Not being Governed: An Anarchist History of Upland Southeast Asia*, New Haven: Yale Press, 2009. I am indebted to James Scott for this reference.
12. Janice Stargardt, 'Burma's Economic and Diplomatic Relations with India and China from Early Medieval Sources', *Journal of the Economic and Social History of the Orient*, vol. 14, no. 1 (April 1971), pp. 38-62; Jacques Dars, 'Les jonques chinoises de haute mer sous les Song et les Yuan', *Archipel*, Année, 1979, vol. 18, no. 1, pp. 41-56; Denys Lombard and Claudine Salmon, 'Un vaisseau du XIIIème s. retrouvé avec sa cargaison dans la rade de "Zaitun"', *Archipel*, Année, 1979, vol. 18, no. 1, pp. 57-67; Lionel Casson, ed. & tr., *Periplus Maris Erythraei*, Princeton: Princeton University Press, 1989.
13. F. Hirth, *China and the Roman Orient: Research into their Ancient and Mediaeval Relations as Represented in Old Chinese Records*, Leipzig, Munich, Shanghai and Hong Kong, 1885, pp. 50, 74-5, 85. The 'water road' linked Ta-ts'in with China through Yungchang-fu and Bhamo. Persia lay on Ta-ts'in's south-east and Parthia on its east. Arabs and Khozar Turks on its frontiers constantly menaced Ta-ts'in in the seventh century as a Chinese encyclopedia of the thirteenth century tells us. See Hirth, 1885, pp. 20, 83.
14. See Rila Mukherjee, 'Mobility in the Bay of Bengal World: Medieval Raiders, Traders, States and Slaves', in *Indian Historical Review* (36.1, June 2009), pp. 109-29.
15. C. Patterson Giersch, *Asian Borderlands: The Transformation of Qing China's Yunnan Frontier*, Cambridge: Harvard University Press, 2006, p. 4.
16. Hirth, 1885, pp. 160-3.
17. Ibid., pp. 42, 45, 47, 70, 82, 173-4. While Hirth claims An-hsi is Parthia, Petech claims that An-hsi might also have been Persia. He also notes that An-hsi was not Parthia proper but the Indo-Parthian kingdom of Gondophares. See L. Petech, *Northern India According to the Shui-Ching-Chu*, Serie Orientale Roma II (Instituto Italiano Per il Medio ed Estremo Oriente, 1950), pp. 15, 70.
18. Hirth, 1885, p. 42.
19. Ibid., p. 178.
20. Hirth, 'The Story of Chang K'ién, China's Pioneer in Western Asia: Text and Translation of Chapter 123 of Ssï-Ma Ts'ién's Shï-Ki', *Journal of the American Oriental Society*, vol. 37 (1917), pp. 89-152.
21. East Asian History Sourcebook *Chinese Accounts of Rome, Byzantium and the Middle East, c. 91 BCE-1643 CE*, by Paul Halsall (July 1998), available at http://depts.washington.edu/silkroad/texts/romchin1.html. Accessed on 17 January 2010. See also Hirth, 1885, p. 39; George

Fadlo Hourani, *Arab Seafaring in the Indian Ocean in Ancient and Early Medieval Times*, Princeton: Princeton University Press, 1951, p. 16.

22. Amitabha Bhattacharyya, 'Trade Routes of Ancient Bengal', in Asok Datta (ed.), *History and Archaeology of Eastern India*, New Delhi: Books and Books, 1998, pp. 157-72, see p. 160.
23. B.N. Mukherjee, 'Coastal and Overseas Trade in Pre-Gupta Vanga and Kalinga', in Shyamal Kanti Chakravarti (ed.), *Vinayatoshini (Benoytosh Centenary Volume)*, Naihati, 1996, p. 181.
24. Wang Gungwu, *The Nanhai Trade: The Early History of Chinese Trade in the South China Sea* (rpt. Singapore: Times Academic Press, 1998), p. 24.
25. Wilfred H. Schoff, 'Navigation to the Far East under the Roman Empire', *Journal of the American Oriental Society*, vol. 37 (1917), pp. 240-9, see p. 243.
26. Hirth, 1885, p. 188.
27. Petech, 1950, p. 74.
28. Hirth, 1885, p. 179.
29. Ibid., p. 198.
30. For Kushana links with Bengal see B.N. Mukherjee, 'Kushana Coins in Bengal: An Appraisal', *Indian Numismatics, History, Art and Culture, Essays in the Honour of Dr. P. L. Gupta*, vols. 1 and 2, Delhi: Agam Kala Prakashan, 1992; Suchandra Ghosh, 'Business in Early Bengal (Pre-Gupta phase): A Numismatic Approach', in Chittabrata Palit and Pranjal Kumar Bhattacharyya (eds.), *Business History of India*, Delhi: Kalpaz Publications, 2006, pp. 77-86; *Marg*, Special Issue, vol. 54, no. 1, September 2002, on Indian terracotta sculpture for Kushana inspired Bengal terracotta, among others.
31. Elizabeth Moore, 'Interpreting Pyu Material Culture: Royal Chronologies and Finger-marked Bricks', *Myanmar Historical Research Journal*, no. 13 (June 2004), pp. 1-57, see p. 10.
32. Bhattacharyya, 1998, p. 160.
33. Sylvain Lévi, 'Notes chinoises sur l'Inde: IV. Le pays de Kharostra et l'écriture kharostr', *BEFEO*, Année, 1904, vol. 4, no. 1, pp. 543-79, see pp. 547-9; Sylvain Lévi, 'Notes Chinoises sur l'Inde. V. Quelques documents sur le bouddhisme indien dans l'Asie centrale (première partie)', *BEFEO*, Année, 1905, vol. 5, no. 1, pp. 253-305, see p. 273.
34. Stargardt, 1971, p. 41; Paul Pelliot, 'Deux itinéraires de Chine en Inde à la fin du VIIIe siècle', *BEFEO*, Année, 1904, vol. 4, no. 1, pp. 131-413, see p. 150.
35. Bhattacharyya, 1998.
36. Stargardt, 1971, p. 42.
37. Dars, 1979, p. 41.
38. Lombard and Salmon, 1979.
39. Schoff, 1917, see p. 240.

40. K.L. Baruah, *Early History of Kamarupa: From the Earliest Times to the End of the Sixteenth Century*, Calcutta: LBS/Gauhati, 1966.
41. Schoff, 1917, p. 246.
42. Lotika Varadarajan, 'Silk in Northeastern and Eastern India: The Indigenous Tradition', *Modern Asian Studies*, vol. 22, no. 3, Special Issue: *Asian Studies in Honour of Professor Charles Boxer*, 1988, pp. 561-70.
43. Schoff, 1917, p. 247.
44. *Peripl. Mar. Erythr*, pp. 63-4.
45. Schoff, 1917, p. 240.
46. Giovanni Antonio Magini, commentary on Ptolemy's *Geographia*, Cologne, 1596.
47. Pierre Duval, *Geographie Universelle*, Paris, 1670 onwards.
48. Guillaume Delisle, *Carte de l'Asie et de la Chine*, Paris, from 1705; Jacques Nicholas Bellin, *Histoire Generale des Voyages* by Abbe Prevost, Paris, 1747-61.

CHAPTER 2

Marsh, Rice and Faith: Aspects of Environmental and Religious Changes in the Early Medieval Surma-Barak Valley*

BIRENDRA NATH PRASAD

In the reconstruction of the history of early and early medieval India, a general emphasis has been on the core, nuclear areas of various regions. Socio-economic and religious dynamics in the areas that are considered to be peripheral have generally not attracted the kind of attention they should have. The persistence of this view may partially be due to a general reluctance to take into account historical implications of the heterogeneity of geographical space. This is despite some excellent observations made by geographers and historians alike. Way back in the 1920s, Arthur Geddes had emphasized the need to understand the evolution of Indian history in terms of interactions between its core 'grain lands' of the middle and upper Ganga Valley, and 'grasslands' and 'forest lands' of the rest of the subcontinent. It was a persistent attempt of the population of the 'grain lands' to expand their subsistence pattern to the 'grasslands' and 'forest lands' and this expansion had significant socio-economic and cultural implications.[1] Later, Richard Eaton argued a similar thing: much of Indian history is marked by a continuous attempt by the settled agrarian population of low-lying plains to expand agrarian frontiers in the outlying jungles. In this expansion of agrarian frontiers, there was a mutual flow of cultures, but the signs and symbols associated with the agrarian population had greater appeal on the other side.[2] B.D. Chattopadhyaya too talks of a persistent interaction between the forested space and cultivated space, which had significant

*Some versions of this article were earlier published in *Journal of Religions of South Asia*, vol. 6.1, 2012.

socio-economic and religious implications for societies on the both side of the continuum.[3]

These impressive studies, no doubt, largely set the framework in which the socio-economic and religious dynamics of many parts of the Indian subcontinent may be studied. In this paper, I will make an attempt to understand some aspects of these changes in the Surma-Barak Valley, corresponding to the undivided Sylhet district in Bangladesh and undivided Cachar district in the southern part of Indian province of Assam. Though not falling exactly within the domain of 'environmental history', this paper will highlight overlapping aspects of the disciplines of environmental history, history of political structures, agrarian history, and history of religions. As the Surma-Barak Valley provided one of the transitional zones through which the plains of Bengal merged with the hills of the north-eastern India (Meghalaya, Tripura and Manipur in particular), this paper has implications for both Bengal and north-eastern India.

SOME GEOGRAPHICAL PECULIARITIES OF THE SURMA-BARAK VALLEY AND THEIR HISTORICAL IMPLICATIONS

In Spate and Learmonth's classification, the area to the east of the Surma-Meghna (Cachar district of Assam in India, and the modern districts of Sylhet, Comilla and Noakhali, and the coastal plains of Chittagong in Bangladesh) forms a 'great embayment of lowland between the Shillong plateau and the parallel ranges which extend from just east of Comilla to beyond the Burma border'.[4] The Meghna-Surma embayment is perhaps the most amphibious part of Bengal during the monsoons, due to high rainfall, interruption of the slopes of the Madhupur Jungle down to the sea, and the pounding back of local waters by the main Brahmaputra-Ganga current.[5] Within this general pattern, a differentiation exists: the Sylhet district is certainly the most amphibious part, not only within this sub-region, but practically within Bengal.[6]

Sylhet, 'the land of winding rivers, swamps and rice',[7] is one of the marshiest districts of Bengal. Large swamps – locally known as *hāors*[8] – are one of the most important characteristics of the landscape. This district, consisting of the lower valley of the Barak or the Surma, is an open alluvial plain, about 70 miles wide, surrounded by the Meghalaya hills in the north and the hills of Tripura in the south.[9] In the west, it opens towards the delta of lower Bengal. The greater part is a uniform plain, broken only by clusters of small sandy hillocks, and intersected by a large number of rivers, watercourses and drainage channels.[10] Annual rainfall is around 150 inches in eastern Sylhet, one of the highest in the whole of Bengal.[11] It could have been higher during the early mediaeval phase when this area was more densely forested. High precipitation ensured a thick forest cover in the past.[12] It imparted a general amphibious look to the landscape for the greater part of the year. In the later nineteenth century, the torrents that 'poured down in cataracts from the hills' during the rainy season, together with the heavy local rainfall, used to convert much of the district into a 'boundless sea of water'.[13] The marshy character of the land is shown in other colonial accounts as well. Lord Lindsay, the British Resident of Sylhet, who came to Sylhet in the eighteenth century during the rainy season, had to sail through a vast tract of water between Dhaka and Sylhet, and the mariner's compass had to be used en route.[14]

The Cachar district is as marshy as Sylhet, if not more; it is more forested, receives higher rainfall, and is under greater tribal influence.

This marshy character had great bearings on the historical evolution of the Surma Valley. That can be seen by comparing the historical experience of the valley with that of early medieval Bengal in general and early mediaeval Samataṭa in particular. In an important study of the political geography of early medieval Bengal, Morrison found that the Bengal Delta had at least four sub-regions: (1) Varendra (covering the areas of north Bengal), (2) Dacca-Faridpur (roughly the historical Vaṅga), (3) areas to the west of the Bhagirathi-Hughli (Rāḍha), and (4) Sylhet-Comilla-Chittagong (variously referred to as Samataṭa or Harikela).[15] His study indicated that in Varendra, Vaṅga and Rāḍha, property relations were fully developed, and culturally they were more or less integrated with the middle Ganga Valley. In fact, they were the 'heartlands of Brahmanical culture in the Delta'.[16] Samataṭa-Harikela had different orientations, economically, politically and even culturally. It had a relatively sparse population, and lacked a long history of individual property rights; hence the land grants were always in favour of institutions or large congregations of Brahmins, never in favour of individual Brahmins. Within the Delta, 'Buddhism had not attracted a major following anywhere except in the lands lying east of the Meghna where it continued to receive benefactions in the thirteenth century'.[17] 'The land that now lies in the modern Sylhet, Comilla and Chittagong districts was the home of people with a culture different from those found elsewhere in the Delta'.[18] It was this land that provided the most fertile avenue for Islamization in medieval Bengal.

Morrison's study is greatly helpful in understanding some peculiarities of the land situated to the east of the Surma-Meghna (i.e. Samataṭa-Harikela) vis-à-vis the rest of Bengal. But, despite providing some macro generalizations, he has not undertaken a micro analysis of the historical and geographical heterogeneity of this tract. We accept his thesis that Samataṭa-Harikela was a periphery within early mediaeval Bengal. But every periphery has its own core, peripheries and semi-peripheries. If the area that constitutes Comilla district today was the 'core' area of various Samataṭa polities,[19] the areas which constituted colonial Sylhet and Cachar districts appear to be the ultimate 'frontier' within Samataṭa-Harikela.[20] After decades of archaeological research and documentation, data from Sylhet is not impressive.[21] We get the same impression from the votive inscriptions on the sculptures of early medieval Samataṭa-Harikela.[22] Numismatic sources indicate the same trend.

This peripherality of Sylhet district becomes sharper due to a poor settlement record in the neighbouring Mymensigh district. Mymensigh district, most of which is located in the Madhupur Jungle tract – an elevated piedmont tract that resisted extensive human occupation till the late nineteenth century – has a very poor settlement record, in terms of settlement sites as well as in terms of sculptural findings datable to the early medieval period.[23]

Situations to the east of the Sylhet district, in the Cachar district, are even worse. Despite unmistakable evidence of early medieval penetration at places like Bhuban Pahar,[24] the larger part of this district remained tribal till the late medieval period, when it witnessed a tribal state formation.

The Surma Valley was subject to divergent political and cultural pulls, and it remained either under the control of the polities based in Kāmarūpa/Prāgjyotiṣa (Brahmaputra Valley of Assam) or Samataṭa. Both states have been described as *pratyānta* (frontier) states defeated by the Gupta emperor Samudragupta. The Surma Valley formed a peripheral portion of these kingdoms. At a later stage, it became a part of those kingdoms which had their core area in the Chittagong coast (i.e. Harikela) and conquered this tract through the Comilla-Noakhali area. For the larger part of its history, this valley remained under the control of the Comilla-based kingdoms. By the last phase of this period, it witnessed a local state formation as well.

This is a short description of the locale – largely marshy; heavily forested; under substantial tribal influence; one of the peripheries within peripheral states – where Brahmanical temples and *maṭhas* emerged and functioned during the early medieval phase. We shall now trace the patterns of interaction between these institutions and other societal institutions in the context of the process of early medieval state formation, consolidation of its resource base and legitimation.

DIVERGENT PATTERNS IN THE NEGOTIATION OF THE FOREST IN THE SEVENTH CENTURY

An active alliance between the state and Brahmanical religious institutions and the Brahmin community is discernible in the Nidhānapur copper plate of Bhāskaravarman of Kāmarūpa (*c.* 600-50 CE), found at Nidhānapur village, 17 miles south-east of Sylhet town. The original grant, issued by Bhūtivarman (*c.* 518-54 CE), the great-great grandfather of Bhāskaravarman, recorded the donation of a large tract of land, the *Mayūraśālmala Agrahāra*, to a congregation of Brahmins on the principle of *bhūmi-chidra-nyāya*,[25] indicating the donation of a tract of land that was not under the plough, where the donees had to initiate or get initiated to agricultural activities. By the time of Bhāskaravarman, the original copper plate was lost, so the donated land became subject to taxation; he therefore renewed it. By this time, important socio-economic changes had taken place in the locality; the document shows the transitions taking place there in a span of some one hundred years. It offers one of the earliest available records for fluvial volatility, its impact on the population of the *agrahāra* and the attempt by this community to cope with this volatility.

The boundaries of the donated land, as mentioned in this copper plate, reveal some interesting inferences. A big *jaṭālī* (*Bignonia suaveolens*) tree marked its northern boundary.[26] Southern boundaries were demarcated by a big hewn-fig tree.[27] On the eastern side, it was bounded by the Kauśikā River, and on the western side by Gaṅgiṇikā.[28] The boundaries refer to elements of natural geography, and the donated tract was not bordered by a settled agrarian tract on any side. That indicates that the locality in which this *agrahāra* was created was originally in a forested tract and prone to forest growth.[29] A large Brahmanical settlement, including a temple, was planted by the state in this largely forested tract. The temple complex appears to be the single biggest landholder in this *agrahāra*. While the maximum share of a Brahmin in the donated land was two *aṃśas* (shares), the temple received seven *aṃśas*.[30] The income from the donated land was to be used by the temple authorities for arranging *bali*,[31] *sattra*[32] and *caru*[33] at the temple. It is apparent that the temple was the nucleus around which this *agrahāra* settlement grew.[34] Here, we have a case of expansion of agrarian frontiers in a largely forested tract, with the temple as nucleus of integration.

By the time this copper plate was renewed by Bhāskaravarman, important changes have taken place. Some potters settled in the north-western side of the *agrahāra*, so a potter's pit is referred to as the north-western boundary.[35] The tank of *vyavahārī* (lawyer) Khāsōka formed the north-eastern boundary.[36] The distinctly non-Sanskritic name Khāsōka may indicate a tribal background or substantial tribal influence. This copper plate shows the interface between the Brahmanical and non-Brahmanical population of this area; a tribal community is being integrated into the Brahmanical world, presumably through the network of the temple and the *agrahāra*.

Some portions in the copper plate were probably not in the original issued by Bhūtivarmana. By the time of Bhāskaravarman, two rivers bordering the village – the Kauśikā and the Gaṅgiṇikā – have either dried up or shifted their course. The Kauśikā shifted its course, giving rise to a *char* (shoal) on the eastern side of the village. The shift of the Gaṅgiṇikā created a *char* on the western side. These riverine shifts created new situations, requiring some new arrangement by the state; hence these lines were caused to be inserted by Bhāskaravarman.

We are not sure of the exact time of formation of these *chars*. Agreeing with Chitralekha Gupta,[37] we may reasonably assume that the *char* of the Kauśikā was earlier than that of the Gaṅgiṇikā, because the western boundary of the village, formed by the *char* of *Gaṅgiṇikā*, is referred to as *adhunā-sīmā-gaṅgiṇikā*, 'Gaṅginikā which is the present boundary'.[38] We don't find the use of this term in the case of the *char* of the Kauśikā. It is also apparent that the *char* of the Kauśikā was larger in area. By the time of Bhāskaravarman, this *char* seems to have become productive, so some sections in the village were probably eager to take a share in the land increased by the drying up of the river. That created a dispute in the village, which was adjudicated by inserting a new passage in the copper plate: 'The produce of the land that is increased by the Kauśikā will go to the Brahmins, the donees of the grant, but the land which is enlarged by the Gaṅgiṇikā shall be equally divided by the Brahmins as recorded'.[39]

Finally, this copper plate provides another important inference: the population of this area suffered from fluvial volatility, but it devised its own mechanism to cope with it. Even the *char* land was reclaimed. This area did not have to await the arrival of Islam for the introduction of settled agriculture or to learn the techniques of coping with fluvial volatility.

The political pattern in the Surma Valley on the death of Bhāskaravarman is unclear. A powerful, semi-independent *Sāmanta* ('feudatory' or 'vassal') stratum emerged, owing nominal allegiance to the paramount ruler of Samataṭa (Samataṭēśvara). This *sāmanta* stratum, to consolidate and expand its resource base or legitimacy, or as an act of sheer devotion, patronized Brahmanical temples and institutions by granting forest land by means of copper plates. Thus the Tippera copper-plate inscription (*c.* 664 CE) refers to Pradoṣaśarman, an orthodox Brahmin, who has caused the construction of a temple of Bhagavata Ananta Nārāyaṇa in a thickly forested portion in the *viṣaya* (district) of Suvvuṅga. Some more Brahmins have settled in the same area and were probably attached to this temple. This copper plate claims that the forested tract where this temple was constructed had no differentiation between 'natural' and 'artificial' (*kṛta-akṛta-avirodhi-āṭavi-bhūkhaṇḍe*).[40] It had a thick network of bush and creepers, and was infested with wild animals – deer, buffaloes, boars, tigers, serpents, etc. – who enjoyed, according to their will, all pleasures of home-life.[41] Pradoṣaśarman approached Sāmanta Lokanātha through a messenger *(dūtaka)* Rājaputra Lakṣmīnātha, for the grant of some land for the perpetual maintenance of *aṣṭa-puṣpikā, bali, caru* and *sattra* to the temple of Bhagavata Ananta Nārāyaṇa, as well as for the maintenance of a community of Brahmins attached to this temple. Sāmanta Lokanātha granted land in the forest region through this copper plate.

The setting up of a temple in a forested region continues the trend seen in some of the Dāmodarapura copper plates of the Gupta period in Varendra, in which common persons take their own initiative in constructing temples in forested tracts. Only later do they approach the state, which grants some *khila* (uncultivated) land on the payment of a sum of money to the state exchequer.[42] We are not sure if Pradoṣaśrman made such a payment; this might not have been required in the much more densely forested landscape of the Surma Valley.

But it is clear that before any endowment by any political elite, he has ventured into this forested tract on his own initiative. The same is true for the community of Brahmins who were probably attached to this temple. Political elites entered the scene only later.

The distinctly non-Sanskritic name of the *viṣaya* (Suvvuṅga) in which land was granted might suggest that it was located on the remote frontiers, in a tribal region. It was in the Suvang area of Cachar district of today's southern Assam.[43] Despite its location in a tribal area, elements associated with the *janapada* society have entered into this area.[44] This forested region was bordered on the south by the limit lines of two villages – Paṅga and Vapikā.[45] On the north, it was bounded by the tank (*puṣkariṇī*) of *mahattara* Raṇaśubha.[46] The word *mahattara* generally refers to the upper strata of peasantry.[47]

This role of temples is apparent also in the Kālāpur copper plate of Sāmanta Maruṇḍanātha (second half of the seventh CE). As it is highly corroded, resulting in the loss of vital data, this copper plate has been deciphered only partially by Gupta. This grant seems to have been made at the request of a Brahmin Jayasvāmin, who had earlier received one *pāṭaka* of *jalāṭavi*[48] (marshy and forested) land and built a temple and installed an image of Bhagavata Ananta Nārāyaṇa.[49] The *jalāṭavi* land granted in the present charter appears to be meant for the preservation of *bali, caru* and *sattra* in the temple and also for the maintenance of certain *traividya* Brahmins.[50] The location of the donated land has satisfactorily been identified in the Srimangala Police Station area of the Sylhet district, on the borders of the Tripura hills.[51] Here, too, a Brahmin penetrated into the forest on his own initiative, got a temple constructed and installed an image. Political elites entered the scene only later. The Ṭipperā and Kālāpur copper plates prove beyond doubt that Brahmanical institutions were one of the pioneers in advancing agrarian and cultural frontiers in the forested tracts of the Sylhet district as well as in the adjoining districts of Assam and Tripura.

COLONIZATION THROUGH STATE INITIATED SANSKRITIZATION

If the Ṭipperā copper plate of Sāmanta Lokanātha and the Kālāpur copper plate of Sāmanta Maruṇḍanātha give a picture of patronage to existing temples built by Brahmin pioneers by the political elites of the area, a different pattern is seen in the Paścimabhāga copper plate (c. 930 CE) of King Śrīcandra of Samataṭa, who also had control over some portions of Vaṅga.[52] It was discovered at Paścimabhāga, a village in the Maulavibazar subdivision of the Sylhet district. Its theatre is thus largely the same as that of the Nidhānpura copper plate, making it an important document to analyse the transitions taking place in this area in a span of some three hundred years. Both are concerned with the state-sponsored colonization of a forested tract through the donation of a large tract of land to a congregation of Brahmins and Brahmanical religious institutions in a largely non-Sanskritic area. In the case of the Paścimabhāga copper plate, we have a case of virtual state-sponsored *janapada-niveśa* (colonization) centring upon temples, *maṭhas* and a huge congregation of six thousand Brahmins. This copper plate is concerned with the donation of three *viṣayas* (districts) – Garalā, Pogāra and Candrapura – together with the tract called Aveḍikā, attached to Sātalavarga within the Śrīhaṭṭamaṇḍala of Puṇḍravardhanabhukti.[53] K.K. Gupta calculated that the donated tract was not less than 1,000 sq. km in area, covering a large section of the southern portions of the modern Sylhet district.[54] It was the single biggest donation to temples, *maṭhas* and Brahmins in all of eastern India, and probably one of the biggest in early medieval India.

These three *viṣayas* were bound in the east by the embankment at Vṛhatkōṭa (big fort), in the south by Mani-nadī, in the west by a canal (*khāṭaka*) called Jujju and the river Vetraghaṅghī, and by Kośiyārā-nadī (the modern Kusiyara River) in the north.[55] This entire tract was granted by the king on the principle of *bhūmi-chidra-nyāya*, which may indicate that a virgin space was being brought under cultivation. It was granted as a permanent gift, with many immunities and privileges, in favour of (temples of) the gods Brahmā, Vaiśvānara (i.e. Agni), Yogeśvara (an aspect of Śiva), Mahākāla (an aspect of Śiva) and to a congregation of six thousand Brahmins.[56] This tract of land was granted to increase the merit and fame of the donor and his parents, in the name of the Buddha.[57] This land was to exclude the land held by a Buddhist establishment (*ratna-traya*) and the land measuring 52 *pāṭakas* of 10 *droṇa*[58] each, which was attached to the boat station of a certain Indrēśvara. The area within the same boundaries was transformed into a *brahmapura* (Brahmin settlement) and given the name Śrīcandrapura, undoubtedly after the name of the king.[59] This *paramasaugata* (a great devotee of the Buddha) king took pride in claiming that this Brahmin settlement was planned and designed (*parikalpya*) by him, so it was named after him. An active role of the king, from planning the creation of this Śrīcandrapura-Brahmapura to its implementation, involving a major administrative restructuring – amalgamating three district-level localities – is more than apparent. A newly conquered area, forested, marshy and heavily influenced by tribal cultures, was sought to be integrated to the core areas of the Candra state through the state-sponsored planting of Brahmanical religious institutions and a huge congregation of Brahmins. Barring the huge size of the donated tract, this generally conforms to the pattern in many other parts of the subcontinent. Patronage to Brahmins and Brahmanical religious institutions was one of the ways through which early medieval Indian states tried to integrate the peripheral areas of their state to the core areas.[60]

The situation is peculiar: a Buddhist king donates more than three *viṣayas* in favour of a large congregation of Brahmins, one *maṭha* of Brahmā, four Vaṅgāla *maṭhas* and even four Deśāntarīya *maṭhas*, while totally ignoring a Buddhist establishment, already present in the same general area. This landowning Buddhist establishment antedated the creation of Śrīcandrapura-Brahmapura and established itself in Sylhet without any kind of state patronage and survived largely due to patronage provided by the local society.[61] It must have played some role in the de-tribalization of the local society, yet Buddhist institutions, as a whole, could not enter into institutional collaboration with the state headed by a Buddhist king in colonizing a marshy and forested periphery and effecting its ritual and functional integration with the core areas of the state. The Sylhet situation may be contrasted with the one in Pagan Burma, where Buddhist Saṅgha provided the institutional nucleus for agrarian expansion, creation and management of hydraulic resources, detribalizatation and integration of turbulent tribal frontiers into the body politic of the Pagan state.[62] This was happening in the same centuries when Buddhism lagged behind in institutional collaboration with the state in Samataṭa in these processes.[63] This failure to enter into institutional collaboration with the state in agrarian expansion in the outlying areas could have been one of the factors in the decline of Buddhism in Samataṭa.

Land grants to Brahmanical religious institutions in Sylhet on a massive scale, as discernible in the Paścimabhāga copper plate, induced some fundamental changes. In this copper plate, one *pāṭaka* was composed of ten *droṇas*.[64] This is a marked departure from the Gunāighar copper plate and Kālāpur copper plate. In both plates, one *pāṭaka* was composed of forty *droṇas*.[65] The Paścimabhāga copper plate indicates an increasing pressure on land as the *pāṭaka-droṇa* ratio has been reduced to 1:10. A significant transformation of the land has taken place. So it should not come as any surprise if we see the evolution of a local state in the same general area in the next century.

CHANGES BY THE ELEVENTH CENTURY CE

That a significant transformation of the land has taken place by the middle of the eleventh century is reflected in another copper-plate inscription from Sylhet district: the Bhāṭerā copperplate inscription of Govindakeśavadeva, *c.* 1049 CE. It was discovered at Bhāṭerā, about 20 miles from Sylhet.

The political situation in the Surma Valley after Śrīcandra is not clear. Around 1049 CE, we see the issue of the Bhāṭerā copper plate by Govindakeśavadeva. It records the donation of 375 *hala*[66] (ploughshare) of land along with 296 houses (i.e. households) in various villages (*nānāgrāme*) to Śiva (i.e. to a temple of Śiva) along with different kinds of attendants belonging to 'subject races'.[67] The absence of any epithet (*mahārājādhirāja*, etc.), either for Govindakeśavadeva or for any of his ancestors, forces us to question the independent status of this dynasty. Nor does the copper plate contain any royal seal. The customary practice of addressing different officials at the time of issue is also absent, and the plate is rather silent on the administrative structure of the state. It appears that the state which Govindakeśavadēva forged was at an early stage of institutionalization. But Śrīhaṭṭa (Sylhet), instead of being just one *maṇḍala* (i.e. Śrīhaṭṭamaṇḍala) within Puṇḍravardhanabhukti, has emerged as a separate political unit, as a state. This copper plate refers to Srīharājya,[68] which is, apparently, an abbreviation of Srīhaṭṭarājya. Govindakeśavadeva is described as Srīhaṭṭanātha.[69] Here we are witnessing the formation of a local state, without much bureaucratic paraphernalia, whose ruler grants a large tract of land to a temple of Śiva, ostensibly for the merit of his parents and himself, as well as for the legitimacy of his rule. His rule extended over at least some portions of Sylhet district, parts of today's Hailakandi and Cachar districts, and parts of northern Tripura.[70] It thus included some areas which have retained their tribal character till a recent past. This is reflected in the language of this copper plate. The first 29 lines are in Sanskrit; lines 29-51 are in a local Bengali dialect; whereas lines 52-5 are in an unknown tribal language, probably Kuki.[71] Thus parts of it were addressed to some tribal audience, in an attempt to negotiate the tribal substrata of the area.

However, a transformation seems to have taken place in the area since the days of the Ṭipperā and Kālāpur copper plates, in which the forested nature of the landscape was the most marked feature. Instead of the donation of *āṭavi bhūkhaṇḍa* (forest land), as in the Ṭipperā copper plate, or *jalāṭavi bhūkhaṇḍa* (marshy forested land) as in the Kālāpur copper plate, or an unspecified category of land, apparently brought under cultivation for the first time, as in the Nidhānpura and Paśimabhāga copper plates, the land granted in this copper plate is measured in terms of *hala*. This land abutted with 'houses', and spread across many villages (*nānāgrāme*). In other words, this temple was granted land along with attendant labour. This was in a swampy area adjoining tribal land. Yet plough agriculture had become so common that land was measured in terms of ploughshares, even in the most forested and marshiest part of Bengal.[72]

The transactional network of this temple, as indicated by the spread of the gift land across a wide area, seems to be widespread. It got two *halas* of land at Kāṭākhāla, identified with a locality of the same name in the Hailakandi subdivision of Cachar district;[73] ten *halas* in the Salachapara area of Cachar district;[74] and many *halas* along with 'houses' in the areas adjoining Bhāṭerā. It was also granted ten *halas* to the west of Sāgara.[75] The translator of this copper plate has rightly equated this with *hāor* – a local pronunciation of *sāgara*, referring to the sea-like swamps.[76] However, even in these deep marshes, some varieties of *boro* rice (a species specific to the marshy areas of Bengal) grow plentifully.[77] Here, we have probably the first recorded evidence of successful negotiation of this swampy landscape in Sylhet.

In Samataṭa, right from the days of the Gunāighar copper plate (*c.* 507 CE), marshy land was granted to Buddhist or Brahmanical religious institutions, yet there is no parallel to this grant of land along with 'houses' in a marshy landscape in all South Asia. A distant parallel is provided by a similar practice in Angkor-period Cambodia. There, whenever a new area was conquered by the king, he tried to bring it under his effective control by planting temples, or bringing the existing temple(s) under the network of the imperial temple of the capital city. If new temples were planted by the state in the newly-conquered area, they were generally granted marshy lands and attendant slave labour. With the help of the slave labour, the temple had to bring the marshy and forested areas under cultivation. This created a new resource base for the state in the long run.[78] In the Bhāṭerā copper plate, the temple of Śiva was granted 'houses' rather than slave labour; that is, members of specified households in the granted villages were required to contribute labour to the temple. This was essential for its survival in a sparsely populated area.

One important differentiation is also discernible: it is only in Sylhet district, especially around Bhāṭerā, that we find references to the grant of 'houses' along with some *halas* of land to the temple. In Cachar district or in the areas of Hill Ṭipperā, only some *halas* of land were granted, not 'houses'. Probably these areas were not settled enough for a grant of household labour to the temple. Here, the temple had to play a more active role on the agrarian frontiers and devise ways to interact with the tribal substrata. This gives significance to the fact that some lines in this copper plate were written in a tribal language, obviously addressed to a tribal audience.

We should also note the total absence of any indication of Buddhist presence in the tracts granted to this temple. In some other parts of early medieval Bihar and Bengal, we see that Buddhist institutions were present on agrarian frontiers and played an important role in detribalization.[79] This does not appear to be the case in the Bhāṭerā copper plate. We have seen that the land granted to the temple was spread across many villages, and no Buddhist presence of any kind is referred to, even indirectly. This may indicate a gradual decline of Buddhism in the area.

The resource mobilization capacity of Govindakeśavadeva, as well as his patronage to Brahmins and Brahmanical temples seems to have increased in the later part of his reign. Thus in the second Bhāṭerā copper plate, issued by his successor Īśānadeva, it is claimed that Govindakeśavadeva undertook the rite of *tulāpuruṣadāna* (donating gold to a Brahmin or a group of Brahmins equal to the weight of the donor). For this nascent state, this ritual must have involved a considerable mobilization of resources. We are also informed that by his *tulāpuruṣadāna*, the Brahmins 'got so much wealth that they were covered with golden jewels' and Govindakeśavadeva became like 'a wish-fulfilling tree for them, and, fully satisfied, they lost the desire to go back to the places of their origins'.[80] We are also informed that he constructed a lofty stone temple for Kṛṣṇa. Leaving aside the usual amount of panegyric in this claim, we may visualize that inviting Brahmins and settling them in this nascent state, and patronage to Brahmanical temples, were among the measures through which he tried to legitimate and consolidate his rule. These acts of munificence must have taken place in the later part of his rule, as they are not mentioned in the first Bhāṭerā copper plate.

Under Īśānadeva, as reflected in the second Bhāṭerā plate, this state came to have an increased administrative apparatus, and this could not have been possible without a further strengthening of its agrarian economy. Thus, the *ākṣapaṭalika* (accountant general) Vanamālikara, who belonged to the Vaidya caste, received two *halas* of land.[81] This copper plate also refers to one Vīradatta, a military commander.[82] These officers of the state are absent in the first Bhāṭerā plate. Īśānadeva also constructed a temple for Viṣṇu.

SUMMING UP THE SURMA-BARAK VALLEY EXPERIENCE

The Surma-Barak Valley experience, arguably the most forested and marshiest part of eastern Bengal, offers some interesting patterns of human attempts of taming the jungle and marshes. In the seventh century itself, we discern two divergent trends. The first recorded evidence (in the Nidhānapur copper-plate inscription) indicates state-sponsored colonization of southern Sylhet centring upon Brahmanical temples and *agrahāras*. But the two other copper-plate inscriptions of the same century display the pioneering zeal of individual Brahmins who penetrated into the forests on their own initiative and constructed temples without any kind of state patronage. These temples established intricate linkages with the society in which they functioned, and catered to some of their needs. In such cases, political elites entered into the scene to patronize them only later, probably to use the societal linkages of these institutions for its own advantage. In the tenth century, southern Sylhet again became the focus of a massive state-sponsored colonization programme, centring on Brahmanical religious institutions and a huge congregation of six thousand Brahmins. This whole operation was carefully planned and executed by the ruling Buddhist king with the aim of integrating this forested and marshy periphery to the core areas of the Candra kingdom. Buddhist institutions failed to enter into institutional collaboration with the state in this important endeavour.

The state-sponsored colonization of southern Sylhet in the tenth century AD heralded some long-term transitions. Emergence of a local state in the eleventh century, which had its main resource base in plough-based agriculture within its territories, was one such transition.

NOTES

1. Arthur Geddes, 'Some Geographical Factors in Indian History', in A.T.A. Learmonth et al. (eds.), *Man and Land in South Asia*, Delhi: Concept Publlishers and ICSSR, 1982, p. 94.
2. Richard M. Eaton, 'Conversion to Christianity among the Nagas, 1870-1971', *Indian Economic and Social History Review*, 21(1), January-March 1984, p.1.
3. B.D. Chattopadhyaya, 'State Perception of the "Forest" and the "Forest" as State in Early Medieval India', in B.B. Chaudhury and Arun Bandopadhyaya (eds.), *Tribes, Forests and Social Formations in Indian History*, Delhi: Manohar, 2004, p. 28.
4. O.H.K. Spate and A.T.A. Learmonth, *India and Pakistan: A General and Regional Geography*, London: Methuen, 1967, p. 583.
5. Ibid., p. 583.
6. Ibid., p. 586.
7. Geddes, op. cit., p. 195.
8. *Hāor* is a local pronunciation of *sāgara*, the Sanskrit word for the sea (K.M. Gupta, 'The Bhāṭerā Copper Plate of Govindakeśavadēva', *Epigraphia Indica* XIX, 1927-8, p. 279). *Hāors* are depressions in the Sylhet plains, in which an enormous amount of water accumulates during the rainy season, so much so that they resemble the sea, hence the name *hāor*. For a more detailed analysis of the *hāors* of the Sylhet district, see Shamsul Alam et al., 'Sylhet and its Evolving Geographical Environment', in Sharif Uddin Ahmed (ed.), *Sylhet: History and Heritage*, Dhaka: Bangladesh Itihas Samiti, 1999, pp. 73-82.They have claimed that out of a total area of 12,569 sq. km of this district, around 6,000 sq. km are covered by different *hāors*. Most of these *hāors* are perennial in nature (pp. 73-6).
9. W.W. Hunter, *A Statistical Account of Assam*, vol. II, Delhi: Low Price Publications, 1990 (rpt.), p. 262.
10. Ibid.
11. Spate and Learmonth, op. cit., p. 575.
12. David Ludden, 'Investing in Nature around Sylhet: An Excursion into Geographical History', *Economic and Political Weekly*, 38(48), 2003, pp. 5082-3.

13. Hunter, op. cit., p. 262.
14. K.K. Gupta, *Copper Plates of Sylhet*, vol. 1: *7th-11th Centuries* AD, Sylhet: Lipika Enterprises, 1967, p. 3.
15. B.M. Morrison, *Political Centres and Cultural Regions in Early Bengal*, Jaipur: Vikash Publications, 1980, p. 38.
16. Ibid., p. 38.
17. Ibid., p. 154.
18. Ibid., p. 119.
19. Birendra Nath Prasad, 'Major Trends and Perspectives in Studies in the Functional Dimensions of Indian Monastic Buddhism in the Past One Hundred Years: A Historiographical Survey', *Buddhist Studies Review*, Journal of the U.K. Association for Buddhist Studies, London, vol. 25(1), 2008, p. 84; idem, 'Monarchs, Monasteries and Trade on an "Agrarian Frontier": Early Medieval Samataṭa-Harikela, Bangladesh', in idem (ed.), *Monasteries, Shrines and Society: Buddhist and Brahmanical Religious Institutions in India in their Socio-Economic Context*, Delhi: Manak, 2011, p. 121.
20. Birendra Nath Prasad, 'Votive Inscriptions on the Sculptures of Early Medieval Samataṭa-Harikela, Bengal: Explorations in Socio-religious History', *Religions of South Asia*, London, vol. 4, no. 1, 2010, p. 29.
21. D.K. Chakrabarti, *Ancient Bangladesh: A Study of Archaeological Sources*, Delhi: Oxford University Press, 1992, pp. 159-60; M.M. Hoque and Seema Hoque, 'Ancient Human Settlement Pattern of Bangladesh: A Preliminary Study', *Journal of Bengal Art*, Dhaka, vol. 2, 1997, 283-300.
22. Birendra Nath Prasad, 'Votive Inscriptions', pp. 27-43.
23. Abu Imam, 'Ancient Sylhet, History and Tradition', in Sharif Uddin Ahmed (ed.), *Sylhet: History and Heritage*, Dhaka: Bangladesh Itihas Samiti, 1999, p. 176; Chakrabarti, op. cit., pp. 170-1.
24. Sujit Chowdhury, 'Bhuban Tirth: A Cult Spot on the Hilltop', in J.P. Singh and G. Sengupta (eds.), *Archaeology of North-Eastern India*, Delhi: Har-Anand in association with Vikas Publishing House, 1991, pp. 16-26; idem, 'The Bhuban Hill in Cachar, Assam: Its Origin and Affinity', in Dillip K. Medhi (ed.), *Man and Environment in Northeast India*, vol. III: *Heritage Issues, Anthropology, Archaeology and Heritage*, Guwahati: EBH Publications, 2008, pp. 35-50.
25. D.C. Sircar, *Epigraphic Discoveries in East Pakistan*, Calcutta: Sanskrit College, 1973, p. 36; translated this term as the 'principle of free enjoyment of land by one who brings it under cultivation for the first time'.
26. P. Bhattacharya, 'Nidhanpur Copper Plates of Bhaskaravarman', *Epigraphia Indica*, XII, 1913-14, p. 79.
27. Ibid., p. 78.
28. Ibid., p. 79.
29. Chitralekha Gupta, 'Aspects of Rural Settlements in the Light of

Nidhanpur Copper-Plate Inscription', in C. P. Sinha (ed.), *Art, Archaeology and Culture of Eastern India, Dr. B. S. Verma Felicitation Volume*, Patna: Bihar Puravida Parishada, 1997, p. 152.

30. Ibid.
31. *Bali* referred to food offerings dedicated to the deity of the temple. It was basically intended to appease or propitiate the god to deter or control malevolent agencies, especially evil spirits (Michael Willis, *The Archaeology of Hindu Ritual: Temples and the Establishment of the Gods*, Delhi: Cambridge University Press, 2009, p. 103).
32. *Sattra* attached to temples became a regular feature of religious life of northern India during the Gupta period, transforming the temple into a virtual community centre. It was an institution providing free feeding and, at a later date, medicines to Brahmins, wandering ascetics and the destitute. For a recent analysis of evolving functional roles and meanings of the institution of *sattra*, see Willis, 2009: 96-108. *Sattras* were designed to support and strengthen the place of the temple and to advance the interests of temple-based theism in Indian society. They seem to have been modelled on the mechanisms organized by the Buddhists to support the Saṅgha and developed as a deliberate counter to them (Willis, ibid., p. 106).
33. *Caru* referred to a *homa* (burnt offering) to the deity of the temple (Willis, ibid., p. 108).
34. Chitralekha Gupta, op. cit., p. 152.
35. Bhattacharya, op. cit., p. 79.
36. Ibid., p. 79.
37. Chitralekha Gupta, op. cit., p. 155.
38. P. Bhattacharya, *Kāmarūpa-Śāsanāvalī*, Rangpur: Sahitya Parishad, 1931, p. 26.
39. P. Bhattacharya, 'Two Lost Plates of the Nidhanpur Copper Plates of Bhaskaravarman', *Epigraphia Indica*, XIX, 1927, p. 121.
40. D.C. Sircar, *Select Inscriptions Bearing on Indian History and Civilization*, vol. II: *From the Sixth to the Eighteenth Century*, Delhi: Motilal Banarsidass, 1983, p. 31.
41. Ibid.
42. R.G. Basak, 'The Five Damodarapura Copper Plate Inscriptions of the Gupta Period', *Epigraphia Indica*, XV, 1919-20, pp. 113-45.
43. N.K. Bhattasali, 1945, 'New Light on the History of Assam', *Indian Historical Quarterly*, XXI, 1945, p. 28; R.M. Nath, *The Background of Assamese Culture*, Shillong: A.K. Nath Publications, 1949, p. 56.
44. It is interesting to note that in developing his thesis of Islamisation of medieval eastern Bengal, Richard Eaton conveniently begins his *The Rise of Islam and the Bengal Frontier*, Delhi: Oxford University Press, 1994, p. 3, by randomly picking some lines from this inscription and inserting some words. It is better to quote him here:

[The Sylhet region of east Bengal] was outside the pale of human habitation, where there is no distinction between natural and artificial, infested by wild animals and poisonous reptiles, and covered with forest out-growth. (insertion his)

He seems to attempt to construct a thesis that this was the case in the whole of pre-Muslim eastern Bengal, which was later won by Islam through the plough. Even in Cachar, the most forested part of Samatata-Harikela, the applicability of Eaton's theory does not appear to be logical. An analysis of the Tippera copper plate inscription shows that the area, despite the heavily forested landscape, was, contrary to Eaton's assertion, not outside the pale of human habitation. His basic premise is not true even for Cachar, leave aside all eastern Bengal. Even when he chooses to generalize the Cachar experience for the entire eastern Bengal, he overlooks the fact that a Brahmin had already constructed a temple there, a community of Brahmins had already settled there, a military chief was already there to patronize them, this forested tract was not far from at least two settled villages, and at least one *mahattara* with his tank was already present in the neighbourhood. This was happening in the Cachar area at least six hundred years before the arrival of Islam.

45. Sircar, *Select Inscriptions*, vol. II, p. 32.
46. Ibid.
47. For an analysis of the role of the *mahattaras* in the rural society of early medieval Bengal, see Sayantani Pal, 'The *Mahattaras* of Early Bengal Inscriptions', *Journal of Bengal Art*, vol. 7, 2002, pp. 277-82. She has observed that the *mahattaras* in the inscriptions of early medieval Bengal represented a class of peasants that had established its leadership in the settled agrarian villages, played prominent role in land related matters and enjoyed social pre-eminence as well (p. 281).
48. K.K. Gupta has completely missed the significance of this term, taking it to mean just *āṭavi* (forested) land. Sircar takes it in the same sense, probably because the original or its impression was not available to him.
49. K.K. Gupta, *Copper Plates of Sylhet*, op. cit., p. 70.
50. D.C. Sircar, *Epigraphic Discoveries in East Pakistan*, Calcutta, 1973, p. 16.
51. K.K. Gupta, op. cit., p. 80.
52. For some earlier analysis of this copper plate inscription, see J.B. Bhattacharjee, 'Land Grants, Land Management and the Nature of Social Formation in Ancient Srihatta', in *Social and Polity Formations in Pre-Colonial North-East India: The Barak Valley Experience*, Delhi: Har-Anand in association with Vikas Publishing House, 1991, pp. 18-40 ; Abdul Momin Chowdhury, 'Tenth Century Sylhet: Reflections on the Paschimbhag Copper Plate of Srichandra', in Sharif Uddin Ahmed (ed.), *Sylhet: History and Heritage*, Dhaka: Bangladesh Itihas Samiti, 1999, pp. 632-43; Abu Imam, 'Ancient Sylhet, History and Tradition', in Sharif

Uddin Ahmed (ed.), *Sylhet: History and Heritage*, Dhaka: Bangladesh Itihas Samiti, 1999, pp. 173-201; S.B. Qanungo, 'Political History of Sylhet: Ancient Period', in Sharif Uddin Ahmed (ed.), *Sylhet: History and Heritage*, Dhaka: Bangladesh Itihas Samiti, 1999, pp. 383-95.

They have provided a general outline of royal patronage received by the Brahmanical religious institutions mentioned in this copper plate. None of them has, sadly, analysed the nature of the Buddhist presence in this area as discernible in this copper plate. Similarly, none of them has attempted to explore why a Buddhist king would donate such a vast area – around 1,000 sq. km, covering more than three districts of his kingdom – to Brahmanical religious institutions while totally ignoring a Buddhist establishment already present in the same general area. For a detailed analysis of the nature of Buddhist presence in this inscription, see 'Some Observations on the Paschimbhag Copper Plate Inscription of Śrīcandra', *Journal of Bengal Art*, vol. 19, 2014, pp. 69-79.

53. D.C. Sircar, 'Paśchimabhāga Copper Plate of Śrīcandra, Year 5', p. 294, ll. 27-8.
54. K.K. Gupta, *Copper Plates of Sylhet*, p. 119.
55. Sircar, 'Paśchimabhāga Copper Plate of Śrīcandra, Year 5', p. 295, ll. 34-5.
56. Ibid., p. 298, ll. 51-2.
57. Ibid., p. 298.
58. The *droṇa* or *droṇavāpa* 'seems to have been originally equal to about five *bighās* or roughly 1.5 acres of land' (Sircar, *Epigraphic Discoveries in East Pakistan*, p. 33). In the context of the Paścimabhāga copper plate of Śrīcandra, Sircar (Sircar, 'Paśchimabhāga Copper Plate of Śrīcandra, Year 5', p. 296; 1973) calculates that one *pāṭaka* was not less than 15 acres.
59. Sircar, 'Paśchimabhāga Copper Plate of Śrīcandra, Year 5', pp. 295-6.
60. For a historiographical review of this process in, see Birendra Nath Prasad (ed.), *Monasteries, Shrines and Society: Buddhist and Brahmanical Religious Institutions in India in their Socio-Economic Context*, Delhi: Manak Publications, 2011, pp. 1-24.
61. The notion of dependence on royal patronage for the survival of Buddhist monasteries is gradually being discarded. For a review of such literature, see Birendra Nath Prasad, 'Studies in the Socio-Economic History of Indian Monastic Buddhism in the Past One Hundred Years: A Historiographical Survey', in idem (ed.), *Monasteries, Shrines and Society: Buddhist and Brahmanical Religious Institutions in India in their Socio-Economic Context*, Delhi: Manak Publications, 2011, pp.27-83. For similar arguments with reference to early medieval Samataṭa-Harikela, see Birendra Nath Prasad, 'Monarchs, Monasteries', op. cit., pp. 116-36; Prasad, 'Votive Inscriptions', op. cit., pp. 27-43. For the need to see the support system of Buddhist monasteries in early medieval Bihar and

Bengal beyond the paradigm of total dependence on royal patronage, see Prasad, 'Major Trends', op. cit., pp. 80-3.

62. Kenneth R. Hall, 'Buddhism as an Economic Force in Pagan Burma', in Nicholas Tarling (ed.), *The Cambridge History of South East Asia*, vol. I, Cambridge: Cambridge University Press, 1992, pp. 240-5.
63. For an analysis of this process in early medieval Samatata-Harikela, see Prasad, 'Monarchs, Monasteries', op. cit., pp. 116-36. It has been noted that most of the royal land grants to Buddhist monasteries in this Samataṭa-Harikela took place in the well-settled area. When Samataṭa rulers granted land to Buddhist monasteries in such well-settled villages, royal legitimacy was the main motive, not facilitating agrarian expansion in outlying areas, for which Brahmanical religious institutions were preferred by kings.
64. Sircar, 'Paśchimabhāga Copper Plate of Śrīcandra, Year 5', p. 298.
65. Sircar, *Epigraphic Discoveries in East Pakistan*, p. 33 ; K.K. Gupta, *Copper Plates of Sylhet*, vol. 1: *7th-11th Centuries* AD, Sylhet, 1967, p. 77.
66. *Hala* as a land measurement unit is still popular in the Sylhet area. K.M. Gupta, 'The Bhāṭerā Copper Plate of Govindakeśavadēva', *Epigraphia Indica* XIX, p. 285, calculates 375 *hala* as roughly 1,312.5 acres.
67. Ibid., p. 295.
68. Ibid., p. 280, verse 5.
69. Ibid., p. 281, verse 20.
70. Ibid., p. 278.
71. Ibid., p. 277.
72. In explaining the massive conversion to Islam in eastern Bengal, the basic argument of Richard Eaton is that in 'much of "eastern Delta", rice agriculture and Islam were introduced simultaneously' (Richard Eaton, 'Who are the Bengal Muslims? Conversions and Islamisation in Bengal', in idem, *Essays on Islam and Indian History*, Delhi: Oxford University Press, 2001, p. 264). It is in this sense that he characterizes Islam as a 'religion of the plough' in eastern Bengal. As per his analysis, eastern Bengal 'experienced a transition to settled agriculture at the time that Islam took hold among common folk' (Richard Eaton, 'Shrines, Cultivators, and Muslim "Conversion" in Punjab and Bengal, 1300-1700', *Medieval History Journal*, vol. 12(2), 2009, p. 208). Before the introduction of plough agriculture by Islam in the area, the subsistence economy of eastern Bengal was characterized by 'fishing, hunting and gathering and slash-and-burn farming' (Eaton, *Rise of Islam in Eastern Frontier*, p. 202). If Islam was the 'religion of the plough' in eastern Bengal in general, this character was most explicit in the tract from Sylhet to Chittagong; hence, within eastern Bengal, Islam had the greatest success here in the Mughal period (Eaton, 'Who are the Bengal Muslims? Conversions and Islamisation in Bengal', p. 274). The evidence from the Bhāṭerā copper-plate inscription indicates that plough agriculture

was known and widely practised, not only in Sylhet, but also in Cachar, almost two hundred and fifty years before the arrival of Islam in Sylhet. His theory of Islamization of Bengal, therefore, cannot be accepted.

73. K.M. Gupta, op. cit., p. 278.
74. Ibid., p. 285, verse 38.
75. Ibid.
76. Ibid., p. 279.
77. Hunter, *A Statistical Account of Assam*, op. cit., p. 266.
78. Kenneth R. Hall, 'The Temple-based Political Economy of Angkor Cambodia', in Nicholas Tarling (ed.), *Cambridge History of Southeast Asia*, vol. 1, Cambridge: Cambridge University Press, 1992, pp. 229-39.
79. Prasad, 'Major Trends', op. cit., p. 83; 'Monarchs, Monasteries', op. cit., idem, pp. 129-30.
80. K.K. Gupta, *Copper Plates of Sylhet*, op. cit., p. 190.
81. Ibid., p. 185.
82. Ibid., p. 186.

CHAPTER 3

Man, Nature and State in Pre-Colonial Kachar

BAZLUR RAHMAN KHAN

Nature generally defines all living and non-living elements of our surroundings including flora and fauna. Man from the beginning has maintained an inseparable relationship with nature and has remained dependent on nature for survival on earth. Nature virtually dominated human life till the discovery of fire and iron. The invention of these two elements set mankind on motion. They started exploring natural resources in different new ways for the fulfilment of their needs. And in this process many societies consciously or unconsciously evolved various methods to use nature prudently. While at the same time, human tendency to have a control over nature encouraged proclamation of right over natural resources like land, forest, etc. Thus a new era of conflict and conciliation between man and environment began. In this new milieu not only society but state too emerged as an actor in influencing nature. However, environment continued to shape the course of human civilization through different means. But with industrial revolution a new form of development took place. To ensure maximum benefit, vested groups started complete destruction of nature. As a result, the centuries old fragile relationship between man and nature entered into a new phase.[1] The relationship between man and nature with regard to Kachar is no different.

Kachar here refers to present Kachar and Hailakandi district of Barak Valley in southern Assam. The district of Hailakandi is recently carved out of the erstwhile Kachar. The study on the origin of the term both Kachar and Hailakandi has revealed that the naming of these places has a very deep relationship with the characteristics of the land. About Kachar, there are two possibilities regarding its naming. Edward Gait, author of the first modern historical account of Assam, is of the opinion that the tribe, Kacharis has given their name to the district of Kachar.[2] The second opinion is that the name has been given to the district by the Bengalis of Sylhet, because it is an outlaying place skirting the mountains. The word 'Kachar' is still used in Sylhet in designating a plot of land at the foot of a mountain. It is derived from Sanskrit 'Kachchha' which means 'a plain near a mountain', or 'a place near water'.[3]

Similarly there are various opinions regarding the origin of the term 'Hailakandi'. According to Rajmohan Nath and others the term Hailakandi derives from the Kuki word 'Halam' which means a small state and 'Kundia' a Bodo-Kacahari word which means a plot of land for temporary ploughing. There are also some other opinions in regard to nomenclature of Hailakandi. One version says that the area was abundant in paddy cultivation; particularly 'shail' peddy was more in production and was the granary of the area as a whole. For that reason it was called 'Shailkandi' – Kundi a Kuki word meaning a 'a bunch' – a land of the Kukis. From this it turns into Hailakandi. The western portion of present Hailakandi was known as Boroibari. It was under the occupation of one Ipra Queen 'Hail'. She was the zamindar of the estate and from her name it became 'Halirkandi' and then turned into Hailkandi.[4]

Hailakandi – a foothill space, though it is difficult to decide which is historically correct yet according to majority opinion the combination of the derivatives of 'Halam' and 'Kundina' was the origin. Both term Kachar and Hailakandi originated in pre-colonial times. However, it was during colonial regime their use became widespread and recorded in the British documents to designate particular territorial unit. When British established their administrative system, they organized *thanas* like Katigorah, Silchar, Hailakandi.

Kachar's Geography

The geography has to do a lot with the environmental history. It played a great role in shaping the destiny of people and their surroundings. Lucien Febvre's pioneer work, *A Geographical Introduction to History*, exposed the relationship between different natural environments and different forms of resource use.[5] The picturesque valley of Barak comprising Kachar plain is the natural extension of the vast Bengal plain. According to Nihar Ranjan Ray, author of *Bangalir Ithihas*, Barak-Surma Valley is the extension of Meghana Valley. There is no natural boundary between these two valleys. That is why the society and culture of east Maimansingh,

Tripura plain is well tied with Sylhet and Kachar that there is no difference that exists between the two. Kachar comprising the Barak plain and the northern and southern foothills is the product of the fluvio-geomorphic processes of the river Barak and its tributaries. The river Barak, while moving westward for a distance of 225 km in Assam through the Kachar district and along the northern border of the Hailakandi and Karimganj districts, builds up its alluvial plain, some time called Kachar plain. The plain is enclosed by hill ranges on three sides – The Meghalaya Plateau and the Barail range of the N.C. Hills district on the north, Manipur hills on the east and the Mizo hills on the south. The north-western side is open to the Kushiyara-Surma plain of the Sylhet district of Bangladesh and Karimganj district while Saraspur-Chatachura, a low hill range, separated Kachar plain from Karimganj district. The Kachar plain is the headword piedmont part of the Barak-Surma-Kushiyara plain, which lies largely in Bangladesh.[6]

River Barak and Kachar

The Kachar plain slopes down gently to the west and the river Barak flows sluggishly in meandering course through it leaving a series of ox-bow like swamps. The immediate neighbourhood of the river represents an active flood characterized by extensive marshy tracts and annual inundation. Occurrence of isolated low hillocks in the plain indicates the erosional activities of the Barak and its tributaries. The western and central part of the plain are built up of the alluvial deposits. Thus the plain is created by both the aggradational and degradational activities of the Barak River system. Tributaries like Chiri, Diksa, Digli, Jiri, Madhura, Jatinga, Larang, etc., from the Barail range of N.C. hills and the Sonai, Dhaleswari-Katakhal, Singla and Longai from southern Mizo hills join the Barak adding considerable volume of water and load of sediments. The Kachar plain bounded by the foothills of the Barail range on the north and foothills of the Mizo hills on south. Kachar plain gradually rises to the north and south and merges with the foothills. The terraces and isolated hillocks (*tilas*) on the interfluves, linked often to the foothills, provide ideal site for tea gardens. The alluvial soils are extensively over the Kachar plains. Because of alluvium left by the rivers after leaving the hills and flowing through the plains these soils receive high fertility. B.C. Allen who composed the *Assam District Gazetteers*, narrated that the Kachar plain was dotted with hollows, beels and swamps.[7]

Climate and Kachar

The climate of pre-colonial Kachar was almost same it is today. The climate of Kachar is a tropical monsoon with predominantly hot and humid summer having high rainfall during June to September (about 4,000 mm) and relatively cold winter. The south-west monsoon penetrate eastward up to the Manipur hills and the Kachar plains receive heavy rainfall. Kachar being a highland on its north, east and south is open on the west to orographic and other cyclonic disturbances of the south-west monsoon. Silchar receives high rainfall in the order of 323 cm respectively on an average annual basis.[8] During the the south-west monsoons to the inconvenience of frequent and long constituted falls of rain, which sometimes commence during the early part of February, and frequently in the following month of March: from this period vegetation develops rapidly, which, in the course of a few weeks, covers the whole of the uncultivated tracts with dense and lofty reed and grass jungles, through which even an elephant penetrates with difficulty, and which forms the favourite haunts of innumerable herds of deer and wild buffalos.[9] The heavy rain causes the nature of Kachar to be bountiful. The high rainfall also has its negative impact in the form of devastating floods. In Hailakandi, during the rains and minor inundations, the *mirasdars* were required to furnish boats for transshipping the thana records.[10] To make matters worse, there were three consecutive unusually wet seasons; added with terrible inundations in 1834 which caused great miseries to the people.[11]

There with great perseverance and toll they raised in the centre of the swamps large hillocks from twelve feet in height, whereon they built their homesteads in the dry weather in order to preserve their cattle and goods during high inundation. In this place they located to the present day, cultivating the swamps with rice and jute and carrying on the occupations of fishing and bird catching, varied with mat and basket weaving, and the cutting of grass for thatching purposes and for the consumption of their cattle.[12]

Nature as Barrier

The large volume of water brought by the Barak and its tributaries enrich the fertility of the land was true but due to the presence of hilly land on the three sides of Kachar plain water logging was very common. So the region was a fertile ground for malarial fever, kalazar, cholera and small pox which usually levied a huge toll on human life. Further, the frequent raids and superstitious customs of the dwellers of the neighbouring hills, the ravage caused by the wild animals, the devastating floods and unhealthy climate had hitherto acted as a serious check on the growth of population.[13] The history of Kachar shows that due to peculiar geographical nature of land not congenial for permanent habitation and the predominance of tribal form of cultivation, permanent settlement all over the plains could not fully develop in the period preceding to Tippera, Koch and finally Dimasa reign. During this period, arable land was extremely scarce due to the presence of thick forests across the alluvial basins of the Barak and its tributaries. So, the Kachar was thinly populated till the arrival of colonial rule. The total population of Kachar at the time of its annexation into British empire was around 50,000 only. Captain Fisher estimated the quantity of arable, but unoccupied land at 18,00,000 *bighas*.[14] The famous saint Hazrat Shahjalal who was associated with the conquest of Sylhet by Sikandar Gazi, sent his disciples eastwards, but it is said that they did not move beyond Bundashil in Badarpur. It may be surmised, not unreasonably, that the tract of the land beyond Badarpur on their eastward journey was full of dense forests not suitable for human habitation. The legend containing the story of Shahjalal's suppression of some giants making regular nocturnal raids on the inhabitants of Badarpur may explain the presence of some tribal folks living in the jungles on the northern bank of the Barak opposite to Badarpur.[15]

The geo-physical nature of the Kachar plain made it the regular prey of devastating floods caused by the Barak and its tributaries. The alluvial basins were very fertile to grow luxuriant vegetations swallowing up the arable land. As a result the village remained thinly populated during the whole of the medieval period. The extension of the Dimasa rule over the Kachar plain in the early eighteenth century, encouragement of migrants to settle in the valley and patronization of them with land grants and other facilities went a long way in re-shaping the relation between man, nature and state.

Forest in Kachar

In the words of Richard Grove we make no apology for devoting so much of this paper to the history of the relationship between forests, people and the state.[16] We don't have any reference about the exact size of forests in pre-colonial Kachar. We have a rough idea about the area covered by forest when the authority of the Company was established in Kachar. We only know that the densely and wooded and mountainous region appears to start at a distance between 40 and 50 miles from the southern bank of the river Barak, inhabited by the Paite Kookis, was a part of the state of Tripura.[17] The forest of Kachar was rich in timber, mineral and tusked elephants and the valley was fertile and the *beels* abundant with palatable fish. Timbers found in Kachar is mainly divided into three broad catergories, called Gundah, Dum, Kari. Gundah consists of Jarols only. Karis consists of smaller trees like Ratta, Pumar, Karil, Kurta, Singra, etc.[18] Elephant was particularly abundant. Author of the seventeenth-century historical account 'Baharaistan I Gaibi' Mirza Nathan mentioned about the richness of Kachar region with regard to elephants. We know from him that when Mubariz Khan and Mirak Bahadur Jalair, two Mughal officials went to the Thana of Bundashil in modern Karimganj, Mubariz Khan thought in his mind that when a new *subahdar* had arrived, it would be well if he could show a record of credible services. He undertook an expedition to Pratapgarh which belonged to the Raja of Kachar. He captured elephants and sent them to the service of new governors.[19] Similarly we know from the same account, when the Raja of Kachar was defeated, he gave 47 elephants to the imperial Mughal forces.[20] Elephants were very common in Kachar even during the initial years of colonial rule. It is reported that when English masters appointed *chowkidars* in every village to report all heinous offences, he was not required to patrol at night since the fear of wild elephants kept the people at home after dusk.[21] The forest also has a place in the mythologies related to the origin of Dimasa-Kachari kingdom.

Besides agricultural production, the chief produce were forest production including ivory, wax, cane, bamboo and timber. There is abundance of proofs that the timber required for boat industries were exported from Kachar. Among other forest produces, *atar* (perfume) producing agar trees were abundant in the Kachar which is proved from the prosperity of Mr Gulu Miya, a trader in *atar* who played a very important role in the politics of the Dimasa kingdom in the closing years.[22]

According to the mythology quoted in Kachari Burunji, the founder of the kingdom of Kachar was Gatotkach of the *Mahabharata* fame.

Similary after the decline of the Ghatotkach family, one Barir-putek became the king of the Kachari kingdom. An interesting story related to his birth and ascendance as a king is narrated in Kachari Burunji. He was a son of a Kachari girl, who was banished the jungle for conceiving a child due to her alleged incestuous relationship with her father.[23]

In between these (territories of Khasia and Kachar) there was another group of people known by the name of Mughals. They lived in that way from generation to generation till they reached this stage. Although the language of these people was akin to the language of the Kacharies, they were all white-skinned and put on big turbans on their heads. They put on their ears big earrings of brass called *tunkal*, weighing half a *powa* and even *powa*. They ate all sorts of animals and vegetables that were available in the world.[24]

Land Use

Under the authority of Tipperas and Koches, there is no evidence of large scale cultivation in the Kachar plains. Here and there in small hillocks or *tillas jhum* culitivation might take place as *jhum* is not the favourite mode of cultivation in the plains. The *jhum* system of cultivation cannot sustain a large number of people because of its inherent weakness and complication. So, the tribes dependent on jhum system of cultivation could not maintain a large population in Kachar. However, they dominated the prevailing agrarian system before the extension of the Dimasa rule over the Kachar. But from a folk story prevailing among the Dheyans, the offshoots of Koch rulers in Kachar, narrated in the Dheyan language, indicates that the use of plough as an implement of cultivation was not unknown to the Rajbanshis living in Kachar even before the settlement of the migrants equipped with comparatively developed method of cultivation based on plough.[25] That the *jhum* system remained an important form of cultivation in the Kachar plain in pre-colonial period is evident from the plot of killing the last Koch king of Cachar hatched by a group of elites in a *jhum* field near Haritakar.[26]

The Dimasa king encouraged migrants belonging to both Hindu and Muslim religious communities from the neighbouring territories presumably for extension of arable land and spreading of plough-based agriculture. That arable land was extended to a great extent as evidenced from the establishment of Kalain, Bikrampur and some other parganas by the migrants. Raja Kirti Chandra Narayana's grant to Maniram Laskar, son of Chand Laskar in 1736 gives an example of the Dimasa Rajas' encouragement to settle Bengali peasants.[27]

According to the estimation of Captain Fisher about 478 miles was arable land of fine quality out of the about 1,008 sq miles tract on the northern bank of the Barak, which is daily becoming more extensively cultivated. In the initial days of English rule in Kachar, on both banks of the Barak, from Badarpur, nearly the whole of to Banskandi, villages have been again established, and the plains, which six or seven years ago were wholly deserted and covered with reeds, now present a scene of fine and varied cultivation.[28]

However, the chief crop in medieval Kachar was rice which was also exported due to surplus production. Pulse and mustard, betel leafs and betel nuts, and cotton were also produced in abundance, U.C. Guha refers to a professional class of Barui living on betel production even before the establishment of the Koch rule.[29]

State Claim Over Natural Resources

Kachar produced ivory, wax, lace, silk, cotton, mules, horses, copper, zinc, lead, silver, gold and rubies. These rajas collected taxes on forest, ferries and cattle, trade, salt-wells. R.B. Pomberton in his report mentioned that timber, rattans, and bamboos found in the inexhaustible forests were always a fruitful source of revenue for the rulers of Kachar.[30] By end of eighteenth-century Kachar grain production became sufficient for export, large quality of grain was annually exported to Narayanganj and Dacca and salt, oil, etc., were received in return.[31] Any man who took articles such as wax and ivory which were considered contraband, into the country as merchandise were required to sell them to the Raja, who fixed his own price and resold them at a profit.[32] Tax was also imposed for the cultivation of poppy, fruits and vegetables for the manufacture of salt.[33]

We know from a letter of Raja Krishnachandra which he addressed to Governor-General Lord Cornwallis in 1790 that the Sylhet collector Henry Lodge was preventing the trade in tusks, wax, cane, and bamboos since he wanted the monopoly of Company in this business. Even the Raja's officers and the zamindars used to make *khedas* for trapping elephants and sell their elephants to the British merchants in Sylhet at attractive prices.[34]

This country consisted mainly of hills and jungles and the ryots subsisted on the sale of grass and bamboos.[35]

State Response to Irrigation

It has already been stated that local-level hydraulic projects such as tanks, wells, etc., were more numerous in early medieval India than supra-local irrigation projects under royal initiatives.[36] According to a tradition, the former Raja of Kachar had artificially opened a river channel called Katakhal which connected Dhaleswari River with the Barak at Sealtekh. But Pemberton in his report mentioned Dhaleswari as the only tributary of Barak from Hailakandi district.[37] The river Dhaleswari originates in the Mizo hills where it is known as Thang. Originally it is used to flow along the western side of the district and fall into the river Barak near Panchgram. A former king is said to have diverted its course a little above Rongpur and the channel is now dried up for a considerable distance of about 1.5 km, after the commencement of a new channel which is called ***katakhal*** and the lower reaches of the Dhaleswari is completely cut-off from the river that originates from the Mizo hills. The Katakhal River flows along the east of the valley and falls into the Barak River near Katakhal railway junction. There are also seven tributaries in the district. Apart from providing a line of water communication for the boat for trade purposes this channel was used by the people for irrigation.[38]

Rulers of pre-colonial Kachar erected embankment on river bank. Two of such called 'Goarer Jungal' were located at a village Hatirhar in Rajnagar pargana. These bunds were raised on the bank of Ghaghra River. Some portions of the embankments were 10 ft wide and 10 ft high.[39] Drains were also created to demarcate the border of states. During the reign of Raja Krishnachandra of Kachar when a dispute developed on the boundary issue, the *amin* of Sylhet dug a drain between the border of Kachar and Sylhet. However, the drain was filled up immediately by the men of the Raja.[40] Tipperas too were interested in the digging of ponds. Old bricks belonging to a Tripuri regime was found near Hailakandi. According to Achut Charan Choudhury, bricks were in used in the stairs of a *dighi* (large pond).[41] In the known period of history most parts of the erstwhile state of Kachar was under Tripuri administration. Existence of Sakala Dighi near Lala is a symbol of Tripuri reign.

Relation with Hill Tribes

People of Kachar had a trading relationship with the hill tribes mainly through the barter systems. There is a tradition that Hazrat Shahjalal visited Deorail, opposite Katigarh in Kachar to save the people of the place from the menace of demons, who very often made life of settled population intolerable.[42] There are many references to raids by predators like Kukis on the plain of Kachar and Karimganj. Later we see the colonial state taking special interest on the settlement of Manipuris whom they considered as the right party to check the frequent raids of hill tribes, who were a menace for the settled agricultural population.[43]

Rituals and Nature

Within the broad bounds of environmental history, there is a cultural space and ideological practice, as expressed through the evocation and representation of nature in art and religion, in myth, in ethics and the law.[44] Since the medieval period, bathing in the water of river Barak has been sacred for the Hindu population of Kachar like many other places of India. Every year thousands of devotees gather at Siddeshwar Baruni Ghat to take a holy dip on the occasion of Shiva Ratri. Similarly, people are also afraid of the river.[45] They worship or invoke the name of goddess, saints for the safety of their journey. In Kachar especially boatmen take the name of the fourteenth-century saint Shah Badar for safe and secure journey whenever they cross a particular point of the river Barak. Similarly fishermen invoke Sufi saint Shah Sikandar, another fourteenth-century Sufi, for his blessings during fishing in the river Barak.[46]

In Kachar a rich set of folk poem is known as the *baromasi*. This is, in fact a popular tradition throughout Bengal. It reflect the impact of the change of nature in twelve months of the year on the mind and body of the womanfolk. The pain of separation forms the husband and the desire of the heroine to meet her beloved is depicted in these *baromasi* songs.[47] The women represented Radha of the mythology and Krshina, her beloved, although they may appear in different compositions under different names.These songs have survived the stress and strain of time and circumstances in the Kachar plain through *dhamail* dance (ballad) of the womanfolk on *navami* during the Durga Puja in autumn season and on occasional Nauka Puja in the months of Karttik and Chaitra. A song by Kavi Krishnamohan describes the plight of the people due to a flood caused by the Barak and its tributaries.[48]

There was a ritual among the Bengali Hindu women of Kachar in the medieval period. After the birth of a child the mother would take her newborn to a nearby tree and utter the desire that the tree should now take care of her infant and in return she would nurture the tree.

The dominant theme of the majority of the folk songs of medieval Kachar is about the infinity of God and unity of religion revealed through the beauty and bounty of nature, ravages of flood, famine and epidemic, and the trials and tribulations, joys and sorrows of life. This is due to the impact of the Bhakti-Sufi movement in that period. Sri Chaitanya, the Swaguna Bhakti saint, hailed from the village of Dhakadakshin in Sylhet, and to Shahjalal, a Sufi saint; Sylhet was the land of his adoption. The origin of folk songs and poems can be traced to the medieval period. According historian J.B. Bhattacharjee, these remained in the memory of the people for a long time and were handed down from generation to generation.

Raymond Alchin says that the aggradation or deposition of silt, in valleys buried plains structure and objects in a relatively short space of time. For example, floods may lay down 5 or 10 cm of silt over many square kilometres in the valley of the lower Narmada and many other rivers.[49] In Kachar, human settlement became deserted on many occasions and led to the development of forests in its place. According to Tripurar Rajamala there were settlements on the bank of the river Rukhini in southern Kachar. But later that particular zone became a part of forest. The depopulation of the place might be because of two reasons – (i) the defeat of the Tippera king by the Koches at the battle of Longai probably in the beginning of fifteenth century or frequent raids by the hill tribes such as Kuki turned the areas formerly controlled by the Tipperas into forest.[50] Similary, during the reign of Govindachandra, after the raids of Manipuri princes, many of the people living in the plains left their home and huts to save themselves from the frequent raids of the hill tribes. The desertion of villages because of raids by the hill tribes and later by Manipuri princes left villages depopulated, agricultural land deserted and peasant migrated to neighbouring Sylhet and other places.

Thus we see the influence of man in the destruction and construction of nature.

NOTES

1. Ramachandra Guha and Madhav Gadgil, *This Fissured Land: An Ecological History of India*, New Delhi: Oxford, 2002, p. 40
2. Edward Gait, *A History of Assam*, London, 1905; rpt., Guwahati, 2005, p. 236.

3. A.C. Choudhury, *Srihatter Itibritta*, vol. I, Dhaka, 1910, rpt., 2004, p. 522
4. 'History of Halilakandi', www.hailakandi.nic.in (Hailakandi District Official Website).
5. David Arnold and Ramchandra Guha (eds.), *Nature, Culture and Imperialism*, New Delhi, 2003, p. 6.
6. K. Bhagabati Avanti, Ashok K. Bora and Bimal K. Kar, *Geography of Assam*, New Delhi, 2007, p. 23.
7. B.C. Allen, *Assam District Gazetteers*, vol. II (Cachar), Allahabad, 1926, pp. 5-6.
8. Avanti, Bora, and Kar, op. cit., p. 31.
9. B.R. Pemberton, *The Eastern Frontier of British India*, 1835; rpt., Guwahati, 1991, pp. 216-17.
10. Jayanta Bushan Bhattacharya, *Cachar Under British Rule in North East India*, New Delhi, 1977, p. 93.
11. Ibid., p. 78.
12. W.W. Hunter, *A Statistical Account of Assam*, vols. 1 and 2, London, 1875.
13. Bhattacharya, op. cit., p. 3.
14. Pemberton, op. cit., pp. 206-7.
15. Sharif Uddin Ahmed (ed.), *Sylhet History and Heritage*, Dhaka, 1999, p. 236.
16. Richard H. Grove, Vinita Damodaran and Satpal Sangwan (eds.), *Nature and the Orient*, New Delhi, 1998, p. 2.
17. Pemberton, op. cit., p. 199
18. Ibid., p. 214.
19. Mirza Nathan, *Baharistan-i-Ghaibi*, vol. I, Guwahati, 1935; rpt., 1992, p. 324.
20. Ibid., p. 326.
21. Bhattacharya, op. cit., p. 94.
22. Ahmed, op. cit., p. 242.
23. Surya Kumar Bhuyan (compiled), *Kachari Burunji*, Guwahati, 1951, p. 27.
24. Nathan, op. cit., p. 225.
25. U.C. Guha, *Kacharer Itibritta*, Guwahati, 1988, p. 38.
26. Bhuyan, op. cit., p. 32.
27. Choudhury, op. cit.
28. Pemberton op. cit., p. 202.
29. Guha, op. cit., p. 26.
30. Pemberton op. cit., p. 207.
31. *FPP (Foreign Political Proceeding)*, 14 May 1832, no. 11, National Archives of India, New Delhi.
32. Bhattacharya, op. cit., p. 132.

33. *BSPC (Bengal Secret and Political Consultations)*, 14 May 1832, nos. 100-7, West Bengal State Archive, Kolkata.
34. Bhattacharya, op. cit., p. 21.
35. D. Datta (compiled), *Cachar District Records*, Silchar, 1969, p. 13.
36. Grove, Damodaran and Sangwan, op. cit., p. 99.
37. Pemberton, op. cit., p. 220.
38. Hunter, op. cit., p. 366.
39. Choudhury, op. cit.
40. Ibid.
41. Ibid.
42. Fazlur Rahman, *Sylhet er Mati Sylhet er Manush*, Maulavi Bazar, 1991, p. 14.
43. Pamberton, op. cit., p. 220.
44. Arnold and Guha, op. cit., p. 3.
45. Sujit Coudhury, *Srihatta Kacharer Prachin Itihash*, Silchar, 2006, p. 134.
46. Rahman, op. cit., p. 17.
47. Amlendu Bhattacharya, *Barak Upatyakar Baromasi Gan*, Silchar, 1972, p. 32.
48. Ibid., p. 54.
49. Bridget Allchin, and Raymond Allchin, *The Birth of Indian Civilization*, London: Pelican, 1968, p. 4.
50. Guha, op. cit., p. 29.

CHAPTER 4

Environment and War: Small Wars in North-East India, 1845-1913

KAUSHIK ROY

INTRODUCTION

By 1849, the British government in India was able to destroy the last substantial independent Indian power and establish control over the subcontinent. British rule in the Indian subcontinent was maintained through a combination of political co-option and coercion. At times, the indigenous social groups were forced to collaborate with the Raj due to pressure exerted by the British-Indian military. The peripheral regions of the British-Indian empire (north-west and north-east India) gave most of the trouble to the British. Terrain, historical context and the cultural characteristics of the people in those frontier regions resulted in more or less continuous uprisings against the British government. In response, the British launched repeated 'butcher and bolt' expeditions.

The 'butcher and bolt' expeditions launched against the Indus tribes in north-west India have come under the scanner of scholarly analysis.[1] However, expeditions against the various north-east Indian tribes are yet to be studied, although one author has recently analysed the political aspects of the colonial and post-colonial state's policy towards the Nagas.[2] This paper turns the spotlight on the British expeditions in north-east India. It begins in 1845 when the *sahibs* first encountered the 'hill men' of north-east India, and ends with the onset of the First World War, as in late 1914 the British-Indian military establishment registered massive changes.

A caveat should be noted in studying such campaigns. The inhabitants of north-east India at that time were mostly illiterate and lacked the tradition of maintaining written records. Hence, our historical analysis is dependent on the sources generated by their enemies, i.e. the files of the military department of British-India, regimental records, private papers of the senior administrators of the Raj, memoirs by the British military officers who participated in these campaigns, and observations by the 'politicals', i.e. civil officials who were in charge of administering the 'hill' tribes of north-east India. This paper is divided into five sections. The first section attempts to locate the theory of warfare in north-east India within the broader theory of 'small wars'. The second section discusses the various sorts of units which were used to wage small wars in north-east India. The third section provides a chronological overview of the various campaigns both from macro and micro perspectives. The fourth section describes the physical geography of north-east India and links it up with the tactics, training and logistics of the small wars conducted in the region. And, finally, the last section compares and contrasts the theory and practice of small wars in north-east India with north-west India in particular and with small wars waged in regions outside India.

THEORIES OF SMALL WARS

From the mid-nineteenth century, British military officers evolved complicated theories about the nature of warfare conducted against rebellious tribes. British officers categorized such irregular wars as small war. Though Colonel Charles Callwell first introduced the term 'small war' in 1896, as we will see various British officers theorized on irregular warfare on similar lines from the mid-nineteenth century. Small wars are now referred to as 'low intensity conflicts', 'counter-insurgency campaigns', 'sub-conventional wars' or 'operations other than war'. During the British Raj, most of the British officers stationed in India focused principally on the Indus frontier when theorizing about small war, and British officers who operated from outside India attempted to generalize small warfare across Africa as well as Asia to produce a coherent body of ideas.

In 1898, Major G.J. Younghusband made a distinction between large-scale combat operations between states and unconventional operations involving the state and non-state rebels. The former he describes as civilized warfare and the latter as uncivilized warfare. Younghusband wrote:

> On every tribe and clan, on every pass and trade route along this immense extent of frontier, the Indian Army has to keep its steadfast watch and ward. Scarce a mile of this frontier but holds an open or secret foe; scarce a year

passes without the necessity arising of armed intervention in one quarter or another. For against the solid wall of British rule the sea of outer barbarism beats ever restlessly. Though the broad strategical principles on which civilized warfare is based throughout the world are the same, yet local conditions so far alter their tactical bearings that methods suitable to the country and the foes to be encountered have had to be gradually evolved in the course of practice.[3]

Colonel Charles Callwell, who can be called 'the Clausewitz of colonial warfare', probably influenced Younghusband. Callwell served with General Redvers Buller's staff in South Africa during the relief of Ladysmith and retired after the First World War as a major-general. He had already retired by 1914 and was then recalled during 1914-15. While Younghusband theorized about uncivilized warfare in India, Callwell philosophized about the nature of insurgencies throughout the British empire in particular and European (especially French) empires in general. In his *magnum opus*, titled *Small War* and published in 1896 (at that time he was serving in the Intelligence Branch of the War Office), Callwell wrote:

Small war is a term which has come largely into use of late years.... Practically, it may be said to include all campaigns other than those where both the opposing sides consist of regular troops. It comprises the expeditions against savages and semi-civilized races by disciplined soldiers, it comprises campaigns undertaken to suppress rebellions and guerrilla warfare in all parts of the world where organized armies are struggling against opponents who will not meet them in the open field.... The expression 'small war' has in reality no particular connection with the scale on which any campaign may be carried out; it is simply to denote ... operations of regular armies against irregular ... forces.[4]

Callwell analyses the nature of small war in the following words:

Whenever a regular army finds itself engaged upon hostilities against irregular forces, or forces which in their armament, their organization, and their discipline are probably inferior to it, the conditions of the campaign become distinct from the conditions of modern regular warfare.[5]

Indeed, small war was intrinsically attritional, given its asymmetrical nature. Callwell warns his readers: 'As a general rule the quelling of rebellion in distant colonies means protracted, thankless, invertebrate wars'.[6] For Callwell, small war, which was equivalent to Younghusband's uncivilized warfare, occurred in metropolitan countries as well as in the colonies. Callwell continued: 'Small wars include the partisan warfare which usually arises when trained soldiers are employed in the quelling of sedition and of insurrections in civilized countries ... and they include punitive expeditions against tribes bordering upon distant colonies.'[7] Callwell wrote that there were two types of small war: hill war and bush warfare. When discussing hill war, Callwell gave examples from the north-west frontier of India, and when elaborating on bush warfare, Callwell had in mind conflicts with the African tribes (such as the Ashanti War). The campaigns of north-east India included elements of both hill war and bush warfare.

Major John Butler of the 55th Bengal Native Infantry Regiment in 1841 was appointed to the civil branch as an Assistant to the Agent to the Governor-General, North-East Frontier. In 1844, he was put in charge of the hill tribes subject to the Political Agent of Upper Assam. Butler noted on the 1845 expedition against the Nagas:

> The object of the expedition was to meet the Angami Naga chiefs, and, by a conciliatory intercourse, to prepare them to co-operate with me in repressing their annual murderous and marauding incursions against our more peaceable subjects; to survey and map the tract of country in question, and to open a regular communication with Manipur and Nowgong, through the Angami country via Dimapur, Sumokhoo-Ting, Poplongmaee, and Yang, which would facilitate trade, improve the condition of the hill tribes, and eventually lead to the abandonment of savage habits, and the peaceable and prosperous settlement of this barbarous tribe.[8]

From an imperialist perspective such as Butler's, the objective of small war was 'civilizing the savages'. Colonel L.W. Shakespear (author of several books on the British-Indian Army's operations in north-east India), writing in 1929, argued on more or less same lines. For Shakespear, British military interventions against the Angami Nagas were attempts to check slave raiding in the districts of Nowgong and Cachar and to establish peace in the borderland.[9]

Winning the hearts and minds of the people was an important aspect of small war. In 1912, Lieutenant-Colonel R.M. Betham of the 101st Grenadiers commented that the subcontinent was full of armed gangs who were engaged in murder, loot and robbery. Betham emphasized that one of the principles of conducting successful pacification operations was not to apply blunt force but to win the trust and confidence of the people residing in the area disturbed by banditry.[10]

One aspect of limiting the infliction of overwhelming force on the 'rebels' was to subordinate the military to civilian command. The use of the army to aid the civil authority was only undertaken on the receipt of a written order from the civil authority. When in north-west India, the army was deployed without civilians in supervisory capacity, the military response was more brutal. However, the strength and composition of the force, the amount of ammunition required and the way in which the pacification campaign was to be carried out, was decided by the military authorities.[11]

In Eric Hobsbawm's view, brigandry constitutes a form of primitive rebellion, or what he terms 'social banditry'.[12] The term bandit is derived from the Italian *bandito* which means a man placed outside the law. *Bandoleros*, the Castilian term for bandits was derived from the Catalan term for armed partisans during unrest and civil conflict which occurred in Catalonia between fifteenth and seventeenth centuries.[13] Hobsbawm elaborates:

> On mountain and in forest bands of men outside the range of law and authority (traditionally females are rare), violent and armed, impose their will by extortion, robbery or otherwise on their victims. In doing so, banditry simultaneously challenges the economic, social and political order by challenging those who hold or lay claim to power, law and the control of resources.[14]

Hobsbawm continues: 'Banditry as an expression of such collective resistance has been very common, all the more so as, in these circumstances, it enjoys considerable support from all of the elements in traditional society'.[15] He adds: 'Poor regions were bandit regions. The months of the farming year when food was scarce and not much farm-work was to be done, were the season for robbing. When floods destroyed the grain, they multiplied brigands.'[16]

Drawing on a classical Marxist framework, Hobsbawm characterizes brigandry as a primitive form of rebellion lacking ideology or means of broader political mobilization, though the bandits retain a heroic stature. Hobsbawm's romantic formulations of these insurgents have led scholars to raise two fundamental critiques of the social bandit thesis. First, bandits may actually work at the behest or at least in the interest of sustaining the local elite and may not fight on behalf of the peasantry. The second critique is that Hobsbawm confuses Robin Hood myths about bandits with what the bandits really did, thereby confusing the actions of the bandits with the social effect of the banditry.[17]

Despite these criticisms, many aspects of the social bandit thesis are applicable in the case of north-east India. Social banditry historically has long been associated with regions far from political concentrations of power. In a detailed analysis of banditry during the Ming Dynasty in China, James Tong demonstrates that nearly all bandit activity occurred in southern provinces, far away from the Imperial palace and the northern metropolitan provinces.[18] This pattern is reflected in modern armed civil conflict, as demonstrated by H. Buhaug and Scott Gates, who find that the majority of armed rebellions occur near border regions, where the reach of the state is limited.[19] In the cases of north-east and north-west India, this pattern was evident in the nineteenth century, as it is today.

As for the notion of social banditry as a form of rebellion, H. Grossman and Paul Collier note, from an economic perspective, then bandits are indistinguishable from insurgents.[20] We follow this perspective in this article. The banditry that took place in north-east India must be placed within the social-political-economic environment within which it occurred. Brigandry is inherently a social-economic phenomenon challenging the authority of the state.

High rainfall in Assam favoured the cultivation of tea, a revenue earning cash crop for the Raj. The British entrepreneurs displaced the 'native' inhabitants, acquired their land and started tea plantations for commercial purposes. The tea estates were located on the higher terraces of the plain, at the margin of the hills.[21] The tea plantation farms were worked with Bihari and Madrasi immigrants. From 1871 onwards, the Lushais (Kukis), Howlong and Sylus tribes raided the tea gardens of the Silchar district of Assam and the Chittagong Hill Tracts (now in Bangladesh).[22] To an extent, Major Butler's assertion was also partly true. Inter-tribal fighting was common. The Kukis used to raid Manipur.[23] And the Angami Nagas fought the Manipuris.[24]

INSTRUMENTS FOR CONDUCTING SMALL WARS IN NORTH-EAST INDIA

During the nineteenth century, an Indian soldier cost four times less than a British soldier in South Asia. This was because the pay of the British soldier was higher than that of Indian troops. Further, the government had to pay for the transport of the British soldier from Britain to India and back to Britain. The British soldier fell ill far more quickly in the climate of South Asia.[25] Britain lacked the manpower to maintain a large army for holding India. Hence, the British had to recruit Indians into the army. The British-Indian army was a long-service volunteer force. The British comprised the officer corps and the rank and file were Indian. In peacetime, about 15,000 Indians were recruited annually from the countryside into the army.[26] Infantry, artillery and cavalry units of the British Army were also stationed in India. The British-Indian army, the British units in India, plus the selected contingents of certain Indian princes known as Imperial Service Troops, together constituted the Army in India.

In 1885, there were 70,000 British troops and 1,30,000 Indian troops in India.[27] In 1912, there were 1,58,603 Indian soldiers.[28] In 1912, each infantry regiment comprised 912 men. The infantry regiments were organized on class and class company base. A class regiment comprised a particular 'martial' group from a particular region, while a class company regiment had two or more martial groups and each martial community constituted one or more company. The Gurkha regiments were examples of class regiments. An example of a class company regiment was the 20th Punjabis, which in 1912 composed two Sikh companies, two Dogra companies and four Pathan companies.[29] From 1796 onwards, the Indians were allowed to become Viceroy's Commissioned Officers (henceforth VCOs). The seniormost VCO in the infantry branch was the subadar-major, who was under the most junior British ensign. After 25 years of service, a sepoy (an Indian infantry private) became eligible for a pension. In 1860, the period was reduced to 20 years of service and in 1912 to 18 years of service.[30]

In 1872, Major-General H.W. Norman (Member of the Military Council of the Governor-General) advised that regular troops should be stationed in Assam, as the region was within the reach of the 'wild' tribes.[31] The senior British officers accepted that breaking up a regiment into several small detachments for a long period in order to conduct policing duties harmed regimental spirit and adversely affected the training of the units for conventional operation against a possible Afghan or Russian attack.[32] Hence, the regular units of the Army in India functioned as the last line of defence. Initially, the military police held the posts and, if they failed, then the local levies (the forerunners of paramilitary formations) rushed in. If the local levies also failed, then the regular army units went to save the situation.

The British raised certain local units for policing north-east India. In 1824, the East India Company raised the 500 strong Manipur Levy. The men were equipped and trained by the British officers and, in the course of the nineteenth century, its strength increased to

2,000 personnel. A few obsolete brass guns were attached to this infantry unit.[33] The Kuki Levy came into existence in 1850, when 200 Kukis were inducted on Major Lister's suggestion in order to assist the armed civil police in securing the frontier and also to give employment to the Kukis living in British-Indian territory.[34] In 1861, the Kuki Levy comprised two subadars, two jemadars, 10 havildars, four buglers, four drummers, one pay havildar and 200 sepoys. The Assam Local Militia (which was established in 1827) comprised one subadar, two jemadars, seven havildars, seven naiks, two buglers, one pay havildar, one drill instructor and 160 sepoys. In 1861, while the annual cost of maintaining the Kuki Levy came to about Rs. 17,708, for the Assam Local Militia it was about Rs. 13,404.[35]

Various types of police units were deployed to maintain order in both the interior of the subcontinent as well as the frontier regions. The district police retained the military organization which they acquired after 1855. While they dealt with crime, military police were deployed against the armed rebels. In 1859, there were about 80,000 military police in India. About 40,000 military police were stationed in the Bengal Presidency and in Punjab.[36] In 1893, General George S. White (Commander-in-Chief of India from 1893 to 1898) noted: 'During the Mutiny the military police had grown into an important force. They were commanded by military officers, had a complete military organization and differed from the native regular soldiers in no respect, except that they were under the civil instead of the military authorities.'[37] In 1893, there were about 45,000 police armed only with swords. However, the military police comprised 17,847 personnel with breech-loading firearms.[38] The British considered that some hill tribes of Assam, like the Cacharis of Cachar district, the Jarwahs, the Garos of Garo Hills and the Nagas, could provide recruits of military value. They were recruited into the Burma Police Battalion as well as the Assam Military Police.[39]

SMALL WARS IN NORTH-EAST INDIA, 1845-1913

After the First Anglo-Burma War (1824-6), Assam came under British control. On 20 November 1845, a company of 100 men of the 2nd Assam Light Infantry under a lieutenant, an apothecary and a sub-assistant surveyor, with Major Butler in command, marched towards Nowgong.[40] The objective was to make a through reconnaissance for preparing a road in the near future and to deter the tribes by a show of force.

In August 1850, about 5,360 Naga warriors opposed the British-Indian detachment of 100 men under Lieutenant Vincent at Konomah Fort. The government ordered a force of 500 men to assemble under Major Foquett of the 2nd Assam Light Infantry with two 3-pounder guns and two 4-inch mortars, to relieve Vincent and capture Konomah. On 24 September, the Agent to the Governor-General warned Butler, Principal Assistant Agent for the North-East Frontier of Assam to the Governor-General, to prepare for an expedition against the Angami Nagas. Due to the emergency which had emerged, the Agent to the Governor-General himself proceeded to the frontier (Dimapur) to lead the expedition. Captain Reed and Lieutenant Bivar, with a detachment of light infantry and two 3-pounder guns, proceeded to Mozomah in November, and by December, having collected 600 coolies, dispatched rice for the troops at Mozomah. Major Foquett, with a detachment and two mortars marched 40 miles from Dimapur to Mozomah on 7 December. Hauling the mortars over the hills proved to be a difficult job. About 8 in the morning of 10 December 1850, a party comprising 354 soldiers with two 3-pounder guns and two 4-inch mortars left Mozomah for Konomah. The fort was constructed of stone and timber. Even when the guns were brought to within 70 yards of the fort, their shots failed to breach the barricade. A deep and wide trench further impeded the attempted escalade of the fort by the troops. However, on 11 December, the Nagas evacuated the fort. The British considered it a victory and then retreated from the region.[41]

In 1871, the Lushai tribes from the region between south-east Bengal and Burma spilled into the British-Indian territories. The British government in India launched two columns: one from Cachar under Brigadier-General Bourchier and another from Chittagong under Brigadier-General C. Brownlow. The Cachar Column comprised half the Peshawar Mountain Battery, one company of Bengal Sappers and Miners, the 22nd Punjab Infantry, the 42nd and 44th Assam Light Infantry, and 50 elephants. The Chittagong column comprised the other half of the Peshawar Mountain Battery, the 27th Punjab Infantry, and the 2nd and 4th Gurkhas. Each infantry regiment was 500 strong and each column was accompanied by 100 armed police. A characteristic of small war was joint operations by the army and military police units. While the regular army units provided heavy firepower, the military police units knew the terrain and culture of the inhabitants. The civil officers who functioned as advisors and channels of communication with the tribes also accompanied the columns. John Edgar, Deputy-Commissioner of Cachar, accompanied Bourchier's column as the civil officer. As there was no road, the soldiers of the expeditions had to construct a road in Lushailand. Between 23 December 1871, when the Cachar column left Cachar, and the end of January 1872, about 110 miles of road were constructed.[42] 'Bobs' Roberts, who accompanied the Cachar column as its Deputy-Quartermaster General, noted in his autobiography:

> The troops worked with a will, and, notwithstanding the vapour-bath like atmosphere of the valleys and the difficult nature of the country, which was a succession of hill-ranges covered with jungle forests, made almost impenetrable from the huge creepers, and intersected by rivers and watercourses, a good road, from six to eight feet wide, was constructed, with a sufficiently easy gradient for laden elephants to travel over. Cutting one's way day after day through these dense, gloomy forests, through which hardly a ray of light penetrates, was most stifling and depressing.[43]

In January 1889, a column about 1,250 strong under Brigadier-General V.W. Tregear, consisting of detachments from the 2nd Battalion, 2nd Gurkha Regiment, the 2nd and 9th Bengal Infantry regiments, 200 frontier police and elements from the artillery and sappers assembled at Rangmati near Chittagong. The objective of this expedition was not only to punish the Lushais but also to establish permanent posts for the occupation of the Lushai region up to the Burma border. To facilitate the mobility of the troops, Tregear was ordered to build a road to Haka in the Chin Hills before commencing the operation, and to establish a series of permanent posts to guard the road. During the winter of 1889, the strength of the column was increased to 4,000 men.[44] In the autumn of 1890, an outbreak occurred in the Lushai Hills and the forts of Changsil and Aijal, which were held by the military police, were attacked. A detachment of the 40th Bengal Infantry was hurried up from Silchar. Thanruma, the village of the leading insurgent chief, was destroyed on 4 October and Aijal was relieved on the following day. On 17 October, the village of another rebel chief named Khalkum was destroyed.[45]

In September 1890, a palace revolution by Tinadrajit Bir Singh, *senapati* (commander-in-chief) of Manipur and brother of the ruler, resulted in the abdication of the *maharaja* of Manipur. As the paramount sovereign power, the British government of India was bound to act. In March 1891, Mr. Quinton, the Chief Commissioner of Assam with 400 Gurkhas of the 42nd and the 44th Bengal Infantry regiments, proceeded to Imphal (the capital of Manipur) in order to settle the affairs of Manipur. Meanwhile, a company of the 43rd Bengal Infantry reached Imphal. The British attempt to arrest the *senapati* on 24 March failed. After sustaining a loss of 40 men killed and wounded, the British-Indian forces retreated to the residency. Late in the evening, Quinton, Colonel Skene and Lieutenant Sampson of the 43rd Bengal Infantry Regiment were seized and executed. The leaderless British-Indian force then retreated in small parties to Kohima, Cachar and Tammu in the Kabaw valley in Burma. On 28 March, Lieutenant Grant, with 50 men of the 2nd Burma Battalion and 33 men of the 43rd Bengal Infantry Regiment, advanced towards Imphal. At Thobal, Grant's detachment was opposed by several thousand Manipuris. On 9 April, Grant's detachment retired to Tammu.[46] Two features are clear. First, the palace revolution of Manipur had popular backing which in turn enabled the *senapati's* party to deploy large number of troops in the field. Doubtless, the people of Manipur hated British intervention and the installation of the puppet *maharaja* at Imphal. Second, because Manipur was a monarchical state, it had a sort of rudimentary bureaucracy to mobilize more forces compared with the numerous scattered tribes of upper Assam.

In response, British-India mobilized a substantial force. In April 1891, the Raj launched three columns into Manipur. The Kohima column under Brigadier-General H. Collett comprised 1,000 men and 3 guns, the Silchar column under Lieutenant-Colonel R.H.F. Rennick had 1,600 men and 2 guns, and the Tammu column of Brigadier-General T. Graham had 320 British and 750 Indian soldiers.[47] The Silchar column marched 126 miles to Manipur, the Kohima column had to cover 105 miles, and the Tammu column covered 68 miles. The general officer commanding Burma organized supplies for the Tammu column.[48] Only the Tammu column faced opposition. On 25 April at Bapam, about 6 miles north of Palel, the Manipuris fought the detachment composed of 12th Madras Infantry Regiment and 2nd Battalion, 4th Gurkha Regiment. The British-Indian detachment suffered 2 killed and 13 wounded. Imphal was occupied, the *senapati* was captured and executed, and the rebellion came to an end. In this campaign, the Nagas supported the British with 250 coolies and also provided paddy for the sepoys.[49] In this case, the British took advantage of inter-tribal rivalries. Several factors, including Naga support, the mistake by the Manipuris to fight a set piece battle at Bapam and mobilization of massive forces, enabled the British to emerge victorious.

Let us assess the impact of small wars in north-east India on particular regiments. The 3rd Bengal Infantry Regiment took part in the Chin-Lushai Expedition of 1889-90 and formed part of the Chittagong column under Tregear. The regiment left Calcutta with a strength of eight British officers, 15 Indian officers, 14 drummers, 34 staff members and 752 sepoys. During a small war, a regiment was occasionally broken up into various details for different duties. On arrival at Chittagong, two and half companies (250 men) under Captain F.B.W. Richardson moved to Duagiri. They participated in the Demagiri expedition on the lines of communication between Rungmati and Sungleh. The northern column was under Colonel Skinner. It moved down from Sungleh during January 1890 by boats and returned to Calcutta through Cachar.[50] There was no rest for the regiment. On 31 March 1891, the regiment left Calcutta for Cachar due to the outbreak of an insurrection at Manipur. But, on its way, the personnel suffered from cholera. The unit reached Silchar and established a military outpost. One month's supplies were stored at Silchar for the regiment. In April 1891, the Sniders of this regiment were replaced by Martini-Henry rifles. This unit returned to Calcutta on 20 May 1891.[51]

On 20 March 1892, four Indian officers and 200 sepoys of the unit left Calcutta under the command of Lieutenant W.P. Anderson for Chittagong. Travelling on steam launches, the detachment reached Chittagong on 23 March. From Chittagong, the 3rd Bengal Infantry detachment went with the frontier police, to Sungleh where a considerable number of Lushais had collected. By launch, the detachment and the frontier police went to Rungmati, where they left a jemadar with 50 men. Then, the party moved by country boats to Duagiri, which was reached on 28 March. On 1 April, at the request of L.W. Shakespear, Political Superintendent of South Lushai Hills, a party of 50 men under Lieutenant F.G. Cardew and Subadar Allah Baksh were dispatched as a mobile patrol in Lushai Hills. On 3 April, information came that about 300 Lushais were trying to cut up the small military outposts along the Duagiri-Sungleh road. The military intelligence assessed that Tuichang outpost, about 9 miles from Demagiri, was to be attacked first. On the morning of 7 April, the post was attacked. Jemadar Hiralal Singh and a sepoy named

Saligram were wounded. Due to their gallantry, they were both given the 3rd Class Order of Merit. However, the small posts along Duagiri-Sungleh road were withdrawn. In May, the monsoon came and the Lushais stopped attacking. Thus, the tribesmen lacked staying power. Without elaborate logistical back up, they could remain in the field only for one month. The regiment came back to Calcutta on 20 July 1892.[52]

In May 1893, about 100 men of the 43rd Bengal Infantry were dispatched from Manipur to punish the Lushai village of Monghan (20 miles east of Imphal). The people from this village had raided the Naga village of Swemi and massacred 300 inhabitants. On 22 May Mongham was reached, the leaders were arrested and the village, along with some other villages in the vicinity, was destroyed. The detachment returned to Manipur in the middle of June.[53]

THE PHYSICAL GEOGRAPHY OF NORTH-EAST INDIA AND ITS INTERRELATIONSHIP WITH THE TACTICS, TRAINING AND LOGISTICS OF SMALL WARS

The British-Indian Army enjoyed massive technological superiority over its indigenous opponents in north-east India. As a consequence of the 1857 Mutiny, the British soldiers were given the latest handguns and the sepoys were equipped with the obsolete models. The .557 calibre Snider was a pattern 1853 rifled musket converted to a breech-loading mechanism and could fire 10-15 rounds per minute. In 1868, the British troops in India were equipped with Sniders. The sepoys retained the muzzle loading Enfields. The Martini-Henry rifle was .45 calibre, with a maximum effective range of 400 yards and was able to fire 15 to 20 rounds per minute. In 1879, the British infantry in India were equipped with Martini-Henry. And the sepoys got the Sniders.[54] In 1888, the Lee-Metford rifle replaced the Martini-Henry. It was a small-bore weapon operated by means of the Lee-bolt action with a magazine underneath. Fired by smokeless powder, it propelled a .303 inch bullet with a muzzle velocity of 2,000 ft per second over a range of 3,000 yards. Because they used smokeless powder, soldiers could fire at the enemy from cover without giving away their positions to the hostile force. In 1891, the sepoys got Martini-Henry and the Sniders were phased out.[55]

The Jarwahs lived in the jungles on both banks of Brahmaputra River in the districts of Kamarupa, Goalpara, Bijnee and Cooch Behar.

Brigadier-General W.J.F. Stafford, who commanded the Eastern Frontier District with its headquarters at Shillong, noted in 1874 that the Garos were a subdivision of the Jarwahs and the Garos of the hills frequently attacked the military outposts.[56] The Garos used straight swords, spears with lozenge shaped tips of iron and crossbows made of bamboo with arrows feathered with leaves kept in quivers covered with fox skin.[57] The crossbow technology probably had filtered into the Garo Hills through south China. The Kachins were armed with the *dah* (also known as *dao*).[58] The Kachin was a generic name given by the British authorities to a conglomeration of tribes, like the Marus, Lashi, Asti, Lepai, Maran, Marip, etc. *Dahs* were also used by the Naga tribes. The *dah* was a long knife or a curved broadsword used by the hill men. The blade was 18 inches long, narrow at the haft, square and broad at the top, pointless and sharpened at one side only. The blade was set in wood and the weapon was quite heavy. The Lushais (a division of the Kukis), who settled in the south of Cachar and Chittagong, used shields made of animal skin, *dahs* (each of whose blade was 12 inches long) and a long bladed two handed Burmese knife. Towards the end of the nineteenth century, they discarded the use of bamboo bows, bamboo quivers and poisoned arrows in favour of British-made flintlock muskets. However, the powder which they manufactured was very weak and for bullets they used bits of hammered iron or lead.[59] In 1841, the Angami Nagas were equipped with spears and a few old muskets.[60] The Shendus of the Arakan hills manufactured gunpowder. Their guns were not of European origin. The stocks were painted red, black and yellow and were highly varnished. The powder flasks were made of horn and inlaid with silver and ivory.[61] One can surmise that gunpowder technology had entered Arakan through south China or through Mughal Bengal in the first half of the eighteenth century. Besides manufacturing firearms and gunpowder, the tribes also acquired firearms by looting the sepoys. For instance on 14 June 1862, in the Jaintia Hills, a party of 12 sepoys who were escorting the coolies carrying provisions was attacked. The tribesmen escaped after looting seven muskets.[62]

The technological superiority of the British-Indian troops, however, did not always translate into military superiority, due to the terrain and climate of north-east India. North-east India comprises the present seven states: Assam, Manipur, Meghalaya, Nagaland, Arunachal Pradesh, Mizoram and Tripura. During the nineteenth century the region was covered with evergreen (rain) forest. Not only did the region receive heavy rainfall, but it was also sparsely populated compared with the densely populated plains of north India.[63] Substantial concentrations of population were found only along the narrow river valleys, such as the Brahmaputra. One of the principal trouble spots was Manipur, which is hilly and covers about 20,000 sq km. Only the Manipur river valley is flat, although surrounded by rugged mountains of heights varying between 2,500 and 3,000 m and covered with forest. Like those of the north-west frontier, the mountains are intermittently cut by deep valleys and narrow ravines. The higher slopes are covered with pine and oaks, and the lower hills with dense bamboo jungle with only goat tracks between them.[64]

The principal river in north-east India is the Brahmaputra, which even at 900 miles from the sea during the summer is broader than the Rhine and the Rhone in their lower courses. The general width of the Brahmaputra is 1,372 m. The rivers are fed by mountain torrents. The Brahmaputra has numerous tributaries and during flood occasionally changes course. The swamps and *jheels* (shallow ponds) of the floodplain are covered with *sal*[65] forest and tall reed jungles.[66] During the summer, intense heat and mosquitoes tormented the inhabitants.[67] The region below 1,525 m was malarial.[68] Some of the most disease-ridden stations in the subcontinent were Kohima, Buxa, Nowshera, and Dibrugarh, where the sick rates annually per 1,000 were 29.2, 28, 27.5 and 26.9 respectively.[69]

Most of the confrontations between the tribes and the British-Indian forces in north-east India occurred in Assam. Assam, according to the British officers, was inhabited by 'barbarous' tribes of Mongolian stock.[70] In fact, Assam was inhabited by the Ahoms, a branch of the Shans of Sino-Burmese borderlands.[71] P.D. Bonarjee, who was a Bengali civilian and worked in the military department, compiled an ethnological survey of various 'martial' tribes of the subcontinent in the last year of the nineteenth century. He assumed that the Assami hill men were a mixture of the aboriginals and the Mongols. Among the Assami hill men, he considered the Cacharis as possessing the best military qualities. The Karens were considered as a Mongol race more close to the Chinese than the Burmese.[72] The Kachins inhabited the mountainous tract in northern Burma. The region inhabited by the Kachins was studded with steep mountainous ranges covered with dense jungle, broken up by precipitous valleys. The Kachins lived under their chieftains known as *duwas*. Among the Naga tribes, the Angami Nagas and the Kukis (Lushais) were considered as the most warlike. The Angami Nagas lived in villages like Khonoma, Mozema, Jotsoma and each of these villages had about 600 to 800 houses.[73] Marcus Franke argues that the Nagas were organized in a clan system which was a sort of segmentary political system.[74] Due to the practice of *jhum* (slash and burn type agriculture) cultivation, the villages were not static. The inhabitants were dependent on the production of bamboos. The bamboos are actually grasses. The stems of bamboo sometimes reach a height of 30 ft. In the hills of Assam and Chittagong, they grew so thickly that it was almost impossible to penetrate the bamboo forest. The inhabitants used bamboos for making baskets, mats, and rafts for crossing the rivers.[75]

Callwell observed that bush warfare occurred in terrain which was full of impenetrable thickets. Hence, loose skirmishing order, emphasizing concealment, and rapid movement constituted the key tactical elements.[76] These principles were imparted to a particular regiment which was deployed repeatedly for small wars of north-east India. On 31 May 1862, Major Campbell, officiating Deputy Assistant Adjutant General, wrote to Lieutenant-Colonel W.F. Nuthall, commandant of the 3rd Bengal Infantry Regiment, that the men should be trained far more rigorously in light infantry and outpost duties. On 17 February 1863, the regiment was inspected at Sitapur in the United Province by Adjutant-General, Colonel E. Haythorne. The inspection report of 3 March 1863 noted that the marching rate of the regiment was slow and the regiment also failed to put out proper flank guards while marching. While the regiment performed quite well in bayonet exercise, platoon firing and forming hollow square, its skill in terms of skirmishing was indeed indifferent. Further, the men failed to utilize the terrain for cover.[77]

The Gurkha units were employed in picquets and escort duties. Escort duties involved guarding the convoys carrying supplies to the column of troops in the field and protecting the bases from marauding attacks by the tribesmen, and picqueting involved establishing small posts at the sides of the roads and mountaintops by the advance guards and the rear guards to protect the main body of the troops while they were advancing or retreating. Combat often involved attacking the tribes who entrenched themselves with field fortifications. The Lushais protected their stockades with *panjis* (bamboo stakes sharpened like bayonets and hardened in fire).[78]

An action between the British-Indian troops and the Lushais was fought on 26 December 1871. Field-Marshal Lord Roberts of Kandahar in his memoirs portrayed the Lushai tactics in the following words:

As soon as we began to draw in our piquets, the Lushais, who had never ceased their fire, perceiving we were about to retire, came down in force, and entered one end of the village, yelling and screaming like demons, before we had got out of the other. The whole way down the hill they pressed us hard, endeavouring to get amongst the baggage, but were invariably baffled by the Gurkhas, who, extending rapidly whenever the ground was favourable, retired through their supports in admirable order, and did not once give the enemy the chance of passing them.[79]

One characteristic of small war was the emphasis on logistics. Camels were not suited to the climate and terrain of north-east India. So, here the army depended on elephants. Each elephant was able to carry 15 maunds (one maund = 80 pounds), while a camel carried four maunds.[80] The height of an elephant used by the army varied between 6 and 7.5 ft.[81] To maintain the elephants, the British government maintained a *kheddah* establishment in Assam.[82] The *kheddah* establishment bought elephants through the lessees who organized the hunting parties in Assam. The lessees were issued licences to catch elephants on the basis that all the captured animals were to be handed over to the deputy commissioner of the district in which the elephants were captured. Then, the deputy commissioner transferred these animals to the *kheddah* establishment, an example of how the Raj's civil apparatus cooperated with its military ventures.[83] In general most of the elephants were retained by the commissariat department in order to form movable columns during particular campaigns and some elephants were attached to the regiments as their organic transport. During 1874-5, 39 elephants were purchased at a cost of Rs. 15,900. During 1875-6, 32 elephants were purchased at Gauhati and were then transferred to Dacca.[84] In 1877, 30 elephants were purchased and of them four died. Each elephant was bought at a cost of Rs. 581 anna 7 (16 anna = Re. 1). The surviving animals were trained in military duties. Special elephants known as koonky elephants were used for training the newly-captured elephants. Each koonky elephant cost more than double the cost of an ordinary elephant. In 1877, two elephants were born in the *kheddah* establishment.[85] In 1877, two elephants were given to the 44th Native Infantry Regiment stationed at Dibrugar and 22 were transferred to the Dacca *kheddah* where they were held for commissariat purposes.[86] In April 1878, nine elephants were confiscated from the chieftains.[87] In 1879, the four regiments stationed in Assam had 32 elephants attached to them. In 1879, the Army in India maintained 1,045 elephants for conducting operations in Burma and in north-east India. The cost of keeping an elephant came to about Rs. 50 per month and the annual cost for the elephant establishment was Rs. 6,27,000.[88] In 1881, the Army in India had 847 elephants and of them 115 were in the Dacca *kheddah*. The commissary general calculated that the army required at least 431 elephants for operations in north-east India.[89]

COMPARATIVE ANALYSIS OF SMALL WARS IN AFRICA AND ASIA

There were certain similarities as well as dissimilarities regarding the small wars conducted in north-east and north-west India. Overall, there were also certain similarities as well as dissimilarities between the small wars conducted in north-east India in particular and the Africa and Asia in general. First, let us compare and contrast the British conduct of small wars in north-east India with that of north-west India.

While the British were afraid that the advance of Russia towards Afghanistan might encourage the Indus tribes to revolt against the Raj, the French and Chinese advance towards Burma also sent tremors among the British ruling elites. In 1893, George S. White noted that the whole north-east frontier was threatened by the Burman and Kachin 'dacoits' who were supported by French intrigue.[90] The British feared that the French in Indo-China had designs on British Burma. On 23 March 1900, George Hamilton (the Secretary of State for India) informed Lord Curzon (the Governor-General/Viceroy of India) that since China was advancing towards Burma, it was necessary for the British government in India to send a costly punitive expedition into north-east India to display British power in order to deter China.[91]

The British in India raised a regional army for dealing with small wars on the north-west frontier. In 1849, after the Second Anglo-Sikh War, the Khalsa kingdom collapsed, and to defend the north-west frontier, an irregular force comprising infantry, cavalry and artillery was raised from the defeated and disbanded army of the Khalsa kingdom. This force comprised four Sikh infantry battalions, six

Punjab infantry battalions and a Gurkha contingent.[92] Originally known as the Punjab Irregular Force, it was later renamed the Punjab Frontier Force (hereafter PFF) and remained under the control of the government of Punjab. In 1886, the PFF was transferred from the control of the Punjab government to the Commander-in-Chief of India. Under Lord Kitchener's (Commander-in-Chief of India from 1902-9) reorganization, the PFF became an integral part of the regular army.[93] The British government in India did not raise any such regional army for conducting small wars along the north-east frontier of India. Unlike in north-east India, the elephants were unsuited for operations along north-west frontier due to the difficulties of feeding them. Here camels were used.[94]

In scale and scope, the expeditions launched along the Indus frontier were much bigger compared with the expeditions launched in north-east India. For instance, the Tirah campaign in 1897 comprised 63,000 soldiers and 118 guns.[95] Such numbers were never concentrated for any operations along the north-east frontier, because the north-west frontier tribes posed a much higher level of military threat. Between 1909 and 1912, the Indus tribes acquired 90,000 modern rifles through arms smuggling and in 1912, the Army in India Committee computed the fighting strength of the Indus tribes to be about 3,34,000 armed males.[96]

Rod Thornton asserts that the British Army has used minimum force in counter-insurgency operations. He has further contended that this characteristic can be traced back to British involvement in the colonies during the late nineteenth century and early twentieth century. Protestant ethics and Victorian values shaped the mentality of the imperial gentlemen officers. At the heart of Victorian values was Christian sentiment. The moral principles of the evangelical Protestant movement that developed during the later seventeenth and eighteenth centuries constituted the basis of British liberalism. The concept of chivalry was inculcated among British officers through the public school system and juvenile literature. The public school system emphasized Christian morality among the Christian gentlemen reared in the duty of chivalry. The ruling class was encouraged to bring the coloured heathens under the orbit of Christian civilization without undue cruelty and excess. In addition, fiction, poetry, drama and paintings spread the public school values of manliness, patriotism, chivalry, comradeship and courage. Rather than unnecessary torture and cruelty, true courage, accompanied by magnanimity and gentleness, were the elements popularized in this way. All these traits were derived from Protestant ethics and refracted and reinterpreted through Victorian sensibilities. The net result was a focus on fairness, chivalry and restraint. Thornton continues that the pragmatic demands of maintaining a large disparate empire with a limited number of British soldiers also encouraged the use of minimum force in order to prevent the alienation of the majority of the empire's subjects.[97]

Overlaying religious ethics with military doctrine is a tricky issue. Indeed, Christian militarism encouraged violent military reaction among the British soldiers during the 1857 uprising.[98] Moreover, small wars were not always 'humane'. Most of the tribes had only scarce economic resources and losing their corn and animals meant collective starvation. A policy of looting the livestock from the villagers and then burning the villages was put into practice when punitive expeditions were launched in both north-west and north-east India. The objective was to deter the villagers from conducting any further anti-government activities and also to inflict punishment on a collective basis. On 5 January 1872, the Sirmoor Rifle Battalion destroyed 3,000 maunds of grain in the various Lushai villages.[99] In the course of operation against the Lushais in 1889, numerous villages were burnt.[100] On 18 October 1897, the village of Dargai was burnt by Gurkha troops after the livestock had been forcibly confiscated from the villagers. On 8 November 1897, 40 villages of Zakka Khel Afridis along with the pine wood forest around them were burnt in retaliation for an attack on a transport column which was carrying DumDum bullets and ammunition for Lee Metford rifles. Lieutenant E.H.E. Collen, a Royal Artillery officer who participated in the Tirah campaign, narrates in his diary that the blaze of the burning villages could be seen from a distance and the sight of burning pleased the soldiers. Collen believed that the brutality of the troops was in response to previous perceived transgressions committed by the Afridis, who were accused of having mutilated the wounded and the prisoners, in addition to not having observed the white flag of truce.[101]

Outside South Asia, pacification campaigns by imperial armies were equally harsh. During the first half of the nineteenth century, Russian commanders deliberately destroyed the crops and villages of central Asian tribes in order to break their spirit. In the eastern Caucasus, the Russians systematically cut down forests and denied grazing lands to the insurgents.[102] Marshal Thomas-Robert Bugeaud (1784-1849. He was sent to Algeria in 1836 and resigned as

Governor-General in 1847) in the late 1840s, while conducting pacification campaigns in Algeria, decreed that the mobile French columns should live off the land. The enemy's flocks and herds were seized to feed the French troops.[103] Between 1891 and 1897, when German East Africa was torn by internal rebellions, the *Schutztruppen* deliberately tried to starve the people. The villages were burnt, the cattle were driven away and the food stocks were plundered to destroy the indigenous mode of life.[104] The systematic and ruthless suppression of the revolt in South-West Africa during 1904-7, by the German security forces, resulted in three-quarters of the Herero and half of the Nama population being slaughtered or starved to death.[105]

H.L. Wesseling's assertion that, compared with the West European context, colonial campaigns were conducted by small European armies holds true for the campaigns in north-east as well as north-west India. Wesseling's second point that the European armies in general enjoyed technological superiority over their colonial enemies[106] also holds water in case of the British-Indian army's small wars in both theatres. In fact, the level of technological supremacy enjoyed by the British vis-à-vis north-east India's tribes was higher than that over the tribes of north-west India. Most of the colonial campaigns in Africa and Asia were conducted by West European armies supported by the 'native' forces and auxiliary contingents of local potentates. During the early nineteenth century, the Dutch colonial army (KNIL) in Indonesia was composed of half Dutch/European and half Indonesian soldiers.[107] After the 1857 'Mutiny', on average there were two Indian soldiers for every one British soldier in South Asia. After 1886, the French decreased the number of metropolitan troops in Vietnam and resorted to the Vietnamization of their security forces by enlisting Annamites and especially the Tonkinese.[108] In the 1890s, about 80 per cent of the French force in Sudan was composed of Africans.[109]

From 1814, in Java, Prince Diapnagara with 5,000 men conducted hit and run attacks against the 12,000 strong KNIL. In response, from 1821 onwards, the Dutch launched movable columns as part of their pacification techniques. Each column comprised 700 men (infantry, cavalry, artillery, pioneers and Indonesian auxiliaries). While advancing into disturbed regions, the columns constructed fortified posts which were stocked with supplies and guarded by garrisons.[110] The tribes of north-east India were never able to deploy 5,000 men but the Indus tribes were able to deploy more than 5,000 warriors at certain moments. Launching movable columns was a standard tactic which the British-Indian Army resorted to while conducting small wars. However, the cavalry was not used in north-east India due to the jungle-clad hilly terrain. In the forests of west Africa, just as in the hill forests of north-east India and Burma, the metropolitan powers encountered ambushes and stockaded positions.[111] Adding to their woes, disease rather than enemy bullets was the principal killer in colonial campaigns. One of the greatest killers of the French soldiers in Vietnam and the British troops in north-east India was cholera.[112]

CONCLUSION

Whether it was South Asia, or South-East Asia or Africa, colonial consolidation depended on the use of European troops backed by loyal 'native' troops. The consolidation of British rule during the second half of the nineteenth century witnessed continuous military expeditions launched especially against the 'border' tribes of both north-east and north-west India, to keep them in line. Given the continuous nature of these operations, the very concept of *Pax Britannica* can be questioned. The ordinary police was useless against the armed tribes of both north-east and north-west India. The only time in north-east India when the British-Indian army was successful was when the Manipuris attempted to stand and fight. Because the British-Indian army was able to engage in more symmetrical conventional warfare, thanks to some extent to the border tribe's development into a rudimentary monarchical state, the Manipuri forces proved to be easy meat for the well disciplined and heavily armed British-Indian units.

Most warfare in north-east India, however, was asymmetric. When amorphous social groupings, such as the Angami Nagas and Lushais, conducted sudden 'hit and run' attacks, the British-Indian army was at a loss. Heavy artillery was useless as the tribes had no cities to defend and the locations of their villages were also temporary. Moreover, hauling heavy guns was almost impossible in the terrain of north-east India. Hills, marshes and thick jungles also prevented the large-scale deployment of cavalry. Hence, for campaigning in north-east India, the infantry remained the 'queen' of the battlefield. In order to avoid ambush, the British-Indian military establishment evolved innovative tactics based on loose order and skirmishing by light infantry. Two characteristics of small wars in north-east India were the use of large number of elephants as logistical vehicles and some sort of civil official supervision of the military operations. In the final analysis, the British government of India was never able to solve the problem of the 'militant' hill men of north-east India. And this problem continues even today.

NOTES

1. See for instance T.R. Moreman, *The Army in India and the Development of Frontier Warfare, 1849-1947*, Houndmills, Basingstoke: Macmillan, 1998; Alan Warren, *Waziristan: The Faqir of Ipi and the Indian Army, The North West Frontier Revolt of 1936-7*, Karachi: Oxford University Press, 2000.
2. Marcus Franke, *War and Nationalism in South Asia: The Indian State and the Nagas*, London: Routledge, 2009.
3. G.J. Younghusband, *Indian Frontier Warfare*, 1898; rpt., Delhi: Anmol, 1985, p. 1.
4. Charles Callwell, *Small Wars: A Tactical Textbook for Imperial Soldiers*, 1896; rpt., London: Greenhill Books, 1990, p. 21.
5. Ibid., p. 22.
6. Ibid., p. 27.
7. Ibid., p. 22.
8. Major John Butler, *Travels and Adventures in the Province of Assam during the Residence of Fourteen Years*, 1855; rpt., Delhi: Munshiram Manoharlal, 2004, p. 12.
9. Colonel L.W. Shakespear, *History of the Assam Rifles*, 1929; rpt., Gauhati: United Publishers, 1980, p. 16.
10. Introduction by R.M. Betham in A.H.M. Simcox, *Memoir of Khandesh Bheel Corps: 1825-91*, Bombay: Thacker, 1912, pp. i-ii.
11. *Army Regulations, India*, vol. 2, Calcutta: Superintendent of Govt. Printing, 1913, p. 109.
12. Eric Hobsbawm, *Primitive Rebels: Studies in Archaic Forms of Social Movement in the Nineteenth and Twentieth Centuries*, Manchester: Manchester University Press, 1959.
13. Eric Hobsbawm, *Bandits*, 1969; rpt., London: Abacus, 2001, p. 12.
14. Ibid., p. 7.
15. Ibid., p. 9.
16. Ibid., p. 10.
17. Anton Block, 'The Peasant and the Brigand: Social Banditry Reconsidered', *Comparative Studies in Society and History*, 14 (1972), pp. 494-502, Pat O'Mally, 'Social Bandits, Modern Capitalism and the Traditional Peasantry: A Critique of Hobsbawm', *Journal of Peasant Studies*, 6

(1979), pp. 489-99; T.J. Stiles, *Jesse James: Last Rebel of the Civil War*, New York: Alfred Knopf, 2002.

18. James Tong, *Disorder under Heaven: Collective Violence in the Ming Dynasty*, Stanford, CA: Stanford University Press, 1991.
19. Halvard Buhaug and Scott Gates, 'The Geography of Civil War', *Journal of Peace Research*, 39 (2002), pp. 417-33. Also see Halvard Buhaug, Scott Gates and Päivi Lujala, 'Geography, Rebel Capability, and the Duration of Civil Conflict', *Journal of Conflict Resolution,* 53 (2009), pp. 544-69.
20. Paul Collier, 'Rebellion as Quasi-Criminal Activity', *Journal of Conflict Resolution*, 44 (2000), pp. 839-53 and Herschel Grossman, 'Kleptocracy and Revolution', *Oxford Economic Papers,* 51 (1999), pp. 267-83.
21. O.H.K. Spate, A.T.A. Learmonth and B.H. Farmer with the collaboration of A.M. Learmonth, *India, Pakistan and Ceylon: The Regions*, 1954; rpt., Delhi: B.I. Publications, 1972, p. 603.
22. Colonel L.W. Shakespear, *History of the 2nd King Edward's Own Goorkha Rifles (The Sirmoor Rifles)*, Aldershot: Gale & Polden, 1912, p. 81.
23. Lieutenant-Colonel B.N. Majumdar, *History of the Army Service Corps*, vol. 2, *1858-1913,* Delhi: Sterling, 1976, p. 251.
24. Shakespear, *History of the Assam Rifles*, p. 18.
25. Kaushik Roy, 'Managing the Environment: Disease, Sanitation and the Army in British-India, 1859-1913', in Ranjan Chakrabarti (ed.), *Situating Environment History*, Delhi: Manohar, 2007, pp. 187-219.
26. Dewitt C. Ellinwood, 'Ethnicity in a Colonial Asian Army: British Policy, War, and the Indian Army, 1914-18', in Ellinwood and Cynthia H. Enloe (eds.), *Ethnicity and the Military in Asia*, New Brunswick/London: Transaction Books, 1981, p. 97.
27. General George Chesney, *Indian Polity: A View of the System of Administration in India*, 1894; rpt., Delhi: Metropolitan Books, 1976, p. 227.
28. *Proceedings of the Army in India Committee 1912*, 3 vols., Simla: Govt. Central Branch Press, 1913, vol. 1-A, *Minority Report*, p. 156, New Delhi, National Archives of India (hereafter NAI).
29. *Army in India Committee, 1912*, vol. 3: *Evidence of Col. L.C. Dunsterville*, p. 897.
30. Ibid., pp. 901, 904; Kaushik Roy, *Brown Warriors of the Raj: Recruitment and the Mechanics of Command in the Sepoy Army, 1859-1913*, Delhi: Manohar, 2008, pp. 153-4.
31. Minutes by Major-General H.W. Norman, 1863-76, Memorandum by Norman on the distribution of the Native Armies of India, 26 September 1872, Bengal, Para 10, p. 320, NAI.
32. *Army in India Committee 1912*, vol. 1-A, pp. 201-2.
33. Majumdar, *History of the Army Service Corps*, vol. 2, p. 250.
34. Shakespear, *History of the Assam Rifles*, p. 22.
35. Military Department Proceedings (henceforth MDP), October 1861,

from Col. G. Balfour, Chief of Military Finance, to the secy. to the Government of India (henceforth GOI), Military Department (hereafter MD), 24 September 1861, p. 426, NAI.

36. Proportion of British to Native Troops in India, Para 39, 28 July 1893, 1Q/10, George White Collection.
37. Proportion of British to Native Troops in India, Para 10, 28 July 1893, 1Q/10, George White Collection.
38. Minute by Pritchard, Enclosure No. 2, 29 August 1893, 1Q/14, George White Collection; K.M.L. Saxena, *The Military System of India: 1850-1900*, Delhi: Sterling, 1974, p. 140.
39. P.D. Bonarjee, *A Handbook of the Fighting Races of India*, Calcutta: Thacker, Spink & Co., 1899, pp. 206-8.
40. Butler, *Travels and Adventures in the Province of Assam*, p. 13.
41. Ibid., pp. 193, 195-9.
42. Field Marshal Lord Roberts of Kandahar, *Forty-One Years in India: From Subaltern to Commander-in-Chief*, 1897; rpt., Delhi: Asian Educational Service, 2005, pp. 310-11.
43. Roberts, *Forty-One Years in India*, pp. 311-12.
44. Major-General D.K. Palit, *Sentinels of the North-East: The Assam Rifles*, Delhi: Palit & Palit, 1984, p. 35.
45. Lieutenant F.G. Cardew, *A Sketch of the Services of the Bengal Native Army to the Year 1895*, 1903; rpt., Faridabad: Today and Tomorrow's Printers & Publishers, 1971, p. 412.
46. Cardew, *Bengal Native Army*, pp. 414-15.
47. Majumdar, *History of the Army Service Corps*, vol. 2, p. 255; Cardew, *Bengal Native Army*, pp. 415-16.
48. Majumdar, *History of the Army Service Corps*, vol. 2, p. 257.
49. Ibid., p. 255; Cardew, *Bengal Native Army*, p. 416.
50. Digest of Services of the 3rd Brahmin, 1861-1914, vol. 3, p. 19. Military Miscellaneous, MD, NAI (certain pages of this regimental record were paginated and in certain cases information was organized under various paragraphs).
51. Digest of Services of the 3rd Brahmin, p. 20; Majumdar, *History of the Army Service Corps*, vol. 2, p. 257.
52. Digest of Services of the 3rd Brahmin, pp. 20-1.
53. Cardew, *Bengal Native Army*, p. 420.
54. Colonel Ali Jalali and Lieutenant-Colonel Lester W. Grau, 'Expeditionary Forces: Superior Technology Defeated, The Battle of Maiwand', in Harold E. Raugh, Jr (ed.), *The British Army: 1815-1914*, Aldershot: Ashgate, 2006, pp. 346, 348, 350; Donald Featherstone, *Weapons & Equipment of the Victorian Soldier*, 1978; rpt., London: Arms and Armour Press, 1996, pp. 20, 24-5.
55. Edward M. Spiers, 'The Use of the Dum Dum Bullet in Colonial Warfare', in Raugh (ed.), *The British Army*, p. 357.
56. Notes and Minutes by Napier of Magdala, Records of Chief Commands,

1865-76, Ethnic Elements of the Indian Army, Armies of Bengal, Bombay and Madras, MSS.EUR.F.114, 5(4), IOR.

57. Wilbrahim Egerton, *An Illustrated Handbook of Indian Arms and those of Nepal, Burma, Thailand and Malaya*, 1880, rpt., Bangkok: White Orchid Press, 1986, p. 87.
58. Captain A. Apthorpe, 'The Kachins and Others: A New Recruiting Area', *Journal of the United Service Institution of India*, XLI (1912), pp. 53-9.
59. Egerton, *An Illustrated Handbook of Indian Arms*, pp. 87-8.
60. Shakespear, *History of the Assam Rifles*, p. 19.
61. Egerton, *An Illustrated Handbook of Indian Arms*, p. 88.
62. MDP, no. 8, From A. Mc. L. Monteath, Under Secretary to the GOI, Home Department, to the secy. to the GOI, MD, 16 July 1862.
63. O.H.K. Spate & A.T.A. Learmonth, *India and Pakistan: Land, People and Economy*, 1954; rpt., Bombay: B.I. Publications, 1967, pp. 76-9.
64. Palit, *Sentinels of the North-East*, pp. 63-4; Shakespear, *Sirmoor Rifles*, p. 82.
65. *Sal* forest is a tropical deciduous (hardwood) rainforest common in South and South-East Asia, dominated by a single tree species, the *sal* tree.
66. Spate et al., *India, Pakistan and Ceylon*, p. 602.
67. Butler, *Travels and Adventures in the Province of Assam*, p. 11.
68. Spate et al., *India, Pakistan and Ceylon*, p. 603.
69. *Army in India Committee 1912*, vol. 3, Minutes of Evidence of Surgeon-General A.T. Sloggett, p. 805.
70. Lieutenant-General W.H. Goodenough and Lieutenant-Colonel J.C. Dalton, *The Army Book for the British Empire: A Record of the Development and Present Composition of the Military Forces and their Duties in Peace and War*, London: HMSO, 1893, p. 448.
71. Spate et al., *India, Pakistan and Ceylon*, p. 600.
72. Bonarjee, *A Handbook of the Fighting Races of India*, pp. 206-9.
73. Shakespear, *History of the Assam Rifles*, p. 16.
74. Franke, *War and Nationalism in South Asia*, p. 6.
75. Spate and Learmonth, *India and Pakistan: Land, People and Economy*, pp. 89-91.
76. Callwell, *Small Wars*, p. 353.
77. Digest of Services of the 3rd Brahmin, para 8, 11.
78. Shakespear, *Sirmoor Rifles*, pp. 82-3.
79. Roberts, *Forty-One Years in India*, p. 315.
80. *Appendices to the Report of the Special Commission Appointed by the Governor-General to Enquire into the Organization and Expenditure of the Army in India*, vol. 4, Calcutta: Govt. Central Press, 1880, Appendix XLV, Memorandum on transport prepared in the office of the QMG in India, p. 1647, NAI.
81. Revenue and Agricultural Department (hereafter RAD), no. 1155, from Col. R. Davidson for Commissary General Bengal, to Col. H.K. Burne, Secy. to the GOI, MD, 10 July 1877, NAI.

82. RAD, no. 1164, to the Commissary General, Bengal, 11 November 1878.
83. RAD, no. 1161, from Commissary General Bengal, 20 June 1878, no. 1163, from Chief Commissioner Assam, 16 August 1878, no. 1157, from Captain T. Deane, Assistant Secy. to the GOI, MD, to the Commissary General, Bengal, 19 September 1877.
84. RAD, nos. 1153, 1154, from Burne to the Commissary General, Bengal, 29 June 1877.
85. RAD, no. 1153, from Col. J.I. Willes, Commissary General, Bengal, to Burne, Simla, 30 May 1877, Progs. no. 1162.
86. RAD, no. 1156, from Captain E.S. Carter, Examiner of Commissariat Accounts to the Controller of Military Accounts, Fort William, 25 August 1877.
87. RAD, no. 1162.
88. *Appendices to the Report of the Special Commission*, vol. 4, Appendix XLV, pp. 1646-7.
89. RAD, no. 1988, from Col. W.C.R. Mylne, Commissary General, Bengal, to Col. G. Chesney, Secy. to the GOI, MD, Simla, 1 June 1881.
90. Extract of a letter from Madras Govt., MD, to the Secy. to the GOI, MD, paras 18, 21; 22 June 1893, George White Collection.
91. George Hamilton to Curzon, no. 12, Hamilton Private Papers, Reel no. 1, Acc. No. 1572, M/F, NAI.
92. Lieutenant-General George MacMunn, *The Romance of the Indian Frontiers*, 1931, rpt., London: Jonathan Cape, 1935, p. 157.
93. MacMunn, *Romance of the Indian Frontiers*, p. 161; Saxena, *Military System of India: 1850-1900*, p. 130.
94. *Appendices to the Report of the Special Commission*, vol. 4, Appendix XLV, p. 1647.
95. Field-Marshal Roberts, 'Memorandum on the Defence of India', in Kitchener Papers, II/50, 176, Roll no. 2, Acc. No. 2094, M/F, NAI.
96. *Army in India Committee 1912*, vol. 1-A, p. 29.
97. Rod Thornton, 'The British Army and the Origins of its Minimum Force Philosophy', *Small Wars & Insurgencies*, 15 (2004), pp. 83-106.
98. Kaushik Roy, 'The Beginning of "People's War" in India', *Economic and Political Weekly*, XLII (2007), pp. 1720-8.
99. Shakespear, *Sirmoor Rifles*, p. 84.
100. Palit, *Sentinels of the North-East*, p. 37.
101. 'Diary of Lieutenant E.H.E. Collen, RA Officer in North-West Frontier Expedition, 1897-98', pp. 16-17, 22-7, NAI.
102. V.G. Kiernan, *European Empires from Conquest to Collapse, 1815-1960*, Bungay, Suffolk: Fontana, 1962, p. 58; Douglas Porch, *Wars of Empire*, 2000; rpt., London: Cassell, 2001, p. 104.
103. Bruce Vandervort, *Wars of Imperial Conquest in Africa: 1830-1914*, Bloomington, Indiana: Indiana University Press, 1998, pp. 62-4.
104. Kirsten Zirkel, 'Military Power in German Colonial Policy: The

Schutztruppen and their Leaders in East and South-West Africa, 1888-1918', in David Killingray and David Omissi (eds.), *Guardians of Empire: The Armed Forces of the Colonial Powers c. 1700-1964*, Manchester/New York: Manchester University Press, 1999, p. 97.

105. Peter H. Wilson, 'European Warfare: 1815-2000', in Jeremy Black (ed.), *War in the Modern World since 1815*, London/New York: Routledge, 2003, p. 211.
106. H.L. Wesseling, 'Colonial Wars: An Introduction', in J.A. De Moor and Wesseling (eds.), *Imperialism and War: Essays on Colonial Wars in Asia and Africa*, Leiden: E.J. Brill, 1989, pp. 5-6.
107. J.A. De Moor, 'Warmakers in the Archipelago: Dutch Expeditions in Nineteenth Century Indonesia', in Moor and Wesseling (eds.), *Imperialism and War*, p. 51.
108. C. Fourniau, 'Colonial Wars before 1914: The Case of France in Indochina', in Moor and Wesseling (eds.), *Imperialism and War*, pp. 78-9; Roy, *Brown Warriors of the Raj*, p. 42.
109. A.S. Kanya-Forstner, 'The French Marines and the Conquest of the Western Sudan, 1880-99', in Moor and Wesseling (eds.), *Imperialism and War*, p. 138.
110. Moor, 'Warmakers in the Archipelago: Dutch Expeditions in Nineteenth Century Indonesia', in Moor and Wesseling (eds.), *Imperialism and War*, pp. 51-2.
111. David Killingray, 'Colonial Warfare in West Africa, 1870-1914', in Moor and Wesseling (eds.), *Imperialism and War*, p. 150.
112. Fourniau, 'The Case of France in Indochina', in Moor and Wesseling (eds.), *Imperialism and War*, p. 83.

CHAPTER 5

The Coming of British Forestry in Assam in the Nineteenth and Early Twentieth Century: Initiatives and Problems

SRIJANI BHATTACHARJEE

The historiography of environmental history has by now established the truism that British forest policies and exercises re/shaped and altered the natural environments of the countries colonized by them. Grazing and monocultural agriculture in Australia, New Zealand, and South Africa necessitated the clearing of native jungles and vegetation which in course of time led to soil salination, erosion and extinction of certain flora and fauna.[1] Conservation of trees of commercial value for future exploitation further resulted in deforestation and extermination of indigenous forest rights. Extending agriculture and trade infrastructure often led to draining of swamps and damming of rivers. In this context, India was no exception. The British Forest Department in India, founded in 1864 by Sir Dietrich Brandis, the first Inspector General of Forests, was an organization which had two perspectives. On one hand, it emphasized on the preservation of trees having commercial relevance for colonial use while on the other it enacted laws to curb the indigenous rights of the rural communities to hunt, graze livestock, farm and resource use in the woodlands under conservation programmes. By the end of the last decades of the nineteenth century, forests in most parts of India were under the authority of the British Forest Department which implemented various laws of conservation and exploitation with the underlying principle of generation of revenue.

In the period under observation, Assam was one of the most blessed regions of India in terms of natural resources when it consisted of all the hilly states of north-east India namely Mizoram, Meghalaya, Nagaland and Arunachal Pradesh except the princely states of Manipur and Tripura. These hilly regions were administrated as districts within Assam and were termed as Lushai Hills district, United Khasi and

Jaintia Hills district, Garo Hills district, Naga Hills district and North East Frontier Agency respectively. The entire region had a huge forest cover with over 80 per cent of its area under forests in the early nineteenth century.[2] In the pre-colonial age, the Ahom rulers exercised authority over the forests and the common people were at liberty to use the forest products. There were practically no proper forest laws and the state's role was restricted to the collection of revenue on some forest products such as aloes wood.[3] The cultivated lands were occupied by peasants and most non-agricultural land was regarded as communal property. The peasants could clear any part of the land for cultivation and did not have to pay any rent or price for it.[4] As a reward for military services, the Ahoms allotted the 'Paiks' (foot-soldiers of the Ahom state) 2 *puras* equivalent to 3 acres of the best rice land free of rent. If personal service was not required he paid Rs. 2 instead. He was also given land for his house and garden for which he had to pay a poll or house tax of 1 rupee.[5] The chief nobles cultivated their private estates with the aid of slaves, i.e. persons taken in war or purchased from the hill tribes, and of their retainers, who were either hill men or manumitted slaves.[6] The Ahom rulers encouraged wet-rice cultivation probably in order to check the migratory nature of the people in the bordering areas. Jungles were often used for the demarcation of boundaries with the neighbouring territories.[7]

With the annexation of Assam to the British Empire in 1826, large tracts of forest lands passed under British protection and Assam was integrated as a part of Bengal. The forests of the vast region were administered by the Bengal Forest Department under the Indian Forest Act of 1865. But soon it was realized that it was impossible to govern the huge region under a single conservator. Gustav Mann was assigned the post of Assistant Conservator of Assam in 1868 and was entrusted with the responsibility of investigating the forests of the region. T. Anderson, the Superintendent of Royal Botanical Garden of Calcutta and Conservator of Forests, Bengal was given the similar task of collecting information about the Bengal region. In 1874, Assam was reconstituted as a chief commissioner's province with Gustav Mann as the Deputy Conservator of Forests of the region.

It is a cliché that forest departments in various parts of the British Indian Empire functioned mainly as organs of commercial usage.[8] This paper seeks to study the formative phase of the forest department in Assam prior to its emergence as a full grown commercial department in the early twentieth century. This paper is an attempt to analyse the initial responses, attempts and mentalities of the colonial state towards the forests of Assam that led to the formal establishment of British Forest Department in the province – the circumstances under which it came into being, and the pattern and character of its administration between the second half of the nineteenth century and the early twentieth century. For the purpose of heuristic convenience the paper has been sub-divided into three sections: first, it probes into the colonial attempts to administer the forests of Assam prior to the advent of British Forest Department in the region. Second, we shall delve into the establishment of the British Forest Department in Assam and its related issues. Finally, we would like to characterize the nature of British Forest Administration in the region in terms of its activities.

EARLY COLONIAL EFFORTS TO ADMINISTER THE FORESTS OF ASSAM PRIOR TO THE ADVENT OF BRITISH FOREST DEPARTMENT IN THE PROVINCE

Soon after the annexation of the province into the British Empire, the Deputy Commissioners stationed in various parts of Assam played a significant role in accumulating knowledge about the natural resources of the areas under their jurisdiction and offered suggestions regarding their commercial utility. They often depended on local use of natural resources to gather information about their respective areas. In 1870-1, the Deputy Commissioner of Garo Hills while acquiring information about the flourishing cotton trade in the region accumulated some knowledge about the timber species existing in the area which according to him if well preserved with all reasonable rights of the Garos could serve as a lucrative source of revenue to the government.[9] Robert Bruce on his visit to Assam to examine the possibility of tea cultivation in the region gave a vivid account to Sir Francis Jenkins, the agent to the Governor-General in north-east India about the brisk pre-colonial timber trade existing in the province.[10] He also listed a set of 23 species of commercial trees native to the forests of the region. Buchanan Hamilton had prepared a 'catalogue of woods' containing 90 species of wood peculiar to the district of Goalpara of Assam which was later on included in the 'List of Indian woods' collected by Dr. Wallich.[11]

In 1850, the first concern was expressed by the colonial government about the preservation of Assam forests when the collector of Kamarupa division reported to the Commissioner of the province that the woodcutters from Bengal had made their appearance in Kamarupa and also in the districts lower down the Brahmaputra in the quest of *sal* (*Shorea robusta*) and exhausted the forests by indiscriminate felling. He had suggested that a tax of Rs. 15 per 100 logs should be levied instead of letting the timber trade remain uncontrolled. It was also recommended that a check should be imposed on the felling of young trees to promote natural regeneration.[12]

During this period, there were multiple authorities exercising their supervision over the forests of Assam. The Deputy Commissioners were in charge of their respective areas. The Public Works Department had some authority over the same as it was the principal customer of forest products at that time for its various developmental works like building of bridges, government houses, etc. It also had to perform the herculean task of clearing the jungles for the construction of public roads. For these purposes, large tracts of forest lands were under its control. Some plots of forest lands were also under the governance of the Revenue and Agriculture Department which was in favour of expanding settled agriculture by clearing forested lands. In 1852 the system of tax collection on woodcutters was abolished and farming out lands to the highest bidder for at least five years was introduced by the Board of Revenue. 'Conservancy measures', they held, 'could be considered after the forests had been cleared'.[13] It was thought that the newly-acquired large tracts of forested or marsh lands could be properly utilized if the areas were brought under settled cultivation. Consequently the immigration of peasants from the neighbouring districts of Bengal was encouraged by the British government. As early as 1832, circulars were issued inviting settlers to Assam through respective collectors to populous districts of Bengal like Dacca, Mymensingh, and Tipperah offering waste lands rent free for a term of ten years after which settlement would be made for the portion brought under cultivation.[14] The ultimate result of this sustained influx of population and the greater significance attached to settled cultivation over forest preservation was the desiccation of some 1.5 million acres of forest into cultivation by 1950.[15]

With the beginning of the tea plantation industry in Assam, the process of land usurpation reached new heights. The British government with the view to expand tea plantation in Assam offered a number of wasteland grant rules on partly or wholly revenue free rates such as the 99 years lease rules, Fee Simple Rules of 1826, and

Revised Fee Simple rules of 1874, etc. The acquisition of wastelands for the plantation of tea often meant cutting of trees, reeds and grasslands in those areas. In the Kamarupa district, valuable sal forests were made over to the Lower Assam Tea Company as wastelands by the Revenue department.[16] Burning of wood for making charcoal required for various activities of tea processing (like artificial drying of tea leaves) was also a widespread phenomenon that severely affected the forests. Major Graham, the Deputy Commissioner of Darrang in 1873 had analysed the prodigal waste of timber for charcoal on gardens with the following words, 'I lately estimated that on a moderate computation 1,000 trees are on an average used yearly in this way alone on each garden, while not a single tree is planted to replace them'.[17]

Apart from these, the system of *jhum* cultivation (variously considered as slash-and-burn, swidden or shifting cultivation) practised by the natives mostly in the hilly areas of Assam was considered as the greatest danger to forests by the British administrators. E.P. Stebbings had vehemently condemned shifting or *jhum* cultivation with the remark, 'The forests of this region had for centuries been devastated by the cutting and burning of the best timber to form ashes to fertilize their wretched fields of half wild grains'.[18] Such a remark was also an expression of the low opinion which the British held about the native tribes of north-east India. So according to the colonial rulers a measure to protect the forests of this region from burning them to ashes was the urgent need of the hour.

Under these circumstances, the British authorities considered the implementation of forest conservancy in Assam as a vital necessity. According to them, if such a measure was not given due importance, the forests of the region would diminish in no time. To quote E.P. Stebbings, 'Those who sit at home at ease and do not penetrate and search the forests are apt to look upon them as inexhaustible, a common term applied to forests, though none can be more inappropriate, but the areas covered with forests are yearly being encroached and the contents fast cleared'.[19]

THE INITIATION OF FORMAL MEASURES TO CONTROL THE FORESTS THROUGH THE BRITISH FOREST DEPARTMENT IN ASSAM

The reports submitted by Gustav Mann and T. Anderson on the forests of Assam and Bengal culminated in the publication of a complete note on the forests of Assam in December 1870 in the resolution to the government of Bengal. These reports represented the first extensive data collection on the forests of the province. The reports made a district-wise study of the natural resources prevailing in Assam by classifying them into (a) *Sal* forests, (b) *Sissu* and *Khoir* forests, (c) Mixed plain forests, (d) Mixed lower hills forests, (e) Pine forests, and (f) Mixed upper hills forests.[20] The beginnings of scientific forestry could be noticed in the gradual deepening of the classificatory base of the forests of the province in the late nineteenth century. Sir Dietrich Brandis, the first Inspector General of Forests paid a visit to Assam in 1879 and re-categorized the forests into (a) Savannah, (b) *Sal*, (c) *Sissu* and *Khoir*, (d) Mixed Deciduous, (e) Evergreen, (f) Bamboo and (g) cane breaks.[21] Sir Berthold Ribbentrop who succeeded him in the same post in 1889 retained the above classification and added pine forests as a separate category.[22] Further changes were brought in such classificatory policies in the twentieth century by M.C. Jacob, the Deputy Conservator of Assam forests in the 1930s. The report submitted by Mann and Anderson in 1870 further emphasized on detailed surveys, identifying and mapping out areas of forests having commercially viable trees which could be demarcated as 'reserves'. In view of the accelerated exploitation of the forests which was taking place in the province prior to the beginning of regular conservancy it was felt that formation of new plantations could be a method of partially stopping its desiccation while simultaneously using the forest resources of Assam profitably. In 1870-1 emphasis was given on starting experimental timber plantations in Assam and accordingly a number of plantations came up such as the rubber plantation in Charduar in Darrang district, teak plantation in Kulsi in Kamarupa and Makumtilla in Lakhimpur, and the Shillong plantation consisting of considerable amount of local pine, oaks, chestnuts, walnuts, eucalyptus, European and Himalayan pine.[23]

In 1874 Assam was reconstituted as a Chief Commissioner's province with a Forest Department created under the provisions of the Indian Forest Act of 1865. For administrative convenience, the province was subdivided into three divisions: (a) Brahmaputra Valley – consisting of the districts of Goalpara, Kamarupa, Darrang, Nowgong, Sibsagar, and Lakhimpur; (b) Surma Valley – comprising the districts of Cachar and Sylhet; (c) Areas under political control – consisting of the hilly districts like Garo Hills, Khasi and Jaintia Hills and Naga Hills. There were some other areas where the forest department exercised limited control such as the *zamindari* areas in parts of Goalpara district, and the areas under political control.[24] The forests under government control were divided into 'reserves' and 'open' forests under the Indian Forest Act of 1865. The reserved forests were under the charge of a Chief Forest Officer where the public use of forest products was prohibited and was solely intended to fulfil the revenue needs of the government. These forests were directly under the governance of the Forest Department. While in the 'open' forests, the department exercised its authority only on the 'reserved' trees while others were open for local use. By 1874, the area of reserved and open forests existing in Assam was 269 sq miles and 422 sq miles respectively.[25] The forests of the region were placed in charge of a Deputy Conservator with an Assistant Conservator for each section. The administration of the hilly districts was carried on with the assistance of political officers. In 1890 the colonial forest authorities started restrictive fire protection in the forests of Assam. The measure was undertaken mainly to regenerate the *sal* forests in the region as it stimulated the growth of new shoots by fertilizing the soil temporarily. It also increased the potash content in the soil by promoting bacterial activity and destroying fungal attacks.[26]

Within a few years of its existence, the nascent Forest Department in Assam witnessed a number of Forest Acts coming into operation in its forest areas. After the Indian Forest Act of 1865, the Indian Forest Act of 1878 was passed which re-notified the existing reserves in the region. Subsequently when the Assam Forest Regulation of 1891 began to function, these reserves passed under its jurisdiction and the local government was empowered to allocate further lands for the constitution of forest reserves. This act also provided for the creation of 'forest villages' to act as a source of labour for the Forest Department.[27] In course of time, a number of forest laws came into force in the region but the Assam Forest Regulation of 1891 was the most important in this regard. In 1905-6, the area under the forest administration of Assam was considerably increased as the region was again merged with East Bengal and renamed as the province of East Bengal and Assam. The districts of Buxa, Jalpaiguri and Chittagong hills were incorporated within the jurisdiction of the Forest Department of Assam. This arrangement was, however, temporary since by 1912 political changes occurred and Assam was assigned the status of a separate province whereby the districts of Buxa, Jalpaiguri and Chittagong hills were transferred to the Bengal division. With the outbreak of the First and Second World Wars, the demand for forest products from Assam increased considerably leading to a greater accruing of forest revenue, more so since the Second World War converted Assam into a war zone directly. Since its inception, the Forest Department was crippled in most of its aspects of administration due to shortage of funds which received a stimulus with the outbreak of the two World Wars.

REFLECTIONS ON THE NATURE OF EARLY BRITISH FOREST ADMINISTRATION IN ASSAM

Horizontally, the nature of British Forest Administration in Assam differed according to the specific regional and spatial setting. The authority of the department in different parts of Assam was not uniform in its various aspects of administration. It exercised a limited control over the forests under the jurisdiction of the *zamindari* areas of Goalpara district and in the hilly divisions of Assam. About half of the forested lands in Goalpara district was under *zamindari* control. In other words, the forest policies adopted by the department were varied in nature with regard to their areas of application. In 1863, the Commissioner of Assam presented a scheme for the preservation of forests according to which the existing system of farming the forests were to be retained in Kamarupa while in the districts of Nowgong, Darrang and Lakhimpur, the fiscal officers-in-charge of the *mouzas* should be instructed to protect the forests from spoliation with the levying of duties varying from 2 annas to Rs. 4 on the cutting of full-sized trees producing valuable timber.[28] The variations in the implementation of forest policies in Assam were not merely in accordance with the needs of the imperial government but to an extent probably they reflected the level of integration of the area under colonial control which in turn depended on the nature of relationships that the colonial state had established with the local communities of the region. Moreover, this period was the phase of gradual territorial expansion of Assam. The annexation of the province to the British Empire in 1826 was soon followed by the occupation of Cachar and Khasi and Jaintia Hills. By 1854, North Cachar Hills was incorporated within the British domain. Garo Hills passed under the British supervision in 1866 and the subjugation of Naga Hills was accomplished by 1889. The process of gradual expansion was accompanied by a number of changes in the administrative spheres which had its impact on every aspect of colonial governance. The system of farming the forests was approved by the Board of Revenue when the forests were divided into 'mahals'[29] and forests were farmed for at least five years. This system was introduced when priority was on the expansion of agriculture by clearing of forest lands and emphasis was laid on the independence of farmers to work in the forests for the purpose.[30] This system was retained in some parts of Assam even after the implementation of British Forest Policy as the British authorities considered that without such measures the resources and condition of the people living in the province could not be improved. The paucity of revenue was also a matter of serious concern for the forest officials during this period. Gustav Mann, the Deputy Conservator of Forests in 1878 was of the opinion that on account of scarcity of revenue resources and consequently limited forest establishments, the demarcation of reserves has not yet been extended to all districts of the province, and Sibsagar, Lakhimpur, and Sylhet have had as yet no professional forest conservancy.[31] Lack of labour for forest works and dearth of forest personnel interested to be employed in Assam were also some of the chief constraints. As a result of these factors, the Goalpara *sal* working plan introduced in 1893-4 could not be implemented properly and was ultimately abandoned.[32] The various plantation programmes like the Balipara Rubber tree plantation, the teak plantation at Kulsi and the Nambor plantation were forsaken prematurely due to lack of finance.[33]

The colonial Forest Department in Assam had to encounter a number of limitations in the way of its establishment in the region. During the period under observation, Assam remained an infrastructural and economic backwater even within eastern India. The region ravaged by Burmese wars and afflicted by numerous incurable diseases was a difficult terrain to deal with. Colonel Jenkins, the agent to the Governor-General in north-east India describes the situation in these words:

When therefore we assumed the charge of the country, nothing could possibly be unpromising than the state of the country. The small remnant of the people had been so harassed and oppressed by the long civil and internal wars that had followed the accession of Rajah Gourinath Singh in 1780 down to 1826 that they had almost given up cultivation and lived on jungle roots and plants, famine and pestilence carried off thousands that had escaped the sword and captivity. All men of rank, the heads of the Great Ahom and priestly families had retired to one district, Gowalpara having with little exception lost the whole of their property.[34]

The infant Forest Department was not organized in many of its aspects and consequently it had to function with the assistance of the Public Works Department and the Revenue and Agriculture Department who exercised parallel authorities over many forested tracts of Assam at that time. In some cases, the approval of the Deputy Commissioners was also required. The main purpose of these departments regarding 'forest use' were quite different from the objectives cherished by the forest department. So often there was a lack of cooperation on the part of these authorities towards the functioning of the Forest Department. Gustav Mann, the Deputy Conservator of the Forests of Assam, while preparing the first forest administration report of the province in 1874 laid emphasis on maintaining a cordial relationship with the civil authorities in order to make the department successful in the province. According to him:

> None of the better forests are given up at all for cultivation until the government forests, both reserved and open are demarcated and this work carried out with much expedition as practicable, since without this there is always great danger of encroachment on the part of forests by the temporary cultivation or alienation of forests by lease or sale.... The chief reason that the Deputy Commissioners had given so little support to forest conservancy is that they do not understand the great influence it has on the welfare of the people and to exclude the civil authorities from it is not a wise policy.[35]

As regards its commercial aspect too, the department had to encounter some restrictions. Assam was one of the lesser known regions of India at that time due to absence of proper communication system. Acute scarcity of labour often posed as the greatest hurdle behind any commercial venture in the province. The amount of forest revenue realized by the department was insufficient to meet its expenditure. Under such circumstances, the smooth functioning of the department in the region was an impossible task. By the later part of the nineteenth century, the construction of railway lines in some parts of Assam, gave a tremendous boost to the growing tea industry in the region. Along with tea, it also stimulated the growth of jute and rice cultivation in the province.[36] In 1883-4, the construction of Dibru-Sadiya railways led to the opening up of tea gardens in the Lakhimpur division. Consequently there was rising trend in the growth of Reserve Forests to serve as stockades of timber required for railway sleepers, tea chests and other commercial enterprises. In 1893, the Assam-Bengal Railways refused to accept the proposals made by the Forest Department which offered to provide supply of 30,000 sleepers to the railways at the rate of Rs. 2-1-6 per sleeper. On the contrary, it purchased Burma sleepers at the rate of Rs. 3 per sleeper at Gauhati. To this, the Chief Commissioner of Assam suggested that the situation would improve if the royalty rate was reduced. But the Conservator of Assam Forests in 1892-3 rendered a different opinion. According to him, the Public Works Department and Railways preferred to work through contractors and obtain supplies from outside the province. Thus the situation, he considered, 'cannot improve as long as this attitude prevailed even if the cost was cheapened by reduction of royalty as suggested by the Chief Commissioner'.[37] Such an approach was also reflective of an uncooperative attitude existing among other departments and commercial enterprises working in Assam towards the Forest Department of the region. As regards the sluggish growth of timber trade in the region, a number of factors played a crucial role. During the period under observation, Assam was regarded as an underdeveloped region of India and the knowledge base about the province was in its infancy. So, when the Forest Department in Assam offered to provide sleepers to railway companies, most of them refused to purchase them as they lacked knowledge about the natural resources existing in the region. The absence of established markets for Assam timbers in Calcutta or elsewhere outside the province was also a major lacuna. The timber plantation programmes of the colonial Forest Department in this period did not prove to be a profitable investment since it was a common assumption of the colonial government and those involved in the wood industry at Calcutta that plantation grown timber from Assam such as teak could never be of the same quality as naturally grown teak from Burma.[38] In addition to these, inaccessible timber reserves and lack of proper export roads in the region contributed greatly towards the slow growth of timber trade in Assam.[39] The tea chest industry in Assam also suffered great losses in this period. The tea companies in the region preferred to import tea boxes from Norway, Japan, Austria, Russia and England rather than availing the local tea boxes prepared by the saw mills working under the supervision of the Forest Department. In 1897, with a view to compete with the imported boxes, the royalty on local boxes were revised but these measures too proved futile in preventing the import of tea boxes in the province. In 1889-90, the sale of local tea boxes gradually declined as the managers of the tea gardens were supplied with imported tea boxes by the Calcutta agents.[40] R.S. Pearson in his note on the tea industry in Assam cited the factors responsible for such an attitude. According to him, the locally manufactured tea boxes were considered inferior to the imported boxes in terms of durability since these were prone to insect attack and tendency to rapid decay. Moreover the *semul* (*Bombax ceiba*) trees situated near the vicinity of saw mills and preferred by tea planters for tea boxes were mostly exhausted by over felling. Therefore, by the last decades of the nineteenth and beginning of the twentieth century, the scarcity of timber and ever increasing distance over which it had to be carried to the saw mills posed a major hurdle in the prosperity of saw mills in Assam.[41] The statement suggests the fact that the forests of the area had long been exploited for internal and domestic consumption to such an extent that *semul* trees had almost diminished from the area. In order to give a fair idea of the situation, Pearson had cited an extract from the note given to him by Mr. Moran of Sissi Saw Mill in the Lakhimpur division which ran as follows:

> The timber supply upto 1905 was within measurable distance from the mills. All the available timber along the banks and within accessible distance from the river has been cut, since then to get Simul wood we had to go to Lalli, 76 miles from the mills, to Dehog and Debong some 90 miles and to Titcoria above Sadiya a distance of about 110 miles from the mills. The result being that the cost of timber had quadrupled; we have had to work timber camps of our own. The loss of timber by the sudden floods in the Brahmaputra is at times also great. In 1907 our camps were several times raided by the Abors, and it is difficult to get native contractors to work on the Lalli and Debong rivers. There are Semul trees in the areas near the above named rivers but the distance from the water ways and cost of carriage is great, and it is almost impossible to bring them out, the expense being prohibitive.[42]

Clearly then, the resource extraction from the forests of Assam began to seem prohibitive due to the physical and financial costs and strain it involved.

The British Forest Department at times also used the forests of Assam to serve *de facto* political ends. The colonial hold over the natural resources of a frontier province like Assam was an essential policy of the British government to make its presence felt at the bordering areas of the region. The actual administrative jurisdiction of the department included the plains districts of Assam whereas the hilly tracts were controlled with the help of political officers. In order to protect the people in the plains districts of Assam bordering the hilly tracts, the department established forest reserves to act as buffer or safe zones. In 1877, a huge forested tract known as 'Inner Line Reserve' consisting of about 509 sq miles on the northern boundary with Cachar in south Assam was created and was managed by the Cachar forest division. In 1904 this reserve was territorially transferred from Cachar to Lushai Hills District in all probability as a measure of protection for the Cachar plains.[43] Unrestricted *jhuming* in these hills was regarded harmful for agricultural sustenance of the plains areas. Forests on the banks of navigable rivers provided the sole revenue generating source since extraction from deeper stretches was financially prohibitive. Here it may be tentatively suggested that the reserve was named as 'Inner Line Reserve' as it served the purposes of the Inner Line Regulation. It was a sort of natural barrier created by the British government between the Lushai hills and Cachar plains to check the latter from resorting to any form of exploitation in the Lushai areas as well as possibly to protect the Cachar plains from Lushai raids.

CONCLUSION

The colonial Forest Department in Assam was thus an integral part of the British imperialistic venture which emphasized on resource use from colonies for its revenue and commercial necessities at various points of time and space. In India, by the later half of the nineteenth century forests emerged as a multidimensional resource base which was to be utilized for different purposes according to their own temporal and spatial contexts. With the beginning of the nineteenth century, expansion of agriculture as a source of revenue gained importance and consequently forested lands were cleared for agricultural purposes. The introduction of railways in course of time created a demand for railway sleepers and timbers suitable for its manufacture were brought under policies of forest conservation. Native use of and access to forests was considered as the greatest threat to the conservationist agenda and consequently bans were imposed on indigenous rights of the forest communities. An urgent imperative developed among the British administrators to preserve the forests of India which would otherwise be destroyed by the indigenous dwellers. Moreover, the vanishing oaks in England needed a replacement which was to be fulfilled by the introduction of forest conservation in India. Plantation of trees having saleable value were emphasized and Indian forests served as a source of revenue and hunting grounds for British *sahibs* during their leisure time.

The colonial Forest Department in Assam in the later half of the nineteenth century came up as an organization inspired by the ideological concern for desiccation of Assam forests carried on by the natives, various administrative departments under the colonial aegis and commercial enterprises working in the province. The underlying principle of 'forest revenue' was not given much hype at the beginning and it was thought that to proceed with the subject in a planned and gradual manner would ensure success. With this long term aim in view, a complete plan on the forests of Assam and Bengal was prepared by Gustav Mann and T. Anderson which contained detailed sketches of the forest types existing in Assam and the demarcation of reserves and areas to be brought under plantation programmes. It also divided the province into administrative segments according to forest types. But these measures could not achieve much triumph at the initial phase as the infant Forest Department in the region had to function under several handicaps which were peculiar to the region. Poor infrastructure in terms of economy and communication along with disease-infested terrain and scarcity of labour were some of the hurdles that had to be dealt with. Lack of knowledge about the natural resources of the region and absence of export markets in Calcutta or elsewhere in the province to deal with products like railway sleepers and tea boxes discouraged the railway and tea companies from purchasing these commodities manufactured under the supervision of colonial Forest Department in Assam. Consequently the department had to suffer commercial loses and work in financial penury. Moreover the British Forest Department at the stage of its inception in the region had to function in collaboration with other departments like Public Works, Revenue and Agriculture. The ambitions of the flourishing tea industry and the wasteland policy of the colonial government in Assam were in stark contradiction with the policy of preservation of forests preached by the colonial Forest Department in the region. The colonial Forest Department utilizing the forests of Assam to play a *de facto* political role was probably a phenomenon specific to Assam. Although the rhetoric of conservation used by the Forest Department in the region formed a part of the global environmental consciousness, in Assam it performed the surrogate role of political safeguards against the hill tribes, especially in the case of the Lushais. In this sense, the forests of Assam constituted pockets of enforced natural barriers to protect the agriculture in the plains from destruction carried on by *jhum* cultivation in the hills.

By the second decade of the twentieth century, certain administrative changes occurred whereby Assam acquired the status of separate province in 1912. The outbreak of the First and Second World Wars produced demands for natural products from Assam and accordingly trade in major and minor forest products from the region received great fillip. Consequently the forest revenue accruing from the region exhibited a rising trend. Measures like the establishment of the Goalpara Tramway project further augmented the scope for exploitation of commercial species existing in the hitherto inaccessible areas. The numbers of reserved forests were increased considerably as the reserved forests existing in the Khasi and Jaintia Hills and Naga Hills were included within the direct control of the British government. Thus, between the second half of the nineteenth and the early twentieth century the feeble Forest Department in Assam plagued by numerous practical hindrances made the gradual transition to a revenue yielding institution of the colonial government. However, we need to reiterate the fact that in all its efforts the professed aim for environmental conservation seldom transgressed the desire for accruing economic benefits.

NOTES

1. *Encyclopedia of World Environmental History*, vol. 1, ed. Shepard Krech III, J.R. McNeill and Carolyn Merchants, New York and London: Routledge, 2004, pp. 169-70.
2. J. M'Cosh, in his *Topography of Assam* estimated that in the 1820s six-eighths to seven-eighths portion of the province was forested.
3. S.L. Barua, *A Comprehensive History of Assam*, Delhi: Munshiram Manoharlal, 1985, p. 241.
4. Alokesh Barua (ed.), *India's North East: Developmental Issues in a Historical Perspective*, Delhi: Manohar, 2005, p. 167.
5. Edward A. Gait, *A History of Assam*, 1905; rpt. edn. 1926, Gauhati: LBS Publications, p. 240.
6. Ibid., p. 241.
7. Barua (ed.), *India's North East*, p. 167.
8. See for example, Mahesh Rangarajan's *Fencing the Forest* for British forest policies in the Central Provinces; K. Sivaramakrishnan, *Modern Forests: State Making and Environmental Change in Colonial Eastern India* for an understanding of the British forest policies and governmentality in Bengal Provinces.

9. Bengal Papers, 1870-1.
10. H.K. Barpujari, *Francis Jenkins Report on the North Eastern Frontier of India*, Guwahati: Spectrum, 1995, pp. 79-81.
11. John M'Cosh, *Topography of Assam*, Delhi, 1st pub. 1837, first Indian rpt., Guwahati: Spectrum, 1986, pp. 36-43.
12. Gustav Mann, *Progress Report on the Forest Administration of Assam 1874-75*, Shillong: Assam Secretariat Printing Office, 1875, p. 1.
13. E.P. Stebbings, *The Forests of India*, vol. III, London: The Bogley Head, 1926, p. 214.
14. H.K. Barpujari, *The Comprehensive History of Assam*, vol. V, Gauhati: Publication Board, 1977, rpt. 1990, p. 48.
15. Richard P. Tucker, 'The Depletion of India's Forests under British Imperialism; Planters, Forests and Peasants in Assam and Kerala', in Donald Worster (ed.), *The Ends of the Earth: Perspectives on Modern Environmental History*, Cambridge: Cambridge University Press, 1988. p. 126.
16. Ibid., p. 215.
17. A. Mackenzie, *Papers Regarding the Tea Industry in Bengal with Notes by J. W. Edgar and Mr Campbell*, Calcutta: Bengal Secretariat Press, 1873, p. 61.
18. E.P. Stebbings, *The Forests of India*, vol. I, London: The Bogley Head, 1922, p. 3.
19. Ibid., vol. II, 1923, p. 415.
20. Ibid.
21. Deitrich Brandis, *Suggestions Regarding Forest Administration in Assam*, Shillong: Govt. of Assam, 1879, p. 2.
22. Berthold Ribbentrop, *Notes on an Inspection of the Forests in Assam during January to April 1889*, Simla, 1889.
23. *Progress Report on the Forest Administration of Assam 1874-75*, Shillong: Assam Secretariat Printing Office, 1875, p. 5.
24. Ibid., p. 4.
25. *Progress Report on the Forest Administration of Assam, 1878-79*, Shillong: Assam Secretariat Printing Office, 1879, p. 1.
26. *Hundred Years of Indian Forestry*, vol. 2: *1861-1961*, Dehradun: Forest Research Institute, p. 156.
27. *The Assam Forest Manual: The Assam Forest Regulation of 1891* vol. I, Shillong: Assam Secretariat Printing Office, 1923.
28. Shrutidev Goswami, *Aspects of Revenue Administration in Assam*, Delhi: Mittal Publication, 1987, p. 119.
29. Mahals were partitions within forests for purposes like hunting elephants by means of stockades or *kheddahs* and extraction of rubber, etc. In this context mahals were created in the forests for expanding agriculture.
30. Ibid., p. 115.
31. Rajib Handique, *British Forest Policy in Assam*, Delhi: Concept, 2004.
32. Regulation on the Falling of Trees other than Sal, Goalpara Division, Assam, 1896.

33. H.P. Smith and C. Purukayastha, *A Short History of Assam Forest Service 1850-1945*, Shillong: Assam Government Press, 1946, p. 12.
34. A.J. Moffatt Mills, *Report on the Province of Assam*, Calcutta Gazette Office, 1854, p. 3.
35. Stebbings, *The Forests of India*, p. 226.
36. Shyam Bhadra Medhi, *Transport System and Economic Development in Assam*, Guwahati: Publication Board, 1978, p. 185.
37. *Progress Report on the Forest Administration of Assam, 1892-93*, Shillong, 1893, p. 4.
38. Goswami, *Aspects of Revenue Administration in Assam*, p. 122.
39. *Quinquinnial Report on the Forest Administration of British India, 1909-10 to 1913-14*, Simla, 1915, p. 23.
40. *The Indian Forest Records*, vol. 5, part 10, R.S. Pearson, *Note on the Tea Box Industry in Assam*, 1913, p. 23.
41. Ibid.
42. Ibid., p. 10.
43. There were only six villages within the Reserve; Saiphum, Mauchar, Tinghmun, Sakawrdai, Bilkhawthlir and Vairengte – each of which was permitted a certain number of houses. In 1947-8 there was a total number of 325 households in the Reserve. Residents were not allowed to cut tree for *jhuming* and had to obtain permission from the authorities to clear bamboo jungles for cultivation. Hunting and fishing within the Reserves were also subject to restrictions. They had to obtain permits for collection of forest produce. Daman Singh, *The Last Frontier: People and Forests in Mizoram*, Delhi: Tata Energy Research Institute, 1996, pp. 28, 38 and 39.

SELECT BIBLIOGRAPHY

Archival Sources

Administrative Reports of the Conservator of Forests, Assam.

Annual Progress Reports on the Forest Administration of Assam from 1890 onwards.

Assam Forest Manual, Assam Forest Regulation 7th of 1891, vol. I, Shillong, 1923.

Quinquennial Reviews of the Forest Administration in British India and in the Province of Assam.

Reports on the Native Newspapers

Notes on the Proceedings of the Conference between the British Authorities and the Lushai Chiefs, 1941-2.

Working Plans of the different Forest divisions of Assam.

The Indian Forest Records, vol. 5, part 10, R.S. Pearson, *Note on the Tea Box Industry in Assam*, 1913.

Brandis, Dietrich, *Suggestions Regarding Forest Administration in Assam*, Calcutta: Calcutta Government Press, 1879.

Mills, A.J. Moffatt, *Report on the Province of Assam*, Calcutta Gazette Office, 1854.

Ribbentrop, Berthold, *Notes on an Inspection of the Forests of Assam during January to April 1889*, Simla: Government Press, 1889.

Ribbentrop, Berthold, *Forestry in British India*, 1900, rpt., 1989.

Stebbings, E.P., *The Forests of India*, vol. I, II and III, London: The Bogley Head, 1922-7.

Hunter, W.W., *A Statistical Account of Assam* vol. I and II, 1st publ. in 1879 and 1887, Delhi: B.R. Publishing, rpt. 1975.

JOURNALS AND SOUVENIRS

Journal of the Asiatic Society of Bengal.

The Special Edition of the *Hundred Years of Indian Forestry, 1861-1961*, vol. I, Dehradun: Forest Research Institute, 1961.

Various articles in the *Indian Forester* between 1890-1950.

SECONDARY SOURCES

Arnold, David and Ramachandra Guha (eds.), *Nature, Culture and Imperialism: Essays on the Environmental Histories of South Asia*, Delhi: Oxford University Press, 1995.

Barpujari, H.K., *Assam in the Days of the Company (1828-58)*, Gauhati: Lawyers, 1963.

———, *Francis Jenkins Report on the North Eastern Frontier of India*, Guwahati: Spectrum, 1995.

Bareh, Hamlet, *The History and the Culture of the Khasi People*, Calcutta: Navamudran, 1967.

Barua, Alokesh (ed.), *India's North East: Developmental Issues in a Historical Perspective*, Delhi: Manohar, 2005

Barua, S.L., *A Comprehensive History of Assam*, Delhi: Munshiram Manoharlal, 1985.

Basu, Nirmal Kumar, *Assam in the Ahom Age 1228-1826*, Calcutta: Sanskrit Pustak Bhandar, 1970.

Chakraborty, B.C., *British Relation with the Hill Tribes of Assam Since 1858*, Calcutta: Firma KLM, 1981.

Chattopadhyaya, Kamaladevi, *Tribalism in India*, Delhi: Vikas Publishing House, 1978.

Choudhury, D.P., *The North East Frontier of India: 1865-1914*, Calcutta: The Asiatic Society, 1978.

Dass, S.K., 'Immigration and Demographic Transformation of Assam, 1891-1981', in *Economic and Political Weekly*, 10 May 1981.

Das, S.T., *Tribal Life in North Eastern India: Habitat, Economy, Customs and Traditions*, Delhi: Gian Publishing House, 1986.

Elwin,Verrier, *A Philosophy for NEFA*, Shillong: Published on behalf of the Advisor to the Government of Assam, 1964.

———, *The Tribal World of Verrier Elwin: An Autobiography*, Delhi: Oxford University Press, 1964.

Gait, Edward A., *A History of Assam*, 1905, rpt. edn. 1926, Gauhati: LBS Publications.

Ghurye, G.S., *The Burning Cauldron of North East India*, Bombay: Popular Prakashan, 1980.

Goswami, Shrutidev, *Aspects of Revenue Administration in Assam*, Delhi: Mittal Publications, 1987.

Grove, Richard, Vinita Damodaran and Satpal Sangwan (eds.), *Nature and the Orient: The Environmental History of South and South East Asia*, Delhi: Oxford University Press, 1998.

Guha, Amalendu, *Planter Raj to Swaraj: Freedom Struggle and Electoral Politics in Assam 1826-1947*, Delhi: Indian Council for Historical Research, 1977.

———, *Medieval and Early Medieval Assam*, Calcutta: Centre for Studies in Social Sciences, 1991.

Guha, Ramachandra, *The Unquiet Woods: Ecological Change and Peasant Resistance in the Western Himalayas*, Delhi: Oxford University Press, 1989.

Gurdon, P.R.T., *The Khasis*, Delhi: Cosmo Publications, 1st pub. 1907; rpt. 1987.

Handique, Rajib, *British Forest Policy in Assam*, Delhi: Concept, 2004.

Hunter, W.W., *A Statistical Account of Assam*, London: Trubner & Co., 1879, 2 vols.

Jacob, M.C., *The Forest Resources of Assam*, Shillong: Govt. of Assam, 1940.

Joshi, M.G., *Mizoram Past and Present*, Delhi: Mittal Publication, 2005.

M'Cosh, J., *Topography of Assam*, 1837; rpt., Guwahati and Delhi: Spectrum, 1975.

McCall, Major Anthony Gilchrist, *The Lushai Chryalis*, London: Luzac and Company, 1949.

Medhi, Shyam Bhadra, *Transport System and Economic Development in Assam*, Guwahati: Publication Board, 1978.

Millington, Powell, *On the Track of the Abor*, London: Smith Elder and Co. 1912.

Mohapatra P.C. and P.M. Mohapatra, *Forest Management in the Tribal Areas: Forest Policy and People's Participation*, Delhi: Concept, 1997.

Reid, Robert, *History of the Frontier Areas Bordering on Assam*, Shillong: Assam Government Press, 1942.

Shakespear, L.W. , *History of Upper Assam, Upper Burma and North Eastern Frontier*, London: Macmilan and Co., 1914.

Shakespear, Lt. Colonel John, *The Lushai Kuki Clan*, London: Macmilan and Co., 1912.

Siddique, Md. Abu B., *Evolution of Land Grants and Labour Policy of Government: The Growth of the Tea Industry in Assam 1834-1940*, Delhi: South Asian Publishers, 1990.

Singh, Daman, *The Last Frontier: People and Forests in Mizoram*, Delhi: Tata Energy Research Institute, 1996.

Sinha, A.C., *Beyond the Trees, Tigers and Tribes*, Delhi: Indus, 1989.

Sivaramakrishnan, K., *Modern Forests: State Making and Environmental Change in Colonial Eastern India*, Delhi: Oxford University Press, 1996.

Smith, H.P. and C. Purakayastha, *A Short History of the Assam Forest Service*, Shillong: Assam Government Press, 1946.

Tucker, Richard P., 'The Depletion of India's Forests under British Imperialism: Planters, Forests and Peasants in Assam and Kerala', in Donald Worster (ed.), *The Ends of the Earth: Perspectives on Modern Environmental History*, Cambridge: Cambridge University Press, 1988.

CHAPTER 6

The Ecological and Social Watershed: Colonial Intervention and Forest Use in Assam

RAJIB HANDIQUE

Colonialism affected different regions of the world differently. Such intervention led to massive changes in the landscape and societies. Ecology may be regarded as the study of the relations between organisms and their environments or of the organism-environment nexus. To what extent an ecological analysis is possible in dealing with complex civilizations still remains a question, although some attempts have been made in this direction. This paper will try to focus on the colonial period of Assam's history as a watershed both in terms of ecology as well as societal changes.

PRE-COLONIAL FOREST HISTORY

The entire north-eastern India forms part of the world's richest bio-geographic area, the Indo-Malayan realm.[1] The geographical position of Assam formed by overlapping mountain chains and the moist tropical climate have contributed in the setting up of a habitat mosaic. It is for such reasons that in a comparatively small area, we find the existence of a number of complementary habitat components such as hills and hillocks as well as water bodies, which successfully create the essential micro-habitats for a large variety of life-forms.[2]

The wealth of species in humid tropical and sub-tropical forests has always fascinated botanists, ecologists, geneticists and students of evolution. However, even in the twenty-first century, we still are not in a position to prepare a complete inventory of all the living organisms from a single hectare of any one tropical humid forest.[3] This is because of the fact that the tropical humid forests are very rich and diverse whereas we are largely ignorant of how the populations of these thousands of species interact with each other. It is for such reasons that there has always been a problem of inventory while undertaking any study of the forests in Assam. The species of trees that find mention in the pre-colonial and colonial sources are not comprehensive enough so as to include trees or other forest produce that existed outside the domain of human use.

This multiplicity of habitats also meant existence of multiple zones for man-nature interaction. Such interaction might definitely have led to development of different cultural traits, customs and traditions that prolonged living in a particular locale normally entailed. This might have also led to creation of exclusive societies with characteristics that differentiated them from the 'others'. It is for such reasons that approximately 240 ethno-linguistic groups of humans live in this area, creating matchless diversity.

The lack of sufficient sources limits our knowledge about the land use pattern in ancient Assam. However, some conjectures are possible based on some geographical realities. The pattern of civilization that had progressed in the western part of India cannot be wholly applicable to Assam. Unlike in many other parts of the world, in Assam, we do not find any significant example of a community that was nomadic and pastoral. This might as well be attributed to lack of grasslands and a climate necessary for supporting such a stage of civilization.

The *Kalika Purana* mentions about a large number of precious trees including *sal* (*Shorea robusta*), *sarala* (pine), *chandana* (sandalwood) and *agaru* (aloewood). The famous epic *Mahabharata* mentions about presents received from Pragjyotisha (one of the historic names of ancient Assam) by Yudhisthira during his Rajasuya ceremony.[4] The presents included among other precious articles, sandalwood skins and heaps of aromatics. Overall, it appears that apart from a few varieties of wood and timber which were used for making houses, palaces and above all boats, not much forest dependent activities seemed to have developed. We may also safely surmise that the forests might have also met many of the medicinal and other important day-to-day needs of the people living in that period in Assam.

The forests of Assam were also very famous for the rich fauna that it supported, and more so for her elephants. Elephants formed an important part of the army of ancient Assam as it had been in several other parts of India. Both epigraphic and literary sources refer to the abundance of elephants in the forests of Assam.[5] The legendary ruler from Assam, Bhagadatta fought in the Kurukshetra war as mentioned in the *Mahabharata*, with troops of elephants and has been credited as 'the best wielder of the elephant goad'. Kautilya mentioned that the elephants bred in the eastern country were probably the best.[6] Kautilya was probably referring to Assam. Kalidasa wrote that elephants were caught in the jungles of Kamarupa (another historic name of Assam).[7] Even the famous Chinese traveller Hieun Tsang who visited Kamarupa around AD 642-3, stated that, there were elephants in herds in the south-east of Kamarupa and so, there was no dearth of elephants for war purposes.[8] It is popularly known that Bhaskaravarman (*c.* 594-650), the greatest ruler of the Varman dynasty went to meet Harshavardhana (606-46 or 647), the great ruler of Kanauj with 20,000 elephants.[9] The number of elephants may be an exaggeration, but is a pointer to the abundance of elephants in Assam.

In the ancient period, as elsewhere in India, the villages of Assam might as well have been divided into three parts: the village proper with the houses and gardens, the arable lands with the cultivated fields and pasture land.[10] Around the agricultural units of a village lay the unused land, and woodlands consisting of belts of fruits, bamboo and the other plants which might extend to some distance so as to reach the boundary of the next village. The pasture land was usually located in the outskirts of the village and sometimes along the boundary of the village and was considered to be common and undivided property of the village. Under such circumstances, forests would have naturally become a part of their communal property.

Medieval Assam witnessed the rise of several important dynasties and kingdoms in the Brahmaputra Valley. It was a period of political consolidation and aggrandisement. During this period cultivation by ploughing was making rapid progress in the valley. The Brahmaputra Valley had been a rich rice bowl that supported the Kamarupa state at one time.[11] With the advent of the Ahoms, the *sali* (wet rice) cultivation received a boost. Embankment and dykes built during the Ahom reign ensured better and stable yields.[12] The *paik* system, which was a means of maintaining a peasant militia in the population sparse region of Assam ensured landholdings for all able bodied men.

In the hills, *jhuming* or the slash and burn cultivation was the predominant mode of cultivation. Animal drawn ploughs could not be used in the hills. However, as Amalendu Guha has mentioned, 'shifting cultivation should be taken more as a concession to conditions of land abundance and the character of the soils than as a device of barbarism'.[13] Terrace cultivation existed side by side with *jhuming* in some hills.[14]

It is reliably known that the Ahom rulers during their heydays realized royalties on timber and elephants. The *Fatiya-i-Ibriah* refers to revenue derived from elephants and certain jungle products.[15]

Assam during the medieval period saw the advancement of agriculture, which probably might have led to the reduction in the forest cover. Moreover, certain villages were known for the production of a specific variety of crops as their nomenclature would indicate. Thus, we have *ambari* (a garden of mangoes) *bansbari* (a garden of bamboos), *panbari* (a garden of betel-leaves), *tamulbari* (a garden of areca-nuts), etc., moreover we have the famous *muga sumonis* of Assam.[16] As such there were some monocultures done for use, and the extent of those were bound to be limited considering the low population figure.

Assam used to export a considerable amount of *lac,* which was of a superior quality to Bengal. According to a table supplied by Buchanan Hamilton regarding Assam-Mughal trade, we find that Assam exported stick lac to an amount of 10,000 maund, valued at rupees 35,000.[17] Even in the earlier period, Tavernier had put down the information that Assam produced an abundance of shellac of a red colour, which was the best of its kind in the whole of Asia.[18]

Medieval Assam did not witness large-scale deforestation mainly because of limited increase in population and also because timber wood were not used for a large variety of purposes. Apart from the very limited threat from extension of agriculture, forests were not subjected to much exploitation. Timber was used only to make houses, furniture and sometimes decorative items, though the state also used it for procuring elephants and making boats for war purposes.

The people of Assam were able to build numerous boats, both in the ancient and the medieval periods.[19] Talish highly appreciated the wooden palace of the Ahom rulers at Garhgaon, and the houses of some nobility. We also learn from the *Fatiya* that the people of Assam could make very beautiful chairs, thrones, boxes, chests and trays all carved out of a single piece of wood.[20] An officer with the title of *kath-barua* was put in charge of the Ahom royal carpentry.[21]

Elephants remained a very important item procured from the forests of Assam. We come to know about a lot of friction between the Ahom representatives stationed at Guwahati and their Mughal counterparts over the *kheddah* operations.[22] The treaty of Ghilajharighat signed on 22 January 1663, which concluded the Mughal expedition under the commandership of Mirjumla, imposed a war indemnity of 20 elephants (14 tuskers and 6 female elephants) on the Assam king. Moreover, the Assam ruler was also to send another 90 elephants during the course of one year in three equal instalments.[23] All these not only points out to the availability of elephants in the forests of Assam, but also indicates the availability of the habitat suitable for elephants.

The forests therefore were a provider of much military equipment as well as articles of daily use. The various kingdoms of Assam did not appear to have a clear-cut and comprehensive forest policy. It was probably the abundance of forests in the region that did not warrant such a policy. However, the Ahom administration did levy taxes on a variety of forest products like aloewood, lac, ivory, etc. The government also appointed officers like the *habiyal barua* and the *kathkatiya barua* to look after forest products and forest timbers respectively. According to the *Tungkhungia Buranji*, *habial barua* was an Ahom officer-in-charge of forests and forest revenues.[24]

As a result of the heavy casualty and dislocation caused by the civil wars, often referred to as the *Moamaria* rebellion that took place in the late 1760s and early 1770s and the Burmese invasions, which took place in the second decade of the nineteenth century, there developed vast tracts of wastelands in the province of Assam.[25] Finally when Assam passed into the British imperial control as per the provisions of the treaty of Yandaboo (24 February 1826), the province with sparse population still had large forested areas.[26]

The following table based on data of 1874-5 (about fifty years after the beginning of the colonial rule), would provide us with a fair idea about the landscape of Assam:[27]

District	*Percentage of area under cultivation*
Goalpara	50.0
Cachar	20.0
Kamarupa	19.9
Sibsagar	17.5
Nowgong	10.3
Darrang	9.5
Lakhimpur	4.2

Even increased activities of the people of Assam during the pre-colonial period did not lead to severe degradation of her forest wealth as early British travellers mention of the extensive wastelands (which included forests) which they saw in Assam during the early part of their intrusion into the country. According to John M'cosh,[28] '...this extensive valley, though some centuries ago richly cultivated by an industrious and enterprising people, is now throughout six-eighths or seven-eighths of its extent covered with jungle.'

Travellers wrote about the *wild* and at places *impenetrable* forests of Assam.[29]

It is therefore, discernible that the history of pre-colonial Assam manifested a close linkage between the people and the environment. Most likely people identified themselves with nature and considered themselves as part of the same. The pre-colonial state was not extractive to the extent of causing any major damage to the environment. People and nature lived in harmony under the circumstances and there was no development of an ideology where forests or for that matter, the natural resources, were regarded as the 'other'. It may aptly be stated that the state and the people of this region, even after meeting their requirements from the forests, might have developed a cultural ecology based on symbiosis and sustainability.

COLONIAL INTERVENTION AND THE CHANGING PARADIGMS

At the time of British occupation of Assam, the province with a sparse population was largely forested. The Britishers carried with them the dominant belief of man's mastery over nature. This perception of superiority was effected largely by events like the Industrial Revolution, the advancements in science and technology and their colonial expansion. The forests in Assam were regarded as obstruction to the prosperity of the empire and came to be gradually exploited for imperial ends by the British colonial administration. It was because of this colonial intervention that forest/land-use in Assam changed its pattern and character and transformed the landscape completely.

The first time forest management was thought of in Assam was in the year 1850, when the Collector of Kamarupa represented to the Commissioner of Assam that the wood-cutters from Bengal, after having exhausted by indiscriminate fellings the *sal* forests in the districts lower down the Brahmaputra, had found their way to

Kamarupa in search of *sal* timber.[30] This intrusion from another province of India for forest resources is symbolic of a process in colonial Assam that was marked by both immigration and deforestation.

Once the necessity of an organized forest administration throughout the country had been recognized, the Government of British India proceeded with great zeal and energy to create and develop a Forest Department for the great work before it. From the beginning of forest administration and conservancy in Assam, there was no change in the main system of managing forests in the province. Although there had often been changes made in details, the fundamental unity of the objectives of forest conservancy in Assam remained unchanged. The aim of the Forest Department from the beginning appeared to be:[31]

First – to secure all the better forests as speedily as possible from further spoliation by having them gazetted and properly demarcated.

Second – To increase the revenue from the Government by all legitimate means, since the financial success of forest management is the only sound basis on which it can be permanently established and maintained.

Third – To protect the areas to be maintained as forest from all that tends to interfere with their highest productiveness.

Fourth – To ascertain by survey as soon as possible the nature and contents of each forest accurately.

Fifth – To divide the forests as soon as practicable into well-defined and manageable divisions, ranges, and beats, because such arrangement is absolutely necessary for systematic forest management, and ensures economy in, and the utmost use of, power.

Sixth – To improve, by sowing and planting as much as ever the income may permit, those forests in which expenditure on such work is most likely to prove remunerative.

Evidently, augmentation of revenue was the main aim of the British interventions in the forests of Assam and we perceive that practically all policies tended in that direction. As in the face of increasing hegemony, taxes came to be imposed on the general population for using forest produce, which so long had been drawn freely.

In the valuable *sal* forests of the eastern *duars*, in the Goalpara district, the Bengal wood-cutters were found exceedingly busy as they cut down whatever they wanted and a great deal more evidently making up for the payment of the annual tax amounting to Rs. 4.4 per axe.[32] That measure led to unrestricted fellings as taxation was done on the axe rather than on the felled trees. This further illustrates the fact that the British forest policy was primarily formulated to earn as much revenue as possible even at the cost of wanton destruction of the forest wealth.

Taxes were further imposed on timber in the form of *gorkhati*, on grazing in the form of *khasury* and on reeds in the form of *bunkur*. The *khasury* was levied at the rate of 2 annas on cows and at 4 annas on buffaloes. *Bunkur* which was usually sold by auction, was a tax levied at the rate of 8 annas on a *dao* and 4 annas on a sickle. These taxes were in addition to the taxes imposed on major forest produce in the form of timber.[33] All these measures aimed at revenue augmentation were unprecedented in Assam.

The colonial government sought to legitimize their hegemony over the forests of Assam through legislations. The Indian Forest Acts of 1865 and 1878, Assam Forest Regulation, 1891, Indian Forest Act, 1927 (this Act was not applicable to Assam), Assam Forest (Amendment) Act, 1931 were some of the important enactments. Of them the Assam Forest Regulation, 1891 had a preponderant effect and was specific to Assam.

Wasteland Grants and the Plantation Industry

Wasteland grants constitute one of the most far-reaching policies of the British colonial administration. It changed the landscape of Assam completely inducting new capital and human elements that had far-reaching impact. As a matter of fact, no land can be termed as waste. However, in face of the huge expanse of forested areas (regarded by many as jungles, as the same were un-administered) and the discovery of tea, imperial interests came to include forests within the connotation of 'wastelands', something that is 'waste' and so becomes necessary to be put to productive usage. One form of productive use of such wasteland was tea plantation. The term 'wasteland' is thus a pointer to the abundance of forests in Assam while at the same time, it could also be used to justify the conversion of the same to productive capacities. The same term (i.e. wasteland) also appears to conform to the colonial construct of wildness and eventual taming of the same. Further, it largely conforms to the notion of 'civilizing mission' of the British Raj.

Wasteland grants made by the colonial government led to large-scale alienation of forest land. With a view to encouraging the growth and expansion of the tea industry in Assam, the British government offered land for cultivation of tea on especially favourable terms, under the various sets of rules introduced from time to time. Thus, we have the Wasteland Grant Rules of 1838 (also known as 99 Years' Lease Rules), Fee Simple Rules of 1826, Revised Fee Simple Rules of 1874 and the New Lease Rules of 1876.[34] It could be noticed that with the exception of lands settled for special cultivation under the New Lease Rules of 1876, lands granted under the older set of rules were either wholly or partly revenue free in perpetuity.[35] The owners of these lands had permanent, heritable and transferable rights.[36] Moreover, the ceiling of such grants was adjusted from time to time to attract more and more speculators to take up wastelands. The ceiling of the grants, which was fixed at 500 acres, was reduced to 200 acres and subsequently to 100 acres in 1856 as per the recommendation of the Commissioner of Assam.[37] The grantees of wastelands were therefore offered maximum possible advantages along with the *de jure* authority over the allocated land.

A large quantity of charcoal was required then in the tea factories of Assam for *firing* and *drying* the tea. In fact, tea industry initially relied a great deal only on charcoal as the source of fuel.[38] Large areas of the grants under forest were used to supply the requirements of wood for fuel and other purposes.[39]

However, it needs to be noted that the colonial masters did not favour making of such grants to the indigenous people of Assam. This may be gauged from the submission made in the Mills report on Assam in 1853, wherein it is stated that the Commissioner of Assam Jenkins had opined that in a country like Assam, where there is super abundance of land and a deficiency of labour, 'I strongly deprecate the granting of waste land to natives of the province except under peculiar circumstances....'

The effect of those favourable conditions was that applications were made for large blocks of land.

The extent of the land alienation might be gauged from the following figures as mentioned in the Annual Tea Report for 1878-9:[40]

District	*Planted (in acres)*	*Not Planted (in acres)*	*Total (in acres)*
Cachar	42,199	92,551	1,34,750
Sylhet	14,713	39,426	54,139
Goalpara	270	737	1,007
Kamarupa	6,999	12,435	19,434

Darrang	14,125	54,485	68,600
Nagaon	10,324	32,695	43,019
Sibsagar	34,194	1,12,877	1,47,071
Lakhimpur	23,781	93,527	1,17,308
Khasi & Jaintia Hills	1,235	836	2,071
Total	1,47,840	4,39,569	5,87,409

It might fairly be said that between 3,00,000 and 4,00,000 acres or approximately 550 sq. miles of land was not really planted, but were in the hands of the planters as allocated grants was forest land and the remainder chiefly grasslands.[41]

There were no inducements for applicants to limit their applications to the area actually required by them, and hence large areas of forest land were alienated by the government for tea plantations.[42] Applications were frequently made for 1,000, 1,500 or several thousand acres by parties who had neither the means nor the intention of bringing more than a few hundred acres under cultivation.[43] Land speculation went on in Assam encouraged by imperial interest. The total number of grants rose from 115 in 1861-2 to 182 in 1862-3 and further shot up to 418 in 1867-8.[44] The practical result of those grants was large-scale alienation of forest land (which would otherwise have been state property) by government than was actually required for the extension of tea cultivation.[45] By 1912, as per the Inspection Report submitted by F. Beadon Bryant it appears that all the areas available within the inner line had been reserved in the Lakhimpur and Sibsagar districts. It is also quite surprising to find that as per Bryant's Report, in the Brahmaputra Valley, reserved forests formed only 8.7 per cent of the total area. As the grantees were mostly European capitalists, it also meant transfer of land (and forest) to foreign proprietary control. The importation of labourers from other parts of India to work in the plantations constitutes another development having wide ramifications.

Agriculture and Forests

Extension of agriculture was actively pursued by the colonial government more as a means of augmenting the land revenue. The forests were considered as an obstruction to agriculture rather than otherwise and consequently a bar to the prosperity of the empire.[46] British authorities were conscious from the very beginning of the fact that unless the vast tracts of wastelands were brought under tillage, neither the resources of the government, nor the condition of the people could be improved.[47] As early as 1832, circulars were issued inviting settlers to Assam through respective collectors to populous districts of Bengal, viz., Dacca, Tipperah and Mymensing offering wastelands rent-free for a term of years after which, settlement would be made for the portion brought under cultivation.[48] Assam's forests had always been put under new pressures when the influx of refugees from East Pakistan moved northwards into Assam. They used to have on their side the general British assumption that settled agriculture was a far more productive and stable means of land (forest) use. In the twenty years ending 1950, the immigrants from East Bengal had turned some 1.5 million acres of forest into settled agriculture.[49]

The following statement made by A.W. Botham in the Legislative Council regarding the Nambor Forest Reserve might be taken as a case in point:[50]

> It does not appear that it was ever the intention of the Government, in throwing open part of the Nambor Reserved Forest for cultivation, that settlement should only be made for ordinary cultivation. In fact, when the proposal to throw open this area was originally framed in 1896, it was supposed that tea planters were the only probable applicants for land in the reserve. The area was not disforested until 1921, and in the notification declaring the area to be disforested (No. 1611 R., dated the 4th May 1921) the reason for the disforestation was stated to be 'extension of ordinary and special cultivation'. The idea that the forest property is more or less inexhaustible is entirely fallacious.

Commercialization of Forests Produce

With the progress of forest administration in Assam, newer and newer varieties of forest trees were sought to be brought under commercial exploitation. With the advance of modern civilization, the demands both of trade and the population increased whereas the forest diminished in size. Railways spread and forest growth disappeared with an incredible rapidity within the reach of the railway lines and even beyond, partly on account of the direct demands made on them (like the supply of railway sleepers) for constructive works and fuel, demands which were frequently met by an exploitation carried on in a reckless manner.

The forest produce of Assam was subjected to very numerous and varied uses. Experiments were conducted on several varieties of trees for discovering the latent commercial value of the woods. Moreover, plywood and veneers, paper pulp, tool handles, gramophone cabinets, decorative furniture, etc., were produced from the trees found in the forests of Assam. *Sati* (*Churcuma angustifolia*) was tested for the quality and quantity of flour extracted from the roots of the local varieties.[51] *Makai* (*Shorea assamica*) was found to yield a very fine transparent resin and attempts were made to find out its economic uses.[52] Experiments continued to be conducted on the latex of India Rubber (*Ficus elastica*). Preparations were made to propagate lac on *arhar* (*Cajanus indicus*) plants by sowing up some 20 acres with that species in the forests of western Bengal and Assam in 1908-9.[53]

Thus, the demand of modern civilization led to greater use of forest resources and the forest produce of Assam got linked to the All India trade and eventually to world trade. The Great Depression of the 1930s which affected the major world economies had significant impact on the forest administration of Assam.[54]

Elephants had always been a source of revenue for the governments in Assam even in the medieval period. In the early years of the Company's rule, *kheddahs* (elephant catching in stockades) were conducted by the government. The right of catching wild elephants later on became a government monopoly. Licenses used to be issued to those who wanted to capture wild elephants through *kheddah shikar* or *mela shikar*.[55] The revenue earned through issue of licenses was put under the head 'minor forest produce'.

Commercialization of the forest resources in Assam remained one of the preponderant features of the British colonial government. However, it was the opinion of most of the earlier British administrators that the forests of Assam did not produce too many valuable timbers, and under the influence of that idea, artificial plantations were developed in the province. The efforts at conservation were limited to regeneration of commercially useful trees that might fetch better returns against the investment. Monocultures seemed to dominate the conservation efforts. Thus it was India Rubber at Kulsi and Charduar, *nahor* in the Nambor. Teak (*Tectona grandis*) plantations were started on the Kulsi River in Kamarupa and on the Dehing River near Makum in Sibsagar district between 1869 and 1872. The plan was to substitute the valueless trees in the Assam forests with a wood really valuable for the numerous kinds of requirements.[56] The experiments with different types of tree plantations were not always successful.

Sylvicultural operations were incorporated as part of forest management in Assam. In the narrower sense, it meant formation, regeneration and tending of forests, or woods, until they became ripe for the axe.[57] This again discriminated for tree varieties with potential for commerce.

The province of Assam was endowed with valuable animals some of whom like the one-horned rhinoceros was native to the forests of Assam. The fauna of Assam was also drastically affected by the British intervention in the forests. It is quite natural that change in the forest cover would lead to change in habitats. The procedure of rewarding the persons who killed animals considered to be dangerous was unprecedented. In fact, there was considerable cost of keeping down wild animals as the government had to spend more than 67.18 pounds in 1865; 401.16 pounds in 1868; 110.18 pounds in 1870; 228.10 pounds in 1871; 227.10 pounds in 1872; 182.15 pounds in 1873; and 362.10 pounds in 1874.[58]

Poaching of Rhinoceros was reaching critical proportions in the early part of the twentieth century because of the great demand of the rhino horn, which was supposed to have some aphrodisiacal properties. The demand of the rhino horn was so much more in China that it caused extermination of *Rhinoceros sondaicus* in Burma except for a few individual specimens guarded by the Forest Department. The China market was after the *Rhinoceros indicus* too and it led to the rise of its prices.[59] However, with the establishment of the Kaziranga and Manas sanctuaries by the 1920s, protection could be provided to the animals that lived there.[60]

Scarcity of labour was always regarded as a big problem by the British for carrying out the forest administration. This problem was sought to be addressed by different means and bartering forest produce for labour was one of them. Moreover, 'Forest Villages' served as an important instrument of the British forest administration, whereby the problem arising out of scarcity of labour was sought to be addressed. The Assam Forest Regulation, 1891 states, 'Forest villages were designed for the purpose of supplying a source of suitable local labour or in the case of temporary cultivation with a view to restocking the areas so cleared and cultivated with valuable species of trees on the *taungya* method'.[61] Accordingly, the Forest Villages could be established on sites, the location of which had to be approved by the Conservator of Forest in writing.[62] Each adult villager of a forest village had to render 20 days of labour per annum at the rate of wages locally current. Adult forest villagers were required to pay for all the forest produce taken by them at ordinary rate then in force at the reserved forest concerned, but could be allowed to remove free of royalty sufficient building materials to erect and maintain their houses and 10 cartloads of fuel annually if they elected to render 10 days of free additional labour.[63]

Under the British administration, the forests in Assam came to be broadly divided into three kinds, viz., Reserved Forests, Village Forests and Protected Forests. According to the Assam Forest Regulation, 1891, the local government might constitute any land at the disposal of the government a reserve land through publication of a notification in the official gazette.[64] Entry to such forests came to be restricted. Any complaint regarding the notification was settled by the Forest Settlement Officer to be appointed for the purpose. Village forests were constituted for the purpose of meeting the needs of village or a community.[65] Protected forests denoted specific trees or a class of trees that are notified for providing protection to the reserved trees from cutting, girdling, marking, lopping, tapping or injuring by fire or otherwise by any person.[66]

Such rules were used to regulate or prohibit the cutting involved in *jhum* cultivation, regulate or prohibit the kindling of fires, and prescribe the precautions to be taken to prevent the spread of fires, regulate or prohibit the quarrying of stone, or the burning of lime or charcoal, or even to regulate or prohibit the cutting of grass and pasturing of cattle, and regulate the payments, if any, to be made for such cutting or pasturing. It was also therein stated that if any person infringed the provisions of protected forests, he shall be punished with imprisonment for a term up to six months, or with fine which may extend up to Rs. 500 or both.[67]

The Assam Forest (Amendment) Act, 1931 added a new chapter to the Assam Forest Regulation, 1891 whereby the local government was given the power to regulate or prohibit in any forest or wasteland, which were not the property of the government, the breaking up or clearing of the land; the pasturing of cattle; or, the firing or clearing of the vegetation through notification when such regulation or prohibition appeared to be imperative in the public interest for the protection of public roads, public bridges, railways and other lines of communication; or for the protection against storms, winds, rolling stones, floods and avalanches; or for the preservation of the soil on the ridges and slopes and in the valleys or hilly tracts, the prevention of land slips or for the protection of land against erosion, or the deposit thereon of sand, stones or gravel; or even for the maintenance of water-supply in springs, rivers and tanks.[68] The local government might do it at its own expense, in or upon any forest or wasteland, such work as it deemed fit. In case of neglect or wilful disobedience of the provisions under the above rules, the government had the power to assume management of the forest. Further, the local government reserved the right to acquire or expropriate any forest for public purpose in the manner provided by the Land Acquisition Act, 1894.[69] The stranglehold of the colonial administration over the forest may be easily gauged under the circumstances.

The colonial period marks a watershed in the ecological history of Assam. It not only changed the landscape but also redefined man's relation with the environment.

POST-COLONIAL CONTINUUM

The British Forest Policy was subsequently followed by the government of independent India. The proprietary rights established by the British over the forests was later on taken over by the Government of India. Forests continued to be treated as a source of revenue. The nexus which had developed during the colonial period between the Forest Department, contractors and the government survived and exploitation of the forests of Assam went on in full swing. Exploitation increased both in terms of extent and means.

As late as in 1993-4, the Government of Assam had issued permits for felling of 2,600 cu m of timber under the Rehabilitation Scheme for the former United Liberation Front of Assam (ULFA) militants; but the actual amount of timber felled was about 7,300 cu m.[70] This clearly indicates the continued use of proprietary powers of the state over the forests to further its own interests. The following finds mention in the Forest Survey of India (FSI) Report, 2005 regarding forests in Assam:[71] 'The loss of forest cover is attributed mainly due to illicit felling in insurgency affected areas of Sonitpur, Karbi Anglong and Darrang districts as observed during field verification by FSI officials.'

Thus, access to forests for exploitation has been controlled by the post-independent Government of India, often to suit political interests.

Shifting cultivation is a common land-use pattern in hilly parts of the state. In a study undertaken by FSI in 1999, it is estimated that during 1987-97 an area of about 0.13 million ha have been affected by shifting cultivation. In the FSI Report, 2005, it is mentioned that some decrease in forest cover has occurred on account of shifting cultivation in the districts of N.C. Hills, Karbi Anglong, Karimganj and Hailakandi.[72]

On the other hand, the area under tea plantations continued to increase and agriculture still remained more extensive than intensive. More food always and necessarily meant more land under tillage. Increase of population as a consequence of immigration from neighbouring East Pakistan/Bangladesh and also from other parts of India increased the pressure on land manifold. Conflicts over land have been regarded as one of the underlying factors behind many ethnic clashes.[73]

It is only with the growing environmentalism of the last decades of the twentieth century that the shortcomings of the British forest policy and its continuance in the post/colonial period came to the fore and became part of a substantive discourse.

In response to large-scale deforestation, certain new policies aimed at reforestation from time to time were introduced in the post-colonial period. New legislations like the Forest Conservation Act, 1980, the Wildlife Protection Act, 1972, etc., were also passed. Creation of forest plantations outside forest areas started mainly in early 1980s. Emphasis of the afforestation activity under social forestry schemes was mainly on the rehabilitation of abandoned shifting cultivation and degraded forest areas. An area of 0.45 million ha was brought under forest plantations up to 1999. To bridge the divide created by the colonial forest policy between the community and the forest, the Joint Forest Management scheme was put into effect in 1998.[74] As on March 2005, there were 503 Joint Forest Management Committees managing about 80,000 ha of forests.[75]

By 2005, there were 5 National Parks and 18 Wildlife Sanctuaries covering an area of about 0.4 million ha constituting about 4.98 per cent of the total geographical area of the state. Total protected area is 0.21 million ha which constitute 2.69 per cent of the total geographic area of the state. Kaziranga, Nameri and Manas Tiger Reserves are located in the state while Manas has also been declared as a Biosphere Reserve, with an estimated area of 2837 sq. km. Kaziranga National Park and Manas Wildlife Sanctuary are also included in the World Heritage sites.[76]

The following table depicts the land-use pattern in Assam at the beginning of the twenty-first century:[77]

Land use	*Area in '000 ha*	*Percentage*
Total geographical area	7,844	
Total reporting area	7,850	100.00
Forests	1,932	24.61
Not available for cultivation	2,531	32.24
Permanent pastures & other grazing lands	163	2.08
Land under misc. tree crops & groves	234	2.98
Culturable wasteland	80	1.02
Fallow land other than current fallows	65	0.83
Current fallows	110	1.40
Net area sown	2,734	34.83

Colonial intervention and post-Independence continuum of policies related to forests changed the landscape and verdure of the province. As already mentioned, tea plantations continued to expand under the new regime. Tea industry also saw increasing use of weedicides and pesticides, creating newer environmental problems. One should not miss the mono-cultured greenery of a tea garden for a natural forest cover.

Introduction of afforestation programmes through schemes like Social Forestry and observance of Vanamahotsav have been efforts to change the situation for the better. However, the psychological breach that developed during the colonial rule with the forests being considered as the 'other' constitute one of the most insidious element of the British forest policy and will take time to get undone. Break with such a colonial past is imperative to reestablish a symbiotic relation with the forests.

SOCIAL IMPACT OF THE COLONIAL POLICIES

Human beings have altered the environment while environmental changes in turn have revised human activity. Changes in subsistence strategies and demography have resulted in both intentional and unintentional modification of the global environment.[78] The awareness of men's dependence upon nature had a long ancestry; but a sense of man as the maker and unmaker of nature has dawned in the industrial/colonial age, with a surprising realization of mankind's own capacity for *mischief and mayhem*.[79]

Environmental relations between man as a member of the

community and the environment have changed over time. Ideologies and perceptions have played a vital role in shaping these relations. The perceptions of dependency or superiority of mankind over nature have changed over time. Natural phenomenon like floods and draughts, desertification and climate change have led to the evolution of environmentalism and the environmental discourse.

In the context of Assam, the environmental relations in the ancient period were more harmonious mainly because of the existing civilizational pattern and the limited population, which did not lead to any large-scale decimation of natural environment. It may be safely inferred that the state did not come in between the community and its access to or use of the bounties provided by the environment. In fact, both the state and the community used the nature's bounty freely.

The medieval period in Assam saw the state putting some restrictions on the use and trade of some forest produce like ivory and aloewood. While both state and the community continued to enjoy the nature's bounty, the semi-tribal and semi-feudal state's polity did not shatter the symbiotic relationship between the community and the forests. We do not find any record of dispute between the state and the community over proprietary rights of forests. At best, the proprietary rights were shared, as access of the general population to the forests was free. The control of the state was mainly restricted to some of the produce or products of the forest rather than on any demarcated physical space.

The colonial intervention shattered the age-old relationship between man and the household of nature. Under the new paradigm, natural resources including the flora and fauna, so long regarded to be nature's bounty that could be used without restriction, came to be regarded as a source of revenue. The state became the proprietor of the forests, and started to determine who was to have access to these resources. The state also determined the parties that could be handed over parts of this property (some of which were also regarded as wastelands) along with proprietary rights if necessary for imperial exploitation. Increase in the area under plantation also meant that there was proportionate alienation of forest land. The relationship between the community and the forest was thus adversely affected in the colonial period and the state came in forcefully (more as a revenue farmer) between the flow of resources between the community and the environment.

The colonial state fenced the forests and controlled entry of the people into them as could be safely surmised from the legitimizing efforts of the colonial regime for exclusion of the common people to the areas under the control of the Forest Department. In other words, proprietary rights over the forests were established on behalf of the Forest Department. British rule in Assam like elsewhere in their empire could be regarded as an elaborate system of resource extraction and allocation, determining who was to have access to the nature's wealth. Thus, the age-old traditional and customary linkage between the people and the forest was shattered under the colonial impact. Forests came to be regarded as an 'other' something that may also be considered as 'virgin' or otherwise, something that may be exploited. The complex of extractive imperial policies which included extension of cultivation (even by encouraging migration), commercialization of the forest produce, encouraging monocultures in regenerative practices, taxation of all available and possible produce of nature like *ekra* (reeds) and on activities like grazing and fishing, coupled with the plantation economy changed the environmental relations and the landscape of Assam beyond recognition.

The colonial policy not only affected the man-environment relations in Assam, but also largely affected the man-man relations. The colonial forest policy along with the other imperial policies sowed seeds of new conflicts over resources. The long-term ill-effects of the colonial forest policy get manifested in the numerous conflicts over resources that took place in post-independent Assam. But, for that, the Indian political elites and bureaucracy that took over the reigns after the British colonial masters were gone, are also to be blamed, as the forest policy, like many other imperial policies were not revised to suit the needs of an independent country with independent needs. It needs to be reiterated that the government of independent India largely followed the colonial forest policies at least till the last part of the twentieth century.

There were intense debates in the Assam Legislative Council (formed in the year 1937) regarding the role of non-indigenous people in exploiting the forest resources of Assam. While raising a question on settling foreigners in several forest blocks in Kamarupa and Goalpara districts, Sri Beliram Das referred to Simons the Deputy Conservator who had opined at the time of settling the blocks in 1932 that foreigners should be excluded, and the people of the province should be given preference as the foreigners were destroying the forests and that the native people were the real watchmen who also had the legitimate rights to get preference.[80] Advantages provided by colonialism helped a particular Indian capitalist class, which included persons like Himatsingka, to practically monopolize the contracts under the Forest Department. Himatsingka used to take contracts both in his name as well as in the name of his men. During 1935-6, it was found that Messrs Himatsingka Timber Limited was responsible for more than 80 per cent of the supply of railway sleepers in Assam.[81]

Questions were also raised in the legislative assembly regarding the Forest Department forcing people in the vicinity of the reserves to work in the forest for the department, when their own fields required attention.[82] It had appeared in a number of cases that the residents of the forest villages were forced to render service to the Forest Department in lieu of taking forest produces such as bamboo, thatch, reeds and wooden ports for domestic use.[83]

Some people in Dibrugarh complained that foreigners were appointed to the subordinate ports like forest guards in the office of the Divisional Forest Officer though there were local people available for the same.[84] There were lot of instances of corruption and harassment of common people by forest officials. They visited the village at their own convenience and used to harass people in search of logs and other items until some gratification was put in.[85]

One of the most far-reaching aspects of the British forest policy was the grazing tax imposed on cattle grazing on the 'unclassed state forest'. Under the Assam Forest Regulation 1891, any person grazing his cattle on the Unclassed State Forest might be made to pay grazing tax. Thus, the tax under the definition could be imposed on any cattle grazing on any wasteland in any village which might be classified as 'unclassed forest'.

There was a lot of debate in the Assam Legislative Council on the question of grazing tax. Moving a Resolution for the abolition of the grazing tax, a member of the Legislative Council, Rohini Kanta Hati Baruah had said,[86]

> Sir, this is not a new resolution before this House. I believe no other resolution than this has come so often before this Council. There has not been a single session without a discussion on this subject. Public opinion on this subject has grown ever since and is now decided. People are vehemently opposed to such a tax. If we look at the pages of the Council proceedings even of the pre-Reform days we find that this tax has been as unpopular then as ever and public opinion on the subject is very much articulate on this.

Native members tried hard to abolish the tax but to no avail. The resolution sought to be passed by them in the Legislative Council of Assam on 24 February 1926 was defeated by a margin of two votes (fourteen to twelve).[87]

However, unlike the grazing tax controversy there was *per se* no concerted opposition to the British forest policy in Assam. It needs to be emphasized that modern environmentalism should not be conjured up in that historical situation. In all possibility, the British forest policy was regarded to be part of their strategy of progress and development adopted by the colonial government. That British forestry was regarded by many in the intellectual circles during the colonial period in Assam as progress, or as part of their civilizing mission, is understood from the writings of that period. In the first issue of *Mou* or 'The Bee', the Assamese monthly published in December 1886, it was stated that, '*bhati savyatar kheti bepar assamot nuhumuia hole eman din hei dekh habir pora mukali nohol heten*' (Assam would not have been freed of its forests if the Western civilization with its agriculture and business had not entered Assam).[88] There were instances when indigenous elites took to timber trade as a profession. Several leading personalities of colonial Assam like Manick Chandra Barooah, Jagannath Baruah et al., were found to be indulging in timber business. Thus, to the natives, the British Forest Policy might have been considered successful, as it tamed what many of the early travellers wrote of as desolate, dreary wilderness of Assam. The colonial policies thus resulted in a cultural learning that was radically different from the pre-colonial society and constitute a paradigm shift of immense proportions.

One of the far-reaching aspects of the British colonial rule in Assam was with regard to the changes in the ecology and the social relations brought about by introduction of the plantation economy. The tremendous impact of the colonial plantation economy is visible even in the twenty first century. The presence of 'wastelands' in Assam, the importation of labourers from other parts of the empire, the advent of merchants from outside who indulged in the trade and commerce relating to the plantations – all contributed to the setting up of a colonial societal framework, where the benefits accruing to the province or to the indigenous populace was very meagre. Under the circumstances, it is found that the 'wastelands' of Assam became the playing field for capital, organization, labourers, merchants, etc. – all drawn from outside. The displacement caused to the imported plantation labourers was huge and after their transportation to Assam, they were made to live a secluded regimented life. Thus neither the immigrant labourers, nor the indigenous people benefited from the plantation economy in Assam. The plantations transformed not only the natural landscape, but also impacted the society and economy of Assam in a significant way. The same colonial plantation economy also contributed in making Assam an enclave of the larger post independent Indian economy.

Thus, the 'influx' of people from the other parts of India to the north-east was a colonial phenomenon. The census reports are replete with statistics revealing the significant inflow of population from other parts of the subcontinent.

Assam's forests also came under intense pressure from extension of agriculture. Revenue maximization being the keystone of the British policies, the colonial administrator encouraged the immigration of people from the more populous districts of East Bengal for extending agriculture.[89] This helped in the conversion of large areas of wastelands into agricultural land that could earn revenue for the government. This process of immigration continued unabated well

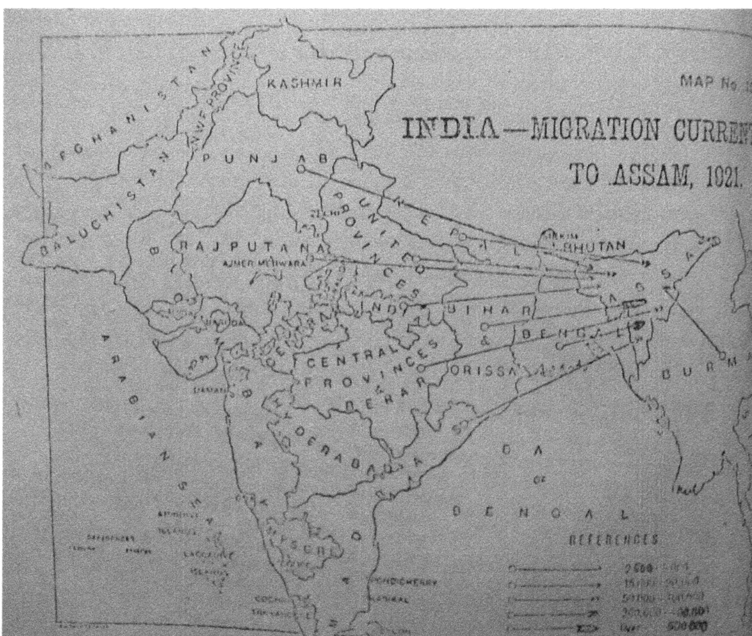

CENSUS OF INDIA, 1921, ASSAM REPORT, SHILLONG, 1922, P. 36.

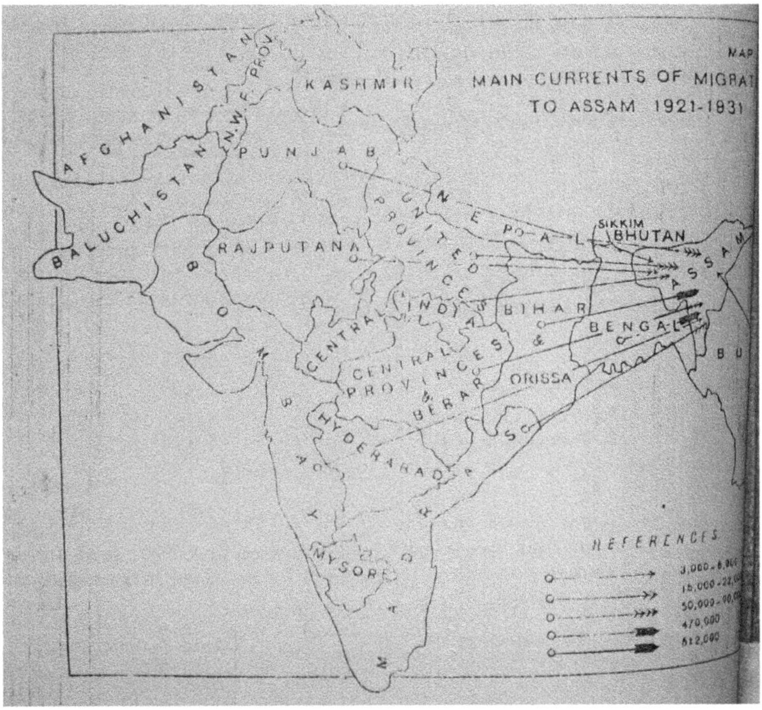

CENSUS OF INDIA, 1931, VOL. III: *ASSAM,* PART I, REPORT, BY C.S. MULLAN, SHILLONG, 1932, P. 41.

into the twentieth century and even the *char* areas came under occupation of the immigrants creating a social problem of huge dimensions. In fact, the *chars* have added a unique dimension to the environmental relations complex in Assam. The *char* areas cover about 4.6 per cent of the total land area of the state whereas the density of population there is 690 persons per sq. km (which is more than double the state average of 340 persons per sq. km).[90] The immigration problem is regarded as one of the primary contributory factors in the politics of identity and ethnic assertion in Assam.

On the other hand, some scholars like Nel Vandekerchkove and Bert Suykens of Ghent University opine that migration itself is insufficient to understand problems like that of violence and conflict in Bodoland. They contend that colonial forestry and tea estates created certain restrictive structures that changed the livelihood pattern of the involved communities. They put the entire development under a paradigm of 'tribal entrapment', where the forest policies and the plantation economy pushed the indigenous population into the periphery of an enclave economy.[91]

We also find that civilizational pressure led to gradual decrease of the natural forest and habitats of the fauna. The man-animal conflicts of the twenty-first-century Assam, especially between man and elephant, have increased over time. Thus, the colonial intervention not only marked an ecological watershed, but equally marked a social watershed in the history of Assam and continues to influence the land and people of Assam even in the new millennium.

NOTES

1. P.C. Bhattacharyya, 'Assam Taken for Granted', in *Survey of the Environment*, 98, Chennai: The Hindu, 1998, p. 83.
2. Ibid.
3. Madhav Gadgil and Ramchandra Guha, *This Fissured Land: An Ecological History of India*, Delhi: Oxford University Press, 1992, p. 208.
4. Sabha Parva XXX 28 as cited in P.C. Choudhury, *The History of Civilization of the People of Assam to the Twelfth Century* A.D., Gauhati: Spectrum, 1966, pp. 349f.
5. S.L. Baruah, *A Comprehensive History of Assam*, Delhi: Munshiram Manoharlal, 1985, p.145.
6. Ibid.
7. Ibid.
8. Ibid., p. 146.
9. Ibid.
10. Ibid., p. 166.
11. Amalendu Guha, *Medieval and Early Colonial Assam: Society, Polity, Economy*, Calcutta: K.P. Bagchi & Co. for Centre for Studies in Social Sciences, 1991, p. 73.
12. Ibid., pp. 73-8.
13. Ibid., p. 4.
14. Ibid.
15. Shrutidev Goswami, *Aspects of Revenue Administration in Assam*, Delhi: Mittal Publications, 1987, p. 113.
16. Baruah., op. cit., pp. 145, ff. The Soom Forests of Assam which were mostly native to the Upper Assam districts, played a great role in production of silk cocoons.
17. B. Hamilton, *An Account of Assam*, Gauhati: Department of Historical and Antiquarian Studies (rpt.), 1963, p. 46.
18. V. Ball, *Tavernier's Travels in India*, II, pp. 28-9, cited in S.L. Baruah, *A Comprehensive History of Assam*, op. cit., p. 434.

19. *Fathiyah-i-Ibriyah* (tr. Jadunath Sarkar), in *Journal of Bihar and Orissa Research Society* (1915), p. 187, cited in S.L. Baruah, *A Comprehensive History of Assam*, op. cit., p. 434.
20. Baruah, op. cit., p. 438.
21. Ibid., p. 255.
22. Ibid., pp. 263-4. *Kheddah shikar* involved capturing elephants in stockades.
23. Ibid.
24. S.K. Bhuyan, *A History of Assam (1681-1826 A.D.)*, Tungkhungia Buranji (rpt.), Delhi: D.K.F. Trust, 1983, pp. 124 and 239.
25. H.K. Barpujari (ed.), *The Comprehensive History of Assam*, vol. V, Guwahati: Publication Board, Assam, 1992, p. 37.
26. B. Ribbentrop, *Forestry in British India*, Simla: Government Press, 1900, p. 104.
27. *Administrative Report, Assam*, 1874-5 (39), as cited in Guha, op. cit., p. 16.
28. John M'Cosh, *Topography of Assam*, Delhi: Logos Publications (rpt.), 1975, p. 13.
29. John Butler, *Travels in Assam,* Delhi, 1994; John M'Cosh, *Topography of Assam,* Delhi: Logos Publications, 1975.
30. Gustav Mann, *Progress Report of Forest Administration in the Province of Assam* (henceforth, *PRFA*), Shillong: Government Press, 1874-5, p. 1.
31. Extract from the Proceedings of the Chief Commissioner of Assam in the Revenue Department, under date Shillong, the 4th October 1879, in *PRFA*, 1878-9.
32. Mann, *PRFA*, 1874-5, p. 2.
33. Goswami, op. cit., pp. 113-14.
34. J.N. Das, *An Introduction to the Land Laws of Assam*, Guwahati: Lawyers Book Stall, 1988, pp. 4-6.
35. Ibid., p. 6.
36. Ibid.
37. Barpujari, op. cit., p. 42.
38. D. Brandis, *Suggestions Regarding Forest Administration in Assam*, Calcutta, Govt. of India, 1879, p. 10.
39. Barpujari (ed.), op. cit., pp. 21-45.
40. Brandis, op. cit., pp. 10-11.
41. Ibid., p. 11.
42. Barpujari, op. cit., pp. 44f.
43. Brandis, op. cit., p. 10.
44. Ribbentrop, *Forestry in India*, op. cit., p. 134.
45. H.K. Barpujari (ed.), *Political History of Assam*, vol. I, *1826-1919*, Gauhati: Publication Board, Assam, 1977, p. 52.
46. H.K. Barpujari (ed.), *The Comprehensive History of Assam*, vol. V, Guwahati: Publication Board, Govt. of Assam 1992, p. 48.

47. Richard P. Tucker, *A Forest History of India*, Delhi: Sage, 2011, p. 166-190.
48. Debates of the Assam Legislative Council, 22 March 1926, vol. VI, p. 481.
49. Mann, *PRFA*, 1879-80, p. 48.
50. Ibid.
51. *Assam Administrative Report 1933-34*, Assam Secretariat Records Office (ASR), p. 20.
52. Mann, op. cit., p. 49.
53. Brandis, op. cit., p. 4.
54. Ibid.
55. William Schlich, *Manual of Forestry*, vol. II: *Sylviculture*, London: Assam State Archives, 1895, p. 1.
56. W.W. Hunter, *A Statistical Account of Assam*, Delhi: B.R. Publishing Corporation (rpt.), vol. I, 1975, p. 25. The value of one pound was equal to about ten rupees at that time.
57. A.J.W. Milroy, *PRFA*, 1929-30, p. 8.
58. Ibid.
59. *The Assam Forest Manual*, vol. I: *Rules for the Establishment and Control of Forest Villages*, vide Notification No. 461R, dated 6 December 1930.
60. Ibid.
61. Ibid.
62. *Assam Forest Regulations, 1891* (National Archives), under section (u/s) 6.
63. Ibid., u/s 30(1).
64. Ibid., u/s 33.
65. Ibid., u/s 35.
66. *The Assam Forest Manual*, vol. I, pp. 21-3.
67. Ibid., p. 23.
68. Express News Service Report in *The Indian Express*, Delhi, 11 April 1995.
69. *Forest Survey of India Report*, 2005, section 8.3.5, p. 56.
70. Ibid.
71. Cf. reference 87.
72. *Forest Survey of India Report*, 2005, section 8.3.4, p. 55.
73. Ibid.
74. Ibid., section 8.3.3, p. 55.
75. Land Use Statistics, Ministry of Agriculture, Government of India, 2005, as cited in the *Forest Survey of India Report*, 2005, as Table 8.3 a., p. 55.
76. Carole L. Crumley (ed.), *Historical Ecology: Cultural Knowledge and Changing Landscapes*, New Mexico: School of American Research Press, 1994, pp. 1-2.

77. David Arnold and Ramchandra Guha (eds.), *Nature, Culture, Imperialism: Essays on Environmental History of South Asia,* Delhi: Oxford University Press, 1996, p. 3.
78. *Legislative Assembly Debates,* vol III, December 1937, pp. 2230-1.
79. Ibid.
80. Ibid., p. 464.
81. Ibid., Question asked by Beliram Das, p. 513.
82. *Report on the Forest Enquiry Committee, Assam,* Shillong, 1929, Assam State Archives, p. 15.
83. Evidence Recorded by the Forest Enquiry Committee, Shillong, 1929, p. 2.
84. *Legislative Council Debates,* vol. VI, Assam State Archives, p. 236.
85. Ibid.
86. Ibid.
87. Ibid.
88. Haranarayan Bora (ed.), *Mou or The Bee,* vol. I, December 1886, Guwahati: Publication Board, Govt. of Assam (ed. S.N. Sarmah); rpt., Guwahati, 2003, p. 1.
89. Cf. nn. 48 and 49 above.
90. Gorky Chakraborty, *Land and Identity Formation: A Narrative on the Farm-settlers in the Char Areas of Assam* in Chandan Kumar Sarma (ed.), Souvenir of North East India History Association, 29th Annual Session, 2008, Dibrugarh, p. 166. *Chars* are riverine islands and Assam abounds in such fluvial formations along the river Brahmaputra and its tributaries.
91. Nel Vandekerchkove and Bert Suykens, 'The Liberation of Bodoland: Tea, Forestry and Tribal Entrapment in Assam', in *Journal of South Asian Studies,* vol. XXXI, no. 3, December 2008, pp. 451-71.

CHAPTER 7

Forests, Fields and Pasture: Environmental and Revenue Debates of Land Usage in Colonial Assam in 1910-1920

SURYASIKHA PATHAK

The colonial period has been a very transformative period, and recent environmental historians have accounted for many changes that have affected post-colonial India in this colonial watershed. The tea gardens, forestry, and extension of agricultural boundaries due to immigration changed Assam from a land surplus region in the beginning of the nineteenth century to a province with unequal land men/labour ratio. Pressure on land kept on increasing for various purposes and as a result of that pastureland suffered. Decreasing pastureland, immigrant professional graziers and taxation levied on grazing all affected the indigenous grazier and cultivator and influenced the policies between the government and the Assam Association. This paper seeks to look into the various kinds of land usage by the colonial government in Assam and in the process how pastureland diminished in the face of expanding tea gardens, wasteland settlement rules, forestry, immigration and how the colonial state exercised political power to control the resources to maximize its revenue earnings.

In the agrarian society of Assam, grazing had occupied an important position as a supplementary economy. *Gorokhias* (the cowherd) are integral to the traditional economy and culture. The integral nature of the cowherds in the traditional agrarian society is apparent in the cultural festivals of the society. During the springtime festival, the *rongali bihu*, a seven-day festival – the first day is dedicated to the cattle and their cowherds. The livestock was mostly composed of buffaloes and cattle. Grazing was generally done on harvested rice fields and in winters in the swamps and marshes, where grasses grew luxuriantly. During the rainy season the villagers experienced hardship regarding grazing their livestock because it tended to fill with water, which rose. In the summer months, there is a general tendency towards floods and so grazing was not possible on the riverbanks, therefore it became necessary to graze in the highlands. During the winters there was excellent grazing in the *chaporis*, the riverine belt and the jungles near it. In Assam, professional grazing was mostly confined to buffaloes because of their being of better breed and the superior quality of milk and milk products. Most of the grassland areas, the *chaporis* in particular are occupied by professional graziers, the majority of whom by the end of the nineteenth century were Nepalese.[1] In the twentieth century due to increase in the immigration and settlement (discussed below) scarcity of grazing land gave rise to tension between the indigenous agriculturist, who had their own cattle to graze and the professional graziers. The root of this conflict was the colonial government's policies of wasteland settlement and forestry as the following discussion would show.

In studying the agitation against the grazing tax in 1912-13 we have to consider the historical growth of grievances of the graziers and the agriculturist against the colonial state. This section of the paper focuses on the changing British policies regarding patterns of land usage since their occupation of the province from 1826 and how it changed the landscape of the province. The charter of 1833 abolished the company's commercial interest and opened the province to the prospects of colonization. The wasteland rules were formulated so that capital can be invested to grow revenue-generating crops. With the discovery of the possibility of tea plantation, wasteland rules were formulated and relaxed to attract planters. As mentioned by Nandita Khaderia, 'utilisation of waste for the purpose of plantation of special crops, which gained popularity from 1840s onwards gave a more definite shape to the objectives behind wasteland settlement. For the development and growth of the tea industry it became further necessary to clear wasteland.'[2] The Assam Company was established in 1839 and by 1859 the number of estates under distinct proprietors rose to the strength of 51. Wasteland settlement rules of 1838 did not attract a great deal of investment. These rules were again revised in 1854 and made less stringent. The new rules provided for a 99 years lease on liberal terms. Initially the minimum area one could apply was 500 acres, which was relaxed to 200 acres. This new rule stimulated a land rush, so by 1859 for every acre planted with tea the planter kept fallow six acres of wasteland in his possession for other purposes including speculation.

Year	*Area under tea cultivation (in acres)*
1841	2,311
1859	8,000

The planters were given revenue concessions and free wasteland grants on long lease provided them many more than mere sites, they contained valuable timber and grasslands. The total area of wasteland settled with the planter in Assam proper was over 3 lakh acres in 1871.[3] By the end of the nineteenth and beginning of the twentieth century, the pressure on land continued to increase. The tea gardens continued to expand at the cost of other activities on the land. In the year 1892-3 the total area under tea cultivation was 5,95,842 acres and area held under ordinary lease for tea being 87,630 acres in the Brahmaputra Valley.[4] The planters had enclosed by 1901some ¼th ofthe total settled area (or 5 per cent of the total area) of Assam proper, under the exclusive property rights. Thereby they limited to that extent the facilities of fluctuating or shifting cultivation as well as of grazing and collecting activities of the local population particularly the 'tribal'.[5]

Stringent land management by the colonial government in the interest of the tea gardens also adversely affected the graziers and agriculturist. By 1901, ¼ of the total settled area (i.e. 5 per cent of the total area) were enclosed by planters, under their proprietary rights. Since large areas of land came under private ownership and if any cattle strayed into their property, it came under the Cattle Trespass Act, 1871. The Chief Commissioner of Assam in 1888 was forced to ask for an amendment of the above-mentioned Act, as he found some peasants in Sibsagar district 'complaining bitterly' and he was sure there were complaints from other quarters also.[6] The Chief Commissioner wanted the Act should be amended and provisions of chapter V of the Act, relating to illegal seizure of cattle should be made applicable to illegal detention upon legal seizure.[7] Due to a loophole in the law, there was a lot of tension between the landowners, planters and the peasants. It was a common practice in Assam for landholders, especially tea planters, when they caught cattle trespassing on their land, they held the cattle till the owners applied for them and made a payment rather than sending them to the pounds as legally stated. But sometimes such a practice was abused. The landowners would occasionally demand more than the prescribed fine of the Act. The cattle owner would bargain and give in rather than sending his cattle to the pound.[8] The cattle owners wanted that there should be some rules against such illegal detention because the law supported the land owner even if the cattle was detained, the land holder was not punished. But sometimes a landholder might make a demand to which the cattle owner might not be ready to accept and the landholders would then keep the cattle in their custody and not send it to the pounds. But the government of India delayed taking action because there was a proposal to amend the laws and the cultivators continued to be harassed.

The land problem was compounded because of immigration. Tea gardens were a major source of immigrations. On expiry of their contracts in the tea gardens many of the labourers settled down in the wastelands as independent peasants. The non-indigenous population appears to have increased from less than 1 lakh in 1872 to around 5-6 lakhs in 1901.

Composition of Population in Assam:[9]

	1891	*1901*
Total population	20,23,703 (100)	21,57,025 (100)
Indigenous Hindu Castes and tribes	15,84,027 (78.3)	15,04,847 (67.8)
The rest	4,39,685 (21.7)	6,52,178 (32.2)

As a result of this there was a greater need for agricultural population to feed the immigrant population.[10] The number of immigrants and ex-coolies continued to increase and in 1915-16 land occupied by them (in acres):

District	*Time-expired coolies*	*Other immigrants*	*Total*
Goalpara	–	30,655	30,655
Kamarupa	1,655	13,571	15,226
Darrang	55,191	35,061	90,252
Nagaon	13,656	19,543	33,252
Sibsagar	60,628	13,560	64,188
Lakhimpur	73,478	16,185	89,663

Source: Report on the Land Revenue Administration of Assam, 1915-16.

The total number of acres settled with time expired coolies and other immigrants being 3,23,700.

By the 1860s forests in the north bank of the Brahmaputra had been worked extensively and heavily by the sawmills established by the Upper Assam Tea Company.[11] So serious was the situation the Bengal government decided to interfere minimally so that forests were not exhausted though it thought 'it may be advisable not to interfere too much as regards petty details with the supply of timber for the general wants of the great tea companies in Assam....'[12] But such exhaustion of forest resources was neither in favour of the companies or the government. The report of 1869-70 again supports the necessity of government control over forests. 'It is to the interests of the companies themselves as much as those of government that the supervision of the state over the working of the forest should be more than nominal ...'.[13] So before a general inspection of the forests in Assam was done in 1868-9, the forest had already been indiscriminately exploited. After the first general inspection of the Assam forests in 1868-9, the climate was found suitable for plantation of various marketable timbers, which was to occupy large areas. Plantation of teak, oak, magnolia, walnut, sal, soom, sissoo, holong, etc., changed the nature of the forest. The Forest Department when clearing lands for these plantations burnt the grasslands and reserved large areas. For example, the soom forests were very lucrative for the British and for that purpose declared as 'reserved' those areas, which had patches of soom forests but also had intermediate open fields, which till then were excellent grazing grounds.[14]

For the purpose of developing Sissoo plantations, Sissoo being in great demand the government adopted a very cost effective method, planting (i.e. sowing sissoo seeds) in the extensive grasslands in the neighbourhood of Brahmaputra, which had been burnt to clear the land.

So the abundant land available to the grazier and the cowherd and even the agriculturist dwindled in the face of expansion of tea gardens and forestry. The impact of decreasing land was felt by the people from the later part of nineteenth century, when the various forest acts came into force, restricting the local people from freely using the forest. Rules made by the government of Bengal under Section 3, Act VII of 1865, for by the administration of government forest in Bengal and Assam. According to it

> reserved forests shall consist of tracts of forests or wastelands, being absolutely the property of the government.... The conservator of Forests and his subordinates shall have entire administration, custody and control over these forests and their products. Within reserved forests, no forest produce could

be removed without general or special authority obtained from the conservator of Forests. There was a notification warning the villagers against trespass or mischief and defining the restrictions imposed on them and the privileges allowed to them within the reserved forests. Conservator of Forests may prohibit all persons from passing through a reserved forest except by authorized roads or paths.[15]

Thus the area available to the villager to graze his cattle or to the professional grazier was more limited due to the creation of reserved forests.

Despite various pressures of ongrowing population nearly all the reserved forest continued to remain close for grazing even during the second decade of the twentieth century. Unreserved state forest, which was open to grazing, was subjected to exploration and valuable areas were to be reserved. And those areas were to be reserved. And those areas of forest (reserved), which were open to grazing, allowed grazing by the neighbouring villagers and professional graziers were excluded. *The Progress Report of the Forest Administration, Assam 1913-14* states that 88 per cent of the reserved forest was closed to grazing, which kept on increasing because in 1916 89 per cent of the reserved forests were closed to grazing.[16] To keep the reserves exclusively for the use of the government, it exempted blocks of reserves near villages to squeeze the various wants of the villagers like timber, firewood, thatching grass and grazing into them.[17]

THE POLITICS OF THE GRAZING TAXATION

The grazing taxation was imposed in 1888 on per head of cattle and buffalo that grazed in the unclassed state forests.[18] As mentioned earlier, already most of the reserved forests were closed to grazing and gradually unclassed state forests were being turned into reserved forests or used for various other purposes, for example expansion of agriculture.[19]

The people who came under the purview of the tax were the professional graziers, some indigenous but mostly immigrant Nepalese. Most of the local people grazed their livestock in the government waste free. Only big landowners and professional graziers grazed in the unclassed state forest. Though grazing in government wasteland was declared free it was indirectly taxed. During the land revenue re-assessment of 1893 when land revenue was reassessed while placing a village within a certain category or class, one factor which aided to workout the relative value was the accessibility to government waste.[20] So two villages which would have otherwise the same rate of taxation, would have different relative value accordingly as they were far from or close to lands furnishing good grazing and building materials.[21] The initial rate of taxation was 8 annas per head of cattle and was collected by the Forest department. In 1907 the tax was increased to Rs. 1 per head of other horned cattle and the tax though assessed by the Forest Department was to be collected by the *mauzadar*.[22] But very soon again in 1912 the tax was suddenly increased which was due to the conflicting interest of the British in Assam.

The revenue drawn from the grazing tax was entirely by taxing the professional graziers, most of whom were Nepalese. There was marked increase of buffaloes grazed by professional graziers, from 12,915 in 1893-4 to 24,257 in 1904-5, in 1911-12 it was 45,893. Though an initial increase might have had government approval, soon the immigration of Nepalese graziers got out of hand and created problems.[23] So great was the influx that Nepalese graziers overran almost all of the grazing area and there being a scarcity of suitable pasture land they tended to be over crowded in certain localities creating problems for the indigenous grazier and the cultivator to graze his cattle. The ryots also complained that the herds of the Nepalese grazier often damaged crops. So, there was social tension directed against the immigrant.[24] Though having a strong revenue interest in having immigrant graziers who would pay taxes as against the indigenous cultivator-cum-grazier the government found such an influx against its interest. First, the government was afraid that such big herds of buffaloes would destroy the unclassed state forest before a proper inspection and reservation was done. In fact, 'in 1912, the Inspector General of Forests after a tour in the province called attention to the damage which was being done to unclassed state forests by herds of buffaloes that roamed unchecked and uncontrolled'.[25]

Moreover evasion of taxes by the professional graziers forced the government to take some steps, regarding the effective collection. Often the government found the *mauzadar* totally disinterested in realizing the taxes, which was quite a hard task because the professional graziers constantly move their cattle to evade taxes.[26] So low was the rate of recovery of the tax that a conference was held at Shillong in 1912 to deal with the problem of the professional graziers and to regulate grazing.

To restrict the mobility of the professional grazier was the main concern because that would make it impossible for them to evade the dues. So the government decided to create reserved grazing grounds, 'for the professional grazier to facilitate control and to prevent their cultivation'.[27] It was also proposed that within the grazing reserves the rates of grazing would be lower to attract the professional graziers to them.[28] The logic was to make them pay even at lower rates rather than have massive evasions. It was instructed that if the professional graziers did not graze in the reserves they should be debarred from grazing cattle in unclassed state forests. To further restrict mobility and thus evasion of taxes, the government prohibited movement of cattle from one grazing ground to another without the prior permission of the Divisional Forest Officer.[29] The sharp increase in the rate of taxation was to dissuade further emigration of Nepalese graziers into the state especially from north Bengal, Jalpaiguri, etc. Moreover the British also had other interest in mind when trying to regulate the grazing pattern of professional graziers for example the reservation of thatch land. The increase in the number of buffaloes necessitated the protection given to thatch. Again there was a possibility of utilizing coarse grasses for manufacture of cellulose for which a demand was made for concessions regarding restriction on grazing because the grass would require protection from fire and cattle, 'as sufficiently intensive grazing dwarfs the heaviest grass'.[30]

The enhancement of the grazing tax though meant for controlling the influx of Nepalese immigrants led to greater evasion and moreover grazing blocks, which was planned took time to be created. So, in view of rising arrears in the collection of the grazing dues the government made an attempt to change the system of collection that was in practice. The government also realized that the *mauzadars* probably takes the slightest interest in the forest matters,[31] and that system of collection of dues by the *mauzadar* can hardly be called successful and was unsatisfactory.[32] So the government in May, 1917 framed new grazing rules whereby it was declared that the duties of assessment and realization of grazing dues with effect from 1 July 1917 was taken away from the Forest Department in order to avoid mistakes due to dual control.[33]

The question of the enhancement of grazing tax brought forth political agitation in Assam under the guidance and leadership of the leaders of the Assam Association.[34] It saw the emergence of organized protest under political initiative, the first phase in the period of national movement when people's rights on the natural resources was discussed. For the indigenous people and even for the British this was not the first instance of protest. From late nineteenth century people had protested and submitted memorials against the forest rules and regulations and the constantly dwindling area meant for grazing. As early as 1886, the Hitasadhini Sabha of Golaghat sent a petition to the Viceroy, 'praying for an alleviation of the hardship alleged to be inflicted on the raiyats of Assam by the operation of several rules and regulations issued by the Chief Commissioner under the Indian Forest Act (VII of 1878)'.[35] It mentions that the government constituted reserved forests in densely populated parts of Assam thereby inflicting hardship and inconvenience on the inhabitants. The reserved forests being at close proximity of the village boundary and *bari* (homestead) there were often cases of cattle straying into the reserved forest and the cattle owner fined. The *sabha* complained that large tracts of forest lands or wastelands, which were situated near or around the neighbourhood of thickly populated villages '...on which the ryots mainly depend for timber or other forest produce or pasture have been or are to be constituted into reserved forests under the Indian Forest Act.'[36] Due to such an Act the ryots would face great hardship and inconvenience. The *sabha* also alludes the statement of Lt. Governor of Bengal on the new wasteland rules in the Bengal Administrative for 1872-3, 'that so long as government reserved for the ryots their fields...the people of Assam...would be greatly benefited and could not be injured by the extension of tea cultivation...'[37] but this was not to be the case in Assam because tea overrode all other concerns of the colonial state. So much so, again during the cadastral survey, before the Assam Valley Re-assessment, 1893, people submitted memorials stating the government have neglected the questions of grazing grounds. It mentioned as a complaint that 'grazing grounds have not been kept for people, but any suitable bits of grassland near villages are not reserved for pasturage but are speedily given away for tea cultivation'.[38] However, in spite of the peasants dissatisfaction, the colonial authorities confirmed the abundance of grazing grounds except in few cases. Most of the grazing grounds were actually government wastes, where cattle could graze free, and which were available everywhere.[39]

The politics against enhancement of the grazing levy was carried on in the Assam Legislative Council. In 1912 the grazing tax was increased to Rs. 8 per head of buffalo and from Re. 1 on per head of other horned cattle. The government advocated the increase because of the manifold growth of cattle, which was seen as a threat to the crops and standing trees. The increased tax would, according to its contention, check the influx of cattle from Bengal. Heightened protest in the legislative politics and the Assam Association against the grazing tax initiated a new spate of political debate in the public arena. The affected sections grievances were articulated in the press too.[40] The pressure on the government resulted in the reduction in the rate of taxation to Rs. 2 per buffalo and 6 annas in 1914. In 1915 an enquiry was instituted under W.I. Arbutthnot, who came to the conclusion that the graziers could pay Rs. 4 per buffalo and 12 annas per horned cattle. But the chief commissioner reconsidered the issue and decided that the fee should be Rs. 3 per buffalo and 6 annas per horned cattle.[41]

The British policy towards the system of grazing demonstrates an inherent bias against it. The argument was that since the cultivator who labours so hard to pays taxes, while the graziers who 'sits idle while his cattle eats the grass the nature produced and possibly his neighbouring crops as well'.[42] Grazing which would not subserve agriculture should not be free. Therefore cattle in excess of agricultural requirements were to be taxed. But though the British allowed bonafide cultivators to graze cattle free of any charge in government waste situated near the villages and the unclassed state forest, often they were also assessed. Often assessment was arbitrary as there was no inspection done and the cattle owner in many cases was not given any notice of the assessment, often failed to raise objections on the wrong assessment.

Amalendu Guha while looking into the question of widespread politicization of grazing tax issue comes to the conclusion that the Assam Association took up the issue because 'the rich peasants and the town dwelling absentee landholders used to invest in a small way in herds of cattle left under the professional graziers care'.[43] The Assam Association wanted that the levy on grazing should be totally abolished and the governement claimed that for the well-being of the indigenous cultivators a high tax should be maintained. But even within the professional grazier policy discrepancy was to be found. The chief commissioner while fixing rates for the professional grazier stated that special pastureland should be reserved for those graziers who supplied all their milk and milk products to the urban areas would be taxed less.[44] This was again an attempt to control the

Nepalese grazier because such professionalism was only present among them and rarely in the indigenous grazier. The Assam Association voiced the grievances of the graziers as a whole and tried to influence the policy making of the colonial state. To some extent it was successful because rates of taxation were contained for sometime and grazing reserves were created before agriculture occupied every inch of the wastelands. The politics of the Association was moderate in nature and obviously did not believe in challenging the state and did not allow extreme steps like breaking the forest laws. During the 2nd phase, i.e. with the coming of the congress and left politics, radical protest finally arrived in Assam.

NOTES

1. The Nepalese came into Assam from the western *duar* side from the nineteenth century onwards. The Nepali migration to north-east was mainly from two sources: Nepal and Darjeeling-Sikkim.
2. Nandita Khaderia, 'Some Aspects of the Rural Economy of Assam: A Study of the Brahmaputra Valley Districts, 1874-1914', unpublished Ph.D thesis, Centre for Historical Studies, JNU, 1992, Chap. VII.
3. Categories like 'wasteland' were constructed by the colonial state. So that abundant land available in the province could be brought under rational and profitable usage, which would bring revenue to the state. What the government termed as 'wasteland' were sparsely forested areas with grasslands, which were till then controlled by the village.
4. *Assam Valley Reassessment Report*, 1893, p. 1. The total area of wasteland statement in 1871 – 3 lakh acres, 1901 – 6.4 lakh acres.
5. Amalendu Guha, 'A Big Push Without a Take Off', in Amalendu Guha, *Medieval and Early Colonial Assam: Society, Polity, Economy,* Calcutta: K.P. Bagchi, 1991, p. 191.
6. Proceedings of the Assam Chief Commissioner, Home (Judical), File No. 240-3, May 1888.
7. Ibid.
8. Pounds were often very far away from the estates so it was problematic for both the landowner and the cattle owner to send or bring cattle from the pound.
9. Assam Census Report as shown in Amalendu Guha, *Medieval and Early Colonial Assam*, p. 194.
10. Large-scale immigration, which included mainly cash-crop producing peasants and tea garden coolies increased the food crop market of the local Assamese peasants. Loaded boats of grains were taken upstream the Brahmaputra River to feed the tea garden population in the Upper

Assam. Arupjyoti Saikia, 'Agrarian Unrest in Assam and the Revolutionary Communist Party of India Kamrup 1945-52', unpublished M. Phil disertation, CHS, JNU, 1996.

11. Proceeding nos. 121-4. PWD/Revenue/Forests- March 1871 (NAI) Progress Report, Forest Department, Bengal, 1869-70.
12. Ibid.
13. Ibid.
14. 'The character of forests varies constantly . . . whilst perhaps one mile may be found to contain a large proportion of useful timber trees, the next 20 may be gone over without noticing anything but useless scrub intercepted by swamp impenetrable cane and other undergrowth or open grass plains with only useless trees not serviceable for firewood.' Quoted from *Progress Report, Forest Department, Bengal 1868-69*, PWD/Revenue Proceedings, nos. 7-12, April 1870.
15. *Progress Report, Forest Department, Bengal 1868-69*, PWD/Forests Proceedings, nos. 7-12, April 1870.
16. *Progress Report, Forests, Assam 1916-17*, p. 6.
17. *Progress Report, Forest, Assam 1911-12*, p. 1.
18. File No. 106. Political History of Assam documents, 1916 (Assam Archive) (hereafter PHA).
19. *Progress Report, Forests, Assam 1911-12*, p. 1.
20. *Assam Valley Re-assessment Report*, 1893, p. 46.
21. Ibid.
22. PHA File No. 106/1916.
23. *Progress Report, Forest, Assam 1911-12*, p. 615.
24. *Progress Report, Forest, Assam, 1912-13.*
25. PHA File No. 106/1916.
26. In 1911-12, it was noticed that cultivators were taking to grazing and graziers to cultivation. The professional graziers often settled down and took to agriculture together with grazing because according to rules any settled cultivator could graze his cattle free in the state forest. *Progress Report, Forests Assam, 1911-12*, p. 6.
27. *Progress Report, Forests, Assam, 1912-13*, p. 10.
28. Ibid.
29. Ibid.
30. Ibid., p. 33.
31. *Progress Report, Forests, Assam, 1915-16.*
32. Ibid., p. 8.
33. *Progress Report, Forests, Assam, 1916-17*, p.12.
34. Assam Association was the first body of Assamese Middle class.
35. Petition of the Hitasadhini Sabha of Golaghat, Home (Forests), Proceedings, nos. 4-9, August 1886.
36. Ibid.
37. Ibid.

38. *Assam Valley Reassessment Report, 1893*, p. 16.
39. Ibid., p. 17.
40. Regional newspapers *Times of Assam*, *Assam Bilasini*, *Assamiya* carried editorials against the grazing tax.
41. Ibid.
42. Ibid.
43. Amalendu Guha, *Planters Raj to Swaraj: Freedom Struggle and External Politics in Assam, 1874-1947*, Delhi: Tulika, 1988, p. 93.
44. PHA 106/1916.

CHAPTER 8

Colonialism and Deforestation in Naga Hills

S. VICTOR BABU

North-east in general and Naga Hills (presently the state of Nagaland) in particular are endowed with rich forest resources. The entry of colonial power in Assam has changed the character of forest resources. Naga Hills formed a district in Assam province. The British regarded the forests as a source of revenue. As a result the colonial power followed a certain policies with a view to exploit the forest resources. This in turn had a tremendous effect on environment, society and the economy. The impact was not the same in the plains and the hills. The Naga were born, grew and lived in the forest. So for them the difference between forest and non-forest (cultivable agricultural land, pasture and forest, etc.) did not exist. Forest was part and parcel of their lives. Hence forest produce was also integral to the lives of hill people. They had unfettered access to the forest produce before the coming of the British. However, the British tried to intervene in the lives of Nagas with its stated mission of civilizing the supposed savage tribes. This paper seeks to explain the way in which the colonial state tried to exert its power and authority on the forest and its produce in the Naga Hills. The first part deals with the constitution of Reserve and various rules which are aimed at controlling the forest produce and third with causes and factors which led to the deforestation in Naga Hills.

Forest always played significant role in the lives of Nagas. It offered a multiple ways of livelihood. Fishing, hunting, gathering and shifting cultivation are part of their lives. Even medicine, fodder and all implements and building materials came from the forest. A variety of leaves, fruits and seeds of various trees and plants in the forest formed the food.[1] They also depended on forest for fodder as it also gave them unlimited grazing ground for their cattle. Besides, Nagas also traded with cotton and ginger and chilies by way of barter along borders.[2] It shows that the forest was part and parcel of their lives. However, once the colonial state established its hold on Naga Hills, conditions slowly began to change.

CONSTITUTION OF RESERVES

The first step in the control of the forest was taken when the British government constituted the forest into Reserve, Protected and District Forests. The tract in the Naga Hills district immediately south of the Sibsagar district and on the road between[3] Golaghat and Samagoodting was declared to be a reserved forest. The Makir Hill, under the Naga Hills district was cleared as reserve on 17 October 1878. Later on some more tracts were added to Makir Hills reserve. The lower Daigrung forest of the Barpathar Mauza in 1883 and the Kaliani of Barpathar Mauza in 1887 were declared as reserved forest.[4] Nambor in 1895 and Desoi Valley was declared a reserve forest in 1902. The Rangapahar was also declared as a reserve in 1916. More and more tracts of forest land were brought under the ambit of reserved forests.

In reserved forests, everything was restricted unless permitted.[5] As for protected forests, everything is permissible unless restricted. The government could declare any class of trees in a protected forest to be reserved from a date fixed by notification and declare a portion of such forest to be closed or prohibit removal of any forest produce. The forest produce, timber or grass was allowed to be procured against a license granted to the inhabitants of the villages or towns in the vicinity of protected forests. Even in village forests, the state retained the authority to cancel or assign the rights to village community through these forests were to provide timber, other forest produce and pasture to the people.[6]

Second, rules for regulating the various activities in the forest were framed from time to time under the Forest Department. In accordance with the policy of the colonial government, T.J. Murry, officiating secretary to the chief commissioner of Assam, promulgated the following 'Rules Regulating Timber-felling'.

(a) As per these rules, timber-bearing tracts were classed as superior and inferior.
(b) Rs. 10 should be charged for every *sal* tree, Rs. 6 for all other reserved trees, and Rs. 2 for unreserved trees used for commercial purpose, such as the manufacture of tea-boxes, sale to timber

merchants, for firewood sold for stationary or marine steam-engines.

(c) The felling of trees on the leaves of which silkworms feed is strictly prohibited.

(d) Any person who wants to fell trees should take permission from the deputy commissioner and pay tax on such trees.

(e) Charcoal should be made in the forest and 2 annas per maund should be charged for charcoal making. For cutting firewood for commercial purpose, one has to pay Re. 1 per month.

(f) Ryots are not to be charged for any forest produce used for their own, except reserved trees.

(g) A list of trees declared reserved in the district of Darrang, Nowgong, Naga Hills, Sibsagar and Lakhipur was issued.

Thus the British tried to extend their hegemony over the forest and their produce in the Naga Hills. They restricted the access of the people to the forest in the name of conservation. People had to pay tax even to graze their cattle. The Colonial government tried to exploit the forest produce to generate revenue and ensure regular supply of timber for ship-building and other activities.

DEFORESTATION

Deforestation started taking place in the Naga Hills precisey because of the demand for timber in Sylhet and East Bengal markets. The growth of tea and coal led to the development ot timber in Assam. There was requirement of timber in large quantities for tea chests, Railway sleepers, planking and posts. Construction and for various uses by local boards and municipalities made exploitation of the existing forest of Assam a necessity. Industries like plywood and timber mills which are forest based also contributed to the depletion of forest resources. In addition, war demand for timber between 1939 and 1945 had also affected certain changes in the method of exploitation. Therefore, timber extration from reserves, unclassed state forest and shared forests and others was 6,905 cu ft in 1939-40 which went up to 10,996 cu ft in 1944-5.[7] This period also saw increase in number of saw mills. Three new saw mills at Digboi, 1 at Sylhet, 1 at Rangapahar, 2 at Jeypore, 4 at Makum junction came into existence. The result of war supply demand was not only to bring additional revenue to the province. But also to encourage and develop local enterprise in the shape of expansion of the business of established timber traders by the creation of small saw mills and small contractors. The Rangapahar saw mill had both saw milling and hand sawing during the early period. It is estimated that quantities of logs cut from 1942-7 was 1,74,833 with Rs. 8,197, 14 anna 0 paisa as royalty.

Besides, Military Department's occupation of reserve forests also led to the decrease of forest. The Manipur road base of the Military Department occupied some areas which fall with in Rangapahar Reserve in the Naga Hills district. It seems that the Army felled a lot of trees without getting permission from the Forest Department for construction of roads and huts. A ranger reported that during five months (from January 1942 to May 1942) nearly 40,000 trees of 6 diameter and above were felled.[8] D.C. of Naga Hills forwarded a claim of the Conservator mentioning the personnel occupied and damages occurred: (a) Military personnel in static campus – for one year 12,300 men were in occupation of the area and claim for firewood was Rs. 30.750 as per the rates decided by the Conservator. About half the personnel were under canvas and claim for bamboos was 6,000 × 50 at Rs. 10 a thousand Rs. 3,000: (b) Indian Tea Association and Indian States Labour personnel were estimated at 10,000 for three years. Claims for pre-wood was Rs. 65,000 and for bamboos Rs. 5,000 (at 50 bamboos a head at Rs. 10 a thousand); (Ch.) Military personnel camping for short period was estimated at a minimum of 20,000 for four months. At Re. 1 per head the claim was Rs. 20,000. The total claim therefore, was Rs. 1,23,750 (i.e. Rs. 33,750 + 70,000 + 20,000). The claim of the D.C. Naga Hills shows that there was a lot of damage and denudation of the forest in the Naga Hills District.

The construction of railway lines had also a considerable impact on the forest of India. However, its impact was not much in the Naga Hills. Dense evergreen forests of Diphu and Nambor reserves in the Naga Hills had to be deforested because of the requirement of strips of land for the Assam-Bengal Railway that passed through the reserves. Two strips of land was deforested for the Assam-Bengal Railway that passed through the reserves. Two strips of land, one 40 acres and 1,189 acres of land which were part of Diphu and Nambor were deforested for the Assam-Bengal Railway in 1895.[9] In 1891 there were 114 miles of railway in Assam. By 1911-12 railway network in Assam covered 871-5 miles. Each mile of railway construction required 860 sleepers and the average effective life of each sleeper was calculated between 12 and 14 years. Then for the railway networks of Assam of 871.5 miles, each mile of railway construction required 860 sleepers and the average effective life of each sleeper was calculated between 12 and 14 years. From this, the extent of destruction of forests can be assessed.[10] Thus the need for timber, railway sleepers, tea box chests and coal mining led to the deforestation in Naga Hills.

NOTES

1. There are a lot of plants which were used as vegetables, see J.H. Hutton, *The Angami Nagas*, Kohima: Govt. of Nagaland, Indian rpt., 1969, pp. 93-4.
2. W. Robinson, *A Descriptive Account of Assam,* Calcutta: MAKAIAS, 1841, p. 244.
3. Extract from the *Assam Gazette*, 12 December 1874, no. 38 of 1874 (Part-A), p. 270.
4. Ibid., later on *jhum* cultivation in the Naga Hills was also restricted through Naga Hills Jhum Land Regulation, 1946. However, this was not discussed in the present paper as it was death by some other works.
5. For the Colonial forest policy in Assam, please see Rajib Handique, *British Forest Policy in Assam*, Delhi: Concept, 2004.
6. Pushpanjoli Deori, *Environmental History of Naga Hills, 1881-1947*, Delhi: Ansha, 2005, p. 80.
7. H.P. Smith and C. Purkayastha, *A Short History of the Assam Forest Service, 1850-1945*, Shillong: Govt. of Assam, p. 54.
8. Genl. and Judl. Dept. Forest Branch, L. No. 156-57/T.S./42, dated 23 May 1942.
9. ASP, Revenue-A, July 1895.
10. Handique, op. cit., p. 96.

CHAPTER 9

State-Science, Hegemony and Shifting the Cultivator: Contesting the 'Anti-modernity' Discourse on Shifting Cultivation in South Asia*

DEBOJYOTI DAS

> It is possible that the progress of knowledge has driven out the idea to a great extent in India, but there are, here and there some few who still argue for forest fires, just as in England some eccentric individuals occasionally question the fact that the earth is round.
>
> B.H. Baden Powell, Colonial Forest Officer, 1876.

INTRODUCTION

The 1990s marked the watershed moment of environmental history of South Asia with the seminal work of Guha and Gadgil (1989, 1992, 1995 and 1997) who for the first time contested 'colonial forestry as progress', as depicted in the writings of the early colonial historians. They amplified the subaltern discourse on the exploitative nature of the colonial state and its rhetoric of 'Scientific Forestry'.[1] These narratives of colonial forestry were later contested by the seminal work of Grove (1995) and his contemporary Sangwan (1996) who debated Guha and Gadgil's central theme on imperial

*The ideas for writing the paper developed during my study and association with scholars in the Science Policy Centre, Jawaharlal Nehru University and continued to grow during the period of my doctoral study in SOAS, University of London. I am indebted to P.S Ramakrishnan, Mahesh Rangarajan, Vinita Damodaran, Rohan D'souza, V.V. Krishna, Pranab Desai, David Mosse, Yohan Pottier, Ranjan Chakrabarti, Kuntala Lahiri-Dutt, Mandy Sadan, Heather Goodall and Barbara Harris-White for their encouragement and support over the years.

environmentalism and their notion of pre-colonial ecology as 'Golden Ageist'[2]. Grove's questions have found echoes in the work of Mahesh Rangarajan, who has raised questions on whether the continuation of traditional land use would have been more effective than the company department and the post 1857 regime in curbing deforestation for timber and other arable cultivation. In fact, Grove's pioneering work on the rise of environmentalism in South Asia *Green Imperialism* (1995), shows the complex nature of the early conservation policy of the British in India which Guha and Gadgil had underplayed in their construct of 'colonial forestry'.[3] The ongoing debate on whether colonialism exploited or marked the beginning of environmentalism in South Asia's colonies, according to Swami (2003), has rather sharpened the research agenda of the subcontinent's environmental history. He essentially argues that the disenchantment between Guha and Gadgil and Grove's work should not be seen essentially contradictory because each highlight a very important aspect of colonial forestry in India and enables a more complex and sophisticated understanding of colonial forest conservation than is otherwise possible.[4]

The ongoing debate within the emerging environmental history of South Asia has sharpened the research agenda to enquire the relationship that developed between the farm and forest; and how the colonial forest officials exercised power through control over forest and its resources. It is within these contextual and historical rhetorics on 'conservation' and 'environmentalism' that I locate the 'anti-modernity' and 'anti–technology' discourses on shifting cultivation that has evolved with the colonial foresters' forest management programme that finds its place till this day in the post-colonial forest policy of South Asian nation states.[5] This phenomenon has underplayed the relevance of shifting cultivation in the life of the swiddeners (*jhum* cultivators) and their bio-physical world. The significance of this study lies in deconstructing the 'romance of modernity' that is often projected by the mainstream culture to be synonymous with values such as 'development', 'growth' 'progress' and of late 'sustainability'. The Malthusian allegory of 'overpopulation' and 'carrying capacity' are put to good use by the post-colonial state through the implementation of newer land use systems, such as what P.S. Ramakrishna has paraphrased 'alternative pathways' to replace and make redundant archaic shifting cultivation and nomadism (field rotation).[6] These policy prescriptions have their colonial roots in taungya farming practiced by hill Karens in Burma, and the *baiga chak* among Baigas of Central India, introduced by British policy makers where shifting cultivation conflicted with imperial appropriation of forest resources.[7] The relentless trials and tribulations of the tribal people practicing shifting cultivation continues till this day right from the hills of Chittagong in present day Bangladesh to the Nilgiris of Western Ghats. The plantation forestry programme initiated by the Left government in Tripura or the multiple land use model developed by the Indian Council of Agricultural Research (ICAR) have all inbuilt within them a 'techno-centric' and managerial understanding of the problems faced by the shifting cultivators. They are integrated with the notion of state control over forest and its resources.[8]

The following paragraphs will unravel the history of British colonialism, its incursion and final control of the forest landscape involving its inhabitants who were nomads. This is not meant to validate the notion of 'golden ageist' attributed by Guha and Gadgil (1995) to the pre-colonial period. However it is argued that state intervention in private forest and in shifting cultivation/grazing land in the pre-colonial period was limited with respect to administrative control and institutional bondage. This understanding is echoed in Sivaramakrishnan's work (1995). Also current researches done by Guha (1999) and Skaria (1999) have shown that the pre-colonial intervention in the forest landscape had a different meaning as the Mughals and the kingdoms preceding them viewed forest differently, often clearing them for military and other strategic purpose.[9]

COLONIAL SCIENCE AND THE IMPLICIT PREDICAMENT OF CONTROL

Before reflecting on the historiography of how colonialism treated shifting cultivation, we need to understand the essence of 'colonial science' and 'colonial knowledge' both as how they were imbibed in the colonies, and how they helped the empire to provide rational justification for its resource plunder from their South Asian colonies. Here I would like to assert that the notion of conflict, primitivism, unproductivity, waste were constructs of colonial interpretation of indigenous knowledge systems that had implicit within them the imperial design of 'control' over native's forest resources. This is not meant to reduce the contribution of colonial naturalists, geographers, geologists and medical officers who pioneered the growth of environmentalism in South Asia through the establishment of botanical gardens and ex-situ conservation. But these noble intentions of colonial conservationists were lobbied down by the colonial administration–bureaucracy, and never echoed in the policy discourse of the colonial government.[10]

To understand the dynamics of colonial forestry we need to understand first 'colonial science' as it evolved under the rubric of state power to implement imperial agenda of scientific forestry or in simpler terms 'regenerative forestry'. Regenerative forestry was the sole long term goal of colonial forestry programme that was operationalized by both in-situ and ex-situ measures of conservation--creation of reserve forests, protected forests and the establishment of botanical gardens to domesticate exotic varieties of plant species.[11] 'Colonial science' was defined as a broad category similar to 'colonial knowledge', which Sivaramakrishnan alternatively calls 'state science'. It is useful to signify a network of ideas and practices that constitute the scientific corpus of colonial governance – in other words technology of power.[12] Clearly colonial science was a body of knowledge, a style of imagining the world and a particular modern regime of representation. The use of the term 'modern' was more ethnocentric, and a systematic design of the colonial state to play down the prudence of indigenous knowledge that was subsequently demonized, condemned and projected as detrimental to development.

Colonial forest officials like Baden Powell were so antagonized by the system of shifting agriculture that they depicted it as anti-modern. In later years the criticism grew, particularly as forest officials became better acquainted with the forest, and with the colonial substitutes to swidden, taungya in Burma and *baiga chak* in Central India. Although it was periodically acknowledged that these scattered hill clearances did not inevitably lead to permanent forest damage or the elimination of teak or sal trees from cleared forests, it was nevertheless a tenet of forest officials that such practices were a threat to forest conservation.[13] Thus we need to focus, not merely on the context of these representations, but on the processes of their composition and deployment.

Initially local colonial scientific societies in India provided the impetus and professional authority necessary to establish the first forest conservation agencies in India to be based on desiccation notion (especially the Bombay Forest Department and the Madras Forest Department).[14] In the early 1850s, however, the proponents of forest conservation on an all India basis found it necessary, in the face of state reluctance to finance such an establishment, to resort once more to a source of metropolitan scientific authority, namely the British Association for the Advancement of Science. In 1851 the BAAS commissioned a full report on the 'physical and economic consequences' of tropical deforestation.[15] This helped to legitimize the theoretical and environmental bases for the subsequent development of an all India forest administration. It created the foundation for a scientific forestry programme that was intrinsically designed to regenerate productive timber wood from the tropical forest where woodlands are not concentrated but dispersed. This was crucial to economies of scale.[16] In Burma, artificial teak regeneration was undertaken to overcome natural obstacles to extraction. The first forest policy of British India (1897), therefore, enshrined principles of state forestry-based on scientific regeneration of forest by adopting in-situ measures of conservation. Similarly, in Burma the colonial state had already introduced taungya among hill Karens in order to prohibit the ancient practice of swidden that threatened the scientific forestry programme. In Central India the Baigas were seeing a similar transformation in the traditional swidden fields. The imperial forestry department created *baiga chak*, a transition camp for the swiddeners to adopt the plough, as the rotation of fields came in direct conflict with forest department regulation of farm forestry.

Politics was internal to the forestry and large colonial bureaucracy. The extrapolation of this politics is informative because it tells us about the enduring mechanism of empire building. Through representation of the forest, definition of expertise and manipulation of local structures of authority, colonial forestry created a body of knowledge about natural resource regeneration for sal and teak forests in South Asia. These frontiers were often the forested fringes of settled cultivators. Managerial knowledge was often defined by the colonial state and the landscape was partitioned into discrete jurisdictions, which were then subject to different modes of management.

Scientific forestry evolved under the rubric of state power that formed the epistemological base for silvicultural practice based on the political rhetoric of conservation. It had twin political goals, (a) management by demarcation and exclusion, and (b) management by inventory and controlled regeneration. This generated conflict between the forest dwellers and the forest as they were denied access to their historically owned commons. The state control became paramount. Sivaramakrishnan in *Modern Forest* (1999), says that the forest keepers started deciding what trees were to be grown where, how and when they would be harvested. It pre-empted the 'tragedy of commons'. The colonial rule projected this as what Bryant terms 'romancing colonial forestry'. Deep within this 'romance' was the draconian state coercion over shifting cultivation that left the hill Keren at the mercy of the British Empire. Similarly Prasad (1994) in her work on the Baigas of Central India shows how the colonial administration entrenched into the life of the shifting cultivators ultimately destabilizing their sustainability that depended not only on *Bewar* (shifting cultivation practiced by the Baigas of Central Province) but also on game and food gathering that were cribbed under the new rules of forestry. Thus the Baigas were systematically marginalized and displaced from their own land which Bryant (1994) rightly calls 'shifting the cultivator'.[17] Colonial science modernized the indigenous tradition of shifting cultivators in Burma by replacing it with the alternative land use system taungya, which led to disempowerment and enclosure of the semi nomadic lifestyle of the hill Kerens of Pegu Yoma.[18]

In the decades following the major restructuring of the colonial forest of South Asia on scientific lines the results were not satisfactory which clearly epitomized the failure of British experts to understand the complex functioning of tropical forest ecosystem. However in the early years of the British forestry programme in the sub-continent, German botanist and foresters were invited to study and frame guidelines for the British Empire.[19] These experts drew their lessons from their experience in temperate forest conservation and hence control of pest infestation, plant succession, did not achieve the desired goals. In many parts of Bengal, Burma, Assam and Sylhet teak and sal regeneration failed principally because of the decline in biological diversity caused by plantation and subsequent pest infestation in tropical forest, that were previously under shifting cultivation. The colonial state tried to cash in its financial losses in Bengal by replicating the success of taungya in Burmese forest, but it failed miserably.[20] Imperial accounts speak of the British forest officials acknowledging the failure of farm forestry which was once romanticized as 'progress' by the colonial forest department. Experienced foresters often confessed in their diaries that it was far from being an 'exact science'.[21] The faith and reliability that was placed by the colonist on occidental science of forestry suddenly seemed to lose its universal validity. The local ecological knowledge that was discarded by the scientific community of 'experts' now seemed to exemplify its relevance in resource management.

COLONIAL FORESTRY: THE POLITICAL ECONOMY OF TIMBER EXTRACTION.

The development of colonial forestry was linked to broader colonial aims and policies regarding: (a) The extension of permanent cultivation and plantation of tea, coffee, rubber, areca nut in the later period; (b) Control over shifting cultivation; and (c) The development of plantation forestry on scientific lines. For this, the colonial governments created their own logic of progress that was guided by the deeper political imperative of control and revenue generation. The concerns over degradation of forests were underpinned by the imperial demand for timber as it extended its hold over the colonies and competed for mercantile trade with other imperialist powers. The transfer of power from the East India Company to the British Empire by the Queen's Proclamation of 1858 ushered a new era of colonial governance in South Asia. It demanded better communication with the provinces as was reflected from the revolt of 1857. Hence the development of railways preempted a new era of colonial forestry that was based on heavy demand for tropical teak and sal that grew abundantly in the deciduous forest of Malabar, Bengal, Assam and Burma.[22] The establishment of the imperial forest department in 1856 was a logical culmination of the need to administer state forest under the empire.

In the early days of British rule the need for scientific management and institution building for scientific forest management did not arise because the colonizers were grappling with the problem of taming the plains. Moreover the earlier notion of forest as waste led to a large-scale clearance. Arthur Wellesley took up strategic denudation in Malabar in 1800-2. The British believed that the forests were lands that had fallen into a state of nature because of inadequate care by humans to clear wild vegetation. For instance, Nathalie Halhead defined the jungle as, 'land left waste for five years'. He was essentially referring to shifting cultivation in the highlands. The jungle was thus seen as a result of the abandonment of cultivation, and was also a place of wild and rare vegetation. The actual records of the new rulers may have been a mixed one, but their ideological animosity towards uncultivated land was very deep. British fiscal pressure often had the unintended consequence of reducing the area under cultivation. In Birbhum, for instance, the proportion of arable land under cultivation declined from 70 per cent in 1771 to 50 per cent in 1776, largely due to increasing revenue demands.[23] The extension of this cultivated acreage was an index by which the British evaluated the success or failure of their policies. Forest was a landscape to be conquered and tamed by the colonist.

New fiscal pressures were only one way in which the British changed the economic relationship with the plains. Imperial conquest of the hills was another means to intervene in the tribal way of life. For instance British military campaign in the Rajmahal hills in 1772-8 put an end to the plunder by the Paharia tribes. It also led to increased immigration of the Santhals who brought the rulers higher revenue.

In Burma, Dr Falcon's 'Report on the Teak Forest of the Tenasserim Province', (Jan., 1851) documented the debacle of *laissez-faire* forestry in British Burma.[24] These views were echoed three decades back by the British surgeon and botanist Dr. Wallich after inspecting the area following the British conquest of Tenasserim in 1826. Dr. Wallich predicted that private forests would 'render fruitless' all attempts to attain timber public works and would destroy a valuable source of revenue.[25] Following the recommendation the imperial government sealed the *laissez-faire* timber trade in the forest of British Burma. As Grove observes, these warnings were published at a time when anxiety over artificially induced ecological changes gave scientists a measure of public influence. In particular by the middle of the nineteenth century, the British Indian Empire had become an established fact; and as the idea of empire took hold, attention turned to the systematic development of the empire. Dalhousie saw the utility of state intervention to protect the forest and ensure their long-term development; and it was in the teak forest of Pegu that the organized system of forest management that included teak regeneration was first developed.

Back in South India, the surgeons of East India Company pitted the stability of the company against the short -term interests of those who cleared woodlands. In particular shifting cultivation locally known as *kumri* in the Western Ghats was indicted for deforestation. *Kumri* cultivators were obviously soft targets because of their condition in comparison with their timber counterpart. Though both were blamed for denuding the land of tree cover, the shifting cultivators felt the burden of government regulations. However, the condemnation of indigenous forest users has to be seen in the wider context of British interaction with communities living inside the forest as forest dwellers – *adivasis* i.e. tribes. Policies vis-à-vis hill people reflected concerns broader than an anxiety about desiccation. The general distrust of such groups led to British efforts to bind them down to plough cultivation or to wage labour. The scientific criticism of hill agriculture gave a sharp edge to existing prejudices against nomadic groups. Anxiety about desiccation did play a role in the ban on *kumri* in Coorg in 1848 and its restriction in Belgham in 1856. But the measures against *kumri* reflected wider concerns about revenue and labour supply. Thomas Cannan, a planter in Canara flanked hopes that the 'savages' who practiced *kumri* would be 'more profitably employed' on public work and plantation. In May 1847 the superintendent of the Shimoga division warned that *kumri* exhausted the soil and prevented coffee from growing on it.[26] Leading proponents of the notion of desiccation, such as Hugh Claghorn and Forbes Royle, shared such views. Their report in 1852 criticized the *kumri* cultivators for 'vagabond habits', low agricultural productivity and destruction of valuable timber.

With the adoption of scientific forestry, forest officials became more critical of 'unscientific' indigenous practice. British assertion of the superiority of scientific forestry functioning through 'working plans', were decidedly paternalistic if not racist. As one British official in Burma remarked 'the paternity of the state in the welfare of its children is surely manifested by restricting the unthrifty methods of a few for the benefits of many'.[27] The use of the term 'many' is a personified rethinking of the lowland population. The colonist didn't see shifting cultivation in cultural relativist terms thus defining customs and practice associated with it (reciprocity, barter, patronage) as essentially regressive, non-remunerative savage practices.

The rationale of scientific forestry first found its full-fledged implementation in the Burmese forestry programme which the British had termed taungya, derived from *taung* (hill) and *ya* (cultivation). It can best be portrayed as a perverted form of swidden where both cash and subsistence crops are grown interspaced with teak plantation. This system of plantation forestry represented a far sighted attempt to establish teak plantations on a long term basis. The colonial forestry scheme projected it as a sign of progress and a system that had evolved without conflict and was above politics. However, recent researches on the political economy of the Burmese forest under colonial rule have documented the coercion used by the state through its institutionalized machinery, the forest department to bring hill Karen under its fold.

The hill Karens initially resented cultivating on taungya fields but the forest department's obsession to create reserve forest forced the Kerens to adopt settled farming as their entry into the wilderness was increasingly made difficult by legislation on forest rights. Bryant (1993, 1994 and 1997) in his research has shown how the hill Karen resistance to the forest department took different forms, and was characterized by what Adas generally termed 'avoidance protest'. In an attempt to deny material resource and labour services to the political and economic elite of the Burma forest, avoidance protest typically involved everyday resistances in the forms of theft and arson, for example.

Yet, the ability of shifting cultivators to resist the colonial state had its limits. As forest officials stepped up the pressure during the 1860s, taungya related offences became the most commonly reported breach of the forest rule. The colonial state was able to intervene in the hills as the pre colonial state was never able to do, and the threat of prosecution for violation of forest law was a vivid and perennial reminder of its power. Against this backdrop of escalating confrontation, the forest department made a strategic concession designed finally to convert the hill Karen over to taungya farming. The breakthrough came in 1869 in the demarcation of a proposed reserve in the Tharrawaddy division in which an agreement was reached between forest officials and the Keren village. This agreement, which provided an exemption from the capitation tax, payment of ten rupees per acre covered with teak, and the provision of land exclusively for Keren use, was a model for subsequent contracts that had both revenue and extractive interests. As the hill Kerens enjoyed traditional rights over the forest they didn't pay tax. With the introduction of taungya both the objectives were fulfilled as the hill Kerens for the first time accepted 'state forestry' in letter and spirit by agreeing to cultivate on government land using advanced methods of land use and agrarian practice, that would help promote conservation and the implicit agendas of state making in the frontier region of British Burma. Such concessions were also initially given to the Baigas, Gonds and Ahirs in the Central Province but were later withdrawn.[28]

However, it must be remembered that taungya plantations were never the principle means by which forest officials sought to ensure future teak supply. It is important to examine why forest officials were keen on taungya farming. The answer lies in deeper socio-political and strategic interests of the British Empire. The British never trusted the hill people. Through short-term concessions they ensured the loyalty of the Hill Kerens who knew the forest well. This political decision served three objectives: (a) revenue generation through settled farming, (b) prevention of nomadic incursions which were considered wasteful and a threat to forest conservation, (c) ensuring cheap labour for plantation forestry and stabilization of the economically important but politically unstable region of Burma.[29]

In a sense, the development of the taungya forestry was paradoxical in that it relied for its success on a way of life that was designed ultimately to eliminate swidden with the introduction of 'scientific forestry'. This, for the colonial forest official scheme was 'progress', a break from the past. Such an instrument of modernity has its own political economy of resource appropriation at the expense of the community of the native forest inhabitants. Obviously it generated conflict and tension as is well depicted in the forest *Satyagraha* (civil resistance) of the 1920-30, in Central India. Rangarajan (1997), states in his study of the Central Indian shifting cultivators that the interest of the swiddeners and forest officials often varied. The British forest officials anticipated that the *baiga chak* would induce in the nomadic cultivators, the notion of progress through the technology of 'plough and oxen', but the swiddeners valued their customary practice over material gains and would often run away from the 'animated modernity' that they strongly believed would destroy their community living. The taboo of the *nat* (god of the teak forest) among the hill Kerens of Burmese highland had for long conserved the valuable teak forest. The colonial foresters discourse eliminated all these indigenous environmental ethics and superimposed their agendas of 'regenerative forestry' through 'working plans' on scientific lines.

SHIFTING THE CULTIVATOR – THE RHETORIC OF MODERNIZATION AND PROGRESS

The casual link that is often cited between deforestation and shifting cultivation in contemporary scientific literature has a Eurocentric bias that has evolved with the domination of South Asia by the British Empire. The history of scientific forestry in South Asia is an illustration of how colonial scientific enterprise was politically and socially furthered. The colonial masters found it to be emancipatory for the natives as it transformed their ways of dependence on land from semi-nomadism to permanent-settled cultivation. Inherent within this logic was the state interest of revenue generation, forest resource appropriation and domination of the cultural landscape that created bonded labourers, cheap (human resource) plantation labour force, indentured immigrants, foot soldiers, informers, construction workers who were inducted to serve the empire. Prasad (1994), Bryant (1997) and Rangarajan (1998) give graphic descriptions of how the emancipatory role projected by colonial forestry had deceptive economic and political imperatives that shelved the tribal ways of subsistence by systematically displacing them from their historically owned commons.

The colonial foresters in their South Asian colonies explained their work as 'progress', a boon of modernity, which was very much a reflection of the discourses in which they lived. Progress was an idea that was central to understanding how Europeans sought to romanticize their conquest of much of Asia and Africa, particularly in the nineteenth and early twentieth century. It was also about the application of Western science and technology to selected areas – agriculture, forestry, communication, transport, etc. In so far as it was allegedly about the promotion of local (as was distinct from colonial) social and economic well being, progress had a moral overtone – it promised to introduce the benefits of Western civilization to the 'less privileged' people of the third world. However, progress was also associated more narrowly with the elaboration of the state, and its functional diversification from about the mid-nineteenth century. The colonial state in the subcontinent (as elsewhere) not only grew in absolute size, but also asserted control over an ever-widening range of human activities. From the viewpoint of its officials, this was summarized in one word: 'progress' – that had political, administrative and cultural significance.

SHIFTING CULTIVATION TECHNOLOGY AND MODERNITY

Technology and modernity are often seen as complementary and shape existing notions of social progress, development and growth. But this close interface of technology with modernity is derived from a certain value system (Eurocentric) that evolved with particular cultures and the prevailing systems of world order (capitalism and imperialism). We have to be mindful while addressing technology issues on the politics of progress, development, modernization and of late sustainability. Why has shifting cultivation technology been looked at as anti-modern and anti-technology both by the colonial imperialist and the post-colonial nation states? There are obvious poetics of politics involved that define the agendas of modernity and shape the knowledge system that are appreciated in the policy discourse. In current anthropological and sociological literature the notion of modernity and its affinity to technology that developed with industrial revolution, often coined as 'technocracy' is being radically reshaped and reflexively examined to understand its implication for human society. Shifting cultivation in this sense has to be seen as a farming practice that evolved at the fringes of civilization and much to the discontent of neo-Malthusian and neo-classical predicament of economies of scale and carrying capacity of land.

In order to understand how modernity and technology co-evolved as determinants, one influencing the other, we have to understand how the definition of modernity has been shaped and reshaped in the discourses on the social shaping of technology, reflexive modernization, neo-Marxism, ecological modernization, postmodern prospective and the demodernization anti-modernization prospective. These discourses have raised questions on the novelty of modernity and have critiqued modernity on the political grounds – the relationship between power and means of knowledge production. Here the contribution of Ulrich Beck to 'Reflexive Modernism' is of specific importance since it reflects on the great modernization project – that is perceived to have ushered in progress. The imperial forestry programme that became the tool of progress and development under the colonial rule and till this day shows several pitfalls that disrupted the subsistence level of the shifting cultivators in the hills and forests of South Asia. To cite a few cases in point, the great depression of the 1930s in America shattered taungya farming in Burma; the elimination of complex sustainable livelihood of the Baigas of Balaghat with the introduction of *baiga chak* and restriction on swidden farming in the sal forest; the failure of rubber plantation as an alternative to swidden in Tripura and Kerala in the recent past because of rubber valorization in the international market (falling prices).

The relationship between modernity and technology can be located in the various definitions of the former that evolved with a Eurocentric bias claiming post-industrial technology as a modern artifact distinct from any other. In fact, modernization refers to a new mode of social organization, a new social order and a discontinuity in history. Danial Lerner exemplified modernization as a current term for an old practice – the process of social change whereby 'less developed' societies acquire characteristics of most developed societies. Inherent in the definition is a set notion of lag, inferiority attributed to other cultures and local knowledge systems that are prefixed as obsolete, anti-modern and anti-progressive. In the literature on modernization, the less developed societies are referred to as traditional (tribal, nomadic, peasant societies). Technology evolved by these indigenous communities through their cognition of nature is looked at by the proponents of modern science as 'anti-modern'. They cannot be retrofitted into the modernized ways of life, evolved through formal or scientific knowledge that claims universal validity. It furthermore refers to a specific mode of thinking in which technology is identified as the central means of advancing the modernization project.

This occidental notion of the link between modernity and technology has been questioned by critics of modernity. Reflective sociologists like Ulrich Beck, Marry Bookchin and Otto Ulrich have directly challenged the knowledge claim that the foundation of ecological transformation proposes to establish.[30] Habermas on the other hand evaluated modernity in the light of its engulfing political economy. He describes modernity as an 'unfinished project' and has attempted to redeem certain elements of modernity. He claims that there has been a one sided emphasis since the Enlightenment, on an instrumental, scientific technological rationality, which has shifted possibilities for expression. The result has been a colonization of the world by an amalgamated system of economy and state, technology and science.[31] In a nutshell it can be inferred that technology and the idea of 'modernity' need to be contextualized in a particular historical and political background.[32]

Contemporary understandings of shifting cultivation in South Asia have a colonial undertone of progress and modernization of the tribal ways of subsistence with greater sophistication and internal logic of Malthusian matrix of overpopulation and resource scarcity. The crisis narrative attached to the practice of shifting cultivation links with questions of food security, environmental degradation, efficiency, and productivity in order to conceptualize it as a 'historical regime of deficit'. It fails to uphold the tenets of modernity that privileges commercialization, commodification, and of late corporatization of agriculture. Taking into account per capita income, productivity of land, man land ratio and swidden cycle, a euphoria is created by econometric data work that quantitatively certifies the inefficacy and non-sustainability of shifting agronomy. The policy discourse like in the colonial framework calls for alternative land use systems that can emancipate shifting cultivators from their state of abject poverty and underdevelopment. The alternative land use models and expert knowledge inherently aim to transform nature by technological intervention, dismantling the indigenous structures and practices – the institutions, little traditions, forms of reciprocity and patronage that web community living. Of late this mechanistic understanding of indigenous traditions have been severely challenged by a school of thought that has revived the significance of traditional ecological knowledge of the indigenous people practicing swidden. This school of *neo-indigenastas* (campaigners of indigenous knowledge system) believes in development from below that is culture specific. In fact they stress on incremental build up on traditional knowledge systems of the indigenous people. They have contested the contemporary notion of modernity that is associated with big science, formal knowledge systems, institutional knowledge productions, technical and managerial solutions that are prescribed by experts to emerging problems concerning agricultural development in the highlands. But these schools of scholars have failed to critique the institutional dominance and state hegemony over the commons. To this Agarwal says that the divide that *neo-indigenestas* create between 'traditional' and 'scientific' is in many ways illusive and underplays the larger political control by the state and the heterogeneity in community whose interests often clash. He argues that development is possible only by paying attention to the knowledge and institutions of the excluded community. *In situ* measures of conservation cannot succeed without indigenous people acquiring control over the use of land on which they dwell and rely. Those who possess knowledge should also have the right to decide on how to save the knowledge and how to use it.

In recent years the radical rethinking of anti-modernity discourse has found lot of revivalist momentum among the *milpa* shifting cultivators of the native Indian population in Mexico and Ecuador.[33] There has also been serious research done on unfolding the prejudiced notions on shifting cultivation technology and efficiency under the aegis of global institutions like the UNESCO.[34] A number of research done by biologists, anthropologists, cultural geographers and ecologists has proved the efficacy of shifting cultivation technology and has dispelled the notions regarding deleterious impact of such farming on the environment. Sanchez (1976), Dove (1981) Slikkerveer (1989), Waerren (1989), Warner (1991), Ramakrishnan (1992), Thapa (1994), Swinclair and Walker (1995), Fox *et al* (2000) in their research findings on productivity, efficiency, succession, sustainability, energy intake, soil nutrient status, runoff and infiltration losses, litter fall pattern in shifting cultivation farms in highlands of the humid tropics have found that banning farming system in areas where the soil conditions are highly acidic, is prone to leaching and heavy run-of.

Ramakrishnan *et al*, (2001) in their research on the secondary forests of the Himalayas show how deforestation is related to external pressure of timber trade for industrial use. When large scale deforestation from outside the region is superimposed upon the demand of the local community for food, fodder and fuel wood, the previously balanced use of forest resources, including the management of swidden fallow of secondary forest, becomes impaired. Thus there are other agents at work that harm the forest ecology more than the practice of swidden which according to Alcorn follow managed deforestation. In another study undertaken by Dvorak (1992) on the economics of shifting cultivation in West Africa, he has shown through a theoretical model that the universal acclamation of soil erosion under shifting cultivation is not true and universal models of soil conservation have systematically destroyed this form of cultivation.

The modernity of any farming practice in most common terms is measured by its productivity. In a study done by Ramakrishnan (1983) on the yield pattern under shifting cultivation – locally known as *jhum* in North East India – very interesting results were derived against the backdrop that *jhum* as an agricultural system is often considered as unviable on economic considerations compared to settled farming methods like terracing on the hills slopes.

Table 9.1 gives a clear indication of the sustainable status of long *jhum* cycle in terms of both input and output vis-à-vis terrace cultivation. While the *jhum* system is exclusively labour oriented which is in a way free to the farmer as it originates within the family

TABLE 9.1: MONETARY INPUT/OUTPUT (RS HECTARE/YEAR) INTO *JHUM*, TERRACE AND VALLEY AGRO ECOSYSTEM (AFTER TOKY AND RAMAKRISHNAN 1981)

	Jhum (yr)			*Terrace Annual*	*Valley Crop I and II*
	30 years cycle	*10 years cycle*	*5 years cycle*		
Inputs	2,616	1,830	896	2,542	4,834
Outputs	5,586	3,354	1,690	3,658	5,565
Net gains/losses	2,970	1,524	794	1,116	722
Outputs/inputs	213	1.83	1.88	1.43	1.14

unit itself, the input into terrace farming, at least a major fraction of it, is in the form of inorganic fertilizers.

To the practitioners of formal (epistemic) knowledge system the definitions of progress and development have relatively Eurocentric connotations. *Jhum* agronomy according to this school of thought is not economic, progressive or modern and needs to be replaced by an alternative system of agriculture. George Basalla, one of the scholars who have traced the history of technology in his most celebrated work, *The History of Technology (1998)* tries to analyse the superiority of any technology and the meaning of development and progress in broader terms. He compares two cultures that grow and consume grain – one using indigenous local agricultural methods and the other modern ones – and resumes the search for signs of progress. Grain yield per acre comes to mind as a meaningful way to assess the relative efficiencies of the two methods of food production. The modern farmer as may be expected clearly emerges as winner in these contests.

If we compare Mexican cut/burn agriculture and contemporary American agriculture practices, in which axe and hoe are used to clear and work on land, the yield of corn weight is 2.8 times higher on the American farm. But this does not reflect the energy expended in each of the two and introduces the bias; high crop yield of the American farm depends on large quantities of energy expended in the form of agricultural chemicals, fuel and machinery. By contrast the Mexican farm crop is raised with not much more energy than is supplied by farmers actually working in the field. When the energy output of the crop is compared with the energy input of the farming practice, the result is startlingly different. On the Mexican farm the energy /output ratio for corn is 11:1 and on the American it is 3:1.

The lesson to be drawn here is that grain yield is a deceptive measure and that agriculture practices must be evaluated in terms of specific cultural attitudes and needs, rather than by some supposedly neutral quantitative test.

Zaros (1993) in her study on shifting cultivators of Madagascar (1896-1940) shows how the neo-Malthusian link between population growth and shifting cultivation negates the need for historical consideration of the political economy of deforestation in specific places. Using concepts drawn from regional geography and political ecology she examines the role played by the colonial state in the organization of land use and agriculture as central to an exploration of deforestation in Madagascar. Almost three primary forests have been cleared from 1895 to 1925 due to the state's economic objectives. Concern prompted a ban on shifting cultivation. A synthesis of political and regional geography perspectives reveal how a consideration of the interaction, among human groups, the environment and social formation is central to a rational explanation of tropical deforestation. Population growth and shifting cultivation, she concludes, cannot fully account for deforestation in Madagascar during the colonial period.

CONCLUSION

The utopia surrounding shifting cultivation that it is anti- modern, unproductive, regressive and non-sustainable comes from a particular historical, political, economic and cultural reality that was shaped by the subcontinent's encounter with Eurocentrism. Industrial revolution seems to mark the divide between the traditional and the modern, and in these ethnocentric terms the colonizers conceptualized the technologies of the orient. Ironically, power played a crucial role in mystifying colonial intervention in the forest landscape of South Asia as progress and a re-orientation towards development of the indigenous ways of livelihood. This romanticism was essential to sustain the project of state making and empire building. A similar path of development has been followed by all the post-colonial nation states in South Asia as it ensured the continuity of state's control over the subaltern population through a vested oligarchy that was served by intermediaries in the forest, industries, transnational companies engaged in timber trade and above all the state bureaucracy. The catchwords that are often used, sustainability, carrying capacity of land, threshold level to show the degenerating implication of swidden cultivation on the environment, have deeper political goals and need to be looked at carefully while discarding a particular tradition of agriculture that has evolved over millennia.

Child (1951) makes a very clear distinction on how technology and modernity have been intertwined by studies on the history of technology. He seeks to exemplify that the most recent revolution that has amplified anthropogenic control over nature, the technological revolution of the late eighteenth century is just one phase of the many revolutions that gave man agriculture, metals, cities and writing, each resulting in the proliferation of the human species. The industrial revolution which was a byproduct of the age of enlightenment and scientific revolution should not be considered as the starting point of modernity; it was merely the latest in the series of technological revolutions that had hastened humankind's progress through the ages. In the twenty-first century technology is increasingly seen as synonymous with modernity and native technologies that are culture specific are seen as outmoded, archaic and opposed to the set perceptions of modernity. Importantly, Basalla argues that neither the historical records nor the understanding of the current role of technology in society justifies a return to the idea that a casual connection exists between advances in technology and the overall betterment of the human race. Therefore the popular but illusory concept of technological progress should be discarded. In its place we should cultivate an appreciation for the diversity of the real world, for the fertility of the technological imagination, and for the grandeur and antiquity.

NOTES

1. See the seminal works of Guha and Gadgil, *The Fissured Land* (1992), *The Unequal Woods* (1992), *Ecology and Equity* (1995), in which they argue that colonial forestry was coercive and exploitative in nature in that they changed forest dwellers' harmony with nature by altering the age old practice of burning forest, restricting game and by creating enclosures that would delimit the nomadic life of the pastoral tribes thus serving imperial interests in forest resource appropriation and revenue generation. Also see similar pioneering work on the history of Burmese forests under the Raj, Raymond L. Bryant (1997), *The Political Economy of Burmese Forest – 1842-1994*, Oxford University Press, Delhi.
2. See, Mahesh Rangarajan (1998), *Fencing the Forest: Conservation and*

Ecological Change in India's Central Province, 1860-1914, Oxford University Press, Delhi, Sumit Guha (1999), *Environment and Ethnicity in India 1200-1991*, Cambridge University Press, Cambridge, and Ajay Skaria (1999), *Hybrid History: Forest, Frontiers and Wilderness in Western India*, Oxford University Press, Delhi. In all these writings the pre-colonial relation between the plains and the highlands in central, western and eastern India have been reviewed and the observation made by Gadgil, that the period up to AD 1800 was a time of 'equilibrium' between man and nature, has been proved erroneous and as mere oversimplified/ uncritical description of the pre-colonial period.

3. See, Richard R. Grove (1995), *Green Imperialism: Colonial Expansion, Tropical Islands Eden's and the Origin of Environmentalism 1600-1860*, Cambridge University Press, Cambridge, pp. 309-71. This book is seminal as it draws references from multiple archives of the Commonwealth without ever losing grip of the central argument on the rise of environmentalism in the colonies. Also see, Richard H. Grove (1998), *Ecology, Climate and Empire: The Indian Legacy of Global Environmental History 1400-1940*, Oxford University Press, London. This work traces the environmental discourse that took place in the sub continent among British conservationists which involved experts from many fields (botany, geology, geomorphology, climatology and soil science) and how these deliberations have shaped the contemporary understanding on the issues of global warming, deforestation and desiccation. Also see, Richard H. Grove, Vinita Damodaran and S. Sangwan, eds. (1998), *Ecology, Climate and Empire: The Indian Legacy of Global Environmental History*, Oxford University Press, New Delhi. In this edited work Grove et al., refer to the environmental history of the sub continent, discussing multiple sets of colonial conservation attempts and the depiction.
4. The complexity in the discourse on colonial forestry need not be overstretched. It comes from a temporal framework and certain changes in the economic interest of the imperialists. Guha and Gadgil looked at a different time frames of colonial history than Grove did earlier – 1400-1800. The year 1857 marked the watershed moment in colonial administration over India. There were three main historical events taking place during the eventful decade of 1850 that made complete control over the subcontinent's forests necessary to build the British Empire. First the development of railways in 1852 generated huge demand for railway sleepers, the need of which could only be fulfilled by optimum appropriation of sub-continent's deciduous teak forests. The growing demand for timber was further complimented by the imperial shipbuilding industry back home. Second, the transfer of power from the East India Company to the British Empire by the Queen's proclamation of 1858, as a consequence of the revolt of 1857, the subcontinent came under the direct control of British administration. Third, the need for revenue generation to sustain

the colonial economy called for greater control and intervention in the forest landscape. It was institutionalized with the creation of the Imperial Forest Department in 1856. Thus the understanding of colonial economy, polity and ecology by Grove and Gadgil seems intrinsically contradictory but they in many ways help to construct a more nuanced understanding of the ideologies of state science, environmentalism, and the political economy of British imperial policy. Also see, P. Swami (2003), 'Environmental History and British Imperialism In India: A Prime Political Agenda', *The Centennial Review:* 3.3, pp. 3-40. In this paper Swami argues that a more deceptive deconstruction of the sub-continent's environmental history remains to be undertaken as in the United States and Europe where a body of research has already emerged that has looked beyond the frontiers of political economy. Also see, K. Sivaramakrishnan, 'Colonialism and Forestry in India: Imaging Past and Present Politics', *Comparative Studies in Society and History*, vol. 37, no.1 (Jan. 1995), pp. 3-40.

5. See, the sequence of articles by Ramchandra Guha that appeared in *Economic and Political Weekly*, R. Guha, 'Forest in British and Post British India: An Historical Analysis', *Economic and Political Weekly,* vol. XVII, (28 Oct.-4 Nov. 1983), pp. 1882-95; and 'Forest in British and post British India: An Historical Analysis', *Economic and Political Weekly,* vol. XVIII (5-12 Nov. 1983), pp. 1940-47. These articles contested and brought forward the colonial misgivings in Indian Forest Act and the National Forest Policy, 1952. See also Ramchandra Guha, 'An early Environmental Debate: The Making of the 1878 Forest Act', *The Indian Economic and Social History Review*, 27, 1 (1990), pp. 65-84.
6. See the book written by P.S. Ramakrishna, *One Sun and Two Worlds: An Ecological Journal.* In this book Ramakrishna uses the term 'Alternative Pathways', to depict the state policy on shifting cultivation.
7. Taungya is a perverted form of shifting cultivation practiced by the Hill Keren of highland Burma, introduced by the colonial government to appropriate Burma's rich tropical teak forests. Such cultivation is a type of dry agriculture combining various techniques: partial forest clearing, multiple cropping, and field rotation, to produce food and cash crops. It soon became a way of life for the Hill Keren but destroyed the modes of self-subsistence. This farming practice which was considered progressive by the forest officials was abandoned by the imperial government in 1935 on the grounds of massive government retrenchment that happened because of the external exigencies of fall in market demand due to the great depression of the 1930s. The *baiga ckak* was a similar kind of *jhumia* (shifting cultivators) resettlement programme.
8. The Indian Council of Agricultural Research has developed a three tier model of land use (field crop-grazing land-agro forestry) for shifting cultivation areas. Its applicability has come under serious doubt – because of its rigidity and non-adaptability by the *jhumias,* as it inherits the same

inappropriate high end technologies that are capital, energy and resource intensive. See, B.N. Borthakur et al. (1983), *A Comprehensive Review on Shifting Cultivation in North East India*, Published by Dr. Baldeo Singh on behalf of Indian Council of Agricultural Research, North Eastern Hill Region, Shillong.

9. See, Skaria's *Hybrid History: Forest, Frontiers and Wildness in Western India* and Guha's, *Environment and Ethnicity in India 1200-1991*. In both these works Skaria and Guha have eulogized the histories of the forest landscapes and how the wilderness – the forest landscape, were perceived and treated by the civilized setteled agrarian communities. They primarily enquired into the pre-colonial relationship between forest inhabitants and the agrarian communities surrounding them.
10. Richard Grove in his work *Ecology, Climate and Empire: The Indian Legacy of Global Environmental History 1400-1900* argues that colonial conservation that emerged in the works of French and German romantic scientists and later in the works of medical officers and naturalists employed by the British East India Company, did not inherently influence repressive agendas of the imperialist powers. Only in its later stages of development did conservatism as a highly bureaucratized justification for state control of land use. Also see Ravi Rajan, 'Forest and Policy of Colonial Agro-Ecology: The Case of Shifting Cultivation and Soil Erosion', *Studies in History*, 14, 2, n.s. (1998). In this paper Rajan endorses Grove's view by analysing the debates of the Empires Forest Conference that were held six times during the period between 1820-50, in various parts of the Commonwealth. The debates of these conferences, he suggested, helped constitute a scientific community with a common commitment to the silvicultural goals of continental forestry.
11. It must be noted that the early period of colonialism, before the establishment of the Forest Department and enactment of the Forest Acts, there was free trade of timber, and indigenous practices of shifting cultivation were combined with it to suggest the need for greater state involvement in the forests that served the long term interest of 'regenerative forestry' for the empire. *De Falcons Report on the Teak Forest of the Tenassariam Province* documents the debacle of *laissez-faire* forestry in British Burma.
12. Here colonial science is seen as a body of knowledge that helped in empire building, was deterministic in spirit, ethnocentric in approach, claimed superiority over native's knowledge systems that was projected as waste, thus helping in legitimizing imperial control and exploitation of native forest.
13. To understand the biases towards shifting cultivation see British officials monograph and books. Brandis, *Teak Forest of Pegu;* B.H. Baden Powell, *The Forest System of British Burma*, Calcutta, 1837; Nesbit, *Burma Under*

British Rule, vol. 2; Stebbing, *The forest of India*, vol. 2; W.H.A. Watson, 'Taungya Cutting', *Indian Forest*, XXXIV (1908).

14. After the 1860s desiccation and 'desertification' fears, incorporated particularly into the forest and land management policies of the British colonial empire, continued to sporadically exert powerful impact.
15. See, H. Clehorn, F.R. Baird-Smith and R. Sreachey, 'Report of the Committee appointed by the British association to consider the probable effects in an economical and physical point of view of the destruction of tropical forest', Report of the British Association for Advancement of Science *(transactions)*, 1859.
16. Teak and sal trees native to the mixed deciduous forests of South Asia, have a limited range, and are only found scattered below an elevation of about 3,000 feet receiving precipitation between 60 to 130 inches per year. Indeed in the so-called teak/sal forests, the tree rarely comprises 10 to 12 per cent of the total forest cover. Thus it became fundamental for the colonial forestry programme to incorporate efficient mechanisms for regenerative forestry.
17. Raymond L. Bryant, in his seminal paper 'Shifting the Cultivator: The Politics of Teak Regeneration in Colonial Burma' uses the lexicon. He exposes the colonial design of timber appropriation through scientific forest management and explores the political economy of taungya farming in colonial Burma.
18. In modern day Burma hill Keren are an ethnic minority fighting for their identity and survival. The contemporary Keren crisis has historical roots in colonial forest policy. The economic depression of the 1930s and the exigencies of the First World War that led to massive retrenchment by the colonial government completely destroyed taungya farming in Burma, which was officially declared defunct in 1935 by the colonial administration.
19. See Ravi Rajan's work 'Imperial Environment or Environmental Imperialism? European Forestry, Colonial Forestry and the Agendas of Forest Management in British India 1800-1900' in which he highlights the expertise of German botanists who were used by the British Empire in the beginning to develop scientific forestry in the subcontinent.
20. For details on how teak plantation failed in Bengal province refer to chapters 7 and 8 of K. Sivaramakrishnan's, *Modern Forest: State Making and Environmental Change in Colonial Eastern India*.
21. One official was candid enough to assert 'no two officers would make the same tree in a given area'. Wimbush paper, under typescript entitled, 'Life in the Indian Forest Service, 1907-1935'.
22. Rangarajan writes that to build a mile of broad gauge rail track required 1,800 to 2,000 sleepers. By 1878 over 2 million sleepers had been used for the construction of railway lines. Other than the Deodar tree, sal and teak were the main sources of wood. See Mahesh Rangarajan's paper

'Imperial Agendas and Indian Forest: The Early History of Indian Forestry, 1800-1878'. Also refer to Brandis, 'Memorandum on the Supply of Railway Sleepers of the Himalayan Pine Impregnated in India'.

23. For further explanation on the political economy of British agrarian revenue generation in Bengal see, chapters 3 and 7 of R.K. Gupta's work *The Economic life of Bengal District, Birbhum, 1770-1857.*
24. Submitted to government in January 1851, it was published along with other papers related to the Tenasserim forests in 'Selection from the Records of the Bengal Government', vol. IX (1852).
25. N. Wallich to Sir A. Campbell, 23 March 1827, quoted by H. Falcon, 23 January 1851 in 'Report on the Teak Forest of the Tenasserim Province', with the other papers on the Teak Forest of India, selected from the records of the Bengal Government, vol. IX, Calcutta, 1852, (hereafter Tenasserim).
26. Supt. Shimoga to Secy. to Chief Commissioner, Mysore, 5 May 1984 quoted in H.F. Cheghorn et al., 'Report of a Committee to Consider the Possible Effects in an Economical and Physical Point of View in the Destruction of Tropical Forest', *Transaction of the British Academy for the Advancement of Sciences.*
27. Refer to the official document, 'Burmese Forest Proceeding (March 2003)'.
28. See the Ph.D. thesis of Archana Prasad on 'Forest and Subsistence in Colonial India: A Study of Central Province', in which she shows that the Baigas were given incentives in the form of bullocks, oxens and even ploughs to practice settled farming within the *baiga chak* formed by the colonial forest department in Balaghat.
29. A point to be noted, that the development of taungya forest took place at a time of considerable political uncertainty in colonial Burma. With the annexation of Pegu at the conclusion of the second Anglo-Burmese War (1852), Great Britain assumed control of a Burmese population whose allegiance was suspected. However, the Kerens who formed an ethnic minority in Burma, had long standing antipathy towards the numerically dominant Burmese population which the British realized could be used to serve imperial interests.
30. Ulrich Beck, Murray Bookchin, Otto Ulrich make a case for de-modernization of the technopolis culture because it creates risk, brought about by ecological transformations, through the intervention of economic institutions (revenue generation), regulatory institutions such as the state and scientific-technology development in formal set up.
31. Implicit in Habermas's understanding of modernity and technology was the presupposition of appropriation and control over the colonized world and their resources through institutional intervention (creation of the imperial forest department, revenue department), low and enactment, transfer of technology, bureaucracy and experts that planned, evolved

and developed agendas contributing to shape a notion of modernity to be exclusively Western. Raymond L. Bryant while discussing the political economy of Burmese forests showed how progress was used as rhetoric to serve colonial interests in forest resource appropriation in Burma.

32. It is in this particular context that I would refer to the works of Guha and Gadgil (1989), Sivaramakrishnan (1995), Bryant (1997), Rangarajan (1998) that help in deconstructing the inherent logic of colonial forest management programme and the political economy of plantation forestry through elaborate working plans that were designed to generate maximum revenue and production of timber through 'regenerative forestry' and afforestation programmes.
33. For example, the Organization of the Confederation of Indigenous Nationalities of Ecuador (CONAIE), and the union of indigenous communities of Glutamate (UGIC), have organized and revived the indigenous subsistence farming practices like swidden and have challenged the modernizing dream of the state. This has turned out to be splendidly successful.
34. UNESCO's Man and Biosphere Programme (MAB) has been funding research in South Asia to develop traditional knowledge systems for subsistence agriculture.

REFERENCES

Adas, Michel. 1981. 'From Avoidance to Confrontation: Peasant Protest in Pre-colonial and Colonial Southeast Asia', *Comparative Studies in Society and History* (April), pp. 217-47.

Agarwal, Arun. 1995. 'Dismantling the Divide Between Indigenous and Scientific Knowledge', *Development and Change*, vol. 26, pp. 431-2.

Ahmed, I. 1999. *Social Geography of India*, New Delhi: Rawat Publishers.

Anderson, David and Richard Grove (eds.), 1987. *Conservation in Africa: Peoples, Parks, Priorities*, Cambridge: Cambridge University Press.

Bassala, George. 1988. *The History of Technology*, Massachetus: MIT Press, pp. 212-13.

Bebbington, Anthony. 1993. 'Modernization from Below: An Alternative Indigenous Development?', *Economic Geography*, vol. 69, no. 3, Environment and Development, Part 1 (July), pp. 274-92.

Beck, Ulrich. 1986. *Risk Society: Towards a New Modernity*, London: Sage.

Bhattacharya, Neeladri. 1998.'Introduction', *Studies in History*, 14, 2, n.s., p. 165.

Borthakur, B.N et al. 1983. *A Comprehensive Review on Shifting Cultivation in North East India*, Shillong: Indian Council of Agricultural Research – North Eastern Hill Region.

Bryant, Raymond L. 1997. *Political Economy of Burmese Forest 1824-1994*, Delhi: Oxford University Press.

Bryant, Philip. 2003. 'Theorizing Modernity and Technology', *Modernity and Technology* (ed. Thomas S, Misa Philip, Byer and Andrew Freeberg), Cambridge: MIT Press, pp. 33-77.

Brandis, D. 1879. 'Memorandum on the Supply of Railway Sleepers of the Himalayan Pine Impregnated in India', *Indian Forester*, IV, pp. 365-83, esp. p. 366.

Cleghron, H. 1861. *The Forest and Gardens of South India, First Annual Report on the Forest Operation in Madras Presidency*, Edinburgh: Allen and Unwin, p. 129.

Cheghron, H.F. et al. 1852. 'Report of a Committee to Consider the Possible Effects in an Economical and Physical Point of View in the Destruction of Tropical Forest', *Transaction of the British Academy for the Advancement of Science*, VII, pp. 78-102, esp. pp. 84-5.

Dverok, Karen N. 1992. 'Resource Management for West African Farmers and the Economics of Shifting Cultivation'. *American Journal of Agricultural Economics*, vol. 74, pp. 805-15.

Gadgil, Madhav. 1992. *The Fissured Land*, Delhi: Oxford University Press.

Grove, Richard. 1990. 'Threatened Islands, Threatened Earth: Early Professional Science and the Historical Origin of Global Environmental Concerns', *Sustaining Earth: Responses to the Environmental Threats*, (ed. J.R. Davis et al.), London: Oxford University Press, pp. 15-16 and 23.

Grove, Richard, R. 1995. *Green Imperialism: Colonial Expansion, Tropical Island Eden sand the Origin of Environmentalism 1600-1860*, Cambridge: Cambridge University Press.

Grove, Richard, H. 1998. *Ecology, Climate and Empire: The Indian Legacy of Global Environmental History 1400-1940*, Oxford: Oxford University Press.

Guha, Ramchandra. 1983. 'Forest in British and post-British India: An Historical Analysis', *Economic and Political Weekly*, vol. XVII (28 Oct.-4 Nov.), pp. 1882-95; vol. XVIII (5-12 Nov.), pp. 1940-7.

———. 1990. 'An Early Environment Debate: The Making of the 1978 Forest Act', *The Indian Social and Economic History*, vol. 27.1, pp. 65-84.

———. 1995. *Ecology and Equity*, New Delhi: United Nations Research Institute for Social Development.

Guha, Sumit. 1999. *Environment and Ethnicity in India 1200-1991*, Cambridge: Cambridge University Press.

Gupta, R.K. 1984. *The Economic Life of Bengal District, Birbhum*, 1770-1857, Bardwan: Oswan Publication, pp. 31 and 37.

Learner, Daniel. 1968. 'Modernization: Social Aspects', *International Encyclopedia of Social Sciences*, vol. 10, p. 386.

Malik, Bela. 1990. 'Hills and Forest Economies of North East India-Mid

19th Century to Early 20th Century', unpublished M. Phil dissertation, Jawaharlal Nehru University, New Delhi.

Mol, A.P.J. 2003. 'The Environmental Transformation of the Modern Order', *Modernity and Technology* (ed. Thomas S, Misa Philip, Byer and Andrew Freeberg), Cambridge: MIT Press, pp. 303-25.

Morehead, F.T. 1994. *The Forest of Burma*. London: Longman Green and Company.

Nesbit, John. 1901. *Burma under British Rule and Before*, vol. 2, p. 58.

Powell, B.H. 1873. *The Forest System of British Burma*, Calcutta: Superintendant of Government Printing and Stationary.

Prakash, Gyan. 1990. *Bonded Histories: Geologies of Labour Servitude in Colonial India*. Cambridge: Cambridge University Press, p. 164.

Prasad, Archana. 1994. 'Forest and Subsistence in Colonial India: A Study of Central Province', unpublished Ph.D. thesis, Jawaharlal Nehru University, New Delhi.

———. 1999. *Verrier Elwin and the Making of Anti-modernity Tribal Identity*, Delhi: Tulika.

———. 1998. 'The Biogas: Survival Strategies and the Local Economy in the Central Province', *Studies in History*, 14, 2, n.s., pp. 325-48.

———. 2003. 'Ecological Romanticism and Environmental History: The Contemporary Relevance of Verrier Elwin', *ALPAJAN*: IV (Oct-Dec.), pp. 25-9.

Rajan, Ravi. 1998.'Forest and the Politics of Colonial Agro Ecology: The Case of Shifting Cultivation and Soil Erosion 1920-1950', *Studies in History*, 14, 2, n.s, pp. 218-35.

Ramakrishnan, P.S. 1984. 'The Science behind Bush Fallow Agricultural System (Jhum)', *Proc. Indian Aad. Sci. (Plant Sci.)*, vol. 93, no. 3 (July), pp. 386-87.

Ramakrishnan, P.S. and S.P.S. Kushwaha. 2001. 'Secondary Forest of the Himalayas with Emphasis on the North-Eastern Hill Region of India, *Journal of Tropical Forest Science*, 31 (40), p. 727.

Ramakrishnan, P.S. et al. 2005. *One Sun the World and Ecological Journal*, Delhi: Oxford and IBH.

Rangarajan, Mahesh. 1994.'Imperial Agendas of Indian Forest: The Early History of Indian Forestry, 1800-1878', *The Indian Economic and Social History Review*, 31, 2, p. 162.

———. 1998. *Fencing the Forest: Conservation and Ecological Change in India's Central Province, 1860-1914*, Delhi: Oxford University Press.

Richards, Paul. 1985. *Indigenous Agriculture Revolution: Ecology and Food Production in Western Africa*. London: Oxford University Press.

Saberwal, V.K. 1998. 'Pastoral Politics: Shepards, Bureaucrats, and Conservation in Western Himalayas'. Delhi: Oxford University Press.

Schat, Johan, 2003. 'The Contested Rise of Modernist Technology Politics',

Modernity and Technology (ed. Thomas S, Misa Philip, Byer and Andrew Freeberg), Cambridge: MIT Press, p. 257.

Sivaramakrishnan, K. 2000. 'State Science and Development History: Encoding Local Forest Knowledge in Bengal', *Forest, Nature, People Power* (ed. Martin Doornbos, Ashwini Seth and Ben White), London: Blackwell, pp. 60-83.

———. 1998. *Modern Forest: State Making and Environment Change in Colonial Eastern India*. Delhi: Oxford University Press.

———. 1995. 'Colonialism and Forestry in India: Imaging the Past and Present Politics', *Comparative Studies in Society and History*, vol. 37, no.1, pp. 3-40.

Singh, C. 1998. *Natural Premises: Ecology and Peasant Life in Western India, 1800-195'*, Delhi: Oxford University Press.

Skaria, Ajay. 1999. *Hybrid Histories: Forest, Frontiers and Wilderness in Western India*, Delhi: Oxford University Press.

Stebbing, E.P., 1881. *The Forest of India*, vol. 2, London: Allen & Unwin, p. 563.

Swami, Praveen. 2003. 'Environmental History and British Imperialism in India: A Prime Political Agenda', *The Centennial Review* 3.3, pp. 112-17.

Taylor, R.H. 'Perception of Ethnicity in the Politics of Burma', *Southeast Asian Journal of Social Sciences*, vol. 10 (1982), pp. 7-22.

———. 1976. 'Politics in late Colonial Burma: The Case of U Saw', *Modern Asian Politics*, 10 (2), pp. 161-93.

Watson, W.H.A. 1918. 'Forestry in Lower Burma', *Indian Forester*, 44, (May), p. 215.

Child, V. Gordan. 1951. *Social Evolution*. New York: Harper and Collins.

Zimmerman, F. 1988. 'The Jungle and the Aroma of Meat: Ecological Themes in Hindu Medicine', *Soc. Sci. Medicine*, 27 (3), pp. 197-215.

Zorosz, Lucy. 1993. 'Defining and Explaining Tropical Deforestation: Shifting Cultivation and Population Growth in Colonial Madagascar (1896-1940)', *Economic Geography*, vol. 69, no. 4, Environment and Development, Part 2 (Oct.), pp. 366-79.

CHAPTER 10

Land Use/Land Cover Change and its Impact on Climate in the Barak Valley, Assam

BASHABI GUPTA

The associations and interrelationships between land use and land cover and climate of the place are complex and many sided. Studies on land use and land cover change (LULCC) exhibit important understandings in forest cover assessments and the concomitant biomass; the regional variations in climate change as well as help in enumerating forward and backward connections amongst LULCC, climate change, and anthropocentric activities of the environment. That the climate system of any place is affected by LULCCs through bio-geophysical, bio-geochemical, and energy exchange processes is a well-established relationship. Changes in land cover affect the reflectance of the land surface, influencing the fraction of the sun's energy absorbed by the land surface and thus affecting heat and moisture fluxes. These processes also create changes in the rate of vegetation transpiration and surface waterlines and cause the division of absorbed surface heat into latent and sensible heat fluxes. Simultaneously, vegetation changes determine surface roughness, thereby, thus air momentum and heat transport. The paper focuses on the land use and land cover changes that have taken place in the Barak Valley of Assam as a case study to bring out such linkages. Barak Valley is taken to be the area that forms the basin of the Barak River, located between 92° 15′ east to 93° 15′ east and 24° 8′ north to 25° 8′ north, an area of 6,922 sq. km. The districts covered under this region are Cachar, Karimganj and Hailakandi. The study examines the historic and current land use and land cover change through analyses of LANDSAT data from GLCF. LULCC is examined through time periods of 1978, 1988, 1998 and 2006. On ground testing has been done by correlating the satellite imagery data with statistical data of land use and cropping pattern change. Rainfall and temperature data has then been correlated with the imageries showing the impact on the climate. This study addresses the spatial and temporal changes of the LULCC components, issues like impact of institutions, land fragmentation and degradation have not been considered here.

RELATIONSHIP OF LAND USE/ LAND COVER CHANGE AND CLIMATE

Land use and land cover are linked to climate and weather in complex ways. Primary linkages are those between land cover and climate which include the exchange of greenhouse gases (such as water vapour, carbon dioxide, methane, and nitrous oxide) between the land surface and the atmosphere, the radiation (both solar and long wave) balance of the land surface, sensible heat between the land surface and the atmosphere, and unevenness of the land surface and its uptake of momentum from the atmosphere. Because of these strong links between land cover and climate, changes in land use and land cover are important contributors to climate change and variability. In addition, changes in land use and land cover, especially when put together with climate variability are likely to affect ecosystems thereby affecting human life.

Impact of the changes in the land use and land cover in any region also requires an understanding of past land use practices, current land use and land cover patterns, and projections of future land use and cover, as well as the interactions between natural and man-made land cover and human activities. Thus climate change is deeply affected by change in land use and land cover, an indicative factor of the balance between man nature interactions. While land use change is often a driver of environmental and climatic changes, a changing climate can in turn affect land use and land cover. Climate variability has shown to have impacted and changed land use practices variably in different areas of the planet, exhibiting differences in micro regional and macro regional vulnerability and resilience.

LOCATING THE STUDY: BARAK VALLEY IN ASSAM

Assam is an important micro-climatic zone. The Brahmaputra which governs most of Assam's climate has little influence here. The effort is to see how in a small micro-climatic zone which is separated from the major influence of the region by high hills forming a bounded area experienced climate variability through change in land use and land cover. The region is divided into three districts for administrative purposes: Cachar, Hailakandi and Karimganj.

The Barak Valley is a smaller river valley as compared to the Brahmaputra Valley and is separated from the Brahmaputra Valley by the North Cachar and the Karbi Anglong Hills. The Barak originates at the western side of Maothana in Manipur and enters this region from Tipaimukh in Manipur and then joins the river Jiri at the Cachar border, flows from east to west in its valley area covering about 8.9 per cent of Assam's total geographical area. Multiple streams join it at different places in the region. The physiography of the Barak Valley is undulating; divisible in three clear zones: the hills and hillocks are known as *tillas* and, the wide plains and the low lying waterlogged areas known as *beels* locally. The hills are rugged in nature as the rivers and streams cut deep gorges through them. The river Barak has shown tendency to shift its course over time, as visible in the valley areas. There are meandering plains towards the north of the Barak River around which cultivation is extensively visible. The low lying *beels* are natural depressions and waterlogged areas are where traditionally paddy is cultivated.

METHODOLOGY

This study examines the historic and current land use and land cover change through analyses of LANDSAT data from GLCF. The imageries have been analysed using ERDAS IMAGINE LULCC is examined through time periods of 1978, 1988, 1998 and 2006. The categories of land use as units of analysis in the imageries are: forest land, cultivated area with irrigation, cultivated area without irrigation, fallow land and grass and scrub land. On ground testing has been done by correlating the satellite imagery data with statistical data of land use and cropping pattern change in the period from 1978 to 2006. Here, the categories of land use classification are used by the Agricultural Census of India. Rainfall and temperature data has then been correlated with the imageries showing the impact on the climate. The land use change was calculated on a point per cent basis. Weavers Method has been utilized to understand the change in cropping pattern along with Herfindhal's Index to understand the crop diversification achieved in the region at different time periods. All of these have been then correlated with the satellite imageries to understand the change in LULCC in the chosen area. Particular emphasis has also been given to the tea statistics which are also indicative of change in the LULCC as well the micro climate.

As the area chosen is the Barak River Valley of Assam, a security classified area as it forms a part of India's international border with Bangladesh meant that the data to be accessed for different analysis used in this paper was hard to acquire. The satellite imageries were a part of the GLCF data which were demarcated on the basis of the latitudinal and longitudinal extent of the region. The statistical data used for calculating land use and land cover change are from the Agricultural Census of India, for the concerned time period. As part of the time period included in this study includes the time period when the state of Assam had been embroiled in political instability, these years have been avoided in the statistical analysis as data was not available for those years.

TABLE 10.1: ANNUAL RAINFALL IN BARAK VALLEY REGION

Year	*Station/District*	*Annual rainfall in mm*
1971	Silchar	2,737.7
1972	Silchar	n.r
1973	Silchar	2,971.2
1974	Silchar	2,536
1975	Silchar	1,355
1976	Silchar	3,919
1977	Silchar	3,455
1978	Silchar	2,837
1979	Silchar	1,792
1980	Silchar	1,789
1981	Silchar	2,361
1982	Silchar	2,816
1985	Silchar	2,353
1990	Silchar	3,246

Year	*Cachar*	*Hailakandi*	*Karimganj*
2003	2,178.0	1,807.0	3,087.0
2007	2,954.2	2,876.5	3,471.5
2008	2,919.7	2,299.9	1,524.8
2009	2,504.4	1,096.5	2,296.6
2010	4,093.9	1,673.0	3,019.9
2011	2,299.0	1,228.1	1,890.5

Source: Agricultural Census of Assam for the concerned years.

CLIMATE OF THE BARAK VALLEY

The climate of the Barak Valley region is warm humid and sub-tropical. In the earlier years the annual average rainfall received was very high almost 3,180 mm with total rainy days of about 146 days per annum. Temperatures ranged from about 25 °C to 40 °C in the summer months and from 10 °C to 25 °C in the winter months. In the past, the average rainfall was high, yet in the recent years there has been a steady decrease of the total amount of rainfall received. This region has also witnessed a steady rise in the summer temperature.

LULCC EVIDENCE FROM SATELLITE IMAGERY

The changes in land use and land cover in the Barak Valley are analysed using GLCF images. The earliest available imagery from open source data is that of 1975. This image given below shows the classification of different land uses prevalent in the Barak Valley region during that time. The areas to the east show dense forest covering about 10.4 per cent of the total area. Cultivated area with irrigation borders the Barak River that forms boundary to the region. Cultivated area

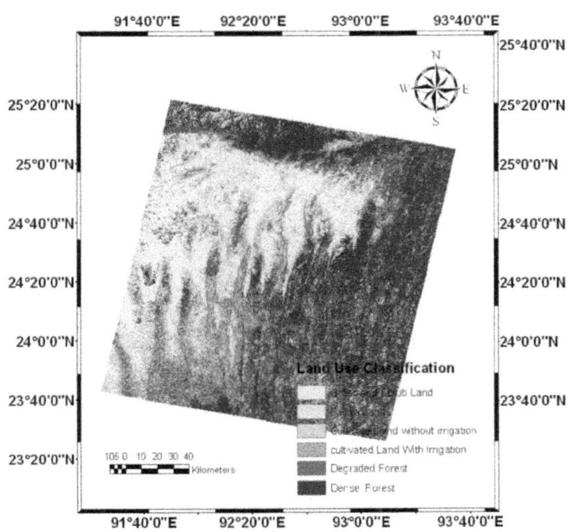

Source: GLCF image from ESRI Open Source Data.

IMAGE 10.1: LAND USE/LAND COVER OF BARAK VALLEY, AUGUST 1975.

without irrigation is about 12.23 per cent of the area, this forms the middle area of the region. There is a presence of marshes and few lakes in the north-west of the Cachar district. Fallow land covers about 22.7 per cent of the area. Grass and scrub land covers the largest area in the region, forming a lock of about 30.33 per cent.

The next imagery from 1988 August shows particular changes that are visible in the region. The region to the east are showing dense forest covering about 6 per cent of the total area, which is a decrease of about 4 per cent in the intervening years. Degraded forest area on the mountain sides covers about 13.5 per cent of the area. Cultivated area with irrigation has increased covering to about 18.5 per cent of the area. Cultivated area without irrigation is about 15.4 per cent of the region. This has decreased in the last decade. There is a evidence of increased siltation of marshes and few lakes in the north-west of the Cachar district. Fallow land has decreased covering about 21.1 per cent of the area. Grass and scrub land still covers the largest area in the region, forming a block of about 25.5 per cent. This imagery shows very clearly that the dense forest of

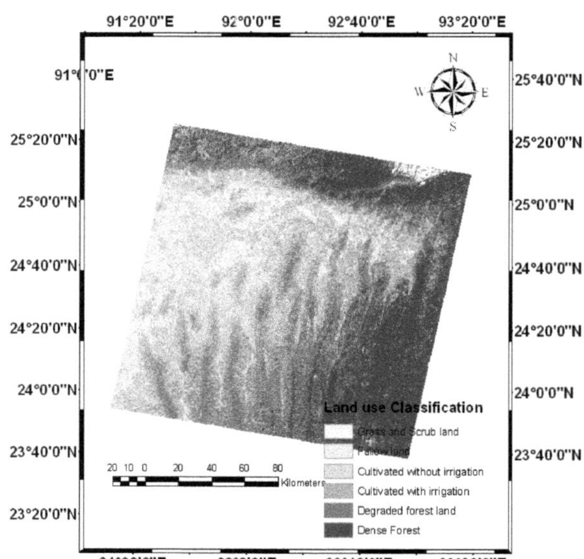

Source: GLCF image from ESRI Open Source Data.

IMAGE 10.2: LAND USE/LAND COVER OF BARAK VALLEY, AUGUST 1988.

1975 has given way to degraded forests and increase in the fallow land of the region. It also shows that the land cover is decreasing, resulting in increase in the regional value of insolation. This is visible in the slow and steady rise in the temperatures prevalent in the region, as well as bursts or higher peaks in the rainfall over the region.

The last imagery is from August 2006. The region to the east showing dense forest has decreased further covering only about 2.1 per cent of the total area. Degraded forest area on the mountain sides has increased significantly and is on the border of becoming scrubland. This covers about 17 per cent of the area. Cultivated area with irrigation has decreased covering about 10 per cent of the area. Cultivated area without irrigation has increased forming about 23.6 per cent of the area. There area of marshes and few lakes in the north west of the Cachar district has also decreased. Siltation has also increased in the Barak River. Fallow land covers about 22.8 per cent of the area. Grass and scrub land still covers the largest area in the region, forming a block of about 25.6 per cent. This imagery shows definitively that the land use in the region has changed. Many of the

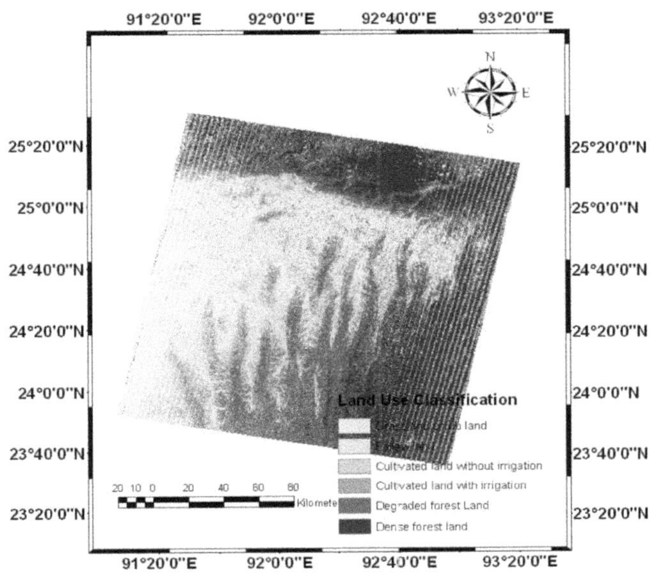

Source: GLCF image from ESRI Open Source Data.

IMAGE 10.3: LAND USE/LAND COVER OF BARAK VALLEY, AUGUST 2006.

areas that were earlier under forests or degraded forests have now been brought under cultivation though irrigation sources are not well developed. This means that the cropped area has increased. This also indicates that the population environment interaction has increased indicating higher population pressure on land as well as increase in total population. The degrading of the forest cover is attested to by the higher levels of siltation in the Barak River indicating

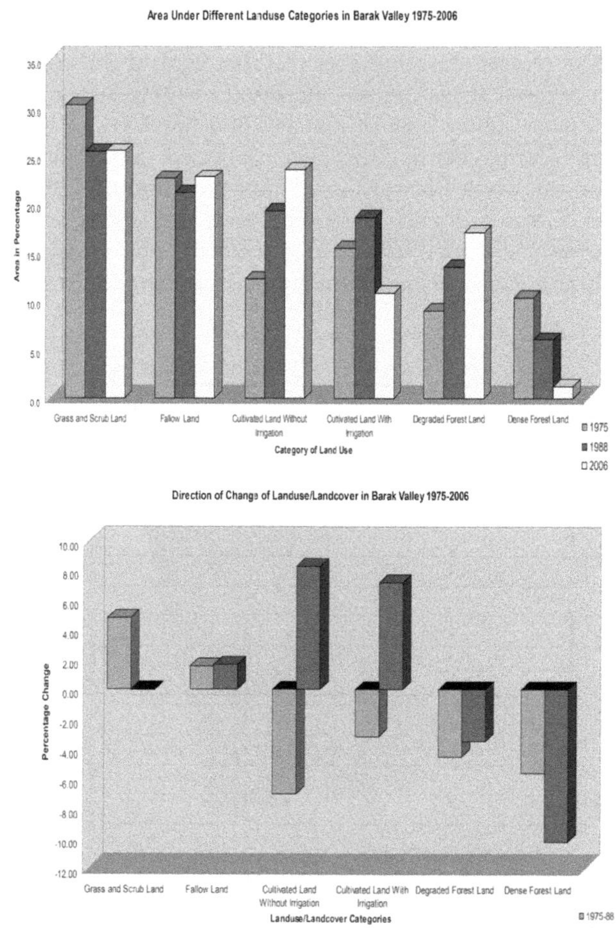

GRAPH 10.1: LULCC AND DIRECTION OF CHANGE AND AS VISIBLE IN THE IMAGERIES IN THIRTY YEARS OF THE BARAK VALLEY.

increased levels of soil erosion in the region. The cropping pattern has also changed in this imagery as evidenced by different types of crops present on ground rather than one or two crops that were visible in 1975. The changes that were visible in 1988 have now been concretized and show a compositely different picture of land use and land cover in the region.

That land use and the land cover change has occurred over time in the Barak River Valley is definitely shown by the imageries, the understanding of its resultant effect on the climate is difficult to say as yet. The total quantum of change in the different categories of land use and land cover as visible in the imageries spanning three decades is given below.

LULCC ANALYSIS OF THE BARAK VALLEY FROM ON GROUND STATISTICAL SOURCES

The imageries have shown a definite change in the land use and land cover pattern in the Barak Valley. The statistical analysis is the correlation of the analysis shown by the imageries covering a 35-year period from 1975 to 2010. Table 10.2 gives the percentage of different land use categories. The table clearly shows that land under non-agricultural uses have increased positively in a steady and enormously significant gain in percentage points which shows that human interference in the ecosystem has been immense in this time period. This is corroborated by the fact that the net sown area has increased whereas all the other categories show decline. The growth of area used for non-agricultural uses also supports the fact this region has witnessed enormous growth of population over the years. The anthropogenic interferences will have created scenarios of LULCC that will be affecting the climate of the region in differential manner over time.

The decline in the category of miscellaneous tree crops and groves as well as current fallows and fallows other than current fallows category also indicates that more land has been brought under cultivation denoting a change in the land use and land cover in the region. This is true of LULCC analysis which is said to be indicative of human, infrastructural and environment interactions at all levels. The increased pressure of population on land resources is also clearly visible.

It is also significant to note that area under forest and permanent pastures report slight decreases during the study period. The satellite imageries show that the dense forests that used to cover the mountain sides in the eastern part of the Barak Valley have now become degraded forests and the ruggedness index of the region has gone up. That the forests have deteriorated to scrub lands and lands used for cultivation without irrigation have increased over time during the study period is clearly visible in the imageries. The on ground evidence comes from the fact that fallow lands in all its categories show a negative growth trend.

The correlation of the data collected on ground as visible in the statistical data for the type of land use is and satellite imageries thus point to similar trends in the LULCC occurring in the Barak Valley region. The figures given below from Figures 10.1 to 10.3 also show the changes that have occurred in the land use pattern in the region for the period 1975-2010. Graph 10.2 shows the trend of change of the different categories of land use in the region in a composite manner for the same time period.

The indication that human pressure on land is increasing is also supported by the fact that fallow lands of all categories added together has decreased substantially over this period as seen in Table 10.3. This shows that land can no longer be left for fallow for any time period as pressure on it is too great indicating high population growth in the region.

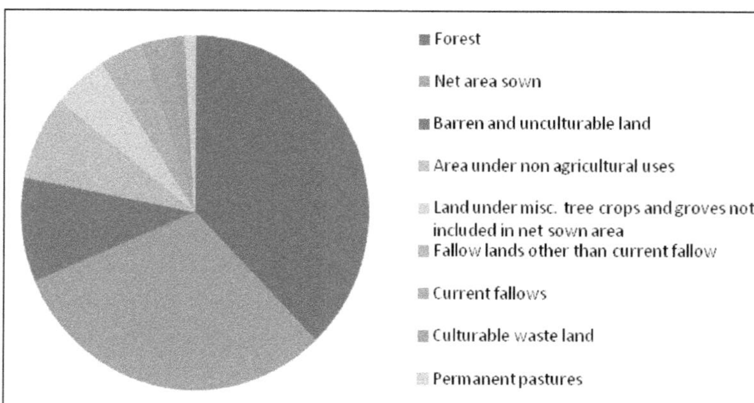

Source: Agricultural Census of India, Assam State, 1975-80, Ministry of Agriculture, Government of India, Computed from Table 10.2.

FIGURE 10.1: LAND USE IN THE BARAK VALLEY IN 1975-6.

TABLE 10.2: LAND USE – PERCENTAGE OF REPORTING GEOGRAPHICAL AREA

Year	*Forest*	*Area under non-agric. uses*	*Barren and uncultur-able land*	*Permanent pastures*	*Land under miscellaneous tree crops and groves*	*Culturable wasteland*	*Fallow lands other than current fallow*	*Current fallows*	*Net area sown*
1975-6	37.79	7.75	9.58	0.95	5.02	1.47	4.08	2.65	30.71
1980-1	38.40	8.70	9.42	0.90	4.35	1.15	2.80	3.25	31.02
1998-9	37.87	10.66	8.65	0.90	4.77	0.64	1.84	1.77	32.90
2000-1	36.82	11.90	8.64	0.90	4.75	0.64	1.71	1.52	33.13
2005-6	38.33	10.39	8.64	0.90	4.75	0.64	1.47	1.68	33.21
2009-10	37.16	15.02	5.53	0.90	3.80	0.64	0.96	1.00	34.98
% rate of change	-1.66	93.88	-42.26	-4.87	-24.23	-56.68	-76.41	-62.25	13.88

Source: Agricultural Census of India, Assam State, Ministry of Agriculture, Government of India, Statistics for the concerned years have been used.

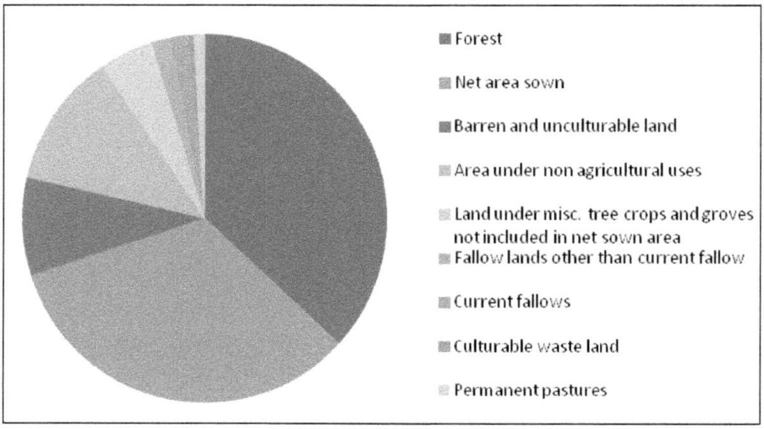

Source: Agricultural Census of India, Assam State, 2000-5, Ministry of Agriculture, Government of India Computed from Table 10.2.

FIGURE 10.2: LAND USE IN THE BARAK VALLEY IN 2000-1.

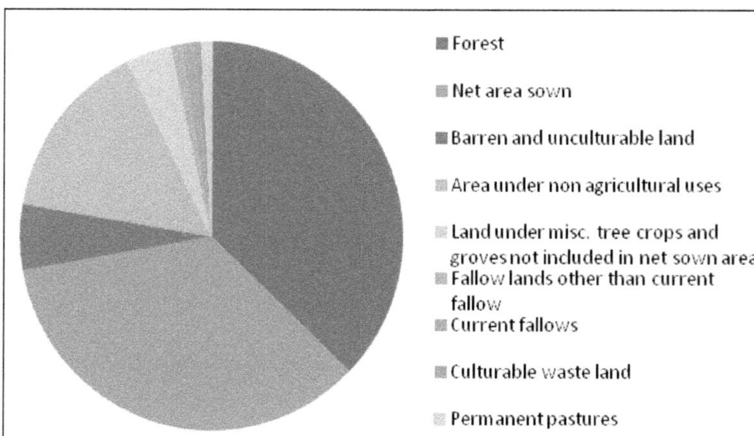

Source: Agricultural Census of India, Assam State, 2005-10, Ministry of Agriculture, Government of India, Computed from Table 10.2

FIGURE 10.3: LAND USE IN THE BARAK VALLEY IN 2009-10.

TABLE 10.3: TOTAL FALLOW LAND IN THE BARAK VALLEY

Year	*Total Fallow*
1975-6	6.72
1980-1	6.05
1998-9	3.61
2000-1	3.23
2005-6	3.15
2009-10	1.96
% rate of change	-70.84

Source: Data has been compiled from Table 10.2.

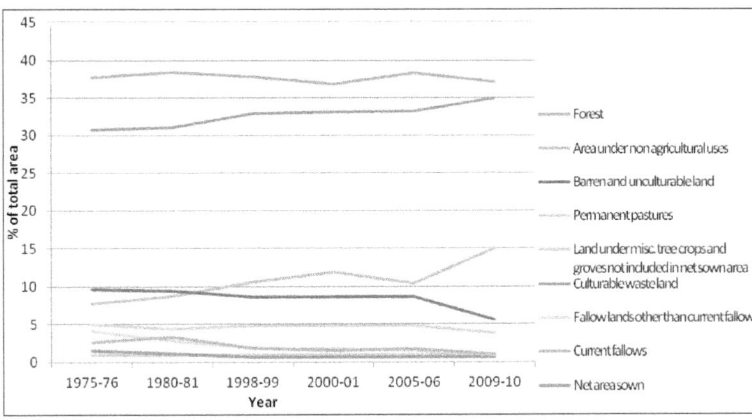

Source: Computed from Table 10.2.

GRAPH 10.2: CHANGES IN DIFFERENT LAND USE CATEGORIES IN THE BARAK VALLEY 1975-2010.

CHANGE IN CROPS AND CROPPING PATTERN AS LULCC ANALYSIS IN THE BARAK VALLEY

The growth of Net Sown Area in the land use change table is an important indicator of LULCC in the Barak Valley. This means that the growth of crops in the area has increased. The type of crop on the ground results in differential climatic conditions. An analysis of change in the crops that are grown in the Barak valley thus becomes important here. Table 10.4 shows the different crops and their areal coverage that have been grown in the area. This area traditionally used to be a subsistence farming area with rice as the major crop.

TABLE 10.4: CHANGES IN AREA UNDER SIGNIFICANT CROPS IN THE BARAK VALLEY

Year	*Rice*	*Tea*	*Other veg*	*Sugar cane*	*Betel nuts*	*Potatoes*	*Other pulses*	*Bananas*	*Rapeseed*	*Other fruits*	*Rubber*
1975-6	78.17	11.02	2.21	1.76	1.17	0.82	0.69	0.58	0.56	0.50	0.00
1980-1	77.21	11.21	1.89	2.28	1.62	0.97	0.54	0.49	0.63	0.49	0.00
2000-1	72.26	10.56	2.30	0.53	3.13	1.59	1.30	1.66	0.88	1.08	0.80
2005-6	68.39	10.17	7.37	0.28	2.76	1.28	2.12	1.44	1.12	0.92	0.76
2009-10	68.73	9.35	6.26	0.21	2.71	1.47	2.09	1.69	0.91	1.06	1.55

Source: Agricultural Census of India, Assam State, Ministry of Agriculture, Government of India, Statistics for the concerned years have been used.

TABLE 10.5: AREA UNDER TEA IN THE BARAK VALLEY (1975-2010)

Year	*% GCA under tea*
1975-6	11.02
1980-1	11.21
1998-9	9.86
2000-1	10.56
2005-6	10.17
2009-10	9.35

Source: Computed from Table 10.4.

The main cash crop was tea followed by sugar cane which had a small presence in the region. Other crops such as vegetables and fruits that form a part of the market gardening were present though minimal area was covered by them in 1975. Together rice and tea accounts for almost 80 per cent of the gross copped area in 1975, this is the combination that has seen the maximum decrease over time. Vegetables and potatoes show slow but definite gain in area covered over time. This indicates that the population living in the Barak Valley has increased leading to an increased demand for vegetables and potatoes. The increase in the acreage under betel nut is an indication of diversification of the cropping combinations being practised. The introduction of rubber in the region poses a challenge to the pre-existing cash crops in the region. The significance of the different crops is that they provide differential heat reflexive values, latent heat exchanges and water usage that are the integral components of climate change. The land cover change is therefore significantly captured by the changes in the crop acreage in any region.

Tea has been considered a strategic crop in that it slowly but significantly helps in changing the microclimatic conditions as well effecting changes in the soil conditions of the region. The slow decline in the area covered under tea indicates that micro-climatic changes are occurring as rubber is found to be replacing it as a plantation crop. Rubber and tea have differential soil, temperature and rainfall requirements showing that there has been a beginning of change in the climatic conditions wherever the change has occurred.

Weaver's method of crop combination analysis (Table 10.6) shows that the Barak Valley area has shifted from a monocropping regime to a ten-crop combination during the time period of the study. The region which used to be rice monocropping area till the 1980s has changed in the 1990s to a ten-crop combination including rubber

TABLE 10.6: WEAVER'S METHOD OF CROP COMBINATION FOR THE BARAK VALLEY 1975-2010

Year	*Crop combination*	*Crops and % area covered*
1975-6	Monocropping	Rice – 78.17
1980-1	Monocropping	Rice – 77.21
2000-1	8-crop combination	Rice – 72.26
		Tea – 10.56
		Betel nuts – 3.13
		Other veg – 2.30
		Bananas – 1.66
		Potatoes – 1.59
		Other pulses – 1.30
		Other fruits – 1.08
2005-6	9-crop combination	Rice – 68.39
		Tea – 10.17
		Other veg – 7.37
		Betel nuts – 2.76
		Other pulses – 2.12
		Bananas – 1.44
		Potatoes – 1.28
		Rapeseed – 1.12
		Other fruits – 0.92
2009-10	10-crop combination	Rice – 68.73
		Tea – 9.35
		Other veg – 6.26
		Betel nuts – 2.71
		Other pulses – 2.09
		Bananas – 1.69
		Rubber – 1.55
		Potatoes – 1.47
		Other fruits – 1.06
		Rapeseed – 0.91

Source: Agricultural Census of India, Assam State, Ministry of Agriculture, Government of India, Statistics for the concerned years has been used.

Note: Only crops with at least 1 per cent acreage to Gross Cropped Area have been taken into consideration.

as a crop with significant cropping acreage. This strongly indicated the increase in the population pressure on land as more and more types of crops are being grown to satisfy the demands of a growing population in the region also signifying agro-economic and agro-ecological change in most significant terms. The change in the crop

TABLE 10.7: HERFINDAHL'S INDEX (HI) OF CROP DIVERSIFICATION

Year	*HI*
1975-6	0.62
1980-1	0.61
2000-1	0.54
2005-6	0.49
2009-10	0.49

Source: Agricultural Census of India, Assam State, Ministry of Agriculture, Government of India, Statistics for the concerned years has been used.
Index Scale: HI of 1 = Complete Specialisation, HI of 0 = High Diversification

combination is important as it indicates that differential land use cover which will affect the climatic conditions as the linkages between land use land cover and the climate of the region will also change indicating the shift in the nature of the prevailing climate. This is a definitive indicator of a change in the major drivers of climatic conditions in the Barak Valley climatic region.

This is supported by Herfindhal's Index of crop diversification (Table 10.7) which shows a high value in 1975 and 1980 showing that there was specialization of cropping in the Barak Valley during that time period. From the 1990s onwards there is a decreasing value of the index indicating that the Barak Valley region is slowly over time moving from a situation of complete specialization to high index of diversification in its cropping pattern. This is also evident in the crop combination analysis given above as the combination increases from an eight-crop combination in 2000-1 to a ten-crop combination in 2009-10. For the cropping combination changes to have become significant means that the changes had started occurring during the 1990s. The similar kind of land use/land cover has changed to differential types, each with its own environmental and anthropogenic interactions. Thus, the climate of the Barak Valley will also vary from place to place in the region, though any particular trend to be termed as a trend needs to be studied in depth some more.

CONCLUSION

There is definite change in the land use/land cover in the region. There is evidence of increased deforestation in the region along with increased siltation of the water bodies. There has been a slow but steady change in the rainfall and temperature regime in the region from 1975 to 2006; temperature has been slowly increasing over the years accompanied by a decrease in the rainfall quotient. There has also been change in the relative humidity values over the different seasons in the region over the same period. It can be said that the climate in the region is displaying instability and flux conditions, which may be said to indicate the beginning of the process of climate change. Creating a holistic understanding of the process of land use change, the significance of variable land use decisions, and the manner in which these decisions are themselves affected by an increasingly variable climate are important to understand the dynamics of climate change. LULCC is a change in the climatic contours that does have long-lasting impacts on the climate system of an area which are required to be understood so as to plan mitigation and amelioration measures.

In addition to being a driver of Earth system processes affecting the climate, carbon cycle, and ecosystems, LULCC is a global change in its own right, requiring its own research foundation. This element provides the scientific underpinning for land use decision-making and projections of future land use, and has substantial benefits beyond climate change assessment and mitigation by supporting a wide array of issues important to users of this information. To meet multiple objectives, the LULCC research will address multifarious questions.

SELECT BIBLIOGRAPHY

Anderson, J.R. et al., 'A Land Use and Land Cover Classification System for Use with Remote Sensor Data', Geological Survey Professional Paper 964, Washington, DC: U.S. Government Printing Office, 1976.

Bhattacharjee, J.B., *Cachar Under British Rule*, Delhi: Radiant Publishers, 1977.

Csaplovics, E., 'High Resolution Space Imagery for Regional Environmental Monitoring: Status Quo and Future Trends', *International Archives of Photogrammetry and Remote Sensing* (1998), 32(7): 211-16.

Foody, G.M., 'Status of Land Cover Classification Accuracy Assessment', *Remote Sensing of Environment* (2002), 80: 185-201.

Gupta, R.P., A.K. Saha, M.K. Arora and A. Kumar, 'Landslide Hazard Zonation in a part of the Bhagirathi Valley, Garhwal Himalayas, Using Integrated Remote Sensing-GIS', *Himalayan Geology* (1999), 20(2): 71-85.

Johnson, Lynn E., *Geographic Information systems in Water Resources Engineering*, 2009, New York: CRC Press, Taylor & Francis Group.

Lillesand, Thomas M., Ralph W. Kiefer and Jonathan W. Chipman, *Remote Sensing and Image Interpretation*, 2004, 5th edn., rpt., New Delhi: Wiley India.

Munsi, M., S. Malaviya, G. Oinam and P.K.A. Joshi, 'Landscape Approach for Quantifying Land use and Land cover Change (1976-2006)', in *Middle Himalaya: Regional Environmental Change* (2010), 10(2): 147.

Saha, A.K., R.P. Gupta and M.K. Arora, 'GIS-based Landslide Hazard Zonation in the Bhagirathi (Ganga) Valley, Himalayas', *International Journal of Remote Sensing* (2002), 23(2): 357-69.

Sachs, J.D. et al., 'Biodiversity Conservation and Millennium Development Goals', *Science* (2009), 325 (5947): 1502-3.

Zhu, A.X., 'Measuring Uncertainty in Class Assignment for Natural Resources Maps Under Fuzzy Logic', *Photogrammetric Engineering and Remote Sensing* (1997), vol. 63 (10): 1195-1202.

CHAPTER 11

Rain, Rain, Come Again: History of Rainfall, Deforestation and Water Scarcity in Cherrapunji, the Rainiest Spot in the Globe

SAJAL NAG

At the beginning of the twentieth century, a major chunk of scientists believed that climates of the world had been essentially constant over at least five thousand years.[1] In the next eighty years the belief was demolished. But we still know far less about the possible effects of past climatic shifts on human activities.[2] Historians have given scant regards to this aspect until in the 1950s and 1960s a number of historians notably Gustaf Utterstrom, Fernand Braudel and Emmanuel Le Roy Ladurie showed some willingness to pay serious attention to the possible effects of climatic change in historical situations.[3] In a subsequent article on the 'History of Rain and Fine Weather', the *Annales* historian Emmanuel Le Roy Ladurie stated that, 'the aim of climatic history is not to explain human history nor to offer simplistic accounts of this or that remarkable episode not even when such episodes prompt us with good reason to reflect upon the great disasters of history . . . (these are merely) spin off of the history of climate'. Ladurie was concerned only with producing a 'clear picture of the changing meteorological patterns of the past ages' in the spirit of 'cosmological history of nature'. In this article we are not concerned with such cosmological history of nature but how climate had influenced the history of Cherrapunji, famed as the recipient of heaviest rainfall in the world and indeed reflect upon the environmental catastrophe that the place came to symbolize. Of course, even in that endeavour we have no pretension to offer conclusive explanation but like Ladurie, 'to supply the natural scientists – meteorologists, glaciologists, climatologists, geophysicists, etc., with archival material' as only a professional historian alone has the key to certain types of data hidden away centuries ago in bundles of illegible old documents.[4]

Indeed that a few drops of more rain can change the destiny of an otherwise non-descript hilly hamlet in remote north-eastern frontier of Indian subcontinent has been nowhere more evident than Cherrapunji, known to be the wettest spot on earth. Such was the power of colonialism that it explored every nook and corner of the globe, brought out its hidden wealth for drainage and left it barren and denuded after complete exploitation and exhaustion.

Cherrapunji is the name of a cluster of hilltop villages situated 51 km away from Shillong, the capital of Meghalaya. It is situated 25.15° north latitude and 91.44° east longitude and 1,330 m above sea level. The name Cherrapunji was actually a construction of the British. It was originally and still addressed by the local people as Sohra which was one of the twenty-five states of the Khasi tribe. It was ruled by an elected chief called Syiem. Sohra was mispronounced by the British as Churra, Ch standing for Sh. Punji was a word used by the Bengalis of neighbouring Bengal district of Sylhet denoting a tribal hamlet or cluster of villages belonging to non-Bengali tribal inhabitants. Sylhet district had several such tribes living within Sylhet like the Khasi, Garos, Kukis and so on. They were addressed as Khasipunji, Garopunji, Kukipunji, etc. Lying on the border of Sylhet they had regular trade commercial relations with each other. Although Sohra was not known to be Shora-punji, it is possible that while informing and directing the British about Sohra, the Bengalis of Sylhet addressed Sohra as a *punji* of the Khasis. The English therefore called it Sohra-Punji spelling it as Churra-punji. Cherrapunji was a later corruption of the same name as till the early twentieth century the British continued to call it Churrapunji.

The British were attracted to Cherrapunji because of its cool climate which was caused by the heavy rainfall it received. All along their colonial empire building endeavour the British had one major adversary: the oppressive tropical heat of the subcontinent. The history of Colonial India is replete with evidence that the British were continuously on the look out for hill tops and cool climate. The establishment of number of hill stations was a result of this. After the Anglo-Burmese War (1824) the British wanted to have a foothold in the north-eastern part of India as well. David Scott, the Agent to the Governor-General proposed to construct a road between the Brahmaputra Valley and Surma Valley to ensure reinforcement. The road had to go through the Khasi Hills even though it was not yet a part of the empire. Scott had an opportunity to reside in the hills while supervising the work. He stayed at Nongkhlaw where he was able to 'eat European air'. But soon the climate posed other health problems. It was during his search for an alternative to Nongkhlaw that he came across Cherrapunji. In fact, Scott was impressed with the climate of Khasi Hills in his first journey to the hills. He found that within six hours off Pandua, there 'was a climate probably superior to that of the Cape of Good Hope in point of coldness and healthiness. The mountains were full of green short grass and the elevation was upwards of five thousand feet'.[5] As far as Cherrapunji was concerned he found the place to be 'two days march in length and one in width was most to table-land- 5 to 6000 feet above sea level'.[6] So impressed he was with Cherrapunji that he was willing to exchange a portion of 'the bold and sterile land for a slice of fertile land below'.[7] He immediately recommended the establishment of a sanatorium in Cherrapunji for invalid soldiers and European Officers working in India for the recovery of their health. Cherrapunji was established as the headquarters of the region from 1831 to 1864 subsequent to which it was shifted to Shillong when the heavy rainfall not only caused health hazards but also inconvenience in executing the administration smoothly. A contemporary record reported,

> Such heavy rains produce extreme dampness which penetrates everything, causes severe soil erosion and floods as the water rush down to the plains. Tables, chairs, benches, etc. must be fixed with bolts. Otherwise they fall to pieces. Iron bolts cannot be used because they rust and become loose. Only wood and brass can be used. It is the same with nails. Shoe nails must be made of wood! Leather articles get mildewed and deteriorated. Books disintegrated and become discoloured. New books no longer new after a rainy season! Clothes, linen, bed sheets and blankets are always damp and have an unpleasant odour. One longs for sunshine in order to bring everything out into the open air to dry. Salt melts and medicines are spoiled. Flour and rice become lumpy unless they are cooled in air tight containers or kept in a heated room.[8]

In fact, the idea of a sanatorium in Cherrapunji also failed as though the inmates recovered their health here, due to excessive rain, gloomy climate and long-stay indoors they either became alcoholic or developed psychological problems. A missionary report recorded,

> The Government headquarters were shifted to Shillong in 1864 on account of the adverse effect which the humid climate and the incessant rains had

on the morale of the British soldiers stationed in Cherrapunjee. Under such trying conditions some even committed suicide.[9]

DISCOVERY OF THE WETTEST SPOT

The earliest reference to the rains of Cherrapunji was made by David Scott in May 1827. In a letter he wrote,

> We had a tremendous storm of hail a few days ago which if it extended so far must I fear have greatly injured our coffee crop. I collected a sufficient quantity to enable me to ascertain the rate at which ice melts and the result leaves no doubt as the feasibility of supplying Calcutta from Churrapunji. The contents of a small bucket weighing about 14 lbs and not exceeding eight or nine inches in diameter took about 40 hours to melt so that a mass of – in every direction would not be extremely consumed in less than about a month and as the voyage might by proper means be performed in fifteen days as sufficient portion of very cargo would reach the presidency.[10]

During one of his subsequent encounters with the rains of Cherrapunji he wrote again, 'We have had almost incessant rains and mists here since the 28th last (May 1827). This is a great drawback on the climate of the place . . . the quantity of rain that falls here in April and May must be at least ten times as much as they have at Nongkhlaw.'[11]

The conjecture about the quantity of rain that fell in Cherra was then begun to be scientifically measured by Mr. Cracroft, 'a gentlemen whose scientific attainment guarantee accuracy of observations which might otherwise appear questionable'. Cracroft commenced a series of observation from June 1832 to determine the actual quantity of rainfall that fell in Churrapunji. The result of is observations were as follows:

	Rainfall at (in inches)	
Months (1832)	*Churrapunji*	*Calcutta*
June	28.580	4.46
July	73.724	4.97
August	52.386	16.44
September	55.309	4.88
Two days on October	15.790	6.90
Total 4 months	225.789	37.45

On enquiry the rain in Cherra was found to be unparalleled in the whole globe. The nearest to this measurement was in Arracan where during the months of July, August, September and October 1825, it was 127 inches and that for the month of July only was estimated at about 70 inches more giving a total of 197 inches for those five months.[12]

This measurement was then compared with that of Malabar Coast, another place where it rains heavily. According to the recorded observation of Professor Forbes, the quantity that falls in a year in that area was 123.5 inches and even this comparatively insignificant quantity was in reality excessive. R.B. Pemberton than ascertained that the only instance that might be considered at all comparable to that of Cherrapunji was recorded by Humbolt in his personal narrative although even that is given in terms which clearly prove some degree of scepticism as to the accuracy of the observation.

Humbolt wrote, 'M Antonio Bernardino Pereira Lago Colonel of Infantry of the Crops of Engineers at Brazil, found that in the year 1821 there were rainfall of 23 feet 4 inches, 9-7 lines, English measure (latitude 2° 29′ South) only at San Luis Do Maranhao'.

He further added,

'We might be inclined to doubt this prodigious quantity of rain yet I am in possession of the Barometric, Thermometric and Ombrometric observation which M Pereira Lago affirms were made by him day to day at those different periods.'[13] These observers also found the reasons for such heavy downpour in Churra. 'If we look to the position of Churra, the extremely precipitated nature of the ascent by which it is attained, the two gigantic valleys of Bogapani and Pian Nullah, which penetrate far into the hills on either side of it. The vast extent and size of the inundations and rivers which deluge the plains immediately below it; the general direction of wind during the monsoon and the altitude at which clouds generally float in the air; it will appear less astonishing that this tract should be peculiarly exposed to the severity of such a discharge than that, the probability of it should have been altogether overlooked though the most experienced meteorologist would have found it difficult to believe that the quantity of rain should so far exceed anything before know, even in a district which like that of Arracan appears still more peculiarly liable to the region of south west monsoon.'[14]

In 1850 Botanist Joseph Dalton Hooker during his visit of Cherrapunji also recorded its rainfall. In his own words,

The climate of *Khasia* is remarkable for the excessive rainfall. . . . Dr. Thomson and I also recorded thirty inches in one day and night, and during the seven months of our stay, upwards of 500 inches fell so that the total annual fall perhaps greatly exceeded 600 inches, or fifty feet which has been registered in succeeding years. From April 1849 to April 1850, 502 inches (forty two feet) fell. This unparalleled amount is attributable to the abruptness of the mountains which face the Bay of Bengal from which they are separated by 200 miles of *Jheels* and *Sunderbunds*.[15]

But still it was not officially declared as the wettest spot in the world. The *Imperial Gazetteer* published in 1908 declared it as the wettest spot only in Asia. 'Cherrapunji is famous as having the highest recorded rainfall of any place in Asia. The annual rainfall averages 458 inches but in 1861 a total of 905 inches fell, of which 366 inches were received in the month of July. In 1876 nearly 41 inches of rain fell in 24 hours.' The cause of this heavy precipitation was also given: 'The Khasi Hills at this point rise straight from the plains and the south west monsoon blowing across the flooded tracts of Eastern Bengal and Sylhet is suddenly stopped by this barrier. The air, which saturate with moisture, rises, cools and is precipitated in the form of rain.'[16] The analysis was subsequently confirmed by modern-day meteorologists: 'Cherrapunji is one of the leading rain receiving places in the world. This is mainly due to its proximity to the towering Meghalaya plateau against which the moisture laden south western monsoon strikes resulting in heavy rainfall.'[17]

HISTORY OF RAIN IN CHERRAPUNJI

Once it was fairly established that Cherrapunji was indeed the wettest place on earth, there were frequent attempts to record the amount of rainfall by different individuals and agencies. Lieutenant Yule in his recording observed that during August 1841 during five successive days 30 inches of rain fell in 24 hours. The total rainfall was 264 inches for that month.[18]

In 1832 Cracroft had given the result of some observation for a few months of the year 1832 from which it appeared that in July of that year the rainfall was 73.724 inches. In August it was 52.386 and in September 55.309. From 1 to 8 October it was 15.790 making a total fall for 16 days of June, the whole of July, August, and September and eight days of October that is a total of 116 days of 225.789 inches. It was an enormous amount of rainfall but still trifling as compared to Yule's statement.

During 1851, Thomas Oldham who was the Superintendent of Geological Survey of India visited Cherrapunji to examine the geological structure of the hills and study the extent, mode and character of its mineral wealth. In course of his exploration he also indulged in meteorological study of Cherrapunji and even recorded day-to-day account of the rainfall for five continuous months. The instrument he used to record the rainfall was Barometer, Thermometer, Wet-bulb-Hygrometer and Pluviometer. While recording the rainfall Oldham had the previous observations of Yule and Cracroft in mind. Although he found the recording slightly 'incredible' it made him prepared for the result. Oldham was aided in his endeavour by Dr. Fayer, the Medical-in-Charge of the Station who carefully recorded the fall. According to Dr. Fayer's records the total fall during the earlier months of 1851 were:

TABLE 11.1: SIX MONTHLY RETURN OF RAINFALL IN CHERRAPUNJI IN 1851

January	.75 inches
February	3.05
March	1.30
April	31.35
May	114.90
June	148.53
Total up to 30 June	299.88

Dr. Fayers also recorded that in the month of December 1850 there was no rain at all. To all these old records, Oldham had his own observation from July to 13 November which added to a total of 592.425 inches. Oldham concluded that

It is certain therefore that these results give a very close approximation, if not a perfectly accurate return of the fall of rain during the year 1851 and thus amounted to five hundred and ninety two inches or to eight fathoms and a quarter of water for it to seems absurd to use a smaller unit in treating of such a enormous quantity. The greatest fall which took place during any one day and night or 24 hours was on the 2nd day of July when 25.485 inches fell between 9 o'clock on the 1st and 9 am on the 2nd. The next largest amount during 24 hours was on the 15th of September when 13.190 inches fell between 9 am on 15th march and 9 am 16th July. The largest continued fall of rain was during August when from 5th to 15th there was uninterrupted fall.[19]

In 1861, 905 inches of rainfall had been recorded, 366 inches of which occurred in July alone. The maximum for a single day was, however, recorded in 1876 when 41 inches of rain fell in 24 hours. It was observed that up to 1905 less than 5 inches of rain ordinarily fell in the four months of November to February and nearly 300 in the three months of June to August. Much of the rain, however, fell at night and the number of hours of sunshine was adequate.[20] In 1899 the annual average rainfall recorded in Cherra was 16,281 mm:

TABLE 11.2: COMPARATIVE RAINFALL AVERAGE RAINFALL IN INCHES

Months	*Shillong 34 years*	*Jowai 30 years*	*Maoflang 14 years*	*Cherrapunji 28 years*
January	0.49	1.07	0.87	0.74
February	0.81	2.04	0.69	2.69
March	1.85	6.30	1.93	11.08
April	4.29	10.46	4.81	32.24
May	10.06	26.18	11.41	51.53
June	16.46	66.15	32.11	105.21
July	13.48	43.94	30.00	109.49
August	12.79	34.74	21.10	76.50
September	14.75	31.66	21.10	53.25
October	6.23	12.69	8.73	13.97
November	0.98	1.44	0.47	1.49
December	0.25	0.75	0.28	0.23
Total	82.44	237.42	131.66	457.80

Although there was a record rainfall in Cherrapunji in 1861 (905 inches), it was broken by a rainy spell in 1974 when there was a rainfall of 961.7 inches (24,554 mm). The Catholic Mission was also given an official hydrometer with which the mission sent reports of the measurement of rainfall once a month to be published in the official gazette. It recorded that the average rainfall for past thirty years had been nearly 12 m (48′).[21] It also recorded that in some years when rainfall was more than 15 m. In the average, however, the annual rainfall in Cherrapunji for the ten years between 1968 and 1977 apart from the fall recorded in 1974 was about 11,897.5 mm. The total fall of rain for Shillong during the same year was 2,954 mm again the heaviest since 1962. At Upper Shillong the annual average was 1968 mm, at Mawryngkneng it is 2,238 mm, and at Mairang 2,743 mm.

THE CLIMATE STRUCTURE

Because of the considerable variations in altitude and exposure, there existed difference in climatic conditions within the Khasi Hills. The low-lying hills and foothills both in the north and in the south were observed to be as low as 50 m above mean sea level while the central range may attain while the central range could attain heights of 1900 m and above. The former have a largely tropical type of climate, with hot and humid summers and pleasantly warm winters. The high hills generally have a salubrious climate through most of the year. The winters can be very cold but since there is little precipitation of moisture during the season, snowfall is a rare phenomenon, the last recorded heavy fall being on 9 January 1899. Hoar frost however lies thick on the ground during the period between late November and late February. At higher altitudes the period may extend well into March and frost were occasionally seen in shady places even at midday. Available records of temperature and rainfall give the climatological tables of only a few places chiefly Shillong (25° 31′N, 91° 53′E; Alt 1500 m) and Cherrapunji (25° 15′N, 91° 44′E; Alt 1313 m).[22] The mean maximum air temperature for Shillong is 21.2 °C and minimum 12.1 °C. The highest temperature recorded during the earlier period was 30.70 °C observed on 2 May 1960 and lowest 2.8 °C on 8 January 1937 and 13 February 1950. Corresponding figures for Cherrapunji were 20.6° and 14.3°. The highest temperature recorded was 30.0 °C on 2 March 1913 and the lowest 3 °C on 16 January of the same year. The relative humidity at these two stations is 67 and 76 per cent respectively. The figures for Shillong recorded at 0830 hrs and 1730 hrs show the mean humidity as 70 and 81 per cent respectively for the period between 1971 and 1981. On the average March is the least humid month and August the most humid, the lowest humidity being in March 1979 (41-53 per cent) and the highest in July 1975 (93-97 per cent); July and August are normally the warmest months and January the coldest in Cherrapunji. The mean maximum air temperature for Shillong during the ten years ending 1979 was 21.6 °C and mean minimum temperature 13.5 °C; for the Cherrapunji during the same period the mean maximum temperature was 21.1 °C and mean minimum 14.7 °C. The temperature seemed to have markedly different from the colonial period to the post-colonial period. From the 1960s temperature had shown rising trend.

For the measurement of rainfall there were two centres during the British rule, one in Cherrapunji and the other in Shillong. Three others have been added in recent time. These are located in Upper Shillong, Mawryngkneng and Mawsynram, all of them in East Khasi

Hills. This is because Khasi Hills receives the heaviest rainfalls which require to be recorded. The Khasi Hills rise abruptly from the plains of Sylhet to act as a barrier to the rain bearing winds of south western monsoon causing them to rise and cool rapidly to be precipitated as rain. In other words Cherrapunji is situated in a strategic location at the head of (present) Bangladesh plains. The south-west monsoon strikes the margin of Cherrapunji-Mawsynram region as it rises abruptly from the plains. The vertical movement of the moist monsoon streams results in heavy precipitation in the escapement region. This type of rainfall is known as *Orographic Rainfall.* This explains why places like Cherrapunji and Mawsynram which are situated almost on the edge of the south facing escarpment received the heaviest amount of rainfall annually, while Shillong on the northern side of the central range has less than a quarter of that.

THE VANISHING RAIN

From the 1940s itself there was a lurking suspicion that that there was a decline in the annual average rainfall in Cherrapunji. It was mainly because of the fact that certain years turned out to be rainfall deficit and quite dry. The winter months were absolutely dry and water short. The streams were drying up and even during monsoon there were acute drinking water shortage. Despite the immensity of problem created by rains for the people, the withering away of the rain was not a welcome development. The receding rainfall meant that Cherrappunji was no more the famed wettest place. It was believed that a nearby village called Mawsynram – about 16 km from Cherrapuji was the new recipient of the heaviest rainfall. Meteorological observation thus began in Mawsynram from 1941 although no regular meteorological office was established there. In fact, the loss of importance of Cherrapuji as the administrative and industrial centre in 1864 had created such an indifference towards it, even the government showed little interest in its development, not to mention in its climate. It was evident from the fact that no regular monitoring of rainfall was done. Even when it was done there were frequent breaks in observation leading to the loss of vital meteorological data. In fact, that Mawsynram received as much rainfall as Cherrapunji was officially observed quite late much later in the 1950s. This was not only due to the use of more efficient ran-gauges but also apathy of the post-colonial state – both local as well as central, environmental concerns. The Colonial government as well as private geologist and climatologists like Thomas Oldham were interested in observing and recording climatic features of the area. It was the British government which established the rainfall measurement centre in Cherrapunji and armed with statistical details established and publicized Cherrapunji as the 'Wettest Spot of the Globe' for the meteorologists of the world.

The annual average rainfall in Mawsynram was calculated from 1941 to 1979 for the initial period. In this period the annual average rainfall was recorded to be 11,873 mm. For the same thirty-eight years Cherrapunji recorded 11,542 mm. There was a difference of 300 mm. The same difference was observed in that average of twenty-six years also. Even taking just the corresponding figures from 1948 to 1957 for which data were available for both places, Mawsynram with an annual average rainfall of 13,978 mm was ahead of Cherrapunji which recorded 12,611 mm.

Observation during the three years from 1975 to 1977 have only established the fact that the amount of rainfall in Mawsynram was quite heavy averaging 9,603 mm compared with Cherrapunji's 11,559 mm although in 1977 Mawsynram did receive 297 mm more. The meteorological facilities have rain defunct in Mawsynram since 1980. So it missed the monsoon of 1995 when Cherrapunji recorded the highest rainfall in a single day in the month of June. That day the rainfall in Cherrapunji was a whopping 1,563 mm. If the concept of average rainfall found deceptive one could compare the annual rainfall too in both the places. In the year 1997 Cherrapunji recorded 8,993.6 mm or rain whereas Mawsynram received 9,609.4 mm. The next

TABLE 11.3: ANNUAL RAINFALL IN SHILLONG WITH COMPARATIVE FIGURES FOR CHERRAPUNJI AND MAWSYNRAM FROM 1969 TO 1977[23]

Year	*Shillong Total*	*Highest (mm)*	*Lowest (mm)*	*Cherrapunji Total (mm)*	*Mawsynram Total (mm)*
1969	1,694.6	402.2 (July)	0 (Feb)	9,140	NA
1970	2,797.5	909.8 (June)	1.1 (Dec)	15,318	NA
1971	1,793.4	435.0 (June)	4.8 (Dec)	16,195	NA
1972	1,684.4	670.5	< 5 mm	NA	NA
1973	2,466.1	747.9 (June)	4.5 (Jan)	10,911	NA
1974	2,954.0	1,086.8 (July)	0 (Dec)	24,554	NA
1975	1,561.5	455.9 (July)	1.4 (Jan)	11,976	10,689
1976	1,461.1	408.2 (June)	2.2 (Jan)	11,012	6,134
1977	2,140.4	453.4 (May)	1.4 (Jan)	11,689	11,986

year the rainfall in both places took a huge qualitative jump to 14,536.9 mm in Cherra and 15,700 mm in Mawsynram. As far as the nature of rainfall is concerned, the daily rainfall was higher in Cherra but the monsoon lasted a bit longer in Mawsynram. Helping it tilt the scales and nudge past Cherra in the annual rainfall stakes.[24]

TABLE 11.4[25]: ANNUAL RAINFALL COMPARISON BETWEEN CHERRAPUNJI AND MAWSYNRAM (APPROX)

Year	*Cherrapunji*	*Mawsynram*
1992	11,000+	9,000+
1993	14,000+	12,000+
1994	11,000+	11,000+
1995	14,000+	14,500+
1996	13,000+	13,000+
1997	10,000+	9,000+
1998	15,600+	14,000+
1999	14,000+	13,000
2000	14,000+	13,000+
2001	12,000+	10,000+
2002	14,000+	14,000+

This is despite the fact that the annual rainfall at Cherrapunji ranges between 6,689 and 16,487 mm with an average of 11,276 mm during the period 1977-88. It was as high as 24,600 mm in 1974 and 22,987 mm in 1987. There had also been a change in the pattern of the distribution of rainfall. It had become less predictable. In the past the heaviest rainfall was invariably in June. In fact, the Khasi name for the month corresponding to June is Jylliew which meant 'deep'. As per oral testimony, during this period there used to be a long spell of ceaseless downpour at the height of the monsoon which the Khasis called *u slap khyndaisngi khyndai miet* or 'Rain of nine days and nine nights'. Such heavy and continuous rain has not been experienced in recent years. It is, however, not yet officially declared that Mawsynram is the recipient of highest rainfall in the world.

Soon afterwards another report indicated that neither Cherrapunji nor Mawsynram holds the record of highest rainfall anymore. The crown was now shifted to a new spot called Wailaleale which was in the Hawaii Island in the USA. Cherrapunji was accorded only a second place as per this report. The data collected from both the places demonstrated that the thirty-seven years average rainfall at Cherra was computed to be 11,161 mm against which Wailaleale had

11,684 mm. Mawsynram was not even considered for the comparison as it was not even known to be the recipient of any great rainfall. The rainfall in Mawsynram was not monitored in the nineteenth century at all as it came to the limelight only in the 1940s of the twentieth century. Both the British and Indian government considered Mawsynram a part Cherrapunji and it was only later that its separate location and identity was recognized in official circles. However, it continues to be neglected. Even now it does not have a regular meteorological office and the task of monitoring rainfall is done by the Public Works Department, that too rather infrequently. A comparison of the rainfall records of all the three spots however show that Mawsynram is still the recipient of highest rainfall in the world and not Wailaleale as claimed.

TABLE 11.5[26]: RESULTS OF RAINFALL BASED ON SHORTER PERIODS OF 26 TO 36 YEARS

Name of Place	*Altitude in metres*	*No. of years*	*Average highest rainfall in mm*
Mawsynram (India)	1,401	26	11,873
Wailaleale (USA)	1,548	32	11,684
Cherrapunji (India)	1,303	36	11,763

According to Whitaker's World of Facts, the heaviest annual average rainfall occurred in Mawsynram (India) which was 11,870 mm a year followed by Tutendo in Columbia with 11,770 mm of rainfall a year. But the record of greatest rainfall still belonged to Cherrapunji with 26,461 mm which took place during 1 August 1860 to 31 July 1861. the greatest rainfall in one calendar month was 9,300 mm which fell in cherrapunji in July 1861. The most rainfall in 24 hours took place in the island of Le Reunion in the Indian Ocean recording about 1,870 mm in 15-16 March 1952. The record of most rainy days in a year is with Mount Wailaleale, in Kuai, Hawaii, USA which was 350 days in a year total a rainfall of 11,684 mm which approached the annual rainfall record.[27]

Since then the spot of the rainiest place has shifted again to Lierro of Columbia. This has recently been established by the National Climatic Data Centre of the United States.[28] But Mawsynram continued to be the second rainiest place relegating Wailaleale to third place. Recently in July 2007 a group of international climatologists gathered in Mawsynram to study actual scientific causes of excessive rainfall in Mawsynram and Cherrapunji and the impact of climatic changes on annual rainfall pattern. They were of the opinion that global change in environment might cause tremendous increase in rainfall in the region. Climatologists Taichi Hayashi of Disaster Prevention Research Organisation based in Kieto in Japan felt that though it is an acknowledged fact that Cherrapunji is one of the rainiest spots in the globe with due impact on the neighbouring Nepal and Bangladesh, there have been no scientific research on the causes of such heavy rainfall so far. The scientist gathered there which include climatologists of the Polish Academy of Science, Warshaw as well Indian Institute of Science, Bangalore, were of the opinion that the instruments used in India to measure the rainfall and meteorological data were old and obsolete. In Mawsynram itself a class IV employee of the Public Works Department has been entrusted the duty of measuring rainfall who uses ridiculous method of rainfall measurement. The acute need is to gather scientific data based on modern state of the art measurement system of rainfall measurement for a proper analysis of the climate in the area.

CAUSES OF THE CRISIS

The fear of decline in rainfall was strengthened by the chronic crisis of drinking water in this spot of heaviest rainfall. It was a classic case of '*water, water everywhere, not a drop to drink*'.[29] In fact, recently environmentalists have begun to call it a '*wet desert*'. All the rainwater just drained away down to the plains leaving very little on the hill tops. The Khasis did not have any rain water harvesting tradition. It proved that Cherrapunji was not always short of drinking water supply and the shortage was a recent development. All the fresh sweet water that nature poured into it went waste. When monsoon disappeared the crises appeared acute. People could be seen descending down to the bottom of hills for natural water-springs to collect drinking water. It was because the population was only few thousands; otherwise the crisis could have deepened.

The drinking water crisis could be due to the decline in annual rainfall. The data showed that the rainfall did not really decline. On the other hand, it increased if not remained constant barring some dry monsoon years. In fact, there seemed to be a rise in rainfall in recent years though not evenly distributed if we compare the amount that fell during the past decades with that of the period between 1931 and 1960.[30]

TABLE 11.6: RAINFALL IN CHERRAPUNJI[31]

Year	*Annual Average Rainfall in mm*
1981	9,236.4
1982	10,467.9
1983	9,772.9
1984	16,673.5
1985	11,798.3
1986	8,132.4
1987	13,136.3
1988	16,021.8
1989	13,460.1
1990	11,598.3
1991	13,494.1
1992	8,536.5
1993	13,155.1
1994	11,190.8

The assigned reasons for the scarcity were that the soil was not able to absorb, retain and store the rain water that Cherrapunji received. The obvious cause was found to be large-scale deforestation resulting in loss of top soil in the absence of which there was nothing on the surface to absorb the water. What could have caused such vast deforestation within hundred years of British discovery of Cherrapunji?

It is of interest to mention that the British entered Cherrapunji in 1828 and a botanical report on the conditions of land in Cherrapunji written as early as 1837 found it already devoid of vegetation. William Griffith visited the hill in September 1837 and reported,

Cherra is situated in a plain surrounded in every direction by low rounded hills except to the east and southeast over which side there is deep ravine, the whole plateau rising considerably towards the north in the direction of Cherra itself. Ravine exists here and there along these and the water courses that the only woody vegetation to be found. The rest of the surface is clothed with grasses of which a number of species exist, they are chiefly Anthropogoneae. Two or three *osbeckias* exist; a *tradescantia* (*T. Septm Clanata*) covers certain patches with its bright blue flower. Three species of *impatens,* two with bright pink flowers are common *spathoglottis* and *Anthogomun* occur in the flat rocks which frequently prevail. Arundinaria is seen every where as well as *smithia* with lotus like blossoms. . . . The woody vegetation consists of Berberis, *Viburuum, Bucklamdia, Cleyera Floribus, Gragrantis, Petalis Sepalis Oppositis, Myrsine* and many others too numerous indeed to mention.

The woods towards Cherra assume that rounded and very determinate form which is seen so commonly in some parts of England. Bucks for instance. None of the trees arrive to any great size. The generality is low, rounded and stunted. It is in these that *Quercus, Vibrumum* and *Padamus* may be seen growing side by side.[32]

He later continued, 'The country immediate adjoining the cantonment is flat and there are rounded hillocks destitute of any covering but grasses and few, half shrubby plants. To the eastward there is a very deep and beautiful valley but this does not contain any large tree.'[33]

Robert Lindsay, collector of Sylhet in 1778 described the barrenness of the Cherrapunji hills even earlier and in most poetic words, 'The *Chunam* or lime rock is washed by rapid stream. A magnificent cataract was seen rolling over the adjoining precipice; the scenery altogether was truly sublime.'[34]

It is evident therefore that the deforestation in Cherrapunji was noticed by the colonial administrators very early even before it was established as the British headquarters. Therefore it is obvious that colonial interference in the local ecology which started in the eighteenth century was not the only reason for deforestation of these green hills. The Geologist Thomas Oldham explained the situation in the 1850s itself in the following terms:

It will not be easy for those who have been accustomed to investigate countries where the average fall of rain amounts to thirty to forty inches, distributed with tolerable equality over the whole twelve months to form a fair estimate of the immense force brought into play in these hills where the fall of rain in 24 hours is not infrequently two feet six inches or equal to the whole years fall in most places in Europe and where the annual fall not distributed over the twelve months but concentrated into four or five amounts to some fifty feet or six hundred inches.

I took an opportunity of visiting one of the streams in these hills after a heavy and sudden fall of rain. The water had then risen only about thirteen feet above the level at which it stood a few days previously, the rush was tremendous. Huge blocks of rock measuring some feet across were rolled along with an awful crashing almost as easily as pebbles in an ordinary stream. In the night a block of granite which I calculated to weigh upwards of 350 tons was moved for more than 100 yards, while the torrent was actually turbid with pebbles of some inches in size suspended almost like mud with the rushing stream.

To the denuding force of this heavy and sudden fall of rain is also due to the almost total absence of any soil in the flats of hills near the southern escarpment. All has in fact been washed away and a thin crop of coarse grass alone finds sustenance on the rocky surface. The marked absence of trees, the growth of which is cut off as with the axe along the edges of every flat is largely due to the same cause but also largely to the blighting storms which sweep over these hills. On the slopping sides of the valley trees grow abundantly and in many places grow luxuriously. There they are sheltered and abundantly supplied with moisture.

But this water-events is degrading not only on the surface of the flats or where in rushing over the precipitious scraps it excavates deep basin beneath, but it pours through the many fissures and clefts in the sandstone and limestone and springs from the solid face of the rock at different levels, tearing with it fragments of the hardest masses and precipitating them into gorges below.

The rapid degradation which these hills must undergo is well shown by the vast amount of suspended matter, which s carried down by the streams which in the drier weather were beautifully pellucid. So turbid and charged with suspended matter [these water bodies are] that a white card is invisible at the depth of one inch and a half, that is, through a stratum of water of that thickness. I have also measured the bulk of such sediments allowed to subside in a carefully divided tube and found it more than once to amount to one-fifth of the total bulk and in one case to very nearly one-third. In all cases this sediment was fine clayey sand. Taking these facts in connection with the enormous fall of rain, it will be readily seen how rapid must be the degradation and denudation of these hills.[35]

In this report Oldham reported that the denudation and deforestation of Cherrapunji was not recent. It was over time and gradual. The culprit was not human but nature itself. It was the heavy rainfall which carried off almost the entire top soil of the hills which was to hold the vegetation.

In the meantime heavy rainfall of the area, rapid waterfalls and swift flowing rivers has caused enormous damage to the already deforested area through erosion leading to complete degradation of the land. It has been estimated that up to about 40 tonnes of top soil per hectare per year may be lost in absence of soil conservation.[36]

There was some vegetation in isolated pockets almost like protected areas in parts of the hills. 'Some of the earlier records of rainfall, vegetation and soil, however suggests that the graminacious vegetation at Cherrapunji has not developed during recent past, rather climate, topography and geology of the area are responsible for the development of this type of vegetation.'[37] The layer of the top soil in these pockets was thick enough to hold vegetation. These islands of forests were like miracles. No wonder these were worshipped by the local people as 'sacred groves'.

It therefore appears that the topsoil was not washed away by rains everywhere. In some parts it remains fixed to the ground. The explanation of this also could be found in the Geological report of Oldham. It was the geological structure of Cherrapunji where the layer of top sol was not only thin; it was loose, rendering it vulnerable to washing away. Any shake of the earth or force of water could easily carry it off its ground. And the force of gushing rainwater was no ordinary force as we could read in Oldham's report.

Oldham explained in his report,

I shall very briefly enunciate a few of the principal conclusion resulting from general view of the previous description of the geological structure of these hills. These are: that the general basis of the range is granite resting upon is a series of metamorphic rocks, gneiss, inicaceous slate, quartz rock, etc. which have greatly altered, disturbed and contorted by the granite. Subsequently to these disturbances and alterations of the older states, these rocks have been subjected to long, continued and great wear and denudation and upon their degraded surface was deposited a series of sandstones and lime stones of varying character but in the aggregate of considerable thickness. Throughout the whole of this series from top to bottom in the conglomerates found at its base in the clean sandstones higher in the series, in the fossil found in these beds, in the irregularity of their development and the constantly repeated occurrence of current marking and 'false bedding, there is sufficient evidence to prove that the entire group, not less than two thousand feet in thickness has been deposited and formed in water of no great depth. The same evidence is extended by the organic contents of limestone. To admit of this occurring there must have been a gradual and continuous depression of the surface within this area, maintained during the deposition of the whole series. These sandstones have subsequently been invaded by other igneous rocks which have been forcibly intruded among them and produced great alteration in their texture and structure and have greatly disturbed their position. There is no evidence at which such intrusion took place, but must have been subsequent to the formation of all of the sandstones.

The whole series has been subsequently elevated until it attained its present position. There is no sufficient evidence to show whether this elevation or rather commencement of this elevation, was synchronous with or not or was caused by or accompanied by intrusion of the trap rocks. The elevation of the rocks to their present position must however have been gradual and long continued to admit of the remarkable conditions under which we found these beds as shown by the many, detached and small outlying portions of these rocks at considerable distance from the main mass.

Coincidentally with and subsequent to this elevation of the hills, en masse, the ordinary atmosphere causes of degradation, which owing to the peculiar climatic conditions of the district are here exerted with great force, have been in operation to produce and modify the present aspect of the surface. And further the action of these forces appears to have been determined as to the direction of its maximum effect by a series of lines of jointing and fracture and occasionally of dislocation or faulting, resulting from the earlier intrusion of the volcanic rocks.

The very gradual and continuous slope of the plains at the foot of the hills show that long subsequently to the period of their elevation, a sea had washed their base and leveled the widely extended flats from which their steep escarpment rise.[38]

The Cherrapunji hills are thus found to be formed mainly of limestone over which the top soil was laid. Because of the limestone base the top soil was thinly layered and loose which made it easy for any violence of nature to shake and uproot it. The perpetual and heavy rainfall for centuries was thus a calamity for the top soil and vegetation of the area. The other calamity which was an occasional visitor was earthquakes. The region is located in the seismographic fault zone and is liable to frequent upheavals. Other than regular, minor earthquakes some of the major earthquakes of the world have taken place in this fault zone. One was in 1875, others in 1897 and 1950. The earthquake that took placed on 12 June 1897 was a great destroyer. It was followed by 5,000 after shocks during the period 1897 to 1902. The result of this earthquake was a huge loss of the top soil from Cherrapunji area. Repeated shaking of the earth continued to make the soil loose to be carried down by the subsequent heavy rainfall. With it went the entire vegetation. Cherrapunji lost about 50,000 *sal* trees in one go by the 1897 earthquake which was an irreparable loss. The impact of other earthquakes have not been estimated but if effects of 1897 were any indication, successive earthquakes over the centuries had really devastated the vegetation and top soil of Cherrapunji. Its impact came to be seen only in the 1940s onwards.

Joseph Dalton Hooker, the environmentalist who visited Cherrapunji in early 1850 reported,

The scenery in (Churra) varies extremely at different parts of the surface. Towards the flat portion, where the English reside, the aspect is as bleak and inhospitable as can be imagined and there is not a tree and scarcely a shrub to be seen, except occasional clumps of Screw-pine . . . Westward the plateau becomes very hilly, bare and grassy. . . .'[39]

Like others he too linked it to the direct effect of heavy rainfall:

The direct effect of this deluge is to raise the little streams of Cherra about fourteen feet in as many hours, and inundate the whole flat; from which however the natural drainage is so complete so as to render a tract which in such a climate and latitude should be clothed with exuberant forest, so sterile that no tree finds support and there is no soil for cultivation of any kind whatsoever not even of rice.[40]

It appeared that the situation was as bad as a century ago. In other words the landscape of Cherrapunji did not differ markedly from what it was a century ago. Scientific studies at Cherrapunji demonstrated that,[41]

(a) The soil depth is poor and in several cases absent.
(b) The severe rains washed way the little soil that is available.
(c) Since plants are fixed and not able to move their growth and in fact very survival has been affected leading to the process of desertification.
(d) The biotic interference was unregulated for long period of time.

The surface of Cherrapunji is characterized by tracts of grasslands on highly drained flats and slopes of hills with small isolated patches of crooked forest occurring frequently in low lying areas such as along the streams and rivulets, and gullies and dykes of hillocks. Because sufficient water and nutrients are available throughout the year and effect of winter storm is less, tree growth is possible on these places.[42] The environmental scientists found that Cherrapunji had a huge barren area of grassy growth with an occasional tree of small girth here and there. This was linked by them to the periodic occurrence of fire in the area.[43] It is obvious it was the result of slash and burn cultivation (*jhuming*) practised widely by the Khasis. This practice requires slashing of jungles to clear fields for farming which was then burnt destroying whatever remained after slashing. The burning also kills the microbial population which provides the fertility to the soil. It therefore rendered the field barren for vegetation permanently. Since *jhuming* has been a centuries old practice, it has ensured the loss of forest cover enormously. Further, the local people rearing cattle had tired to obtain the fresh flush of edible growth which is highly palatable for cattle. This can be said to be true in case of Cherrapunji where there is occurrence of annual fires. At Cherrapunji burning of the dried vegetation during dry winter months (January-February) has been an integral component of the socio-cultural milieu of the people. The impact of fire on the eco-system is profound and its consequence are dependent on its intensity and frequency, proportion of bio-mass that is burnt, the onset of monsoon and total precipitation. The direct influence of fire on vegetation was the conversion of dried shoot and dead remains on the ground surface into ash and other combustion products. The extent to which organic matter is transformed into depended on a number of factors such as intensity and duration of fire, fuel load, moisture content in the fuel, weather and topography. After fire the nutrients locked in organic matter may (a) be deposited as ash on the soil surface; (b) held up as charred but not completely burned material; (c) lost to atmosphere through volatilization. At Cherrapunji, study of soil properties immediately after burning aboveground vegetation showed an increase of phosphorus and Cations and a decrease in Carbon and Nitrogen contents in the surface soil.[44] Rainfall that followed fire was of particular importance because it caused heavy loss of nutrients. At Cherrapunji a major portion of rainwater is lost from the system by way of run off and the loss of percolation through soil profile is relatively less important.[45] Besides these effects, fire seemed to be responsible for bringing about change in species composition of the community by causing death of those species which propagate mainly through seeds.[46]

The modern-day environmental scientists explained,

> Besides these natural environmental factors, cutting of trees and frequent burning of grasslands by local people during later winters, before the onset of monsoon have also contributed substantially to the degradation of land and vegetation at Cherrapunjee. On account of these activities and hilly terrain, major part of rain water is channelised though overland flow causing heavy sediment and nutrient losses. Coal and limestone mining and change in land use pattern due to unprecedented rise in population have also accelerated the pace of degradation of natural resource of the entire southern parts of Shillong plateau including Cherrapunji.[47]

What proved damning for Cherrapunji, after devastation there have been no efforts at eco-restoration. Cherrapunji was thus a calamity resulted by the combined efforts of men, nature and tradition.

COLONIAL DRAIN OF WEALTH

Geologist Thomas Oldham's trip to Cherrapunji in 1851 was not an innocent academic exercise. He had to gone to survey the reported mineral wealth which was already being mined and exported by the

European traders from the Sylhet frontier. There were very large deposits of limestone in Cherrapunji. Besides there were other mineral deposits like coal, granite, iron and petroleum. Even before the British formally conquered the Khasi hills they had begun to trade the Khasi limestone and iron. The Khasis of Cherrapunji themselves were living off crude mining of lime and iron and trading them in Sylhet traditionally. From the earliest days of British rule the lime quarries of the Khasi hills formed one of the principal attractions of Sylhet.

The lime trade drew a large of number of Europeans to that district and it is to the indiscretions of these persons that some of the earlier Khasi forays were attributed. Robert Lindsay, collector of Sylhet in 1778 was largely interest in business and he described the source of his wealth to the limestone of Cherrapunji. He said 'The Mountains was composed of the purest alabaster lime and appeared in quantity equal to the supply of the whole world'.[48]

Of the trade of Sylhet district he observed that,

The only great staple and steady article of commerce is Chunam or lime. In no part of Bengal or even Hindustan is the rock found so perfectly pure or so free of alloy, as in this province. Therefore Calcutta is chiefly supplied from here. This branch immediately attracted my attention and I was led to investigate how far the trade could be improved or extended. I found it had hitherto been occupied by Armenian Greeks and Europeans. But to a trifling extent only. While I had so greatly the advantage over them from the command of the currency, that It was evident, the trade might soon centre with me and it accordingly did so.[49]

Lindsay's business experienced some vicissitudes owing to the violent conduct of the Khasi Chiefs but limestone no doubt contributed largely to the fortune that he was able to accumulate in Sylhet. At the end of the eighteenth century the lime trade of Sylhet-Cherrapunji passed into the hands of the Inglis Family (Inglis and Co.) who enjoyed the monopoly over it for many years. The founder of the firm was George Inglis who died in Chatak in 1850 after a residence of fifty-six years in the district. He was succeeded by his son Harry Inglis who also had the absolute monopoly of lime trade for sometime. In 1858, W.C. Allen, a Commissioner of Revenue complained of excessive price of limestone due to the practical monopoly enjoyed by Inglis and suggested abolition of that monopoly. The government then decided to reserve one quarry for departmental operations. Three years lease of the remaining quarries were to be put up for auction subject to the provision that no more than three quarries were to be held by the same interest that quarries which were not worked could be resumed. The experiment did not, however, work as Inglis and Co. arranged to purchase the whole of the output of the lessees and thereby retain its monopoly. A system was then thrown open to the general public and royalty levied at the rate of Rs. 20 per 1,000 maunds of stone exported. Half the royalty was taken by the Syiem of the area. The lime quarries were situated all along the southern face of the hills from Lubha River on the east to the Maheshkhali River on the west. During 1876-7 the estimated export was 16,00,000 maunds valued at Rs. 4,80,000.[50]

Petroleum was found in the valley of Khasimara River on the southern border, little west of Shella. G.L. Garth was licensed to draw petroleum from this field from 1902. Coal also occurred near the top of the isolated ridge between Cherrapunji and Maomluh. It was first worked in 1840 by Captain Lister, the Agent for the Peninsular and Oriental Company. Next year Messers Gisborne and Co. took over for two years. In 1851 they transferred their rights to Moran and Co. Between 1850 and 1855 about 5,100 tons of coal was extracted. The coal had found ready sale at Dhaka and elsewhere at 8 annas for maund. The average quantity exported into Benal was about 25,000 maunds valued at Rs. 12,500. Even when the trade died out by 1866-7 the export was of 2,956 maunds.[51]

Then there was iron which was found in the form of fine sand, consisting of minute crystals of *titaniferous magnietic oxide* which were found in large deposits near Mylliem, Laitlyngkot, Nongkrem and so on. It was carried to other parts of Khasi hills for smelting. The iron export in 1858 alone was 45,000 maunds.[52] Such enormous mining pursuit which was unscientific and anti-environment was largely responsible for the rest of the deforestation, soil erosion and conversion of vegetation into unproductive wastelands. Meteorologists assert that it is the forest that plays a vital role in impelling the clouds to cause rainfall. In the absence of adequate forest cover weaker monsoon winds were hardly impelled to cause rainfall and this was one of the reasons for the reduced average annual rainfall. Thus the violence on Cherrapunji was not just by nature but also by greedy and unsympathetic colonialists.

CONCLUSION

Cherrapunji was a sleepy hill top village in the remote north-eastern frontier of India. The colonial search for a cool place suitable for European sensibilities led to its discovery. In course of their stay the

British also discovered that it was the wettest place on earth receiving the heaviest amount of rainfall. But the rainfall proved to be too hazardous to run administration smoothly. The British therefore abandoned Cherrapunji and escaped to the safety and serenity of Shillong. But by then their agents had ripped open the heart of Cherrapunji and took away the last of its mineral wealth and left it barren and waste. It proved ruinous for a place whose geological and climatic pattern had already ravaged its vegetation. A time came when the European colonialists, traders, miners and speculators and their agents and collaborators all left. The only thing left were the Khasi tribals and their rain in Cherrapunji. The Europeans had done one thing; they made Cherrapunji famous by announcing it to be wettest place in the globe. The publicity attracted a steady stream of visitors, scientists and tourists to the spot to witness the rainfall. With no farming possible in this barren land, and saddled with exhausted mines, rainfall soon emerged to be the only industry in Cherrapunji. They virtually lived off the rain. The revenue earned from the visitors who came to see the rain was one of the major sources of their livelihood. But with rumour of dwindling rainfall and Mawsynram turning out to be the new wettest place this source of livelihood too was threatened. All they could do was hope and pray for the rain not to go away.

NOTES

1. H.H. Lamb and M.J. Ingram, 'Climate and History', *Report on the International Conference on Climate and History, Climatic Research Unit, University of Norwich, England, 8-14 July 1979*; also reproduced in *Past and Present*, no. 88, 1980, pp. 136-41.
2. Ibid.
3. Gustaf Utterstrom, 'Climatic Fluctuation and Population Problems in Early Modern History', *Scandavian Economic History Review*, no. 3, 1955, pp. 3-47; Fernand Braudel, *The Mediterranean and the World in the Age of Phillip II*, trs. Sian Reynolds, 2 vols., London: University of California Press, 1972, vol. I, pp. 267-75; Emmaneuel Le Roy Ladurie, *Times of Feast, Times of Famine: A History of Climate Since the Year 1000*, trs. B. Bray, London: N.J. Doubleday, 1972.
4. Emmanuel Le Roy Ladurie, 'History of Rain and Fine Weather', trs. Ben and Sian Reynolds, in Maurice Aymard and Harbans Mukhia (eds.), *French Studies in History*, vol. 1: *The Inheritance*, Hyderabad: Orient Longman, 1988, pp. 192-214.

5. *Bengal Secret and Political Consultations, 2 April 1824, nos. 16 and 10. Scott to Swinton, 21 and 24 March 1824*, C. Baker, *History of the Catholic Missions in North East India*, Shillong: Vandrame Missiological Institute, 1980, p. 280.
6. Ibid.
7. Ibid., he later retracted his word 'sterile' when its mineral wealth was discovered.
8. C. Becker, *History of the Catholic Missions in North East India*, Shillong: Vandrame Missiological Institute, 1980, pp. 201-2.
9. Ibid., p. 208.
10. *David Scott to Lamb, 8 May 1827.*
11. Ibid., *10 June 1827* cited in R.B. Pamberton, *Eastern Frontier of India*, Calcutta, 1835, rpt. Delhi: Mittal Publishers, 1979, p. 247.
12. W. Cracroft, *Transaction of Medical and Physical Society Journal*, vol. III, cited in Pemberton, op. cit., p. 248.
13. Cited in Pamberton, op. cit.
14. *Humboldt's Personal Narrative*, vol. 6, cited in Pamberton, op. cit., p. 249.
15. Joseph Dalton Hooker, *Himalayan Journals: Notes of a Naturalist in Bengal, The Sikkim and Nepal Himalayas, The Khasia Mountains etc.*, vol. II, London: John Murry, 1855, Indian rpt. Delhi: Today and Tomorrows Printers & Publishers, 1980, pp. 283-4.
16. *Imperial Gazetteer of India*, Govt. of India, 1908.
17. E.P. Philemon, *Cherrapunji: The Arena of Rain*, Gauhati: Spectrum, 1995, p. 3.
18. Lt. Yule 'Notes on the Khasia Hills and People', in *Journal of the Asiatic Society of Bengal*, vol. XIII, p. 612.
19. Thomas Oldham, *On the Geological Structure of Part of the Khasi Hills*, Calcutta: Govt. of India, 1854 (Appendix).
20. B.C. Allen, *Gazeteer of Khasi Jaintia and Garo Hills*, Shillong: GSI, 1905, p. 30.
21. C. Becker, *History of the Catholic Missions in North East India*, Shillong: Vandrame Missiological Institute, 1980, pp. 201-2.
22. The data above are based on observations made between 1931 & 1960 and between 1971 & 1981.
23. *Megahalya District Gazetteers: Khasi Hills District*, ed. I.M. Simon, Shillong: Govt. of India, 1991.
24. Govt. of India, Meteorological Reports cited in Binoo K. John, *Under a Cloud: Life in Cherrapunji, the Wettest Place on Earth*, Delhi: Penguin, 2004, pp. 135-6.
25. Data collected from Shillong Science Centre, NEHU Campus, Shillong.
26. *Mausam*, Meteorological Journal of Govt. of India, New Delhi, no. 43, 3 July 1992.
27. Russel, *Whitakers World of Facts*, Delhi: Penguin, 2007.

28. Reported in *Dainik Jugashankha*, Guwahati, 23 July 2007, under the caption 'Meghalaye Oti Borshoner Karon Khotiye Dekhte Antorjatik Bigyanidr Bhir'.
29. There was a moving documentary film on the water crisis of Cherrapunji by Chidananda Dasgupta as well as Ecologist P. Ramakrishna of Jawaharlal Nehru University, New Delhi.
30. *Meghalaya Gazetteer*, op. cit., p. 27.
31. The Indian Meteorological Department, Regional Office Guwahati, reproduced in *The Sentinel*, 10 October 1994.
32. W. Griffith, *Journals of Travels in Assam, Burma, Bootan and Afghanistan*, 2 vols, Calcutta: Bishop College Press, 1847.
33. Ibid.
34. Lord Lindsay, *Lives of the Lindsays or Memoir of the House of Crawford and Balcarres*, vol. III, London, 1849.
35. Thomas Oldham, *Memoirs of the Geological Survey of India*, Calcutta: GSI, Govt. of India, vol. 1, part I, p. 174.
36. D.N. Borthakur, 'Eco-Restoration of Cherrapunji Plateau', in B.K. Tiwari and Surendra Singh, *Ecorestoration of Degraded Hills*, Shillong: Kaushal Publication, 1995, pp. 3-8.
37. R.S. Triparthi, Uma Sankar and H.N. Pandey, 'Present Status and Strategies for Ecorestoration or Degraded Ecosystem at Cherrapunji', in B.K. Tiwari and Surendra Singh, ibid., pp. 23-50.
38. Oldham, op. cit., vol. I, part II, p. 168.
39. Hooker, op. cit., p. 279.
40. Ibid., p. 284.
41. B.S. Corrie, 'Eco-Restoration Technologies: A Basic Approach', in B.K. Tiwari and Surendra Singh, op. cit., pp. 13-21.
42. Triparthi, Sankar and Pandey, 'Present Status and Strategies for Ecorestoration or Degraded Eco-system at Cherrapunji', op. cit., pp. 23-50.
43. Ibid.
44. S.C. Ram and P.S. Ramkrishnan, 'Vegetation, Biomas and Productivity in Serial Grassland of Cherrapunjee in North-Eastern India', in *Vegetatio*, vol. 84, 1988, pp. 47-53; S.C. Ram and P.S. Ramkrishnan, 'Hydrology and Soil Fertility of Degraded Grassland at Cherrapunjee in North Eastern India', in *Environ.Conserv*, vol. 15, 1988, pp. 29-35 cited in ibid.
45. Ibid.
46. Ibid.
47. Ibid.
48. Lindsay, op. cit.
49. Ibid.
50. W.W. Hunter, *Statistical Account of Assam*, vol. II, Calcutta, 1879; rpt., Guwahati: Spectrum, 1998, p. 234.
51. Ibid.
52. Ibid.

CHAPTER 12

Challenging Times, Challenged Body: Decolonization, Displacement and Disease among East Pakistani Refugees in South Assam, 1947-1954

BINAYAK DUTTA

Authoring the official History of Relief and Rehabilitation Programme of the Government of India, post-1947, U. Bhaskar Rao, observed:

> For many years past it has been the fashion to speak of the refugee from East Pakistan as a creature apart. Often he is held up as an object of derision and contempt, where his counterpart on the west is sung of in paeans of praise. Yes, the comparison does not flatter him. He is dubbed a bundle of apathy impervious to the rehabilitation effort bestowed upon him. And the severer critics proclaim, he is rebellious and obstructive. Yet, how thoughtless and cruel all such comment is. It hardly takes into account the peculiar lineaments of the eastern tragedy.[1]

This initial paragraph of the much quoted text, sets the tone for any discussion on the life and living conditions of the East Pakistani refugees in eastern India, who had come into those areas which formed part of the Indian dominion to escape varied forms of persecution in East Pakistan after the Partition of India. Though official estimates, built up through census enumeration and registrar procedures, put the tally of East Pakistan refugees in Assam at about four hundred thousand,[2] it is now popularly admitted that these figures are contested and the actual number of refugees in Assam was much higher. South Assam, especially Cachar had to bear a major brunt of refugee rehabilitation, in view of its close cultural and religious affinity with the neighbouring areas of East Pakistan. However, in spite of a continuous stream of refugees coming into this area, there was very little initiative and innovation, among the representatives of the Indian state to ensure these refugees adequate and hygenic rehabilitation. The result of such lackadaisical approach was the conversion of refugees and their camps into fertile grounds for disease and epidemics resulting in large-scale mortality. This paper, in light of the above assertion, seeks to argue two major points. In the first case, it seeks to establish connectivity between improper and inadequate rehabilitation measures and human health and mortality. In the second, it seeks to critique post colonial relief and rehabilitation policy of the Government of India between 1947 and 1954. These dates are not comprehensive points of closure but signposts, adopted for the convenience of research; the first being the Partition of India and the second being the year of the Third Refugee Conference of Cachar, which was held on 8 and 9 November 1954.

DECOLONIZATION AND DISPLACEMENT

Though Cachar had its 'own culture, tradition and history',[3] there was little doubt that in case of Partition of India and the displacement of people, thereafter, it would play an important role in the process of rehabilitation.[4] It was therefore a matter of little surprise that Hindu refugees from East Pakistan chose to migrate to Cachar, an area acknowledged in official circles also as a predominantly Bengali district.[5] A non-official report of the situation also echoed similar strains of thought while observing that,

> Herein this district of Cachar, bordering Eastern Pakistan, the refugee problem is as old as Noakhali riots in 1946 whence influx of refugees started. Then came the partition in 1947 on August 15, since when Hindus from East Bengal districts of Pakistan have been, as if, in a ceaseless flow of stream coming to Cachar.[6] The political situation in East Pakistan was extremely hostile to the religious minorities, who found their life and property endangered in an 'Islamic state'.[7] Officials and ministers who were close to the Prime Minister were also aware of this situation and was candid in their reports that, the policy of the Government of Pakistan, notwithstanding its official rhetoric of safeguarding minority lives, was to ensure that non-Muslims do not live or stay back in the newly created state.[8]

Official Reports on displacements and refugee rehabilitation was candid about the perception of horror that had crystallized into the minds of the Hindu displaced, who had left their ancestral homes in East Pakistan and moved into the refugee camps in the Indian union. Discussing the same U. Bhaskar Rao, noted that, 'The horrors of Partition had been burnt into their memories, nothing could lure them back to the hell whence they had escaped with the skin of their teeth'.[9]

The response of the Pakistani authorities were extremely hostile towards the Hindus who constituted the minority in the new state of Pakistan. U. Bhaskar Rao, in his *The Story of Rehabilitation* observed, 'If we are to go by Pakistan's behavior patterns, not perhaps until every one of the original 12 million Hindus in that region had been driven out, not until the protagonists of the two nation theory have accomplished their dream of an exclusive Islamic state,[10] would the Pakistani state rest in peace.'

In these circumstances, the Government of India officials were candid about the fact that, if they were to go by Pakistani behavioural patterns, the situation was ripe for a large-scale exodus of population to the Indian dominion. It was acknowledged by Sri Prakash the Governor of Assam himself that, in view of the growing tension, the Indian government had to be prepared for, 'further and more exodus of Hindus from East Bengal'. In the report that Sri Prakash sent to Ajit Jain and to Nehru, he pointed out that, 'There are 45 lakhs of Hindus in the East Bengal districts contiguous to our borders on Assam; and any day they might be moving. . . . I have personally no doubt that most of them will come away. . . . And that we shall have to be prepared to receive them.'[11]

The apprehensions of officials came true and since 1947-8, i.e. immediately after the Partition of India, the minorities of East Pakistan were steadily displaced from their homeland. The critical situation was ably summed up in a non-official report from Cachar which recorded, that, 'This district was for the matter of fact over-flooded by refugees: refugees and refugees everywhere in the district sheltered in school and college buildings, other public and private houses, railway stations and even in open air tents'.[12]

In spite of early warnings, the Indian state was unprepared to meet the refugee crisis in the east, especially south Assam. Notwithstanding warnings such as, 'I fear I cannot indulge in any wishful thinking that it will not be so',[13] no proper planning for the relief of these refugees could be made in these areas. The authorities were at one level clueless and at the other helpless to plan a definite relief and rehabilitation programme. Meher Chand Khanna, the Relief and Rehabilitation Minister, Government of India was very forthnight when he observed, 'we will try to provide for the four million here. . . . The only trouble is that I am never sure that four million is the final figure. Our planning is at the mercy of the Pakistan Government. . . . What are we to do?'.[14] It is statements such as above which exposed the lack of preparedness of the Indian state to meet the problems of refugee relief and rehabilitation. While uncertainty of the actual numbers of refugees made planning an uphill task, the linguistic antagonism between the Assamese leader of the Congress who formed the government in Assam and the Bengalis (who were the predominant community in south Assam and the refugees who were streaming into Cachar) made matters worse. Cachar had to alone shoulder one-third of the total refugee population that had trooped into Assam. This is only going by the official statistics, though unofficial sources reported the presence of about 4,00,000 refugees in Cachar alone. It is this combination of lack of preparation at the level of the government and the linguistic and ethnic antagonism at the level of the state and the people that made Refugee rehabilitation of the displaced a non-starter from the very inception. As a result, the central authorities were clueless and the state government of Assam left the refugees at lurch to rehabilitate them by 'clearing available forests' and lands which were essentially unhabitable and 'unsuitable for occupation'.[15]

Reports on the refugee situation often described the sordid living conditions and the failing health of the refugees residing in the refugee camps. There were three types of refugees in Cachar. In the first category were those who resided in the refugee camps since their displacement in 1947-8. In the second category were those who resided in the Indian Tea Association rehabilitation camps and in the third category were those who made their own arrangements to stay in Cachar (non-camp refugees). This study makes an attempt to study the fate of all the catagories of refugees in Cachar. While the refugees were pouring in almost everyday, those already existing in the camps were succumbing to the vagaries of nature and disease which were breaking out almost on a daily basis. While starvation deaths were common, epidemics broke out in almost every camps in Cachar and Karimganj. Disease like malaria, typhoid and pox were common disease which themselves were reflected deplorable condition of refugee life. Disease were one of the biggest killers in refugee camps in Cachar and Karimganj. The local press, regularly carried reports of the deplorable living conditions prevalent in the camps. *The Chronicle*, published from Silchar, noted with concern that, 'Reports of heart rending misery arising out of disease, starvation and death of the displaced Persons from all the corners of the district of Cachar was daily pouring in. . . .'[16]

The epidemics that broke out in the refugee camps were a result of non-availability of clean drinking water, lack of proper drainage and sanitation. In the Duhalia camp which was a part of the Karimganj sub-division, there were reports of outbreak of Malaria in the colony.[17] Pox epidemics broke out in the 'Manipuri Bustees' in areas adjacent to the Duhalia Refugee Hills Colony. While epidemics were rampant, there were no medical facilities, and reports in the local press were extremely apprehensive about the future of the people living in the camps. One of the local newspaper pointed out that, 'It is feared that if this state of things continues, all the refugees at Duhalia will be swallowed up in the belly of death. Same is the condition of other colonies. It is high time to provide emergency relief and to invite Red Cross units or havoc overtakes the district.'[18]

Officials of the provincial and central government fought while the displaced battled for life, with death being a daily experience in the refugee camps.[19] The memorandum submitted to A.P. Jain pointed out, 'There is at least one death in average daily. . . .'[20]

Instead of providing relief to the dying displaced people residing in the camps, the officials were more interested in a game of one up man ship. Sri Prakash in his report to Pt. Nehru explained the helpless situation as he witnessed during his visit to Assam in 1950. At page 3 of his report he observed, 'Mr. Chatterjee was constantly at pains to tell me that the work in Cachar was very much better than the work in Goalpara or Kamrup which we visited. The officer of the Assam government were equally keen to assure me that their work was as good as, if not better than, the work done in Cachar.'[21]

DISPLACEMENT AND DISEASE

It is now fairly well established that quality of human life, health and mortality is dependent in his relationship with his environment, which plays a very important role in determining how human beings behave, relate to one another and organize themselves.[22] In this context it is pertinent to agree with a historian who has very aptly summed up that 'Epidemic disease are more often than not functions of environmental decay and ecological disruption'.[23] By 1950, the inflow of refugees were such that the post-colonial state was left with little choice but to engage in large scale efforts at refugee relief and rehabilitation. Serious differences of opinion between the state government and the central government officials led to the central government directly taking over the relief and rehabilitation programmes to be undertaken in Cachar, while the refugees' rehabilitation in the rest of the State of Assam was the responsibility of the state government.[24] Contrary to claims of officials of the central government, relief camps and permanent rehabilitation sites in Cachar were tales of neglect and lacking organization and coordination between various levels of officialdom. A case in point was the Masimpur Destitute Home. The houses were leaking, rice supplied there was rotten and the beaten rice (*chira*) and the jaggery (*gur*) given to the inmates were unfit for human consumption. There were patients everywhere, in every house, but bereft of food or medicine. The people's suffering because of state apathy was aggravated by red tapism and bureaucracy. Sri Prakash the prime minister's friend himself was forthcoming about the abysmal situation in the refugee rehabilitation network when, in a letter to Pandit Nehru, he observed that, 'there is a lot of red tape that holds ups grants of many to the Government there for rehabilitation. Balachandran gave some illustrations and Chatterjee agreed that that was so. Balachandran writes to Chatterjee at Calcutta and Chatterjee then sends his proposals to Delhi where it takes a long time to take things through. . . .'[25]

Besides red tapism and bureaucracy, the camps themselves were organized in a shoddy manner which made them fertile grounds for disease and mortality. A memorandum submitted to S.P. Mookerji in May 1950, from Cachar, very candidly observed that, 'The actual condition of these refugees excepting a very small percentage, who have somehow managed to earn their living, is extremely miserable'.[26]

The same memorandum gives graphic details of the situation to point out that there was no proper rehabilitation scheme till May 1950, which could provide proper relief to the displaced. There was no arrangement for food, shelter or medication and the helpless people were passing their days with the hope that the government would come to give them relief. The memorandum pointed out that, 'Without proper food and shelter, without adequate clothing, broken down physically and mentally these helpless thousands are at the end of their resources and passing their miserable days in the slight hope that the Government will come to their rescue.'[27]

However, the attitude of the state and its government was far from friendly and the Revenue Department, Government of Assam, came out with a circular which prohibited the settlement of refugees in normal habitable land in the districts of Assam.[28] Therefore there was no alternative for the refugees but to be forced to find shelter and habitation in lands within forests and tea gardens where the climatic conditions were not very good for human habitation.[29] The Assam government from the very inception was unsympathetic to the refugee cause. While the first reaction of the provincial government was to deny the existence of refugees in Assam,[30] they were forced to acknowledge the refugee problem in 1948. The Assam government was determined to deny the refugees any habitable land. As a result, land unsuitable for cultivation and habitation, either being rocky barren hillocks or low marshy lands, inundated by heavy rains and full of wild beasts, leeches, snakes and poisonous insect were selected for the settlement of refugees.[31] Wild beasts regularly ravaged those areas where the camps were established. One such camp was the Kalinagar refugee rehabilitation scheme which had to be finally abandoned because of the 'recurring ravages by the wild elephants'.[32] While the temporary housed were destroyed by wild animals,[33] the area was inhospitable and insect prone the semi-forested lands given to the refugees for habitation exposed the refugee to health hazard and diseases which they were not equipped to counter. The death of a refugee at the Madrassa camp in the Arunaband Tea Estate due to insect bite exposed the failing rehabilitation arrangement.[34] Many of the refugee camps were flood prone. The ITA refugee camp at Gumrah marshes, under Katigora police station were easily flooded after the rains. As a result, the houses and paddy crops were regularly destroyed leaving the 183 refugee families ill-nourished and famished. As the report of the General Secretary in the 3rd Cachar Refugee Conference noted, 'The colonies that we have visited recently represents such heart rending scene – people famished and just like living skeletons deprived of all relief, even medicines. . . .'[35]

In some cases, the areas allocated for rehabilitation camps by the state government were susceptible to erosion by the local rivers, which broke into its banks. Such predicament was the regular fate of the Chandighat-Khagrahban ITA colony. Parts of it were eaten up by the local river, Madhura. There was no doubt in public perception that, the areas allocated for refugee rehabilitation in Barak Valley were unsuitable for human habitation and a breeding ground for disease and death.[36]

Thus the ITA scheme came into being, which provided for refugee rehabilitation in the waste lands of the tea gardens under the Indian Tea Associations in Cachar was doomed to failure since inception. Living in these camps were like life in 'veritable hell', where 'distress of the worst type over took the refugees'[37]. The memorandum submitted by the refugees to S.P. Mookerji pointed out that,

In most of the gardens they were most unsympathetically treated, in many cases they were kept in huts not fit for human habitation, amidst dense forests abounding in ferocious wild animals,[38] with the result that most of them left the camps and turned into beggars. These refugee camps were veritable breeding grounds of disease and epidemics, a point that draws attention to the relationship between displacement and disease among these refugees in south Assam. These tea garden camps were mostly malarious, exposing the sheltered to the vagaries of malaria, which flourished through the mosquitos breeding abundantly in the marshy lands in which the camps were located. There were virtually no treatment or proper medical facilities for the diseased and infirm. Most of the refugees in these camps suffered from starvation as well, which made their bodies weak and susceptible to disease like beriberi, gastric pains and ulcers which led to their death. A case in point was the Ghongoor camp where the diet supplied was much below the sanctioned ration of 6 chhattak of rice and one chhattack of dal per person per day. A memorandum that was sent to the authorities, virtually pleaded that the 'lives of the inmates cannot be saved unless the quantity and the quality of their food be improved.'[39] The fates of the refugees in other camps were no better. An unofficial Report was very candid when it opined that, 'Hunger, disease and death have been the fate of these unfortunate victims of Indian freedom.'[40] Many of these refugees, who had come from urban centers and towns of East Pakistan,[41] and hence were unaccustomed to living in forests and marsh lands, felt prey to the vagaries of their new life. Even for agriculturists, who formed a sizeable part of the displaced population, the new sites of rehabilitation were mostly 'unsuitable for habitation and cultivation being either rocky barren hillocks or low marshy lands easily inundated by ordinary rains. Besides, their inhospitable topography, these sites were located in distant, 'out of the way places', full of wild beasts, leeches, snakes and insects. It was of little surprise that infant mortality was increasing with every passing year, with an average of one death a day. An important element of this deplorable situation was total absence of health care and timely medical treatment for afflicting diseases. An interesting case in point was the death of a small child at the Madrasa camp of the Arunaband Tea Estate, as a result of insect bite[42]. It is evident that the refugee camps were not only congested but also ill-equipped to meet the calamitous situation that confronted them. The arrangement in these camps, were inadequate and distribution of unbalanced diet and unhealthy conditions of living contributed to the deterioration of the general health of the inmates. A memorandum submitted to A.P. Jain, the Hon'ble Minister of GOI by the All India Women Council on 18th of June 1950 pointed out that better arrangement needed to be made for proper ventilation in camps, arranging sanitations, diet and medical health besides proper care for expectant mothers and new born children. But it was clear that none of these issues received the attention that it deserved. A telegram sent to A.P. Jain, with copies to the Prime Minister, noted with concern that, there was widespread suffering in the refugees camps of south Assam, because of starvation and inadequate medical support which was resulting in large scale adult and child mortality.[43] As late as July 1950, the Secretary of the Central Refugee Board, Silchar informed the controller of relief and rehabilitation, Silchar that the situation in the Dullavsherra camp in the Patharkandi sub division was precarious. The letter was vivid in its description when it observed that due to malnutrition and want of food, clothing and medical assistance the refugees are dying in large numbers. During the last three months men, women and children numbering above four hundred had already died and more are on the verge of death. Relief and rehabilitation programme in Cachar was unplanned and marked by rampant corruption: as a report pointed out, it was, 'Waste of public money and bungling in name of doing some good things. Success as claimed by officials is only on paper. . . .'[44]

At this point, it is pertinent to make a reference to Alfred Crosby's monumental work *Ecological Imperialism* where the author draws the readers attention to the death of all the Ameri-Indian slaves in Spain, 'because the land did not suit them'.[45] Situation for the refugees in Cachar were no better. The refugees were placed as such in areas where the climate conditions were not good. It was evident that the working of the official relief and rehabilitation machinery had no coordination with the refugees, who were after all supposed to be the beneficiaries of the programme. A memorandum submitted to Government of India from Cachar pointed out that, 'A regrettable feature in the working of the services is a complete lack of co-operation with the people'.[46]

The programmes were designed in a manner that, it could neither facilitate the rehabilitation of the displaced nor provide any relief to them. A majority of the displaced were middle class townsmen, who belong to varied urban professional classes such as doctors, traders, school teachers, clerks, lawyers, artisans and craftsmen, who had no previous experience of forest dwelling. They were unable to find suitable employment in the areas where they were rehabilitated. Without adequate technology or government supports, the refugee efforts to reclaim land and engage in settlement of a semi-urban settlement failed. Moreover their settlements exposed them to epidemics of dysentery, diarrhoea and pox which resulted in heavy mortality. Initiatives to start business by giving some loan also ended in failure. Some of the families within the ITA colonies who were promised loans of about Rs. 350-400 were provided delayed installments. The state government stopped all other relief measures, including medical aid to them which made their life miserable. In spite of the best effort their business initiative failed due to lack of auxiliary state supports to them and their lack of experience. They had to be rehabilitated in other refugee colonies. The urban professional classes who were accustomed to town life were mostly unable to adjust to the hostile environment in which they were placed. This was highlighted in a speech delivered by Sri Suresh Chandra Deb in parliament where he observed, 'Taken to jungle there was no arrangement for sanitation. There was no drinking water. There was no land.'[47]

The residents fell easy victims to malaria, diarrhoea, dysentery, cholera, typhoid, naga-sore, etc. Reports revealed that by July 1950, at Cheragi, located near Dullavcherra pointed out that, of the 500 refugees stationed there, 50 had already succumbed to death due to want of food and malnutrition and of the remaining 450, 148, inmates including children were afflicted by several ailments. The situation in Gambhira Tea Estate was no better with fifteen refugees dead and 60 per cent of the inmates of the camp suffering from various diseases. These reports though specific to certain camps were representative of the general conditions of refugee rehabilitation in south Assam. Local newspaper reports of the period point towards large-scale misery of the refugees arising out of disease starvation and death from all corners of the district of Cachar. *The Chronicle* an English daily published from Silchar in its issue dated 13 June 1952, was vivid in its description of the morbid camp life when it pointed out that, 'Malaria, typhoid, pox, etc., have broken out in epidemic forms in and around many colonies. But medical aid is not yet given'.

This story which was a report from the Duhalia camp was more or less representative of the situation in all the camps of Cachar. The situation for non-camp refugees was no better. For those refugees who were turned away from the camps due to shortage of space and facilities, and who had tried to make their own arrangements, were also passing their days in starvation or near starvation. Many displaced persons, including children died of malnutrition. In spite of such morbid reports, the responses of the authorities were most unsympathetic. It was pointed out in a memorandum therefore, 'Reports of starvation are and were submitted to the Controller of Relief and Rehabilitation who is the principal authority on Cachar but with no visible results.'[48] The same reports also goes on to add that 'The Government is, as a rule, indifferent and dilatory'.[49] 1952 witnessed a big spurt in inflow refugees into Eastern India. It was, as U. Bhaskar Rao, put it, 'The frantic rush for sanctuary before it was too late'.[50] In spite of their experience with refugee rehabilitation, the state initiates were left wanting when the steady stream of refugees went on to become a flood. The colonies represented, 'heart-rending scene – people famished and just like living skeleton deprived of all relief even medicine'.[51]

Besides the ITA Scheme camps, the other Rehabilitation camps at Katirail, Kinnarkhal, Bishnunagar, Gandhinagar, Sanbeel East and South, Ghungoor, Maijaon, Panchagram and Ramkrishnanagar fared no better. These camps were located in areas which were abandoned and unfrequented by people in the neighbourhood as they were either deep in the forests infested with wild animals, high hillocks or low lying marshes easily inundated by rains in the monssons – in other words, 'unsuitable for human habitation or cultivation'.[52] As a result of such rehabilitation measures, 'There occurred large scale deaths on account of diseases like Dysentery, fevers, diarrhea, pox, etc'.[53] By 1953 the rate of influx of refugees 'showed a steady upward trend'.[54] By 1954, displacement of people rose from thousands to lakhs.[55] As Bhaskar Rao, put it,

> Week after week, month after month, year after year, they came, regardless of the hardships they might have to endure in this country'.[56] For these non-camp refugees, life was even more difficult. Most of them did not take shelter in any of the camps but made arrangements by themselves. Private initiative at rehabilitation was a result of state apathy. The emergence of slums was a significant development in Cachar after 1950. The urban refugees, unwilling to live in the barren and marshy lands established squatter colonies that had no concept of proper drainage or sanitation. The refugees had no means to construct proper houses with adequate urban facilities. The 3rd Cachar Refugee Conference Report was graphic in detail about such private initiatives. It noted that, '*Bastis* have been established in rural and suburban areas where closely constructed houses without drain or road have created a conjested unhealthy environment'.[57]

Reports pointed out that their conditions were as miserable as the camp refugees. 'Many are at starvation levels and proceeding towards death inch by inch'.[58] The situation was so morbid that, there was tremendous criticism of the Relief and Rehabilitation officials, some of whom were subsequently transferred from Cachar. By February 1953, the responsibility of Relief and Rehabilitation in Cachar was transferred from the central to the state government. But the lives of the refugee hardly experienced any improvement. People continued to die of lack of medical facilities. A report in a local newspaper in 1954, highlighted the case of Krishna Nath and Tara Charan Deb of the Gambhira Tea Estate who died 'without any medical aid'. This report went on to add that. 'Similar deaths are being reported from different other tea garden colonies where medical aid had long been stopped to the refugees by the garden authorities'.[59]

With the state government stepping in, the refugees were further subjected to neglect and hardship. The unconcerned attitude of the state towards the refugees was not only reflected in the reticence of the state government to sanction habitable land for the displaced but also in their lack of response to the failing health-care systems in the refugee camps. Health care had emerged as one of the key denominators of state attitudes towards the refugees, over which much politics was played. As a response to the state apathy the refugee organization demanded the continuance of central government control over the rehabilitation programme in Cachar. This was strongly opposed by Members of Parliament from Assam such as Debakanta Barua and Jogendra Hazarika who during their tour of Cachar, were openly unsympathetic to the refugee cause. They were more than willing to rid Assam of those refugees who were critical of the state government. In his response to the local press one of the Members of Parliament was candid enough to observe, 'Those who demand centre should better be sent to Tripura, Manipur and the Andaman'.[60]

Considering the relentless clamour, among the refugees for better health-care responses from the state, it was tragic that all such demands were deliberately ignored as part of the politics that was played over refugee rehabilitation. It was as if the government was making a deliberate effort to make living and livelihood impossible for the refugees. Starvation led people to indulge in hazardous practices such as consumption of poisonous roots and leaves which compromised their health. A report from Maniknagar Tea Estate pointed out that, 'Some families have been suffering from various diseases for having eaten *kachu, palui*, etc., in exchange of rice which they cannot procure. . . . People being exposed to storm and showers of rain have been taken seriously ill. Treatment is but an apology.'[61]

Advertisements issued by medical stores in local newspapers can also be used as a source to comprehend the status of public health in an area of study. The deteriorating conditions of public health-care system and nature of disease can be seen from the hoards of advertisements issued by the medical stores in newspapers which catered to the refugee cause. *The Chronicle* published from Silchar, by Sri Premendra Mohan Goswami, carried these advertisements almost on a daily basis between 1952 and 1955. Once such regular advertisement was by Arogya Niketan, situated at Hospital Road Silchar which had one N.C. Deb as the visiting physician. A specimen copy of the same is given below:

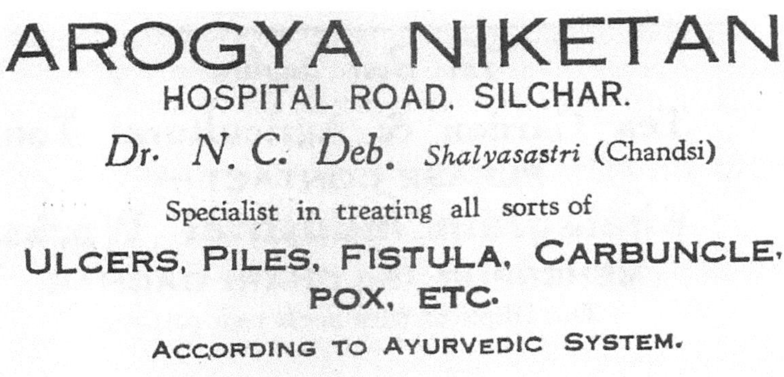

Another such advertisement was that of Pitambar Ayurvediya Oushadhalay, where the visiting doctor was one Kabiraj Prafulla Chandra Acharjee.

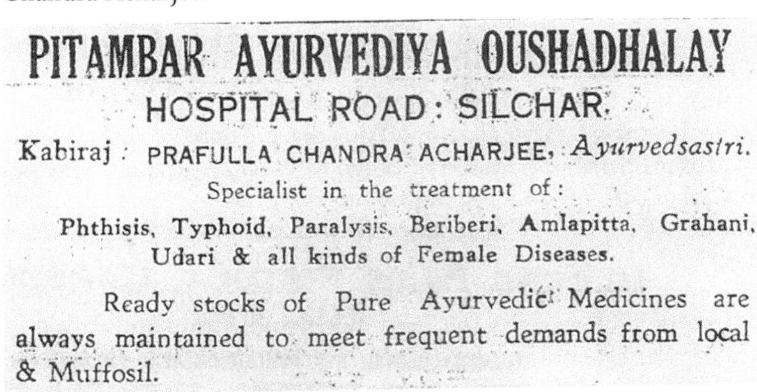

A close reading of both these advertisements clearly highlight their connect with the medical problems faced by both camp and non-camp refugees in Cachar. It was as if these doctors and the medical stores were tailored to meet the refugee predicaments. The diseases which generally afflicted the refugee populations like typhoid, malaria, dysentery, gastric ulcers, pox, etc., was highlighted in the advertisements as the specialization of the doctors attending these medical stores. These shops and others like them spared no effort to attract the refugee population through their publicity efforts. When government health-care system was in shambles, private and retired medical practitioners and doctors of traditional and alternative medicine began to provide succor to the ailing refugees. The second advertisement stood out because of its effort to highlight their abundant stock of medicine to 'meet frequent demand from local and muffosil [*sic*]'.[62] It is clear from such advertisements that diseases broke out regularly among the people in the camps around the Silchar town which led to frequent demands for medicine. It could also be pointed out that the regular medical facilities were beyond the reach of the refugees who often turned to these Ayurvedic medical practitioners to cure their ailments. Government health-care systems in Cachar was non-existent for the refugees who died in hundreds due to inhospitable rehabilitation schemes.

The story of decolonization, displacement and rehabilitation in Cachar is, in itself, a story of state neglect, denial and politics over health care. A perusal of the unofficial reports and archival materials at hand, expose the connectivity between policies of a disinterested state and failing health-care systems among the people of the region under study especially its displaced refugees. The evidences at hand also bring to light the impact of forced displacement and unplanned rehabilitation on community health-care systems and individual health. The records also reveal the inability of displaced refugees to adjust to their new habitat. These refugees thus turned into the vagaries of life in their new home. It is ironical that the fate that befell the Ameri-Indians in Spain five hundred years ago would now befall the refugees in Cachar, though in a different context just as the Ameri-Indians, who died in Spain unable to adjust to their new land,[63] thousands of East Pakistani refugees perished in Cachar, unable to adjust to their new environment and inhuman living conditions. In the context of a large political crisis as the Partition of India, the critical role of health care system in proper human rehabilitation could hardly be over-emphasized. In spite of advance warning and premonitions of the impending disaster, records indicate, that, the post colonial Indian state both at the federal and the provincial level failed to rise to occasion and mitigate the hardship of the people who had already suffered the vicissitudes of political machination in colonial India. Victims of colonial games of power again fell victims to post colonial politics in which environment and health care played pivotal roles. This story is an attempt to relate displacement and its related policy in India to the health of the displaced and in the process question the claims of post colonial Indian state of providing secured life and livelihood to its citizens.

NOTES

1. U.B. Rao, *The Story of Rehabilitation*, New Delhi: GOI, p. 141.
2. Ibid., p. 147.
3. Statement of Nibaran Chandra Laskar, dt. 13 June 1947, in S.P. Mookerji Papers, File 40, NMML.
4. Ibid.
5. Sri Prakash's letter dt. 14 August 1951, File 40, S.P. Mookerji Papers, NMML, p. 4.
6. Gen. Secy's Report on 'The Condition of Displaced Persons', in the 3rd Session of Cachar District Refugee Conference, 8-9 November 1954, Silchar.
7. J. Bagchi et al., *Trauma and Triumph*, Kolkata: Stree Publications, p. 169.
8. Sri Prakash to Nehru, op. cit.
9. *The Story of Rehabilitation*, op. cit., p. 143.
10. Ibid., p. 144.
11. Ibid.
12. 'Report on the Condition of the Displaced Persons', 3rd Refugee Conference, Silchar, 1954.
13. Sri Prakash, op. cit., NMML.
14. Rao, *The Story of Rehabilitation*, GOI, p. 147.
15. Sri Prakash, op. cit., S.P. Mookerji Papers, File No. 40, NMML.
16. Rpt. in *The Chronicle*, dt. 13 June 1952.
17. Ibid.
18. Ibid.
19. The Cachar District Branch of the All India Women's Council, in its Memorandum to the Hon'ble Member of the Rehabilitation Sub-Committee of the standing Finance Committee of the GOI, dt. 3 June 1950, A.P. Jain Papers, NMML.
20. Ibid.

21. Sri Prakash, op. cit.
22. R. Chakrabarti, *Situating Environmental History*, Delhi: Manohar, 2007.
23. 'A Samanta Plague and Prophylactics: Ecological Construction of an Epidemic in Colonial Eastern India', in R. Chakrabarti, ibid., p. 221.
24. Sri Prakash, op. cit.
25. Ibid.
26. File 40, S.P. Mookerji Papers, 1950, NMML.
27. Memorandum dt. 27 May 1950, S.P. Mookerji Papers, File 40, NMML.
28. Letter No. R.S. 195/47/188 dt. Shillong 4 May 1948 from Secy. Rev. Dept. to Deputy Commissioner Goalpara, Kamarupa, Darrang, Nowgongm Sibsagar, Lakhimpur and Cachar ref in Report dt. 8/9 November 1954, Cachar District Refugee Conference.
29. D.K. Chakraborty's letter to the Controller of Relief and Rehabilitation, GOI, Silchar, File 40, S.P. Mookherjee Papers, NMML.
30. Rep. on the condition of the displaced persons prepared by the General Secretary of The Cachar District Refugee Association for the 3rd Cachar District Refugee Conference, 1954.
31. Ibid.
32. Ibid.
33. A problem which was acknowledged by Sri B.N. Mukherjee, during his visit to Kalinagar, ibid.
34. Memorandum of the Cachar district branch of the All India Women's Council to Sri A.P. Jain, op. cit.
35. Report of the General Secretary, op. cit.
36. Ibid.
37. File 40, S.P. Mookerji Papers, NMML, op. cit.
38. Ibid.
39. Ibid.
40. 'Report on the Condition of Displaced Persons', Cachar District Refugees Conference, 8 & 9 November 1954, Silchar.
41. Memorandum of the Central Refugee Board, Cachar dt. 30 May 1950 to Gopinath Bordoloi, File 40, S.P. Mookerji Papers, NMML.
42. File 40, S.P. Mookerji Papers, NMML.
43. Dilip Chakraborti's telegram to Jain, copy to S.P. Mookerji, SPM Papers, File 40, NMML.
44. Report of the General Secretary to the 3rd Cachar Refugee Conference, op. cit.
45. Page 198, Cambridge: Cambridge University Press, 2004.
46. Memorandum of the Cachar Branch of the All India Women's Council, op. cit.
47. *The Chronicle* in its edition, dt. 11 July 1952.
48. Report on relief and Rehabilitation by the Ratabari Thana Refugee Committee, S.P. Mookerji Papers, No. 40, NMML.
49. Ibid.

50. U. Bhaskar Rao, *The Story of Rehabilitation*, p. 145.
51. Report of Gen. Secretary in the 3rd Cachar District Refugee Conference, 1954.
52. Ibid.
53. Ibid.
54. Rao, op. cit., 145.
55. Ibid.
56. Ibid.
57. Reports of G.S. at 3rd Cachar Refugee Association Conference, 1954.
58. Ibid.
59. *The Chronicle*, May 1954.
60. Ibid., 9 January 1953.
61. Ibid., 22 May 1953
62. Ibid., 25 July 1952.
63. Crosby, *Ecological Imperialism*, op. cit.

CHAPTER 13

The Empire as a World of Sport: Aspects of Hunting in Colonial Assam, *c.* 1850-1900

BIPUL CHAUDHURY

> There is no country not even Africa where there is more and varied game than Assam and Burma. The people of Assam, debased as they are, are preferable to Africans in General, and all Europeans who have come in contact with the Bermese prefer them to most Asiatics. . ., but the Assamese are only fit to be slaves, and will do nothing unless driven.[1]

The colonial intervention with the forests of Assam is marked by an important breakthrough in the evolution of modern forest policy in the province. But the colonial state till 1900 had no concrete notion about the protection of nature and wildlife, rather it viewed it only as a source of revenue and entertainment. Even after the establishment of reserve forests, the killing or the hunting process did not cease. The ethnographic writings of the colonial officials in the nineteenth century reveals rather an opposite picture as both the nature and environment were situated as unending reserves even after the wastelands settlements and repeated flow of immigration. Forest also became at one hand an obstacle to the notion of Western progress and at the same time an instrument to display British masculinity to the natives. The Colonial Forest Policy guided by the notions of power was instrumental in large-scale deforestation and killing of innumerable wild animals. This has long-term impact in the ecology of the province.

This paper tries to critically examine the notion of 'hunting' that the colonial officials utilized in Assam through the writings of nineteenth-century travellers. This topic has not evoked much response from the scholars as it should have in the Assamese historiography.[2] It will basically concentrate upon the Brahmaputra

Valley prior to the establishment of the Kaziranga Wild Reserve due to availability of sources.

Hunting is as old an activity as human existence itself. Human society has tried to cope up with its relationship with the animals either through killing or taming them for personal comfort. With the expansion of the human civilization or habitat the animals had always to face the growing appetite of the humans. Wildlife has always evoked a mixture of fear and curiosity as well as the urge to kill them for sport.

The British Empire building project involved a metanarrative in which 'landscape, races and ideas on civilization with theories of evolution and progress went in a linear scale'. Hunting played a crucial role in it by providing the scope not only to expose the hidden treasure or bounties of the nature but also to utilize them for the benefit of the empire. In other words hunting fell within broader logic of colonialism. Hunting in colonial times therefore not only served the pleasure of the colonial officials but also served as instruments to expand new territories and control the people living in the fringe. In addition hunting also served the purpose of displaying the valour of the Englishmen who frequented the unconquered nature sometimes alone and sometimes in group with the entourage of native servants.

Moreover many colonial officials believed that wildlife was a kind of obstacle to the human habitat and this could only be reduced by hunting. In the words of Capt. Jenkins,

> Of the wild animals we have heard of every species, elephants, rhinoceros, buffaloes, tiger, leopard, jackals, and numerous kind of monkeys. They all commit serious depredation on the crops, and more particularly the elephants, which often demolished granaries in the open day to get at the grain and slat.[3]

COLONIAL STATE AND THE FORESTS

The colonial state took a keen interest in the affairs of forests. While the earlier native rulers were not so dependent on forest as a source of revenue the colonial state exercised several levels of controls over the forests. In order to welcome the English capital into the province a series of wasteland settlements were contracted by the state. In these wastelands there were also huge amounts of natural flora and fauna apart from animals. The planters were also very enthusiastic hunters and many of the ethnographers and hunters were in close terms with them.

In order to extract maximum revenue from the forest the colonial state reserved particular areas where private contractors were leased the rights to utilize the resources unhindered. This trend continued during the entire colonial period without any break. The native traders and a section of the immigrants were also involved in it.

THE *KHEDA* OPERATION

One of the important colonial interventions in the forests of Assam was regarding the elephants. The elephants due to their ability of negotiating the jungles, their tusks and necessity to the hunting operations received maximum attention from the colonial state. The colonial state itself maintained several elephants to run different tasks due to the bad transportation system. Moreover the elephant from Assam had great demand in the neighbouring areas and trade in it was very lucrative from the pre-British period. Till 1874 there were no restrictions on catching elephants and both the government and private entrepreneurs were fully involved in it.

After 1874 the government created 'mahal or operational partition in the districts and the right of elephant catching in those tracts was sold in auction'.[4] The novelist Amitav Ghosh has narrated similar experiences in colonial Burma.[5] Several native entrepreneurs were also involved in these elephant catching ventures known as the *kheda* operation. In these operations the role of the mahuts was very important who apart from catching elephants also played the important role of trainers. Therefore the image of the Mahuts in the estimate of colonial hunters was dominant as without them there would be no sports.

THE ENGLISHMEN AS THE IDEAL HUNTERS

The accounts relating to hunting in the then nineteenth-century Assam was mainly written by men who were not professional hunters like Jim Corbett. To them it was a hobby as well as their duty in the province. But the task of hunting was not easier for them to carry and narrate to English readers. First, they had to constantly show to the natives that they were technologically, mentally and physically stronger to the latter. Second, they also had to show that shooting is not merely the hunting but is a big game. Third, they also had to convince their readers at home that their accounts were reliable without losing the spirit of hunting. For example, Col. Pollock and W.S. Thorn in their work wrote:

> Neither Mr. Thorn nor I pretend to be learned naturalists, but we have been keen sportsmen and kept our eyes open, and have studied the manners and habits of the animals we have hunted, and we flatter ourselves that many points which we have noted have been ignored or overlooked in the best Natural Histories. . . . There are would-be sportsmen who have spent most of their time in mercantile pursuits in Rangoon, Moulmein, and Bassein, and, who, having shot a snipe or two, think they know everything that is to be known with regard to sport. Hence they criticize, as Munchausen, the records of adventure and exploits that transcend the limits of their narrow experience, and wax anonymously wrathful with sportsmen who are not ashamed add their names to what they relate. In reply to the criticisms of such, my colleague and I have merely to say, in anticipation that our records are not taken from our diaries, and are as accurate as they can be made.[6]

These accounts also served the purpose of travel guides to future visitors and hunters. The ideal hunter should also think about his own safety. Col. Pollock and Thorn advises the young English hunters in these words,

> Should the sportsman be the only armed European present at a drive, he should see that he is posted in the best position, which is usually the centre. Two stops, some fifty or hundred paces oft, should also be placed in likely spots on high right and left. These two men should be instructed to turn inwards, any animals which may appear in front of them, so as to afford the sportsman a shot.[7]

These books contained several sketches and photographs to depict the visual reality. They constantly refer to dangers and obstacles involved in a place like Assam and suggested precautions against these. They repeatedly emphasized that hunting was no easy game and it needed strong masculine qualities. To remain physically and mentally strong was the first priority of these writers. They also emphasized about the foods to be taken during the hunt. While Pollock and Thorn abstained from drinking, Col. Cutter was not averse to it while on camp.

HUNTING AS A SPORT AND THE GREAT GAME

Colonial Assam presented so many opportunities for the English hunters not to be confined only to only few hunts. They vigorously indulged in several hunting practices although elephants, rhinos and tigers were their great sports. The vocabulary they utilized for their hunt is illustration of their spirits. For example, Col. Pollock and Thorn while describing the rhino hunt mention,

> I fired on the mass before me, and as the smoke cleared away, a very large rhinoceros rushed into the open and got another bullet in its shoulder. He pulled up. I dropped the discharged weapon and took up another, gave him two pills in the chest; he swerved and ran off, squealing awfully. On hearing this noise my steed right-about faced, and raced for her life, and could not be stopped for some time. So I went back to the bheel and took up the trail, and soon came upon the rhinoceros stone dead. Its horn was not long but very massive, weighting in *seers*. We got men from the nearest village, who were thankful to get the flesh, cut off the head and took off the shields.[8]

This account mentions the fact that a section of the natives were not bothered about the nature of the flesh and free from many caste prejudices.

Although 'exciting', hunting the rhino was no easy matter due to its size and power. John Butler has narrated the risk involved in it as,

> The squeaking grunt of this beast is peculiarly sharp and fierce and the elephants become so alarmed that few wait its approach in the shape of a charge but mostly quit the field with the utmost speed scarcely giving the sportsman time to have a shot. If the rhinoceros succeeds in overtaking the elephant, it inflicts terrible wounds on the haunches of the latter with its 'mouth, and with the horn on its nose endeavours to rip up the belly of the elephant. Of all the animals of the forest, the rhinoceros is most feared, from its destructive powers; and, as it possesses an enormously thick skin, it requires a good gun or rifle to bring it down. Nevertheless, we have known several rhinoceroses killed with one ball, if hit in a vital part; otherwise, as with the buffalo, ten or fifteen balls may be fired without effect.[9]

Tiger

After elephant and rhinos the hunters in Assam were interested in tiger hunting. The usual process of killing tiger was to surround the hunt through elephants and shoot. For this the hunters usually utilized the services of the 'beaters' (who made great noise through beating jungle grass) and drummers. But this was also no easy task as Butler writes,

> At times, a tiger, being surrounded by a field of elephants in a small patch of high grass, shows great sports; for as often as he is beaten up by the elephants, he turns round and with a tremendous roar rushes across the plain

towards the nearest one, and jumps upon its head or stem; the elephant then becomes dreadfully alarmed and screeches out in the most terrific manner shaking its body with all its power, to free itself from the claws of the enraged monster clinging to it. In this predicament the sportsmen is helpless; as from the violent motion of the elephant all he can do is to hold fast to the howdah, for if thrown out he would be torn to pieces; but a skilful sportsman, on perceiving the tiger's approach towards his elephant, will generally stop the rapid charge of the tiger by one or two well-directed shots, which will either prove fatal, or so cripple the beast as to render his efforts to charge futile.

Few elephants can be brought to stand repeated charge of a tiger; if the sportsman fail to shoot the tiger in the first charge, the elephants instinctively seems to lose confidence, and no exertions on the part of the mahut can induce the elephant again to encounter the danger of a second charge, by advancing to beat up the tiger concealed in the grass; a tiger's charge is always desperately fierce, and seldom met without making its pursuers feel the power of its fangs and claws, and causing fatal accidents.[10]

The hunters also enjoyed hunting wild buffaloes although it was not a great game like killing elephants, rhinos or tigers. Yet it did involve some risk as the wild buffalos could charge at the hunters if they were not careful. Same also applied according to T.T. Cooper regarding bear hunting.[11] Priority for hunters also depended upon individual personality. For example, according to John Butler, 'The most pleasant sport in Assam is deer shooting: all kinds are found in great numbers, and in open plains many may be killed in a day.'[12]

Fishing

Fishing was another activity in which the hunters involved themselves throughout the year. As the province has great water resources the hunters were naturally attached to it. T.T. Cooper has described in details the fishing particularly the *masher*.

Bird Hunting

The hunters also enjoyed killing birds in innumerable numbers including wild hens and ducks. They relished the dishes prepared with them by the Indian cooks who always accompanied them.

HUNTING AND RACE

The practice of hunting was very intricately linked with the idea of English racial superiority to the native. T.T. Cooper illustrates this phenomena regarding pig sticking in these words, 'The savage and determined gameness of the boar was only equalled by the horseman's cool daring; and I think, of all manly and brave sports, that of pig sticking, as practised by the English *shikaries* in India' [stands out].[13] With regard to the native submission or obedience and ferocity they were variously classified as savage, barbarous and lazy. Ajay Skaria has also shown in the context of the Dangs of western India the process of colonial classification of the Indian tribes. But at the same time the English hunters were helpless without the support of the natives. The native with their thorough knowledge of the topography and vegetation apart from the animals had several advantages over their masters. This over dependence on native knowledge and labour also at times proved as obstacles to the hunters.

Sometimes the natives also deceived them and they had to swallow their pride. For example, Col. Pollock and Thorn have mentioned how the village *mahajan* fraudulently charged more prices from them. In their own words,

> We had great difficulty as usual in getting supplies, not because they were scarce, but because the Mouzadars forbid the villagers to sell except through them. They ought to have known me well by this time, as I had been there more than once and had always paid their own prices with my own hand to prevent speculation by our servants. They also knew Seetaram and Sookur well; but the Assamese are only fit to be slaves, and will do nothing unless driven.

Not only the *mauzadars*, the natives as a whole, posed other obstacles to the hunters. Col. Pollock and Thorn further mention that,

> The Assamese people are difficult to deal with; the people are debased, given to debauchery and opium, and it is impossible to depend on them. Daily payments are very objectionable, as a great deals sticks to the palms of the subordinates. I introduced the contract system, paying for heavy embankments only after measurements; but I ran great risks, as I had to advance often many thousands of rupees to get reliable men to take up the work on my own responsibility and risk, and I got very little thanks for my pains.

Therefore the estimate of the natives varied according to the moods of the narrators. Sometimes, these hunters also had to seek cooperation from the native chiefs and here their estimates became very positive.[14]

But, the hunters did not enjoy the dominant status among the native higher castes and they had to adjust with it. Here their accounts became similar to the Christian missionaries who also had to face similar situations. For example, Col. Pollock and Thorn complained,

'There are namghurs, but often they are in the heart of a village, and not pleasant places to put up in; and besides, the Hindoos are not like Burmese, who welcome visitors, whilst the former would be insolent if they dared.'[15] This inverse relation is an interesting feature of British colonialism in India. As a result, they had to come into contact with the different tribal communities like the Kacharis who were relatively free from many of the caste prejudices of the higher castes.

Although hunting was not uncommon to the natives, many of them were puzzled with the English hunters unending appetites for the wild sports. Col. Cooper mentioned one such encounter after a tiger hunt through the words of one of his servants, 'Truly master, you Englishmen are curious men. Do you really feel a pleasure in such dreadful scenes as these? Truly suppose I never have see this, my no can believe. Ah, Chinamen never can do this kind of business, he heart too small.'[16]

HUNTING AND PROGRESS

Since hunting was intricately linked with the colonial notion of progress, these writers tried to defend their activities as progressive. It was part of the colonial civilization process. They believed that with gradual clearing of jungles, Assam would emerge as a prosperous area fit for cultivation and industry. They therefore welcomed the entry of English private capital in the province through tea gardens and coal and petroleum industries. Besides, some of the writers themselves were involved in different ventures in the province. The colonial state also in many cases patronized hunting to accelerate the growth of population in the province. Till the nineteenth century there was virtually no ban on killing animals in the province. In Lakhimpur district people were rewarded for killing snakes. In the early nineteenth century there was a reward of Rs. 5 per head to kill a tiger.[17]

CONCLUSION

The romantic notions of the jungle and the hunters have become an essential feature of the colonial past along with the specific dress and traditions. The hunters were technically not soldiers in many cases but their dress and ideas show a clear link with the latter as the defender of the interests of the empire. Hunting also became a symbolic representation of the empire and English masculinity. The contemporary British press and public opinion also supported and promoted the ventures of the hunters. The image of hunting as mentioned earlier was also essential for the maintenance and integrity of the empire as it showed that the English supervision or control was necessary for the progress of the natives who otherwise would have been in a lower scale of civilization.

It is difficult to make an estimate about the damage that the colonial hunters have done to the ecosystem of the province due to lack of necessary data. But it was substantial and given the trend started by them the province has lost innumerable animals for the pleasure of few humans. In fact, in the nineteenth century there were no idea about animal rights and it would be wrong to blame them. Moreover, the natives were also no less to be blamed for the steady loss of animal habitats. The English methods of hunting were imitated later by nationalist leaders like Tarunram Phukan and others. But the damage done by the English hunters were more than the natives as the accounts of the nineteenth-century writers clearly testify.

The problem aggravated due to the colonial government's exclusive concerns about timber and except the elephants and the rhinos it was not seriously interested in the protection of animals. Only after independence the government became more aware of protecting the tigers.

NOTES

1. Col. Pollock and W.S. Thorn, *Wildsports of Assam and Burma*, London: Hurst & Blackwell, p. viii.
2. See for example, Rajib Handique, British Forest Policy in Assam, Delhi: Concept, 2004 deals primarily with the forest policies of the British but the issue of hunting is ignored.
3. Quoted in Arupjyoti Saikia, *Jungles, Reserves, Wildlife: A History of Forests in Assam*, Wildlife Areas Development and Welfare Trust, Assam, 2005, p. 259. Also see Oscar Flex, *Assam*, 1864, pp. 64-8, translated from German by Salim Ali, Gauhati: Assam Sahitya Sabha, 2012.
4. Handique, ibid., p. 34. Some English hunters were amazed at the nature of the elephants. For example, Pollock and Thorn op. cit., p. 42 mentions, 'I have never known an elephant that could be invariably depended upon for dangerous shooting; they are like women – "Uncertain, coy, and difficult to please"'.

5. Amitabh Ghosh, *The Glass Palace*, pp. 89-102, Delhi: Harper Collins, 2000.
6. *Wildsport of Assam & Burma*, op. cit., pp. viii-xi.
7. Ibid., p. 408.
8. Ibid., p. 434.
9. Butler, *Travels in Assam*, pp. 218-19, 1854, London: Smith Elder & Company.
10. Ibid., Polloc and Thorn, op. cit., mentions that 'In Assam they (tigers) are more plentiful than in Burma and more get-at-able', p. 52.
11. T.T. Cooper, *The Mishimi Hills*, 1873, p. 63; rpt. Delhi: Mittal Publications, 1995.
12. Butler, op. cit., p. 219.
13. Cooper, op. cit., p. 23. For a different perspective see, Rudyard Kipling's story, *The Tomb of his Own Ancestors*, pp. 79-103, Kipling's *India*, Delhi: Roli Books, 2012.
14. Wildsports, p. 453, also see Cooper, op. cit., p. 141. But in some cases where the native princes or zaminders whose fortunes were interlinked with the colonial state, they tried to keep in good touch with the masters through hunting. For example, The Maharaja of Cooch Behar in his book *Thirty-Seven Years of Big Game Shooting in Coooch Behar: The Duars and Assam, A Rough Diary*, published in 1908, Bombay shows his hunting expeditions only with the Europeans. This is reflected in other princely areas of India. For example, see *Exotic Aliens: The Lion and the Cheetah in India*, Valmik Thapar, Romila Thapar, Yusuf Ansari, Delhi: Aleph Books, 2013, pp. 159-80.
15. Wildsports, op. cit., p. 438, was forced to make an agreement with the Namghar authorities that he can only take shelter in it during the 'heat of the day or in case it came on to rain'. But he could not dine inside but outside under the shade of a tree.

    When the English hunters missed their targets they had to face humiliations from the native aides. In their own words, 'The beaters regularly laughed at us every time we missed, and I have no doubt thought us fools for trying to shoot such small birds on the wing. I fancy we were the first Europeans they had ever been out with, and had never seen bird shoot flying.' p. xix.
16. Cooper, op. cit., pp. 31-2.
17. Arupjyoti Saikia, op. cit., p. 261. By the twentieth century, however, the tone of some of the hunters who wrote their adventures changed a bit and they became 'Gentlemen Hunters' who hunts only to protect the people but not to kill animals for sports. For details on this issue see Fiona Natasha Mani, 'British Hunters in Colonial India, 1900-1947: The Gentleman Hunter, New Technology, and Growing Conservationist Awareness', published in *Pakistianiaat*, A Journal of Pakistan Studies, vol. 4, no. 1, 2012, pp. 69-87.

CHAPTER 14

Colonizing the Wild: British Policies towards Wildlife in Assam, 1874-1947

GEETASHREE SINGH

Wildlife is a part of human ecology and they live in close proximity. They did not affect the life of each other till their food chain was disturbed but once it was they started preying on each other. The human-animals conflict existed since long back. However, prior to British rule the conflict between human and wildlife was not huge because people did not interfere much in the wildlife habitation. After the annexation of the province the British government started a tug of war against wildlife as it was considered as hurdle to the extension of cultivation. But the process of the destruction of wild animals did not start abruptly as Mahesh Rangarajan argued that the British rulers were initially concerned with eliminating carnivores and collecting trophies.[1] The commodification of wildlife and need for extension of cultivable land led the adaptation of measures for the extermination of wildlife. British government introduced the system of reward giving, appointed *shikaris* and distributed guns for the destruction of wildlife.Similarly, Ramachandra Guha and Madhav Gadgil also argued that

> the British, as proponents of *shikar* on a large scale, had very little interest in wildlife-conservation. The consequences of record-breaking *shikar* sprees and habitat destruction were apparent by the time India gained independence. The tiger population, estimated at 40,000 at the turn of the country, had slumped to 3,000. The cheetah was extinct in 1952. Other large mammals, such as the elephant and rhino, had disappeared from areas in which they were formerly quite numerous, while the Asiatic lion survived only in the Gir Forest.[2]

The Christian Missionaries records also reveal the decrease of the wildlife population. According to one missionary record, 'Only a few years ago it was considered unsafe for anyone to come here even in daylight. Wild animals were very numerous. Now there are thousands of settlers located on these rich lands.'[3] Though the casualties by wild animals cannot be ignored but the statistics shows that the destruction of the wild animals was more in comparison with the casualties by the wild animals. Through this paper an attempt has been made to study the British polices towards wildlife and its impact.

BRITISH POLICIES TOWARDS WILDLIFE

The desire for exploitation of forest resources and clearance of jungle for cultivation led the British government adopt measures for the extermination of wildlife. Wild animals like tiger, buffalo, stags and other animals made the cultivation difficult which was main source of revenue.[4] The British officials argued that the killing of wildlife was needed for the safety of life and property. This led the British government to initiate various measures for the destruction of wildlife. At the initial stage, there was debate among British officials as to what measures to be adopted for the destruction wildlife. After some of the earlier experiments the Government of India as well as the provincial governments recognized the giving of rewards as effective method. Reward giving became the most popular method of the destruction of wild animals during the British rule. Prior to British rule the reward giving was never practised by any ruler. Mahesh Rangarajan argued that the system of reward giving for the destruction of wild animals was 'utterly unknown to the original rulers of India'.[5] The British began fresh infringements on the animal world with their systematic measures of extermination.[6] The introduction of reward involved the local inhabitants, *shikaris* called from neighbouring provinces, in the process of extermination of wildlife primarily for the sake of rewards and second, for trade purpose. Mahesh Rangarajan argued that

> Bounties aimed to eliminate cattle-marauding tigers. Saving draught cattle would help extend the area that was under the plough. Fewer tigers meant more cultivation and more revenue, their elimination a blessing of imperium after the elimination of an oriental despot. Unprecedentedly, larger rewards were given out for killing tigress, and special prizes for finishing off cubs. This was to be a war where no quarter was given.[7]

Large sums were given for the destruction of females and cubs of wildlife to stop the reproduction of wildlife. The pattern of use of weapons changed with the introduction of modern weapons. Prior to the British rule, the local inhabitants used traditional weapons like bow and arrows, spear, and *daos* through which not many wild animals could have been killed but the supply of modern weapons like gun and rifles made the killing of wild animals easier than ever before. The use of poison for killing wild animals was also practised during British rule. This resulted in the destruction of wild animals in large numbers.

The scale of reward varied from animal to animal. Reporting on the measures adopted in the province for the destruction of wild animals, the Secretary to the Chief Commissioner stated the following measures – different rates of rewards were paid for the destruction of wild animals according to the nature of animals. For example, the highest reward paid was for the destruction of rogue elephant, viz., Rs. 100. The lowest reward paid was Rs. 2 for the destruction of hyenas. The paying of rewards also depended on the nature of destruction in any district. For the destruction of a full-grown tiger Rs. 25 was paid in North Cachar Hills, Sibsagar, Lakhimpur, Garo and Naga Hills but in other district only Rs. 20 was paid. For the killing of a leopard Rs. 5 was paid in all districts of the province, for wolves and bears Rs.10 was paid. For the destruction of snakes rewards were not paid in all the districts but in some districts like Gauhati and Sibsagar a reward of 2 *annas* was paid. Other than, reward giving the gratuitous distribution of guns and ammunition in Assam Valley, Khasi and Jaintia Hills districts for the protection of human lives, cattle and crops from wild beasts also caused the destruction of wild animals in large numbers. The free licensing of guns also fostered the destruction of wild animals.[8] The appointment of the professional *shikaris* was very important as the success of reward giving mostly depended on the existence of the professional *shikaris* in the province as there was no native *shikaris* in Assam. The use of poison like 'cobra poison' and *dakara* (aconite), was also in practice for the destruction of wild animals.[9] Apart from these, sports by the British officials and elite class also contributed to the destruction of wild animals. According to Rangarajan, 'the deliberate and organized destruction of carnivores under government patronage was a novel feature of British period'.[10]

BOUNTY KILLING

The practice of reward giving was started by the British since 1840s. The inference of British government in forest for timber and other natural resources brought the wild animals in open country and that caused menace to human life and their property. Wild animals were also a hurdle in the extension of tea plantation. The colonial projects like means of communication, particularly roads and railways, led the government to adopt measures for the killing of wild animals. The practice of the reward giving for the destruction of wildlife was popular during British rule. But there were no accurate statistical records to conform the number of wild animals killed for sports. Mahesh Rangarajan argues that 'bounties were not the sole or the major cause of decline, but they are too an important factor to be left out in a story of the past'.[11] The practice of reward giving was introduced as a measure to encourage people towards killing wild animals. The reward giving was practised since Assam was under Bengal presidency. Though the scale of reward paid for the destruction of wild animals was much less prior to 1874, still the total amount paid was much higher than the amount paid after the formation of the Forest Department in Assam. An amount of Rs. 16,713, Rs. 14,148, Rs. 17,064 was paid as reward in 1866, 1867, 1879 respectively. After 1874, however, there was a gradual decline in the amount of rewards given. A sum of Rs. 10,640; 10,210; 8,385; 7,022 was paid in 1877, 1878, 1879, and 1880 respectively. There was decline in the number of wild animals killed for reward after the formation of Forest Department. This is evident that a total of 4,381, 2,712 and 2,752 wild animals were reported to have been killed in 1866, 1867, 1868 respectively for rewards. On the other hand after 1874, a total of 7,72; 800; 772 wild animals were reported to have been killed in 1875; 1876 and 1877 respectively for rewards.

Other than 'bounty killing' wild animals were also killed for trade. However, the statistics of the wild animals killed for reward was under reported. People from interior places did not take the trouble of reporting the killing of wild animals as the market value of dead wild animals was more than the amount given as reward. F.C. Daukes, Secretary to Chief Commissioner of Assam, reported that, 'tigers, leopards, bears, and other animals are frequently shot by persons who do not take the trouble to obtain the government reward or to report having shot them, and professional *shikaris* often find it more profitable to dispose of the animals killed by them to private persons than to bring them into the station to obtain the rewards. These cases are seldom reported.'[12] Moreover trade in wildlife brought more sum than the amount paid as rewards. The reward for killing poisonous snakes was not given prior to 1874 but later a small amount of two *annas* was introduced in some of the districts for the destruction of snakes.

SCALE OF REWARD

A good sum of amount as reward was given for the destruction of wild animals as noted above. It varies according to animal and district. The rewards were given occasionally for killing those wild animals which were more destructive in a particular district. Each Deputy Commissioner had freedom within the limits of his allotment to pay rewards but the rate should not exceed the amount specified in the annexed schedule for the destruction of especially dangerous animals or of particular kinds of animal in certain localities. Deputy commissioners were permitted to authorized subordinates – districts superintendents, assistant superintendents, inspectors of police, sub-inspectors, head constables, tahsildars and *mauzadars* to certify the deaths of wild animals. Deputy commissioners and sub-divisional officers were allowed to pay the rewards on the production of such certificates together with the skulls of the animals killed.[13] In other parts of the provinces, rewards were paid on the certificates of police, revenue and magisterial officers.

TABLE 14.1: THE AMOUNT PAID AS REWARD MOSTLY REMAINED THE SAME EXCEPT ON CERTAIN OCCASIONS AND IN CERTAIN DISTRICT THE AMOUNT MOSTLY GIVEN

Wild animals	*Districts*	*Rs.*	*A.*
Tiger (full grown) [rate to be doubled when special need exist]	Sibsagar, Lakhimpur, North Cachar, Garo Hills and Naga Hills	25	0
Ditto	All other districts	20	0
Leopards	All districts	5	0
Wolves (rate to be double when necessary)	Ditto	10	0
Bears	Darrang and Sibsagar	10	0
Ditto	Other districts	5	0
Hyenas	All districts	2	8

Source: NAI, Home, Public-A, 1881, October, File No. 104-117.

For cubs and young ones, half of the rates for full grown animals were paid.[14] In the case of a rogue elephant a reward of Rs. 50 when the animal causes injury to crops or houses and property and if it was destructive to human life an increased reward of Rs. 100 was given. If the animal was a tusker the tusk became the property of the person who killed him.[15] The reward was offered with a description of the elephant killed had to be notified in the local Gazette and also locally at the offices of the Deputy Commissioner and at all police stations. The paying of reward was also informed to Chief Commissioner.[16] For the destruction of venomous snakes an amount of 2 *annas* each were given within the limits of the Gauhati and Sibsagar municipalities.[17] However, there was no specific policy to distinguish between venomous and harmless snakes in paying rewards.[18] Government of India distributed the book by Sir Joseph Fayrer *Thanatophidia of India* for the identification of common classes of deadly snakes. The clearance of jungle and under growths received attention in localities where snakes were more than usually numerous.[19] Government of India insisted on clearing of surroundings to kill snakes.

In Karimganj subdivision, rewards were granted for the destruction of wild pigs at the rate of Rs. 1-8 for full grown animals, Re. 1 for half grown and 8 annas for young ones. The same rates were extended to the Sunamganj subdivision during 1894. In the North Lakhimpur subdivision, a reward of Rs. 20 was sanctioned for any wild buffalo, as declared to be especially dangerous. For the destruction of wild boars which were proved to be dangerous to human being, a reward not exceeding Rs. 1-8 per head was paid in all the districts. After 1894 the North Lushai Hills were brought under the operation of the reward system. A rate of Rs. 25 for the destruction of each full grown tiger was sanctioned experimentally for a period of two years.[20] The rates for killing tigers and wolves were doubled whenever, according to Deputy Commissioner, 'special need exists for so doing'.[21] In 1891 the rate for killing tigers ranged from Rs. 50 to 100, which was normally ranged from Rs. 20 to 25.[22] The reward for the destruction of tigers in Sibsagar, Lakhimpur, North Cachar, Garo Hills and Naga Hills was Rs. 25 but because of the disturbances by the wild animals special reward was asked by the Comptroller of Assam. The reward was thus, extended to the double rate for tiger i.e. Rs. 40 or 50 by the Deputy Commissioner.[23] Thus, an amount of not less than Rs. 25 and not more than 50 could be rewarded for killing a tiger. In the year 1904 the rate for reward was increased

TABLE 14.2: THE SCALE OF REWARD PAID FOR THE DESTRUCTION OF WILD ANIMALS IN 1904

Wild animals	*Districts*	*Rs.*	*A.*
Tiger full grown	Sibsagar, Lakhimpur, North Cachar, Garo Hills and Naga Hills	25	0
Tiger cubs	Ditto	12	8
Tiger full grown	Other districts	20	0
Tiger cubs	Ditto	10	0
Leopard, bears and wolves	All districts except Lushai hills	10	0
Lepard, bears and wolves cubs	Ditto	5	0
Leopard, bears	Lushai Hills	5	0
Lepard, bears and cubs	Ditto	2	8
Hyenas	All districts	2	8
Hyena cubs	Ditto	1	4
Wild dogs	Mokochang subdivision and Naga Hills	3	0

Source: Assam Executive Manual, 1905, p. 131.

for some wild animals and was made more specific, as shown in Table 14.2.

Rewards were not given for all the cases of wild animals killed but a distinction was made between killing for self-protection and killing for sport. A lump-sum grant was placed annually at the disposal of each animal. Within the same limits a Deputy Commissioner had to get approval from the Commissioner, in special cases of rewards in excess of the rates laid down. Man-eating tigers or rogue elephants might constitute special cases. The 'political officers' could also grant rewards on those lines subject to budget and allotments.[24]

The special rewards were also paid occasionally for the destruction of specific wild animals in some districts. A special reward was sanctioned on a experimental basis when the situation arose for the destruction of a particular animal depending upon the disturbance caused. A special reward of Rs. 40 was paid for the destruction of a man-eating tiger in the district of Kamarupa, and a reward of Rs. 50 for the destruction of a rogue elephant in the Golaghat subdivision. In 1881, Rs. 8, 4, 2 was sanctioned respectively for the destruction of boars, sows and sounders in Sylhet district.[25] The discontinuation of awarding for the killing of a particular animal led to the cease of reporting about their death. The Secretary of the Chief Commissioner of Assam viewed that in 1880 the rewards for wild buffaloes having been discontinued because the number of wild animals killed were considerably diminished.[26] On the other hand, the number of persons killed and cattle destroyed by wild beasts and snakes were increased. Bounty killing played a vital role in the destruction of wild animals. However, the increase in rewards did not affect much the killing of wild animals for instance, in 1880 the scale of rewards for the destruction of bears was increased from Rs. 5 to 10 for Darrang and Sibsagar districts. In Darrang district the number of bears killed was only eight in excess of the figures of the year 1879, and in Sibsagar five bears were returned as destroyed during 1880 against none in 1879 which was not much in comparison to the previous year.[27] The wild pigs committed great damages in Sylhet district. Rewards were sanctioned for killing wild pigs in Karimganj but not in the Sunamganj subdivision of Sylhet which was singularly affected. In this division wild pigs caused a greater number of deaths annually and huge damage to crops. To deal with this rewards for the killing of the wild pigs was extended to Sunamganj sub-division.[28] The killing of wild animals can be observed till 1947. In 1944-5 a total sum of Rs. 440 and 12 *annas* was given as reward in the Lushai Hills for killing 7 tigers, 65 wild dogs, 7 leopards, 1 king cobra and 3 cobras.[29]

AMOUNT SPENT ON REWARD

Statistics revealed the nature and amount of rewards given for the destruction of wild animals for 1875-1927. The rewarding giving caused a large number of killings of wild animals. Mahesh Rangarajan argued that the 'there is no question that it tipped populations over the edge in places where habitat was under increased pressure. In fact, the numbers of animals killed for rewards were often a good index of the land deforested for agricultural expansion'.[30] The available statistics shows that a sum of Rs. 6,12,665 was paid for the destruction of 1,68,112 number of wild animals including snakes for a period of fifty years from 1877 to 1927. Out of it Rs. 5,95,955 was paid for the destruction of 78,010 number of wild animals and only Rs. 16,710 was awarded for the destruction of 90,102 number of snakes. The number of animals killed for reward was possibly only a fraction of actual number of wild animals killed. Officials recorded only those cases for which reward was paid. Delay in claiming the reward meant the killing went unrecorded.

For the destruction of a snake on an average only 19 paise was spent. No rewards were given for the killing of snakes in the province till 1880. Only in parts of Sylhet district higher rewards were paid for the destruction of snakes. A reward of Re. 1 was offered by the North Sylhet Local Board for each poisonous snake. This high rate of reward was introduced in 1893, previous to that, no rewards were offered. In spite of this the number of snakes destroyed fell from 495 in 1892 and 289 in 1893 to 99 in 1894, and the amount of rewards paid was also fell from Rs. 45 in 1893 to Rs. 9 in 1894 in this subdivision. The Government of India expressed that no general system of rewards for the destruction of snakes was of much practical efficacy.[31]

Highest amount was paid for the destruction of tigers which was at Rs. 3,37,125, followed by amount paid for the destruction of leopards at Rs.1,65,738, followed by amount paid for the destruction of bears at Rs. 70,179, followed by amount paid for the destruction of elephants at Rs. 7,044, followed by amount paid for the destruction of wolves at Rs. 244 and lastly the total amount paid for the destruction of hyenas was Rs. 52. Other than these, occasionally rewards were paid for the destruction of wild pigs, rhinoceros, wild boars and jackals, etc. In 1882 a sum of Rs. 545 was paid for the destruction of buffaloes, wild boars and rhinoceros. For the destruction of a mad jackal a sum of Rs. 5 was paid in 1885 in Kamarupa district and for wild dogs Rs. 3.8 was paid in 1886. In 1900, a sum of Rs.23.8 was paid as reward for the destruction of 91 dogs in Kamarupa district. An amount of Rs. 5 was paid for the destruction of a single wild dog in Sibsagar and Rs. 6 was paid for the destruction of 2 wild dogs in the Nowgaon district in 1901. In Darrang a sum of Rs. 2.8 was paid for the destruction of a wild dog in 1894. No reward were paid for the destruction of jackals in Sylhet but in Darrang district a sum of Rs. 15 was paid for the destruction of 2 jackals. Some amounts were paid in Sylhet district for the destruction of wild boars which was not paid in other districts. A amount of Rs. 38.8 was paid for the destruction of 514 wild boars in 1895 in Sylhet. Thus, the amount varied from district to district depending on the atrocities by any particular animals in any particular district.

The maximum sum was spent on the destruction of tigers and leopards, because the atrocities perpetrated were more by these animals. 93 per cent of the cattle and 24 per cent of humans were reported as killed by tigers and leopards. Occasionally the rates for the destruction of tigers and leopards was also doubled which in turn increased the destruction of these animals for reward. The bear was

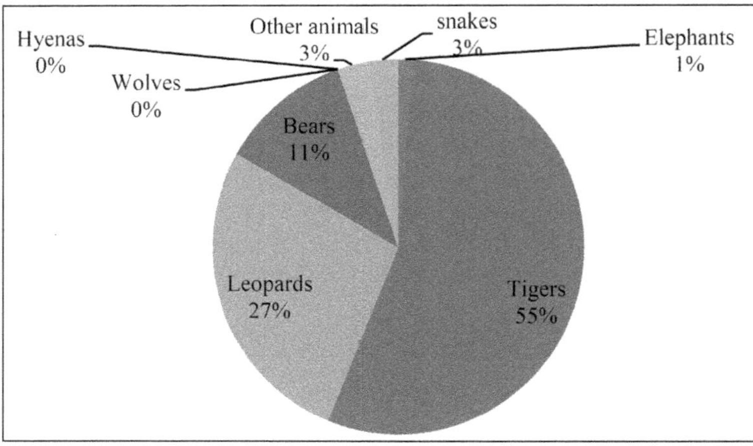

Source: NAI, Home Public A, Report of the measure adopted for exterminating wild animals and poisonous snakes in British India, 1877-1927.

CHART 14.1: THE AMOUNT OF REWARD PAID FOR THE KILLING OF WILD ANIMALS IN THE PROVINCE OF ASSAM (1877-1927)

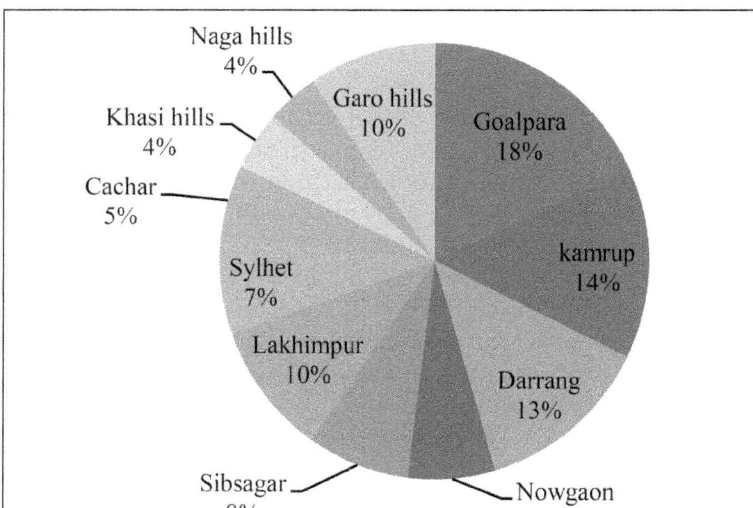

Source: NAI, Home Public A, Report of the measure adopted for exterminating wild animals and poisonous snakes in British India, 1877-1927.

CHART 14.2: THE AMOUNT OF REWARD PAID FOR THE KILLING OF WILD ANIMALS IN VARIOUS DISTRICTS OF ASSAM (1877-1927) next in the list as 11 per cent of the total amount paid for the destruction of wild animals was paid for the destruction of bears. Though it was not much destructive for the cattle as it is reported to have killed only 0.12 per cent of the total number of cattle destroyed by wild animals but it was dangerous for human life. It is reported to have killed 14 people (app.) every year. In case of the destruction of snakes the amount paid for its destruction was very less and that too was paid only in some districts of the province. The amount paid for the destruction of snakes started only in 1881. The amount was paid for the destruction of poisonous snakes only. Rewards for the destruction of poisonous snakes were paid by Chairmen of Local Boards in the plains districts and by the deputy commissioner or sub-divisional officers in the hill districts. Municipalities were not required to pay rewards. The scale of payment sanctioned was Re. 1 for each Ophiophagus and four *annas* per head for any of the following five species – Cobra, Krait (*Bungarus caruleus*), Sankin (*Bungarus fasciatus*), Russel's Viper (*Daboia russellii*), Kupper or Phursa (*Echis carinata*). Rewards were not paid for any other species of snakes.[32] It is reported to have killed the highest number of people, almost 53 per cent of the total number of people killed by wild animals, still not much rewards were sanctioned for its destruction. One per cent reward was also paid for the destruction of wild elephants though it was mostly preferred to capture them than to kill. But in the case of rogue elephants certain amount were paid for its destruction as it proved dangerous for human life. It is reported to have killed 20 people (app.) each year. It also destroyed crops, paddy fields and granaries, etc. Other than these, 3 per cent of the reward was also paid for the destruction of other animals in some specific district, like for snakes and wild boars in Sylhet, for wild dogs in Kamarupa, Sibsagar, Nowgaon and Darrang, etc. Killing for reward was not the only force at work, killing for trophies reached unprecedented levels during British rule.[33]

USE OF MODERN WEAPONS

One of the reasons for frequent killing of wildlife was the liberal issuance of gun and hunting licenses. Pre-colonial weapons like bows and arrows, spear, *dao*, etc., did not cause much destruction to wildlife but after the British came into this province, guns were made available for the people to kill wild animals. This made the killing of wild animals much easier than the earlier. The increase in the destruction of wild animals was more particularly after the distribution of guns among the villagers. In the initial years of the distribution of guns it has been found that most of the gun licenses were given to cultivators in order to protect their crops, cattle and their life, who rarely went in search of game or participated in wildlife hunting. C.J. Lyall, Secretary to the Chief Commissioner of Assam, viewed that, 'many of the guns in use can hardly be described as weapons of precision. Flint-locks and match locks still abound among the rustics who live on the borders of the great forests of the province, and these are used quite as often for scaring away, as for slaying, the nocturnal depredators of the ryots' crops.'[34]

In 1884, the Government of India sanctioned 40 muskets for distribution to such persons as were likely to make use of them in Assam Valley districts for their protection and their crops from wild beasts. Out of these 40 guns, 38 were distributed in various districts. After use of these guns one tiger, five buffaloes, five pigs, and thirteen deers were killed by two guns issued in Lakhimpur, while in Nowgaon a total of ten guns, succeeded in killing only one tiger, one bear, seven pigs, and one deer. The twenty muskets which were distributed in the Khasi and Jaintia Hills was not used much but only one leopard was killed. Though guns were distributed the tribes mostly used traditional methods kill and catch wild animals. Two leopards were caught in a trap near the deputy commissioner's bunglow in Shillong during the winter of 1884.[35] The government of India recommended the killing of wild animals by guns as it was gratuitously distributed, the reason for this could be firstly if they killed with guns it was more responsible and the killing of wild animals could be recorded. Moreover, it was easier to kill wild animals by using firearms. However, Babu Bipin Chndra Pal argued in the INC session of 1886 that the Arms Act prohibited the use of arms by countrymen. Cultivators appealed the government to protect their crops from the ravages of wild animals especially by tigers and leopards for the Arms Act deprived them of means by which cultivators could protect their crops and themselves.[36] Gradually it was realized that the guns should be distributed among the cultivators to protect their crops and their lives. In 1902 a resolution was taken in Allahabad session of INC that the rules under the Arms Act should be amended as to make them equally applicable to all residents in or visitors to India without distinction of creed, caste to ensure the liberal concession of licenses wherever wild animals habitually destroy human life, cattle or crops, and to make all licenses granted under the revised rules of life-long tenure revocably only on proof of misuse and valid throughout the provincial jurisdiction in which they were issued. In 1891 guns were distributed in various districts under the Arms Act in form XI, i.e. for the possession of arms and ammunition for the purpose of the destruction of wild animals or protection of crops. However, The Commissioner of Assam Valley had objection on the free grant of gun licenses. In his words

> I am altogether opposed to the granting of licenses for more than one year. In this frontier province it is necessary to exercise strict check on the trade in arms and ammunition. The only check we have or can have is that we compare the endorsement on the backs of gun licenses with the entries in the vendor's books. Unless gun licenses are filed annually, no proper examination of the endorsements on these can be made.[37]

He feared that guns and ammunition could be misused if it were supplied without restriction. However, gun licenses and guns were distributed and used by the British officials to kill wild animals which led to the killing of a large number of wild animals.

Guns were mostly used by *shikaris* and license holders for killing of game for trade and not for the protection from wildlife. In addition to the free grant of licenses under the Arms Act (1878), government guns were gratuitously distributed to persons living in dangerous localities for protection from wild beasts. It was not only used for the purpose for which it was given out but it was used for the purpose of sport and pleasure.[38] Moreover, prior to 1889 Provincial Government had not given any instruction for the use of these licenses. In 1889 instructions were issued to the district officers to exercise strict supervision over the holders of the government guns, so as to secure the object for which they were distributed, i.e. the destruction of wild animals. Later it was required for the holders of each government gun to kill in each year a certain number of noxious animals for which rewards were paid under the penalty of having the gun taken away from him.[39] But no rules were made to restrict the use of the government guns for game hunting which led to the large number of killing of wildlife for hunting for which no record is available.

The result of the liberal distribution of guns could be seen as in 1894 though the total number of wild animals killed was almost same of that of 1893. A total of 1,608 wild animals were killed in 1893 and 1,606 in 1894. But of the larger number of 'other animals' 524 wild boars were destroyed in Sylhet and Garo Hills, report shows the number of wild boars killed was more than in 1893. In the words of the Secretary to the Chief Commissioner of Assam, 'this increase is said to have been chiefly to the more liberal grant of gun licenses and hunting licenses in the year under report'.[40] Eight weapons were needed for killing a single animal, which shows that the licenses were in most cases not held by persons who used the weapons habitually for the purpose of hunting or even for self-protection, but more commonly for show and the name of the thing though district officers were instructed to search more diligently for man of *shikari* class, and to offer them licenses and assistance in pursuing their profession and keeping down the wild animals which caused serious loss to life and property.[41] Licenses under the Indian Arms Act were given and the number of licenses was steadily increased by 1887. Government guns were also distributed gratis for protection against wild beast in infested localities. It was, however; observed from the returns received from all districts in which government guns were given out that these guns were more frequently used for purpose of sports and for the killing of buffaloes, pigs and deer for sale than for the destruction of dangerous animals.[42] Guns were distributed for keeping down the number of wild animals when it was a danger to life and property. During 1884 thirty-one guns were distributed in four districts of the Assam Valley and with these 156 wild animals were shot.[43] In 1886, 52 guns were distributed with the help of which 201 wild animals were killed, most of these were pigs and deer, but in Nowgong 12 tigers and in Sibsagar 7 tigers were killed with these free guns. On some occasions the killing of wild animals was necessitated for the safety of crops, cattle and human lives and the killing of wild animals was appreciated by people. The Deputy Commissioner of Lakhimpur writes – 'when I was at Sisi and Dhemaji last December, the people were loud in their expressions of gratitude for all the good that the guns (two in number), which I had given out for that part of the district, had done, especially in respect of the slaughter of wild pigs'.[44]

INVITING THE PROFESSIONAL *SHIKARIS*

Appointment of the professional *shikaris* for keeping down the number of wild animals was common during British rule. There were attempts to encourage men of *shikari* class to keep down the wild animals. However, very few natives of the *shikari* class were in the province.

It was confirmed by Colonel Pollock, Madras Staff Corps, during one of his hunting expedition in the province said that, 'we had no shikaris, as none exist in Assam'.[45] Thus, *shikaris* from neighbouring province, Bengal were called up to Assam to keep down wild animals. Earlier also *shikaris* used to visit the province in search of wild animals. In Goalpara alone a few men of the *shikari* class, from the district of Purneah (Bengal), came in search of game. They were induced to take out licenses for a term of five years.[46] These *shikaris* visited Goalpara as it was near to Bengal but Cachar and Sylhet, being on other side were not visited by these men and thus the British government called up *shikaris* from Purneah (Bengal) to these districts to keep down wild animals. These *shikaris*, however, used gins, poisoned arrows, and other primitive contrivances rather than guns.[47] The use of traditional weapons by the *shikaris* was also because killing by firearms had to be registered and they could not be sold in the market.

Even the reward giving was not successful to control the wildlife in the absence of professional *shikaris*. The Secretary to the Chief Commissioner of Assam viewed that 'The success of the system of rewards, in fact, depends a good deal upon the existence of a professional *shikari* class, who can be attracted by them to engage in the destruction of wild animals as a means of livelihood'.[48] Even the increase of the amount of reward paid was not successful in keeping down the wild animals in the absence of professional shikaris.[49] In case of elephants the highest reward of Rs. 50 and 100 was offered for the destruction of mischievous or dangerous 'rogue' elephants but it did not produce any significant effect. Similarly, the increased reward offered for bears in Darrang (Rs.10, instead of Rs. 2-8) was attended in 1883 with an absolute decrease in the number of bears destroyed.[50] In 1882, 41 bears were killed in Darrang district which decreased to 33 in 1883. The killing of wild animals brought large sum of amount for the *shikaris*. In 1883 the *shikaris* from Purneah and the neighbouring parts of Bengal hunted in the district, and made large bags but their absence in 1884 led to the decrease in the amount of rewards. In 1884 Rs. 9422-14 were paid as reward against 10864-13 in 1883.[51]

In addition to the professional *shikaris* tribal chiefs were also volunteered by British officials to hunt down wild animals. The Dolloi or the chief of Nartiang, in the Jaintia Hills volunteered to hunt down wild animals particularly large tigers which were found near the highways to the plains of Nowgaon. Arms and ammunition were also supplied to them by the government.[52] Occasionally, the Kacharies also used to trap or poison wild animals for rewards. In Mangaldai in 1885 a party of Kacharies brought 9 tigers, 6 bears and 2 leopard skins as a result of a month's operations with poisoned arrows in their *mauza*.[53]

Shooting parties were also organized to keep down the wild animals. In 1894 in Lakhimpur, shooting parties were organized for the pursuit of some tigers, which killed many cattle on the churs of the Brahmaputra, near Dibrugarh.[54] Police parties were also given the task of keeping down the number of wild animals. In 1894 a police party was sent to Khasi and Jaintia Hills to kill a man-eater which reported to have killed 4 people but it was without any success.[55]

Other than these the killing of wildlife for sports by British officials also contributed to the destruction of wildlife as they did not observe the true sportsman's rules or ethics. 'The Deputy-Commissioner remarks that tigers and other animals are constantly being killed by Europeans, but as no application is made for reward, nothing is known of the occurrence'.[56] E.P. Gee viewed that true hunting for sports when licenses were obtained and shooting rules were observed was never a depletory factor, on the other hand the presence of genuine sportsmen in a forest area on a regular basis could be a deterrent to poachers. He also viewed that, 'but in a country like India where wildlife has been so much consumed that there can be no more shooting'.[57] The large-scale destruction of wild animals in Assam was because of the impact of British policies. However, the elite class and native tribes also participated in it. The hunting was a part of tribal culture. But the common Assamese people did not participate in the process of the extermination of wild animals.

IMPACT ON WILD ANIMALS

The policies of government of India led to the destruction of a large number of wildlife and also brought some of the animals on the verge of extinction. As argued by Mahesh Rangarajan that 'The British came to Indian subcontinent with a long history of systematic campaign to exterminate carnivores in the British Isles'.[58] Balakrishna Seshadri argued that, 'nowhere in the world has destruction of the natural wilderness – the habitat of wild life – proceeded with such speed and totality as on the Indian subcontinent. It has been the most decisive factor in the catastrophic diminution of India's wildlife – within and outside the sanctuaries – in the last twenty-five years'.[59] The clearance of jungle was mainly to provide timber for the newly constructed railways. In the initial years of the British rule wild animals were seen as pest whose elimination was encouraged with monetary incentives. Each year around thousands of wild animals were killed for rewards. According to the available statistics a total number of 1,68,112 wild animals including snakes were killed during 1877-1927. Out of which 90,102 were snakes which is 1.1 per cent of the total number of snakes killed in India and 78,070 were wild animals which is 9.2 per cent of the total number of wild animals killed in India. Out of 78,070 wild animals 21,541 leopard, 17,316 tigers, 12,823 bears and 155 elephants were killed. Wolfs or hyenas were very less in Assam Valley unlike in other provinces of India where the British government attempted to exterminate the wolf along with the tiger and leopard. In Assam the destruction by wolves or destruction of wolves was very less. Only 48 hyenas and 53 wolves were reported to have been killed during 1877-1927.

Other than these wild boars, wild dogs, wild pigs, *gharial* (crocodile) was killed in large numbers. The killing of these animals was not properly reported. The reason for it might be the absence of rewards for the destruction of these animals. Whenever rewards

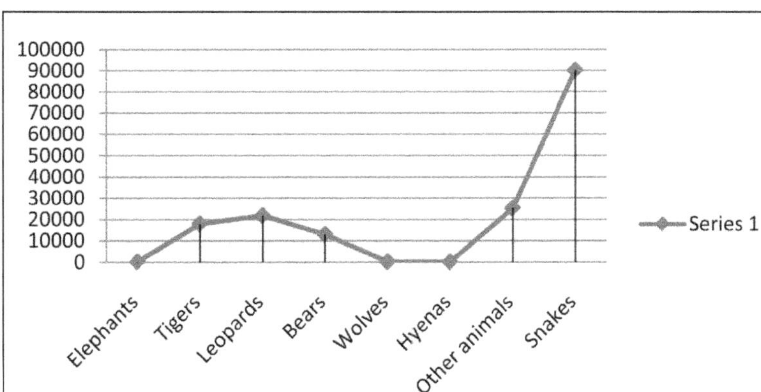

Source: NAI, Home Public A, Report of the measure adopted for exterminating wild animals and poisonous snakes in Britsih India, 1877-1927.

CHART 14.3: THE TREND IN THE DESTRUCTION OF WILDLIFE (1875-1927)

TABLE 14.3: THE DESTRUCTION OF WILD DOGS

Year	1913	1914	1915	1916	1917	1918	1919	1920	1924	1926
Wild dogs	108	123	115	164	156	133	104	131	117	154

Source: NAI, Home Public A, Report of the measure adopted for exterminating wild animals and poisonous snakes in British India, 1914-1927.

were granted by the government the killing of these animals were reported. In 1900 a reward of Rs. 23 and 8 *annas* was paid for the destruction of 91 wild dogs in Kamarupa district. The killings of wild dogs were not properly reported during early years. Table 14.3 shows the destruction of wild dogs in Assam.

Wild boars were also killed in large numbers, 600 in 1912, 691 in 1913, 949 in 1914, 1390 in 1915 and so on. Occasionally buffaloes and crocodiles were also killed. Buffaloes were also killed occasionally, 94 and 21 buffaloes were killed in 1912 and 1913 respectively. 'The extermination of the arna or the great wild buffalo often found enthusiastic support among rice-growers and cattle-herders in the wet savannahs along the Brahmaputra and the Ganga rivers'.[60] Occasionally crocodiles were also killed for rewards like 3, 21 and 54 crocodiles were killed in 1913, 1914 and 1915 respectively. In 1926 five wild pigs were killed. The lack of proper reporting of these animals could be observed. Elephants were mostly captured and not killed because of its strategic needs. Though reward was given to kill rogue elephants but the killing of elephants was discouraged and in some case fined. In Nowgaon *shikaris* were fined for the one unclaimed killed elephant.[61] Still the killing of 155 elephants for reward was recorded. An average of 3 elephants were killed each year for reward during 1875-1927. Tigers, leopards, bears were mostly destroyed for reward. A total of 17,316 tigers were killed during 1875-1927 with an average of 333 per year. In 1921 the highest number of tigers were reported to have been killed, 619, and the lowest number of tigers were reported to have been killed in 1924 which was 175. Among all the wild animals, leopards were reported to have been killed in the highest numbers at an average of 414 per year. The highest of it were killed in 1902 which was 618 and lowest in 1875 which was 150. Bears were also destroyed in large numbers. A total of 12,823 bears were reported to have been killed from 1875-1927 with an average of 247 per year. The highest of it was killed in 1927 which was 621 and lowest in 1876 which was 46.

The statistics varied from year to year. Though the total number of wild animals destroyed was less during 1877 than the preceding year, still it could be noticed that the more ferocious and destructive kinds of animals were accounted for in 1877.[62] In 1877, 434 tigers were killed against 410 in 1876, 188 leopards were killed in 1877 against 175 in 1876 and 58 bears were killed in 1877 against 46 in 1876. Highest numbers of wild animals including snakes were killed in 1893. It was 11,051. But this was because that year 9,443 snakes were killed and only 1,608 wild animals were killed. It was in the year 1915 that the highest number of wild animals were reported to have been killed. Out of it 533 leopards, 327 tigers, 253 bears, 9 elephants, 3 hyenas, 1,390 wild boars, 115 wild dogs, 54 *gharials* and 376 unidentified animals were killed. The rate of destruction of wild animals was very high. Sometimes the destruction of a single species in a single district almost doubled the total number of wild animals destroyed. In 1881, 555 wild pigs were destroyed in Sylhet by the frontier police under the direction of the Deputy Commissioner of Sylhet which led to the increase in the number of wild animals killed from 541 in 1880 to 1,176 in 1881.[63] Thus, the destruction of wild animals was in large numbers. The number of wild animals killed for reward was no doubt very large, still many went unrecorded like those which were killed for sports or for horn and hides.

Thus, the colonial rule witnessed huge destruction of wildlife. The need for the extension of tea cultivation led the British government to adopt measures like rewards giving, sanction of special rewards, liberal distribution of guns and gun licenses, calling up of professional *shikaris* and use of poison. This resulted in the killing of a large number of wild animals, as the given figures indicate. The method of killing of wild animals changed with the British rule. Earlier traditional arms like bows and arrows, spear, *dau*, etc., were used for hunting but availability of gun during British rule made it easier to kill wild animal. Because of the wholesale killing of wild animals in the province elephants, rhinoceros and leopards were brought to the verge of extinction.

NOTES

1. Mahesh Rangarajan, *Fencing the Forest: Conservation and Ecological Change in India's Central Provinces, 1860-1914*, Delhi: Oxford University Press, 1996, p. 139.
2. M. Gadgil and R. Guha, *This Fissured Land: An Ecological History of India*, Delhi: Oxford University Press, 1999 pp. 232-3.

3. D. Downie, 'Do Missionaries Die Young', *The Baptist Missionary Review*, June 1915, vol. XXI, no. 6, p. 256.
4. Gunnel Cederlof, *Founding Empire on India's North-Eastern Frontiers 1790-1840: Climate, Commerce, Polity*, Delhi: Oxford University Press, 2014, p. 183.
5. Rangarajan, *Fencing the Forest*, p. 145.
6. Anon, 'The Game and Game Laws of India', *Qly Review*, 1888, vol. CCCXXXIII, p. 91, cited from M. Rangarajan, op. cit., p. 145.
7. M. Rangarajan, *India's Wildlife History: An Introduction*, Delhi: Permanent Black, 2005, p. 23.
8. NAI, Home, Public A, December 1885, File No. 69-101.
9. A.M. Smith, *Sports and Adventure in the Indian Jungle*, London: Hurst and Blackett, 1904, pp. 103-4.
10. M. Rangarajan, 'Computing the Numbers of Tigers Killed for Rewards in the British India: 1875-1925', Nehru Memorial Museum & Library, New Delhi, 1996, p. 6.
11. Rangarajan, *India's Wildlife History*, p. 32.
12. NAI, Home, Public A, December 1890, File No. 360-407.
13. *Supplement to the Manual of Local Rules and Orders Made Under Enactments Applying to Assam to the 31st March 1901*, Shillong: Assam Secretariat Printing Office, p. 132.
14. NAI, Home, Public A, October 1881, File No. 104-117.
15. NAI, Home, Public, December 1890, File No. 360-407.
16. *Supplement to the Manual of Local Rules and Orders Made Under Enactments Applying to Assam to the 31st March 1901*, Shillong: Assam Secretariat Printing Office, p. 132.
17. NAI, Home, Public, December 1885, File No. 69-101.
18. NAI, Home, Public A, October 1903, File No. 237-235.
19. NAI, Home, Public, September 1895, File No. 211-247.
20. Ibid.
21. Ibid.
22. NAI, Home, Public, November 1892, File No. 227-260.
23. ASA PRFA, Assam Secretariat Proceeding, Home–B, proc. November, 921/923, March 1895.
24. *Manual of Executive Rules and Order in Force in Assam*, Shillong, AGP-1928, Department, General, Section XII.
25. NAI Home, Public A, December 1882, File No. 332-370.
26. NAI Home, Public A, October 1881, File No. 104-117.
27. Ibid.
28. ASA, ASP, Home, Public A, May 1894, File No. 151-156, Sub: Extension to the Sumanganj Subdivision of the scale of rewards sanctuary for the destruction of wild pigs in the Karimganj subdivision.
29. MSA, General department, CB-54, G-668, 1946.
30. Rangarajan, *India's Wildlife History*, p. 32.

31. NAI, Home, public, September 1895, File No. 211-247.
32. *Supplement to the Manual of Local Rules and Orders Made Under Enactments Applying to Assam to the 31st March 1901*, Shillong, Assam Secretariat Printing Office, p. 132.
33. Rangarajan, *India's Wildlife History*, p. 33.
34. NAI, Home, Public, December 1882, File No. 332-70.
35. NAI, Home, Public, December 1885, File No. 69-101.
36. Indian National Congress, Proceedings for the Year 1886, Calcutta.
37. NAI, Home, Public, October 1891, File No. 316-353.
38. NAI, Home, Public, December 1890, File No. 360-407.
39. Ibid.
40. NAI, Home, Public A, September 1895, File No. 211 to 247.
41. NAI, Home, Public A, October 1881, File No. 104-117.
42. NAI, Home, Public A, November 1889, File No. 236-269.
43. NAI, Home, Public A, December 1886, File No. 795.
44. NAI, Home, Public A, December 1887, File No. 126-164.
45. C. Pollok, *Incident of Foreign Sport And Travel*, London: Chapman & Hall, 1984, p. 42.
46. NAI, Home, Public, December 1882, File No. 332 to 70.
47. Ibid.
48. NAI, Home, Public, December 1884, File No. 109-140.
49. Ibid.
50. Ibid.
51. NAI, Home, Public, December 1885, File No. 69-101.
52. NAI, Home, Public A, December 1882, File No. 332-70.
53. NAI, Home, Public A, December 1886, File No. 795.
54. NAI, Home, Public, September 1895, File No. 211-247.
55. Ibid.
56. NAI, Home, Public A, December 1884, File No. 109-140.
57. E.P. Gee, *The Wildlife of India*, Delhi: Sterling Publishers, 1986, p. 8.
58. Rangarajan, *Fencing the Forest*, p. 145.
59. Balakrishna Seshadri, *The Twilight of India's Wildlife*, London: John Baker Publishers, 1969, p. 13.
60. Rangarajan, *India's Wildlife History*, p. 29.
61. NAI, Home, Public, December 1886, File No. 795.
62. NAI, Home, Public A, December 1878, File No. 244-280.
63. Ibid., File No. 795.

CHAPTER 15

Encountering Floods: Colonial State and the Flood of 1916 in the Surma-Barak Valley of Assam

MONISANKAR MISRA

INTRODUCTION

Socio-economic formation in a particular geographical space is always dependent on the type of climate and topography of the prevalent area. Human history is replete with examples of ancient civilizations mostly growing in and around sources of water, namely rivers, seas, lakes, etc. Such sources of water provided sustenance to these civilizations by helping agriculture and communication. Abundance of rainfall was and is a crucial factor that contributed to civilizational growth. For example, Indian civilization over the centuries has depended on timely monsoon and agricultural calendar of Indian peasants evolved as a response to it. But there is also another side of the story. Excess of rainfall have caused largescale flooding leading to destruction of not only property but also human and animal lives. The Andhra flood of 2009 is a case in point. But still, mankind over the centuries in every part of the globe had devised means to cope with natural calamities. It had shown more 'prudence' than 'profligacy' in dealing with 'nature' in pre-industrial/colonial age. However, with the coming of the industrial age, first in Europe and then gradually spreading to other parts of the globe since the nineteenth century, led to a change in the mentality of the people, particularly those in power. A new found confidence in science and technology began to shape their attitude. Developments in science and technology created an illusion that humans can control anything under the sun and be the master of all. 'Nature' was now to be controlled and 'natural resources' were now to be extensively harnessed and exploited for the use of man. In short, 'nature' is to be made subservient to 'humans'. Natural calamities such as floods were now begun to be viewed as obstacles to progress and development. Presence of large-scale forested areas was considered as impediments to the spread of agriculture. Trees became valuable only as timber and state supervision was used for their synchronized and planned felling. All these ultimately led to deforestation, air and water pollution and unsuccessful attempts at controlling rivers by building large dams in different parts of the globe. In the name of progress natural drainage systems were undermined across the planet when railway and road networks were built across flood plains creating more problems and solving none.

Such ideas of dominance over nature came to India with the British. The colonial rule indeed marked a 'watershed' in the environmental history of India. Forests of India virtually disappeared under British supervision to meet their imperial and capitalist needs. Not just forests, but rivers in India were also began to be controlled and worked upon by building extensive networks of embankments and irrigation facilities disregarding the character of the riverine landscape. All these have resulted, as Rohan D'Souza have pointed out, in making 'flood dependent' agrarian regimes to 'flood vulnerable' ones. The people of India were accustomed to annual floods and devised ways and means to mitigate their effects. It became part of their traditional wisdom. Moreover the silt which the inundations brought helped in fertilizing the agricultural fields. But the British had different ideas. They considered floods mainly as a problem and an obstacle in realizing full revenue. So they made attempts to regulate rivers and control floods.

In the context of Indian history, environmental history is comparatively new. It was only in the 1980s that it started getting a proper shape. The colonial impact on Indian forests became the major thrust area of research. Ramachandra Guha and Madhav Gadgil[1] were the pioneers in this field. However, other aspects of ecology remained understudied. In the late 1990s 'water' in colonial India in its variegated aspects came under sharp focus of historical investigation. Rohan D'Souza[2] examined the British attempts at flood control in the deltaic Orissa and thereby opened up new vistas of research in environmental history in India.

The time has come to extend the scope of such researches to include other parts of India such as the Brahmaputra and the Surma-Barak valleys of north-eastern India. The agrarian economies of these valleys have since time immemorial depended on these rivers. Both the river valleys suffer from extensive flooding almost annually.

However, in the second decade of the twentieth century, there were three consecutive massive floods in 1913, 1915 and 1916 in the Surma-Barak Valley. The ferocity and magnitude of which were unprecedented in the annals of the valley and the common people as well as the emerging nationalist intelligentsia started alleging that such floods were ***unnatural***. The traditional coping mechanisms failed in front of such continuous and fierce onslaught of nature's fury. The present paper will try to capture this moment of the past of Surma-Barak Valley when the colonial state faced a severe critique from the nationalist intelligentsia as well as from the European tea lobby, but obviously for different reasons, over the issue of a 'natural' calamity, and how it responded to that criticism.

PHYSICAL FEATURES OF SURMA-BARAK VALLEY[3]

The Surma-Barak Valley during colonial period comprised the districts of Cachar and Sylhet. It was and is an alluvial tract dotted over with small hills and marshy hollows called *haors*. The river Barak or Surma is the chief river which enters the valley from Manipur at the extreme north-east corner and flows south west into the Meghna. The Barak assumes different names before it meets Meghna. At Bhanga Bazar, beyond Badarpur junction it divides into two branches, the Surma flowing north and the Kushiara south. In the early part of the twentieth century, Kushiara became the main stream instead of the Surma which was gradually silting up. The Surma and the Kushiara reunite near Markali. The lower part of the valley is extremely deltaic in character and main rivers split up and reunite, forming many channels. In the beginning of the twentieth century, the population was still sparse particularly in the Cachar district which afforded people to migrate to neighbouring higher or less affected areas in times of heavy inundation.

All the plains portion of Sylhet and Cachar were formed by successive deposits of silt brought down by the Barak and its numerous tributaries like Longai, Manu, Khowai, Juri, Katakhal, etc., from the surrounding hills. The marshy hollows or *haors* play a very important role by absorbing excess flood waters from the river Barak. Some of the important *haors* in the Surma-Barak Valley include Chatla, Hakaluki and Bakri *haors*. During the rainy season these *haors* give the appearance of a vast sheet of water like a sea. In fact, the word *haor* is a derivative of the word 'sagar'. The northern and western parts of the Sylhet district and the central portions of the Cachar district, particularly the areas in and around Bakri and Chatla *haors* are more susceptible to floods as they are more low lying. In addition the mean elevation above sea level of the Surma-Barak Valley is much lower than the Brahmaputra Valley. The cold weather zero of the Surma at Sylhet was only 22.7 ft above sea while that of the Brahmaputra at Gauhati was 148.36 ft at the start of the twentieth century.[4] As a result of which the river Surma was and is very sluggish and tortuous in its movements and leaves a rich deposit of silt in its banks thereby gradually raising the height of the banks. These raised banks are actually used for building habitation sites from a very ancient time and it still continues. The small hillocks (*tilas*) which are spread throughout the valley acts as places of refuge in times of flood. The extremely flat character of the landscape makes it difficult for the flood waters to recede early and any artificial obstruction could only further worsen the situation. This is not to deny the fact that embankments were not built in Sylhet in pre-colonial times. Rather embankments on rivers such as Surma, Kushiara and Manu were very old investments and reinforced by successive generations of rulers in Sylhet region to prevent the land being washed away.[5] As the valley is covered from three sides by hill ranges, the hill rivers when in spate bring down a lot of water which causes flood in the plains even if there is no rainfall there.

The hill ranges around the Surma-Barak Valley experienced one of the heaviest rainfalls at the beginning of the twentieth century. For example, at Cherrapunji in the Khasi Hills, the average annual rainfall is 458 inches and was considered in the last century to be the wettest place on earth. The rainfall in the Surma-Barak Valley is also very heavy, amounting to between 100 and 150 inches annually in Cachar and the southern part of the Sylhet district and between 200 and 250 inches in northern Sylhet along the foot of the Khasi Hills.[6] Owing to this heavy rainfall in and around the valley flooding is a common feature and the British also realized this fact quite early.

EARLY ENCOUNTERS: BRITISH AND THE FLOODS PRIOR TO 1913

The district of Sylhet came under British rule in 1765 when the Mughal emperor Shah Alam granted Diwani to the English East India Company. On the other hand, Cachar was annexed in 1832 when its last ruler Govinda Chandra died without leaving any heir to the throne.

In both the districts immediately after their occupation the British had to face some major inundations. Throughout the 1770s, 1780s and 1790s, Sylhet was visited by mighty floods. The British took up the task of constructing and renovating embankments on the Surma, Kushiara and Manu, after the severe flood of 1784. However, this did not improve the situation and the floods did not abate. The British soon realized that because of the enormity of rainfall, the low level of the country and the complicated character of the drainage system, any attempts to train the rivers would be superfluous. Consequently the embankments were allowed to fall into disrepair and by 1905 only one dyke on a portion of the Surma River was officially maintained.[7] This British apathy in maintaining embankments throughout the nineteenth century was strongly resented by the zamindars. A.J.M. Mills writing in the mid-nineteenth century also opposed the construction of canals, irrigation works or other protective measures. It may be mentioned here that Mills was voicing his concerns at a time when in 1850-2, the district of Sylhet faced a major flood and fresh proposals were put forward to build embankments.[8] The 1870s and 1880s again witnessed some major floods in Sylhet.

The district of Cachar also faced devastating floods in the 1830s which forced the British to reduce the revenue demand of the district by a new settlement in 1839 made by J.G. Burns. In this district also we find the British very cautious in making any hydraulic interference. There was no plan of flood protection or river training for the Cachar district throughout the nineteenth century. As the district was sparsely populated the colonial state was more concerned in inducing peasant migration into the district and increase agricultural output.

The greatest flood which engulfed Cachar in the nineteenth century occurred in 1883 when the whole district virtually became a vast sheet of water and rice and other food products had to be imported from Bengal to relieve people.[9] The earthquake of 1897 did not have much of an impact on the drainage system of the valley except for making river Kushiara the main channel of the river Barak.[10]

THE CONTEXT

Assam and more particularly, the Surma-Barak Valley were visited by three years of exceptional floods in 1913, 1915, and 1916. Of these the last two were especially destructive to crops and property causing distress amounting almost to famine and necessitating extensive relief measures on the part of the British government.

The flood of 1913 was regarded as the 'highest flood since 1883' in Cachar.[11] It occurred due to continuous rainfall in Cachar and the surrounding hills since 28 June. The river level at Silchar which was only 60.52 ft above the mean sea level on 29 June 1913 rose to 74.72 ft on 5 July. It was the highest level reached since 1883. In the Hailakandi subdivision, there was more distress due to overtopping of Katakhal which carried the flood waters of Lushai Hills. The *aman* and *aus* paddy of both the Sadar and Hailakandi subdivisions suffered extensively. The loss of cattle was also severe. However, human mortality was only twelve at Cachar and none at Sylhet. At the height of the flood people took refuge in temporary *machans* and *tilas*. There was luckily no shortage of rice in the district except in the Bakri *haor* region of Hailakandi subdivision where rice was sent by boats by district authorities. The flood waters started receding from 6 July and distribution of rice at relief centres was stopped from 11 July. In Sylhet district the worst affected parts were the Jaldhup thana of Karimganj subdivision and Golabganj thana of Sadar subdivision. Significantly, at the latter thana it was reported by the Deputy Commissioner of Sylhet that greatest harm was done to crops because of insufficient waterways in the railway line between Sylhet and Fenchuganj. Agricultural loans were distributed where necessary.[12]

The year 1915 was again a year of disastrous floods for both the districts. During May to July, both Cachar and Sylhet virtually remained under water. In Cachar continuous heavy rainfall for more than two weeks led to a rise in the Barak and Katakhal rivers. The rainfall at Silchar for the week ending on 5 June was 13.03 inches and that of Hailakandi 21.20 inches which was heavy by any means. The river level at Silchar reached 72.82 ft on the 9 June.[13] The greatest damage to crops was done in the villages around Bakri *haor* of Hailakandi subdivision and the three paraganas of Jatrapur, Phulbari and Rajnagar in the Sadar subdivision. In these localities more than 75 per cent of the crops particularly *aus*, *dumahi* and *asra* varieties were destroyed.[14] However the town of Silchar virtually escaped inundation except for the low lying areas.[15] By the end of June water receded to normal levels. But, even before people could get a breather, another flood of still greater vicissitude visited Cachar district in July. In a letter dated 13 July 1915, H.A.C. Colquhoun, the Deputy

Commissioner of Cachar informed the Commissioner of the Surma Valley and Hill districts that by 12 July, the level of the Barak reached 77.43 ft which was 2.71 ft higher than that of the floods of 1913. This time almost the entire town of Silchar was submerged.[16]

On the other hand, the southern portion of Cachar plains escaped lightly as the rivers flowing from the Lushai Hills did not rise to any great extent. The central portions of the district suffered most and nearly all the villages were drowned. A number of houses were washed away completely and *aus* and *asra* crops and *sali* seedlings were almost entirely destroyed. Interestingly mortality among cattle and human beings was not very high. In all 35 deaths occurred and about a thousand cattle were reported to have died mostly because of starvation owing to the lack of fodder. In the north Cachar Hills excessive rains did damage to jhum crops through landslips which also blocked the hill section of Assam-Bengal railway which was reopened only in July 1917. The distress was so much that the government postponed the first installment of land revenue for 1915-16 which fell due on 1 August.[17]

The fate of Sylhet was no different as has been mentioned already. Continuous rainfall started in mid May and by early June, the Surma River was in spate. The rivers from Hill Tipperah brought down flood waters which further worsened the situation. It was categorically reported that the flood waters from Hill Tipperah were initially banked up by the railway line and the roads and by the high waters in the bigger rivers and gradually they were overtopped and lands in the southern part of the district which were usually free from inundation became flooded totally destroying the *aman* paddy. By the middle of June, however the water started receding raising prospect of magnificent *sali* crop. But all hopes were belied when from the end of June began a fresh downpour of rain creating a fresh flood situation. 'This time the floods came almost entirely from the east.' The Surma and the Kushiara rose with great rapidity to a height greater than that of 1913 and throughout the central portions of the district the entire paddy that were resown after the first floods was destroyed, most of the seedlings were drowned and many of the villages had to be deserted. There was large-scale loss of cattle and stored paddy. There were also reports of human casualty. It was estimated by the government that half the normal area under *aus* and more than half of *aman* was destroyed by the first flood and the second flood in addition did considerable damage to *sali* seedlings. It was further reported that out of the 16,00,000 acres of agricultural lands in Sylhet not more than 7,00,000 acres would ultimately become available for late sowing as there was no possibility of immediate retreat of the flood water.[18] As relief to the distressed, the government distributed Rs. 19,57,430 as agricultural loans and Rs. 1,52,087 as gratuitous relief by the end of revenue year 1915-16.[19] The basic purpose of the government to provide such extensive relief was to induce and encourage the peasants to start cultivating at the earliest which would minimize the loss of revenue.

Just as the previous year, within a span of few months a still greater flood visited Cachar and Sylhet in the month of October in 1916. This time the flood was caused by a cyclonic storm which passed over the Surma-Barak Valley between 2 and 9 October. Although the rainfall at these districts were not exceptional, the flood waters that came from the hills particularly Manipur and the Lushai Hills through the rivers Jatinga, Sonai, Katakhal and Barak created havoc in the plains. At Silchar, the highest flood level on 11 October was 78.46 ft which was more than 1 ft above the last year's flood level.[20] The worst affected parts in the Sylhet district were the Karimganj subdivision, Jaintia Paraganas, Golabganj thana of North Sylhet subdivision, Kulaura, Rajnagar, Kamalganj thanas of South Sylhet subdivision, and the town of Karimganj and the villages around it which became totally submerged causing serious damage to winter rice, both broadcast and transplanted.[21] In Karimganj sub division it was reported that more than '10 *annas*' of the winter rice was destroyed. It was further pointed out that the 'country (w)as so water logged that probably no test or relief works such as the construction of roads or digging of tanks could be undertaken before January'.[22]

The town of Silchar was again fully submerged leading to considerable damage to Local Board roads and bridges. However, the northern portion of the district did not suffer much. The worst affected parts of the sadar subdivision of the district were Leberputa, Haritikar, Katigora, Phulbari, Jatrapur, Rajnagar, Barakpur, Rupairbaly and Bonraj where '12 to 14 *annas*' of standing paddy were lost. It was calculated by the officials that '10 *annas*' of crops were lost in the district. In The Hailakandi subdivision, the low lying areas surrounding Bakri *haor* suffered most due to the flood waters of Katakhal. Both the *aus* and *sali* crops were totally lost.[23]

The loss of rice crop in Cachar district alone was estimated at something like Rs. 35 lakh. Tea gardens near Chatla *haor* such as Chincoorie, Kathal, Silcuri, Rosekandy, Borajalinga, etc., also suffered losses to a great extent. Comparatively speaking the flood of 1916 was more severe in Cachar than in Sylhet, especially its western portion. Surprisingly loss of human lives was only nine in Cachar and none in Sylhet. The agricultural loan and gratuitous relief were provided to all classes of people including the '*bhadralok* class' whose distress 'knew no bounds'. In Cachar these amounted to approximately Rs. 4.5 lakh, where as in Sylhet, it was around Rs. 11 lakh.[24]

THE ALLEGATION AND THE RESPONSE

Three continuous and large-scale flooding in a span of four years obviously created a lot of apprehension in the minds of people. The emerging nationalist intelligentsia of Assam started voicing their concern as to why was there such repeated massive inundations in the valley. Floods were not exceptional in Sylhet and Cachar districts but the intensity of 1913, 1915 and 1916 floods were unprecedented in the annals of the valley. The traditional coping mechanisms of the people failed in the face of such tremendous onslaught of nature's fury and they virtually became fully dependent on state relief measures. There was a growing feeling that these inundations were caused more by human and preventable factors than natural factors such as excess rainfall. The most important issue which troubled the nationalists was how far the colonial intervention in the drainage system of the Surma-Barak Valley brought about these flooding. The floor of the Assam Legislative Council became the site of critiquing colonial rule and policies as here they could directly confront the British.

However, the first salvo was fired by an Englishman named A.J.G. Cresswell. Immediately after the floods of 1913 he raised the question as to whether floods in Sylhet were more due to railway embankments between Fenchuganj and Sylhet and the silting up of river channels. W. McM. Sweet, replying on behalf of the government in the Council categorically stated that the floods were chiefly the results of abnormal rainfall. Although he did recognize the fact that at least 'locally in part of the Sylhet district they were aggravated by the Sylhet-Fenchuganj road and railway embankment'. It was further informed in the Council that the road would not be restored to its earlier height so as to pose any obstruction in the free flow of flood water in future.[25] It was probably the first instance when the colonial government in Assam accepted *albeit* reluctantly its role in aggravating flood situation.

After the calamitous floods of 1915 and 1916 the Indian members of the Council also started raising issues concerning colonial role in the making of these floods. On 23 October, 1916 Babu Ramanimohan Das a member of the Assam Legislative Council asked the government if it was planning to investigate the causes of repeated floods in the province. He further went on to ask whether the floods were due to incessant downpour or to any breach of any natural or artificial bunds in the Hills. He also demanded from the government information about the possible steps to prevent such catastrophe in future. But as was in 1913, so also in 1916, the government response was that excessive rainfall caused the successive floods. The British were in no mood to accept any allegation forthcoming from the Indians. The question of holding investigations also did not till then get any importance in the official circles.[26]

Meanwhile, conflicting viewpoints appeared in two newspapers about the real cause of floods. One of the newspapers blamed the recent flooding in Cachar to heavy precipitation in the surrounding hills of Khasi & Jaintia, North Cachar, Lushai and Manipur. It was alleged that the enormous quantities of silt which was being brought down from the hills and were deposited in the lower reaches of Barak River and the Ganges estuary almost every year had actually made the outlet to sea of most the rivers going further and further away and as a consequence rivers were mostly widening and shallowing creating more opportunities of bigger floods in the future.[27] On the other hand, another newspaper namely *Capital* virtually ridiculed the very idea that the railway and road embankments had caused flooding, an idea earlier floated by one F.J. Ede, a consulting engineer in the provincial administration in the columns of same newspaper. However, his other suggestion of building protective ring embankment around Silchar to protect it from recurrent floods was not only supported by the editors of *Capital* but was promoted as the most viable measure against floods for the whole plains of Cachar. It further opined that there would have been no floods in Sylhet had *bunding* being resorted to. In the end it urged the government to enquire into the 'sources and causes' of recurrent floods.[28] Interestingly however, H.A.C. Colquhoun, Deputy Commissioner of Assam 'strongly deprecate(d)' the proposal of *Capital* 'to enclose the whole course of the Barak with *bunds*'. He feared that 'if this were ever done, our last state would be worse than the first'.[29]

Apparently the government tried to take a firm stand in opposing any idea that any bursting of 'natural or artificial obstruction' in the flow of the rivers from hills had caused recent floods in Cachar. Nevertheless letters were sent by B.C. Allen, Chief Secretary to the Chief Commissioner to the Commissioners of Assam Valley Districts and Surma Valley and Hill Districts as well as to the Political Agent of Manipur enquiring about the same on 27 October 1916. The commissioners and the Political Agent in their reply basically supported the proposition that it was abnormal rainfall and nothing else which caused the recent floods in the Surma-Barak Valley. The Deputy Commissioner of Cachar and the Superintendant of the Lushai Hills effectively 'dispose(d) of the theory' that obstruction in any of the hill streams had caused floods. However, W.T. Reid, the Commissioner of the Surma Valley and Hill Districts pointed out in his report that

> a disquieting feature in the situation is that when the recent floods occurred, the Barak and Surma rivers were all below their rain level, while the big haors in the Sylhet district were far from full. Notwithstanding all these the flood water did not flow off until irreparable damage had been done to the crops. Whether or not the levels of the main rivers in the Surma valley are altering and drainage is less effective than it used to be are questions for experts to decide.[30]

Surely the opinion in the government circle was divided. The Chief Secretary to the Chief Commissioner believed that it was only rainfall that was to be blamed. However Chief Commissioner A. Earle himself favoured the idea that there might be other factors beyond rainfall which needed proper enquiry.[31]

In the mean time the Government of India in a letter dated 5 December 1916 to the Chief Commissioner of Assam asked him first, to take early steps to investigate the causes that led to exceptional floods and second, to suggest possible remedial measures to mitigate the effects of floods in the region.[32] The pressure of the nationalist intelligentsia also started mounting when no less than three members viz., Radha Benode Das, Ramani Mohan Das and Munshi Riaz Baksh of the Assam Legislative Council again inquired the government whether any full scale enquiry would be conducted to ascertain the real causes of inundation in the Cachar and Sylhet districts.[33]

Under the circumstances, F.O. Lechmere-Oertel, Chief Engineer and Secretary to the Chief Commissioner in the Public Works Department was asked to prepare a detailed report on the floods in the Surma Valley which he duly submitted in November 1917 to the provincial government of Assam. While preparing the report Oertel also took cognizance of the views expressed in the Surma Valley Railway Conference which held two meetings at Sylhet and Silchar between 21 November and 25 November 1916 under the presidentship of Sir Robert Gales, Chief Engineer, Railway Board. Oertel was also a member of the Railway Conference. This conference was organized chiefly to look into the allegation made by the nationalists and others that roads and railway embankments which were thrown across the lines of drainage by the colonial government over the past few decades had blocked the passage of the flow of water and thereby intensified the impact of floods. The specific subjects for discussion in the conference were as follows:

1. a. General question of waterways in railway banks in the Surma Valley.
   b. Waterways on the Sylhet-Fenchuganj section of the Assam-Bengal Railway.
   c. Waterways on the Fenchuganj-Kulaura section of the Assam-Bengal Railway.
   d. Complaints regarding waterways in railway bank between Udna and Gandhi bridges near Satgaon railway station on the Assam-Bengal Railway and over Palki river near Shamshernagar station.
2. a. Possibility of railway extension to Sunamganj and Mohanganj.
   b. Determining the best route for a line from Sylhet to Therriaghat whether via Companyganj, Chhatak or Dwara.
   c. Headway of bridge over Surma for selected route.
3. Waterways on the Badarpur-Silchar section of the Assam-Bengal Railway and whether the railway bank is intensifying the floods in the Cachar district.[34]

After a thorough discussion, the conference virtually admitted the fact that insufficient waterways in the railway embankments did increase the possibility of flooding and recommended that all the railway embankments in the Surma-Barak Valley should be provided with waterways on a scale to ensure that in years of normal flood no such raising of the water level on one side would occur that would cause material damage to crops on that side. Consequently, more waterways and openings were suggested for both the Sylhet-Fenchuganj and Fenchuganj-Kulaura section of the Assam-Bengal railway. Moreover, it was categorically stated that no extension of railways should be allowed beyond Chhatak via Sunamganj to Netrokona across the Sylhet swamps on account of the interference with natural drainage. The proposed railway from Silchar to Dwarband was likewise vetoed at the conference. But on the question of insufficient waterways in the Badarpur-Silchar section of the Assam-Bengal Railway and their probable effects on drainage on and off the Chatla *haor*, the conference suggested a separate investigation to be jointly conducted by the officers of the Public Works Department and the Railways. It was also asked to look into the feasibility of removing Hatiya rocks in the mouth of the Gogra River which was blocking the discharge of water from the Chatla to Gogra.[35]

It may be noted that the Chatla *haor* region was a very important component part of the colonial economy as many of the tea gardens were located around it. It was known in the official circles as Chatla Bil Tea District. Many of these gardens suffered extensively in the recent floods and pressure from the tea lobby for protective measures was very obvious. The members of the Conference made it a point to discuss the problems of tea estates arising out of floods with R.S.J. Hickman, the Chairman of the Chatla Bil Tea District Committee before finalizing the report.[36]

As proposed, the separate investigation was conducted jointly by S.G. Butler, Executive Engineer, Cachar Division and T.G. Cule, Assistant Engineer, Assam-Bengal Railway in the first half of 1917 to enquire into the flood condition of Silchar town and the Chatla *haor* area. Its report was discussed in another conference held at Silchar on 24 July 1917. Oertel also participated in its deliberations. In the meeting it was 'agreed', on the one hand, that railway bank between Silchar and Tillain *tila* did not materially increase the floods at Silchar or at Chatla region nor did it obstruct 'to any appreciable extent the subsidence of the flood waters'. On the other, however, it urged upon the government and the railway authority to provide one opening of 30 ft span on the Cachar Trunk Road just opposite the railway bridge which already had an opening of three spans of 30 ft located about half a mile from Silchar railway station to improve the flow of water from Barak through it. Otherwise, it held the view that the Cachar Trunk Road was considerably below the level of the railway bank and the high floods could easily pass freely over it. Similarly, it was decided to blast away the Hatiya rocks to a depth of 8 ft to ease the flow of water from the Chatla to the Gogra in order to relieve the floods around Chatla and Silchar. Some more minor waterways were recommended in the Chinkuri, Kattal, Dwarband and Sonabari-Narsingpur roads to enable the spill waters from Barak and its tributaries to have a free passage.[37]

As can be seen Oertel was deeply involved in the workings of both the conferences. Therefore, it comes as no surprise when we find that he incorporated in his final report most of the suggestions made by these conferences regarding the waterways in rail and road banks in the Surma-Barak Valley. Besides, he advised the government, that any future expansion of road and railway networks in the valley should be made only after a careful consideration of their possible effects on the drainage of the country. In addition to abnormal rainfall, which he considered to be the primary cause, he blamed extensive *jhuming* practised in the surrounding hills as a determining factor in causing floods in the plains. According to him, *jhuming* had led to forest depletion at the headwaters of rivers coming from the hills. The forests, he opined, acted as 'sponges' which retained the rain and slowly soaked it into the soil. The absence of forest cover had resulted not only in the rapid discharge of flood water but also denudation of soil on the hill sides causing landslips. Thus to him it was to the hills one must go in order to control floods in the plains and suggested the banning of *jhum* cultivation and the burning of trees in the hills as well as creating reserve forests and 're-afforestation' to protect the forests 'at the headwaters of rivers'. Moreover, land reclamation by silt deposit known as *bonificazione* was considered by him to be an important instrument in raising the level of the land and thereby reduce the risk of flooding. He requested the government to take all possible means to promote the process of *bonificazione* and discourage any measure which could come in its way. Moreover, according to him, roads in the low lying deltaic part of the Surma- Barak Valley, 'should usually be kept below high water level', so that floods could spill freely over them and breach them where necessary. Further the government should observe and record flood gauge readings regularly to assess the degree of the rise of riverbeds.[38]

CONCLUSION

The above discussion brings out certain important aspects of the history of colonial Assam in the first half of the twentieth century. Till now the historians have stressed only the political or economic critique of the British rule by the nationalists. That a 'natural phenomenon' such as flood could become a site of contestation for legitimacy was hardly ever thought of. But there is no denying the fact that floods in colonial Assam and the British policy towards it offered the nationalists a scope to develop a critique of colonialism which was unique and very novel. For the colonial rulers floods were simply a hindrance in affecting a full realization of revenue. But for the inhabitants of Cachar and Sylhet it was a question of death or survival. They could clearly realize that the whole character of inundation was changing slowly but steadily under the gaze of colonial state. The areas which were never flooded before now became flooded even with normal rainfall. The ferocity of the floods of 1913, 1915 and 1916 in the Surma-Barak Valley was considered unparalled in the history of the region and believed to be caused more by the policies of the British who had built high road and railway embankments across flood plains which had induced quick accumulation of water and slow discharge and thereby increased the intensity of floods for a longer period of time causing more damage to crops, property and human and animal lives. The need for investigation also arose because of pressure from the tea lobby. Thus two contradictory forces – the nationalists and the tea lobbyists – operated to force the British to identify the causes of floods. The British officials had to walk on a tight rope. They not only had to defend themselves but also at the same time satisfy the British planters.

These they did quite remarkably by holding so-called scientific enquiries as has been stated above. The findings were a foregone conclusion. Hence, the attempt to put all the blame to abnormal rains, a natural occurrence, as the determining factor and over which it had no control, comes as no surprise. No doubt lack of sufficient waterways and *jhuming* in the hills were recognized as possible factors that might have aggravated the flood situation in the province but in the end these were only considered as secondary or peripheral factors. In this connection it might be mentioned here that nowhere in Oertel's report was suggested the idea of lowering the high level of existing railway embankments, the chief object of nationalist critique. He knew it very well that railway lines were the life lines of colonial economy and administration and therefore no suggestion should be made to lower its height which might hamper its smooth functioning, particularly in the rainy season. Very soon his report was put into cold storage as when in 1929 another Commission was set up to enquire into the floods of Assam, the same terms of reference reappeared. Thus, the first major policy intervention of the British regarding flood control in Assam ended in a failure because of lack of sincerity on the part of the British as well as its reluctance to admit its fault.

NOTES

1. Ramachandra Guha, *The Unquiet Woods: Ecological Change and Peasant Resistance in the Himalayas*, Delhi: Oxford University Press, 1989; R. Guha and Madhav Gadgil, *This Fissured Land: An Ecological History of India*, Delhi: Oxford University Press, 1993.
2. Rohan D'Souza, *Drowned and Dammed: Colonial Capitalism and Flood Control in Eastern India*, Delhi: Oxford University Press, 2006.
3. The description of the physical features of Surma-Barak Valley have been compiled from F.O. Lechmere-Oertel, *Floods in the Surma Valley: Their Causes and Remedies*, Shillong: Government Press, 1916; *Report of the Administration of Assam for the Year 1911-12*, Part II (Report), pp. 1-3, W.W. Hunter, *A Statistical Account of Assam*, vol. II, Delhi: Spectrum Publications, 1998 rpt.
4. *Report of the Administration of Assam for the Year 1911-12*, part II (Report), pp. 1-3.
5. David Ludden, 'Investing in Nature around Sylhet: An Excursion into Geographical History', in *EPW*, 29 November 2003.
6. Lechmere-Oertel, op. cit.
7. B.C. Allen, *Assam District Gazetteers*, vol. II, *Sylhet*, Calcutta: Caledonian Steam Printing Works, 1905, p. 49.
8. Hunter, op. cit., pp. 380-1
9. Revenue and Agriculture A, July 1883, Nos. 11-17.
10. Lechmere-Oertel, op. cit.
11. *Statesman*, 6 July 1913.
12. Revenue B, October 1913, Nos. 428-73.
13. Revenue A, September 1915, Nos. 62-128.
14. Ibid., Nos. 129-49.
15. Ibid., Nos. 62-128.
16. Ibid., Nos. 129-49.
17. Ibid.
18. Ibid., Nos. 177-210.
19. *Resolution on the Land Revenue Administration of Assam for the Year 1915-1916*, p 3.
20. Revenue A, November 1916, Nos. 56-91.
21. *Resolution on the Land Revenue Administration of Assam for the Year 1916-1917.*
22. Revenue A, November 1916, Nos. 56-91.
23. Ibid.
24. Lechmere-Oertel, op. cit.
25. *The Assam Gazette*, part VI, 1914, p. 21.
26. Ibid., part VI, 1916, pp. 87-8.
27. *The Statesman*, 25 October 1916.
28. *Capital*, 26 October 1916.

29. Revenue A, June 1918, No. 18
30. Ibid., Nos. 1-72.
31. Ibid., No. 23
32. Ibid., No. 13.
33. *The Assam Gazette*, part VI, 1917.
34. *Proceedings of Surma Valley Railway Conference* in Revenue A, June 1918, No. 20
35. Ibid.
36. Ibid.
37. Appendix B of the *Proceedings of Cachar Flood Conference* in Lechmere-Oertel, op. cit.
38. Lechmere-Oertel, ibid.

CHAPTER 16

Environmental Impact of the Great Earthquakes of 1897 and 1950 on North-East India

SHYMANANDA BHATTACHARJEE

If not from antiquity, as the record reveals, since historical times North Eastern Region of India has obviously been continuing as a mute spectator to a series of devastating earthquakes, and not to speak of the later ones. The historical records of *Ahom* Kingdom alone would be sufficient to place the region as one among the severe-most seismic zones of the World. However, based on other seismic records of early colonial period and the era of post instrumental recording including those of two great ones – widely known as the Shillong Earthquake of 12 June 1897 and the Assam earthquake of 15 August 1950, both measuring 8.5 on the Richter Scale – a more or less well accepted plate tectonic model has also been worked out by now for the region. As the general understanding goes – tectonically north-east India is located in between the two sets of active plate boundaries also forming a part of the great Alpine Himalayan Seismic belt. North of this region is wholly bounded by the Himalayas, i.e. the junction of Indo-Eurasian plates and in the east down south-east, the region is surrounded by another plate junction popularly known as Indo-Myanmar plate junction and towards both east-south east and north direction Indian plate is going below the neighbouring plates. In between the plate junctions, the part of Indian plate with its raised Shillong plateau and the tectonically guided mighty Brahmaputra is virtually compressed to a high degree from both the sides and appears to be pushed more from the south east direction there by making the region a super seismic area already recording a number of seismic events of all categories from micro to the great ones.

The region also being located in the thrust areas of south-west monsoon accommodating Cherrapunji, the place of highest rainfall in the world, is rather compelled to bear a huge amount of rainfall every year. Thus, the topography of the region, which many a times have been shaken by earthquake has to further bear the perennial downpour, occasionally intense rainfall, to actually readjust itself almost after every major and great seismic events, i.e. the earthquakes having magnitude of more than 7.0 and above on the Richter Scale. As has already been mentioned above, only during little over last hundred years the region has been shaken by two of the greatest known earthquakes of the globe.

Though *Ahom Buranjis* have recorded a number of major earthquakes including some of their other impacts but regarding their impact on topography of the region, the *Buranjis* are not that explicit. However, during the last phase of Ahom rule, the Assam earthquake of 1762 had certainly made a considerable impact on the topography of the region at least in the southern Assam. This seismic event which originated somewhere in Arakan and was recorded in Chittagong after travelling through erstwhile Lushai Hills, i.e. modern Mizoram.

> By the Chittagong earthquake of 1762, several Hills are described as having been rent as under, sinking down and stopping up the river.... Thus, these examples sufficiently illustrate the extent to which landslips occur during earthquake shocks and furnish striking indications of the great energy of the disturbing forces in operation.[1]

LANDSLIDES AND SINKING OF LAND MASS

Great Shillong Erathquake of 1897

During the 1897 earthquake huge landslides took place in the Shillong Plateau. In Shillong itself four or five major landslides were visible. At places hill debris had fallen from steep *nala* banks, carrying trees and undergrowth with them, and subsequently marked as patches of red soil on the hill. The measure of the largest slides was about 300 feet both in width and height.[2]

On the way to Cherra from Shillong, portions of the road in between 17th to 24th and 29th to 32nd miles went down the hillside bodily, thereby completely disrupting the road link. The impact of the earthquake on Cherrapunji was devastating.

> As regards Cherrapunji and the numerious villages in that quarter, the

apprehension continued much longer. As there was no doubt that the most serious damage had occurred in that neighbourhood, I obtained the Chief Commissioner's permission to despatch Mr. Rita, Subdivisional Officer of Jowai, to Cherrapunji, where the descent of hills is absolutely abrupt, and the country consists of narrow plateaux intersected with valleys from 2,000 to 3,000 feet in depth. At the same time, I despatched Inspector Naba Kishore Dutta with Rs.1,000 to Jowai to endeavour to get up rice from Jaintiapur in Sylhet as a precautionary measure, and in order to restore confidence in that direction.[3]

At Shella too the destruction was chiefly from the landslides. The Laitiam village, where the death toll was 86, was situated almost directly below Mawsmai falls thus suffering primarily from the landslides.

The Green Hillock surmounting the vertical sandstone cliffs of the falls have been shot over so that now there is a long red landslip extending for about a mile horizontally from near the village of Mawsmai along the top of the cliff to the eastward. The western and greater portion of the village of Laitiam was overwhelmed by this shower of loose earth, which must have been dislodged instantaneously. A similar phenomena occurred at Lawshainai, further up the deep gorge which runs from near Tharia to Dympep, 17 miles from Shillong, which has resulted in forming a fine cataract by the denudation exposure of precipitous cliffs of sandstone. Fortunately there was no villager below.[4]

At Kdait village 2 houses were completely shattered by a landslip killing all the 8 members. Similarly at Maomang village 8 deaths took place in their millet field by landslips. The villages lay in the deep valley of Wah Ru between the Nongkredem, Thanjinath ridge, and the central ridge, which commencing at Suair, ran south, opposite to and beyond Cherapunji and was divided from Cherapunji by another deep valley, which ended at Dumpep and Suair.[5]

Under the Palasbari tahasil in Kamrup district, one village, named Sapartari, in mauza Chayani subsided to some extent and was over flooded. The people took shelter in another village. In the same tahsil, chars in Brahmaputra were reported to have subsided. In Chhaygaon Pantan mauza a village named Lankhar was reported to have sunk down a few feet and the people, with their cattle, took shelter on the hillside. Coolihati village near Sessamukh and Pakergonah, south of Sessamukh subsided. Village Garigaon, in mauza Ramsa along the Brahmaputra also sunk down a few feet.[6]

In 1897 earthquake landslips being very common were visible

from Tura in almost every direction with fewer number to the north. This happened wherever the ground was steep and not formed of solid rock. At Tura the landslips were mostly in the southern side of the station and southern spur suffered most. There was a huge slip to the south of DC's bungalow, the whole hillside from the head of the *nala* to the parade ground on the western extremity of the spur had slipped down more or less. The inspection bungalow and charitable dispensary situated on small spur displayed similar effects. On the south sides, half the knoll, on which the clerk's houses were built came down. On the northern face landslips were fewer and smaller, only a few rocks had fallen. The spur on which the mission compound was located suffered least but the high hill behind that was scarred all over.[7] Cracks were very common and seen everywhere, particularly around landslips and along the upper edges of sloping ground. Their direction followed the line of the hills. In certain cracks a walking stick could be pushed down to depths of 2 to 3 feet. On the level crests of the spur far from any sloping ground cracks developed in various directions.[8]

In Goalpara there had been considerable sinking of the land in various places, and formation of large cracks in all directions. Subsidence of the bank near the old jail brought the Brahmaputra river dangerously near the bazaar at Dhubri. Huge fissures running east and west were to be seen everywhere at Goalpara town.[9]

The Great Assam Earthquake of 15 August 1950

The landslide area of the region due to the 1950 earthquake mostly spread over between the 94°E longitude, i.e. Ranganadi in the west and to 96°E longitude in the east. Immediately to the east of 94° longitude landslides were seen on the outer hills only. In the inner ranges much land sliding was not noticed to the west of the Subarnsiri, but eastwards landslides increased progressively. The worst affected area was between the Dihang and the Dibang Valleys.[10]

In the epicentral tract

> the region that had suffered extensive land sliding is about 200 miles long and about 60 miles wide comprising an area of about 12,000 sq. miles. As a considerable portion of this region consists of high hill slopes, the total land surface can safely be assumed to be not less than 18,000 sq. miles. From the air-reconnaissance it appears that at least one-third of this area is affected by landslides, say 6,000 sq. miles.[11]

It has also been described as:

In the Lohit Valley the line of erosion extended up to the McMohan line. South of the Lohit, the landslides extended up to the valley of New Dehing. The length from the Ranganadi to the east of Lohit valley is about 200 miles. The height of these hills ranges from the foothills upto 15000 ft. The landslides are more prominent on the southern face of the hills from Subansiri to Dehang Valley.The hills in the Mishmi range have irregular features and so the landslides here are also irregular.The landslides are not confined to the soil cover with vegetation but also include rock formation in many places.[12]

While calculating the volume removed as a result of landslide, the average depth taken was only 10 feet and thereby the volume of debris slashed down the hill was worked out to be at least of the order of 60,000 million cubic yards.[13]

No landslides were reported from the Patkai Burma range south of Noa Dihing, or anywhere in the Naga hills to the south-west of the Patkai hills.[14]

Alluvial plains in the immediate neighbourhoods of the epicentral tract of the great 1950 earthquake were affected severely. Thus, the worst affected areas were the Saikhoaghat, Sadiya, Margherita, Ledu and Jorhat and many other areas in the North Lakhimpur subdivision. In many places subsidence occurred near fissures and sand vents. Fissures and sand vents had a more or less linear arrangement in a number of localities and in some cases continued for a few miles along the same alignment. As usual most of the fissures and sand vents ran parallel to the banks of the existing river and *nalas*, others occurred along the old abandoned courses of rivers and streams. For example the long line of fissuring and subsidence which passed through the Jorhat town marked the old course of the Bhogdoi river.[15] Some fissures had opened and closed. In North Lakhimpur a nine year old girl was caught in a fissure which immediately closed up burying her alive.[16]

Fissures on the ground were also seen in and around the Rima village. Long fissures were cutting across the stoney field, mostly running parallel with the banks of the river, past or present. Fissures were distributed unevenly – in some places numerous fissures lay very close, elsewhere they were far apart. These cracks were seldom more than a few inches wide and two to four feet deep. Sinking of land was also visible here and there in the area.[17]

IMPACT ON WATER BODIES: RIVERS, STREAMS, *KHALS*, *BILS* & THE LIKE

Earthquake of 12 June 1897

The earthquake of 1897 had significantly affected the water bodies of the region. Filling up of tanks, wells, *bils* as well as beds of the streams by the ejected sand was the most common feature that the water bodies of the region exhibited after the earthquake. The earthquake had raised the beds and depressed the banks of rivers in a number of cases. The effect was more prominent in case of small rivers than large ones. Rivers of small width was blocked up and sometimes their courses changed.[18]

The rivers in the northern part of the Sylhet District, which lies more than four thousand feet below Shillong plateau on the immediate south of Khasi and Jaintia Hills were mostly affected by over siltation and that too, the rivers to the west of the Peini River suffered much more than others.[19] Bifurcation of rivers, just where they emerge from the hills into the plains were very much evident after the earthquake. The Punatirth River, the Bhoishekhali, the Chella (or Shella) or Bogapani, the Dolai or Therria and the river Harryganj which rises in the Khasi and Jaintia Hills and falls into the Surma river after entering through the northern border of the Sylhet are examples of this kind. This was due to the post earthquake incessant rainfall in the southern parts of Khasi and Jaintia Hills. The floodwaters, therefore, rushing out of the very steep hills first spread over and then, ran in one or more channels towards the Surma. The rivers at the bifurcation were thus, found to be much wider than where they fell into the Surma. After the earthquake these rivers became very shallow and during the subsequent floods they were the worst sufferers.[20]

The channels which were very little affected during the earthquake were entirely filled in with sand during the subsequent floods. Two rivers of this district viz., the Bogapani or Chella river and Dolai or Bholaganj along with Kulsi river in Darrang district, Noanadi in Kamrup district, the Gara and the Pagla in the Goalpara district were the examples under this head.[21]

Effects on the water bodies of the region caused due to the great earthquake of 1897 were analysed and certain definite remarks and observations made.[22] Some of important categorization made on the basis of detailed scrutiny and observation are given below:

(i) *Beds of the channel became new.* In a few cases, river beds were raised to the same level as the surroundings and banks also collapsed thereby leaving a part of the river entirely dry. The course above the dried part were then diverted, sometimes falling into the old bed lower down and at others, those followed a different course altogether. The Jia Rowta in Darrang, the Krishnai in Goalpara and the Moheskola in the Sylhet district were examples of the former kind and the Kulsi in the Darrang district, the Noanadi in the Kamrup district and the Gara in the Goalpara district were the examples of latter kind.

(ii) Rivers like the Brahmaputra gave very little idea as to the raising of the bed by earthquake. However, the heavy scouring action of the river was referred to as the possible cause for the same.

(iii) Possible causes for the raising of the river beds were identified. First, from the analogy of the filling up of the *bils*, tanks and wells with sand springs, one of the causes of raising of the river beds could be taken to be sand springs. Immediate drying of the Daiphong in the Darrang and Titamari in the Nowgong after the earthquake was the result of such sand springs only. The same might have contributed to the formation of the sand bars. Another cause might have been the upheaval of the bed during the earthquake. The bed of one *khal* at Pykerati village in the Sunamganj subdivision of the Sylhet district and that of another *khal* near Jamadarhat in the Goalpara district were raised. The other principal cause was the deposit of silt and debris brought down by floods. The fourth cause and a very important one was the sinking and slipping in of the banks into the bed of the river causing great effect particularly, in case of rivers of small dimension. Thus, raising of river beds might have been the result of either the joint or separate action of the causes condensed and outlined here under:

    (a) sand springs during earthquake;
    (b) upheaval or swelling of beds;
    (c) silt deposit during subsequent floods;
    (d) falling in of banks.

(iv) The banks of rivers, *khals*, *bils* and hollows were much fissured and had sunk and slipped into the respective bodies during the earthquake. These depletion and sinkages of river banks became very fatal and dangerous to the countryside. In absence of any banks and dykes some of the areas got totally exposed to flood water and suffered great loss. The southern part of the Goalpara district lying to the west of Lakhimpur and the Barpeta subdivision in the Kamrup district were in grave danger as a result of this.

Earthquake of 15 August 1950

The great earthquake of 1950 had a remarkable impact on the rivers of the North Eastern corner of the region in and around the epicentral zone.

Immediately after the primary shock several tributaries of the Brahmaputra river, particularly the Subansiri, Dibang and Tiding were blocked by landslips caused by the violent shaking of the earth. The slip-dam formed out of the huge landslides at Subansiri lasted for four days and ultimately burst out causing widespread havoc to the east of the Subansiri, inundating about 800 sq. miles and thus causing heavy destruction to some villages, tea gardens and other cultivated lands. This flood took about 500 lives.[23] The Kabuli river which was only a small spill channel of Subansiri and was only 250 feet wide in 1947 doubled in width following the earthquake and the subsequent flood because the river was carrying half the discharge of Subansiri.[24]

After the earthquake at Passighat, there was no water in the Dihang river owing to landslides in the upstream thus having created a dam. The water in this huge river, swollen with the rains, accumulated for approximately twenty-four hours before the dam burst carrying all before it and flooding the land adjacent to the river for many miles.[25]

Dihang, the largest tributary of Brahmaputra had been appreciably silted up at and below Passighat and a good deal of erosion had occurred at Passighat. Maximum depth of erosion was 700 feet threatening the town itself. The river had also eroded many large areas around 14th mile of the road to Passighat, necessitating the diversion of the road further inside.

During the rains of 1951 the Subansiri river twice completely changed its course in the plains of North Lakhimpur. At the beginning of the year it followed its old course, with slight change since 1950. By August 1951, all these channels were dry, and a new and a large channel had formed between

Koyam and Baligaon. Then in mid-September, it entirely altered its course westwards, engulfing most of the tea estates of Pathalipam. Vast areas of forest and cultivated rice fields were destroyed during the vagaries of this large river.[26]

This earthquake had profound impact on the river system of the Lohit District for many cascading torrents either altogether dried up or ceased to flow except for a trickling thread of water. Some of the rivers changed their courses considerably while some other seasonal channels were swollen into mighty rivers.[27]

The load and volume of debris, which was collected by the river Brahmaputra owing to this great earthquake and as observed, would surely take considerable period of time to clear up its bed.

Optimistic opinions are that normal condition in Brahmaputra are not likely to materialise for two to four years, other opinions give a period up to not less than ten years. The optimist base their opinion on the supposition that the deposited silt will remain practically static and the river will score a channel for itself through this deposit. Monsieur A. Normandin with a life time of riverine experience reduced his opinion to a mathematical basis and holds that many year will pass before normal conditions materialise and that in the interim there will continue to be disturbed conditions. He gave a period of ten to fifteen year for stabilisation. Col. F.J. Salberg whose acquaintance with the Brahmaputra, goes back to the great flood of 1906 has also recorded his views in a most interesting note and while he records the opinion that there is no question that in time Brahmaputra will re-establish its old regime, he also records that it is impossible to say how long this will take. He also records that in his view, flooding will not occur in the Dibrugarh or Jorhat areas but will occur further down the river.[28]

The silt and debris deposited to the river beds of the extreme corner of the North East and upper Assam after the 1950 earthquake, not only changed the course of many of those effected rivers, but actually the impact was so much that it altered the topography of the region. An observation to that effect is quoted below:

The silting up of this river beds in North East Assam has considerably altered *the* topography of that part of India. The *Lohit at Sadiya*, where it is two miles wide, was believed in March, 1951 to have silted up to the extent of four or five feet; and the *Brahmaputra* at *Murkong Selek* to the extent of eight to ten feet, at *Dibrugarh* some six or seven feet. In addition to this, the adjacent country-side is estimated to have subsided some four or five feet during the actual earthquake, thus affecting a general levelling-out of the area – a stern foreboding of floods in subsequent years, as has already been experienced in 1951.[29]

AGRICULTURE

Earthquake of 12 June 1897

The region suffered a huge loss in agriculture due to the 1897 great Shillong Earthquake, which was further compounded by the flood that almost accompanied the disaster.

Earthquake caused ejection of sand through sand springs in the plain areas, more so in the open cultivable fields – the amount of sand being substantially large. In hill areas destruction arrived through landslides.

Since, there were two floods led by the great earthquake of 1897, their impacts on the ground were superimposed in the district. Large chunk of sand was ejected through the fissures caused by the earthquake. The sands were then deposited over the crops thereby destroying a huge quantity of *ahu* and *bao* crops in the district. The deposits of sand were most extensive in the *mauzas* of both banks of Brahmaputra belonging to the district where the fluctuating cultivation of *ahu* and mustard were carried on. Dakhin Sarubangsar, Pub Chamaria, Paschim Chamaria on the south bank of Brahmaputra were the *mauzas* which were severely affected and Dakhin Barkhetri, Chunga, Barpeta, Bagribari, Rupasis, Bhabanipur, Sarukhetri and Paka were on the north bank. The damage done by the floods which followed the earthquake was much greater than that caused directly by the earthquake.[30]

Mr F.C. Henniker, ICS, Officiating Director, Department of Land Records and Agriculture, Assam while forwarding Mr Lees' report to the Secretary of the Chief Commissioner of Assam made his stand clear regarding the comparison, whether the damages to crops were because of earthquake or flood.

4. The actual damage attributed to the earthquake directly or indirectly is of various kinds. They were:
   (i) Deposits of sand ejected from fissures in the earth at the time of the actual earthquake (worse in Kamrup than in Nowgong).
   (ii) Floods which actually destroyed or damaged crops, cattle and granaries. These floods are said to have been higher than before (vide for instance paragraph 4 of Mr Lees' report). The cause apparently was destruction of river banks and the elevation of river beds, causing rivers to quit their beds and wander over the countryside. This was especially the case with the Pagladia in North Kamrup and the Kopili in Nowgong, besides the Brahmaputra itself.

(iii) Deposits of sand left by the floods referred to Mr Lees remarks, in paragraph 3 of his report, that it is often impossible to distinguish between sand so deposited and that ejected from the soil by the earthquake. I gather, however, that generally the floods deposited the greater quantity. The point, however, is not material. The effect upon the land is the same in either case. Practically, therefore, the damage was only caused in two ways, but it is generally alleged that the earthquake was directly or indirectly the cause of both in the year 1897.[31]

Earthquake of 15 August 1950

Assam Earthquake of 1950 caused landslips of a very great dimension. Those huge landslips had effected the river system of Assam and hence the cultivation in two ways – direct effect and long term indirect effect.

Direct Effect: The river Subansiri was blocked by landslips and logs. But the block could not remain for a long period and eventually burst. The bursting of the block in a length of 15-20 miles, flooded an extensive area along the north bank to a width of about 3 miles on the right and 2 miles on the left. Thereby a large part of the flooded area was silted up by the sand deposit rendering that unfit for cultivation.

Indirect Effect: Raising of river beds of most of the rivers of the upper Assam and of Brahmaputra had certainly warranted floods of bigger dimension for the following few years.[32] As was apprehended, the very next year i.e. in 1951 there was a devastating flood of record dimension in June-July followed by another of similar intensity which took place in September of the same year. This was mainly due to two distinct reasons: firstly rapid runoff of water from the mutilated hills and secondly the incapability of the river to hold more water in the absence of any depth. The two floods of 1951 along with the one of 1950 had destroyed the agricultural crops and thus the produce of the region to its extreme.

The rivers of north-east India were largely affected by the great earthquakes of 1950 and there were different opinions of the experts about the future behaviour of the rivers including that of the mighty Brahmaputra. A few exact opinion of the experts have already been quoted above. One more opinion was that: ‘He also records that in his view, flooding will not occur in the Dibrugarh or Jorhat area but will occur further down the river.'[33]

If vis-à-vis this, the extent of 1951 flood of Assam is seen, the strength of the opinion becomes evident.

> This flood of June-July moved slowly down to Brahmaputra Valley of Assam inundating the north and south banks as it went. Travelling by air from Dibrugarh to Gauhati on July 20th I observed that the flood had receded in Upper Assam, but in Nowgong and Kamrup districts the whole plain from the Himalayan foothills in the north to the Khasi and Jayantia Hill in the south appeared to be a continuous sheet of water, with only trees and the roof of houses showing.[34]

Thus it could be seen that the theatre of at least one flood immediately after a year of that great earthquake had been shifted towards lower Assam. The spread of agrarian field being much wider all along the Brahmaputra valley covering almost the entire State of Assam from upper to lower Assam, the loss of agriculture in 1950 itself was quite huge. Thus it is seen that the flood, another very known calamity of Brahmaputra Valley of the region seems to have a close relationship with the earthquake of the region. In all probability the recurrence of flood in Brahmaputra which has become a regular feature of the region over the years in recent times has its root in the great Earthquake of 1950 and so the subsequent earthquakes has become more devastating for the people of the region virtually changing the over all environmental set or to be precise the eco-system of the region in the long run.

GENERAL IMPACT ON THE ECO-SYSTEM OF THE REGION

In the 1897 earthquake, landslides carrying trees and the other under growth along the southern fringe of the Shillong Plateau as has already been described above had been of a very large dimension. The fissures and cracks that developed on the plateau including the Garo Hills due to this earthquake, made the ground very loose, hence, prone to further quick erosion by the subsequent heavy rainfall and after-shocks. This had obviously resulted in denudation of the hills to a great extent and which in turn had great impact in progressively reducing both the flora and fauna in parts of Shillong plateau and Garo Hills. As recorded, this plateau received around 5,000 after shocks in between 12 June 1897 to 1902 and the obvious result was a huge loss of top soil from the Plateau, particularly Cherra area of the Shillong plateau where the landsslides were great due to the main shock of 12 June 1897. Repeated shaking of the ground continued to make the soil loose to be carried down by the subsequent heavy rainfall in the area. Over the years the loss of top soil has been so much that Cherrapunji is now called a wet desert. In all likelihood the present day Cherra area has become so, owing to its devastating start of loss of top soil in one go with that great earthquake of 1897. The loss of 50,000 sal trees by the side of Jhira lake due to this earthquake had been another irreparable loss.[35]

It was but obvious that the Assam Earthquake of 1950, which had brought down over 60,000 million cubic yards volume of soil along with its dense greenery had along with it damaged a substantial quantity of flora and fauna of the extreme north-eastern corner of the region. 'From the air-reconnaissance it appears that at least one-third of this area is affected by landslides, say 6,000 sq. miles. We have no data regarding the depth of the landslides. The region was covered by tall trees and thick vegetation which are all gone.'[36]

Another important opinion expressed in this respect:

> Official sources estimated the number of deaths as 1,526 and stated that from 25 to 35 percent of livestock, including the interesting gayal or *mithun* (formerly classed as a distinct species, *Bos frontalis*) in the Abor and Mishmi hills, were destroyed or washed away. But as these hills constitute a wild and inaccessible region, no degree of accuracy is possible in computing the amount of damage done there.[37]

The eye witness account supported the view. They often described the same effect as they saw, huge amount of uprooted trees flowing along the Brahmaputra for months together even years. 'Trees and other vegetation of all types from various altitude were torn down and swept away by the rivers. Many of these trees were of coniferous species. A major portion of the driftwood could not be salvaged in the plains, and has passed beyond the Indo-Pakistan border on its way to the sea.'[38]

Mammals in the epicentral tract were the worst victims. By conservative estimate, some 40-50 per cent of the wild animals were certainly killed. Among those affected were the vanishing/endangered Musk Deer (*Moschus moschiferus*), the rare and interesting Takin (*Budoreas taxicolor*), as well as Serow (*Capricornis sumantraensis*), Goral (*Nemorhaedus*), Gaur (*Bos gauras*) and other animals. Due to the subsequent flood of 1951, which was an indirect effect of the earthquake,[39] wild Buffalo (*Bubaus bubalis*), Gaur (*Bosgauras*), Samber (*Rusa unicolor*), Swamp Deer (*Rueervus duvaucelli*), Hog Deer (*Hyelaphus porcinus*) and others were believed to have suffered greatly.[40] It was feared that the Lalli Game Sanctuary, a *chaporee* situated between the Lalli and Dihang rivers formerly teeming with wild buffalo and various species of deer were totally destroyed. Even in July 1951 only about eighteen wild buffaloes in very poor condition could be observed from the air. The floods of September, which completely submerged those *Chaporees*, must have completed the destruction of all wild life which could not escape from these riverine areas.[41] The tigers of the Saikhowa and Dibru Reserved Forests were believed to have been mostly destroyed by the flood of 1951. Birds were also affected to a considerable extent by this devastating earthquake.[42]

Fishes in all the rivers from the Subansiri in the west, to the Lohit, and possibly the Dehing in the east were believed to have been totally destroyed by the liquid mud mixed with decaying vegetation, which came with the phenomenal flood waves after the bursting of the dams.[43]

Capt. Kingdon-Ward, Botanist who was camping at Rima, almost in the epicentral zone of the 1950 earthquake during the event while commenting on the volume of floral loss due to this earthquake in and around its seat of occurrence related the periodic burning of forests going on in the area to that great seismic event:

> It would be incautious at this stage to state categorically that the annual burning of the pine forest for the last fifty years, between Walong and Rima, was responsible for the huge damage done in the arid Lohit Valley, but it seems certain that any further burning will prove completely disastrous. Even without the annual fires, the Lohit Valley is likely to be a perilous place for some years.[44]

The devastating impact on ecology that the great earthquake of 1950 had brought in to the extreme Northeastern corner of this region was further recorded in a government document of Arunachal Pradesh in specific terms:

> The devastations in the wooded hills and valleys brought down countless tons of logs and timbers and vegetations over an wide area were absolutely destroyed as though they had never been there. It was a shocking spectacle, for the entire faces of the hills were peeled off, leaving not a shred of vegetation from the top to the bottom, range after range was stripped off, and hardly

any tree was visible where there were deep forests. The devastating earthquake of 1950 laid many parts of the land bare and desolate.[45]

The floods of 1951 in Assam occupies a special position and for its level of inundation it owes much to that great earthquake of 1950. During the second flood of the year in September 1951, it was officially reported that some 2,000 sq. miles of upper Assam was under water.

Vast timber forests holding valuable plantations of hillock (*Dipterocarpus macrocarpus*) and extensive *chaporis* of thatch, were irretrievably ruined, and much of the wildlife contained therein was destroyed.[46]

OBVIOUS PROJECTION

As has been seen North East India, being a zone of very heavy rainfall had suffered great loss additionally due to repeated earthquakes particularly by the two great ones. The devastation on environment so initiated in the region has had a long term consequence and it seems almost obvious that the same is being continued even now. The Cherrapunji area, which suffered extensive landslides during 1897 earthquake had in one go lost a huge amount of greenery. Therefore, it won't be unjust as already derived that 1897 earthquake has a definite role in determining the present environmental status of Cherrapunji turned 'wet desert'. Thus, the long term effect of 1897 earthquake could act as a guide to judge the long term impact of the 1950 Assam Earthquake in and around the epicentral zone. As a result of the 1950 earthquake, the river Brahmaputra had to bear a colossal deposit of silt and other debris accompanied by the indiscriminate felling of trees. This obviously led to the apprehension regarding the future role of this mighty river in the region. The apprehension found its expression in the words of E.P. Gee as:

> The gradual westward movement of the colossal silt deposits down the Brahmaputra Valley may be completed within a decade or two. But the partial denudation by the earthquake of the hillsides in the catchment areas of the rivers Subansiri, Dehang, Dibang, Lohit, Dehing and all their tributaries, assisted by the indiscriminate felling of forests in all the tribal areas of Assam through the system of jhuming (shifting cultivation), will continue for a long time to cause greater and more accelerated floods in the plains. And until new and deeper channels can be formed by the rivers of these alluvial plains, the widespread flooding experienced in 1951 will be an annual occurrence

and may even worsen. It will probably take some hundreds of years, if not considerably longer, before any satisfactory amount of vegetation can again cover the hillsides mutilated by the earthquake.[47]

As is known, denudation of hilly region has cumulative role and that becomes more so if the hilly area lies in a zone of intense rainfall. It triggers the loss of top soil at a faster rate. The hilly region in turn fails to hold water and so the water comes rushing down to the plains, thereby enhancing floods to the adjacent plain areas down below. The top soil thus eroded, gets accumulated in the river bed, thereby further raising the river beds contributing directly to the cause of flood in the region. If Cherrapunji be any lesson then the rate of loss of top soil after the great earthquake of 1950 along with the rainfall from the hilly epicentral zone obviously warrants a critical watch for hindering any further recurrence of wet desert in those areas of the region. Earthquake, the potential natural disaster of the region is thus a great threat to the ecosystem of the region and demands introduction of continuing educational programme to educate the masses in the region to save its greenery at all cost. For the region, the aforestation is necessary not merely for protecting the region from the envisaged green house effect but for sheer survival of the life form in the region, where Cherrapunji is just a minor hints.

Hence, the great traditional cultural practise of saving the greenery in the name of 'Sacred Forest' needs to be propagated all along the length and breadth of the region and which should be made mandatory particularly for the hilly areas of the region with all seriousness. Adequate earthquake awareness for the region should be a household cultural practise there. People of the region will have to learn to live with earthquakes with all the possible modern and traditional inputs.

NOTES

1. R. Beird, 'Memoir on Indian Earthquake', *Journal of Royal Asiatic Society*, no. 156, 1844, p. 969.
2. R.D. Oldham, 'Report on the Great Earthquake of 12th June 1897', *Memoirs of Geological Survey of India*, vol. 29, Calcutta, 1899, rpt. 1989, (here in after referred as memoirs of Oldham), p. 6.
3. J.C. Arbuthnott, 'Report by the Deputy Commissioner, Khasi and Jaintia Hills', Appendix III in E.A. Gait's 'Report on the Earthquake of 12th June 1897', Proceedings of the Chief Commissioner of Assam, Home, June 1898.

4. Ibid., p. 28.
5. Ibid., p. 29.
6. P.R.T. Gurdon, 'Report by the Deputy Commissioner, Kamrup', Proceedings of the Chief Commissioner of Assam, Home, June 1898, p. 19.
7. A.A. Howell, 'Report by the Deputy Commissioner, Garo Hills', Proceedings of the Chief Commissioner of Assam, Home, June 1898, p. 48.
8. Ibid.
9. H. St. P. Maxwell, 'Report by the Commissioner, Assam Valley Districts', Appendix III in E.A. Gait's 'Report on the Earthquake of 12th June 1897', Proceedings of the Chief Commissioner of Assam, Home, March 1898, pp. 5-6.
10. L.P. Mathur, 'The Assam Earthquake of 15th August 1950', M.B. Ramchandra Rao, *A Compilation of Papers on the Assam Earthquake of August 15, 1950*, The Central Board of Geophysics, Pub. No. 1, Calcutta, 1953 (hereinafter referred as *Rao's Compilation on 1950 Assam Earthquake*), p. 59.
11. Ibid.
12. G.R. Garg, 'Earthquake of August 15th and its Effect on the Topography, the Regimes of the Rivers in North East Assam and Damage to Roads', *Rao's Compilation on 1950 Assam Earthquake*, pp. 65-6.
13. Mathur, op. cit., p. 60.
14. Ibid.
15. Mathur, op. cit., p. 58.
16. Ibid.
17. F. Kingdon-Ward, 'Assam Earthquake 1950', *Himalayan Enchantment*, John Whitehead (ed.), London, 1990, Chap. 20, pp. 236-40.
18. Pandit Matadin Sukul, 'Report by Pandit Matadin Sukul on the Effect Produced by the Earthquake on the Levels, Drainage and Navigation of Certain Parts of Assam', Ch. III, para 17.
19. Ibid., Ch. X, para 87.
20. Ibid., Ch. III, para 20, subpara 3.
21. Ibid., Ch. III, para 18, subpara 4.
22. Ibid., Ch. III.
23. M.C. Poddar, *Rao's Compilation on 1950 Assam Earthquake*, p. 41.
24. Garg, op. cit., p. 68.
25. Ibid.
26. E.P. Gee, 'The Assam Earthquake of 1950', *Journal of Bombay Natural History Society*, vol. 50, no. 3, p. 633.
27. Ibid., p. 12.
28. C.H.T. Seignior, 'Assam Earthquake', *Rao's Compilation on 1950 Assam Earthquake*, p. 62.
29. Gee, op. cit., pp. 631-2.

30. D.H. Lees, 'Report by Mr D.H. Lees, ICS on the Circumstances of the Raiyats of Kamrup and Nowgong District', *Proceedings of the Chief Commissioner of Assam, Revenue and Agriculture*, June 1898, p. 4.
31. F.C. Henniker, 'Report by the Deputy Commissioner, Lakhimpur, Dibrugarh', p. 1.
32. Gee, op. cit., p. 106.
33. C.H.T. Seignior, 'Assam Earthquake', *Rao's Compilation on 1950 Assam Earthquake*, p. 62.
34. Gee, op. cit., p. 104.
35. *Memoirs of R.D. Oldham*, p. 144.
36. Mathur, op. cit., p. 59.
37. Gee, op. cit., p. 630.
38. Ibid., p. 633.
39. Ibid., p. 632.
40. Ibid., p. 634.
41. Ibid.
42. Ibid.
43. Ibid., p. 633.
44. G. Kindenward, 'Caught in the Assam-Tibet Earthquake', *National Geographic*.
45. S. Dutta Chowdhury (ed.), *Lohit District Gazetteer (1978)*, p. 12.
46. Gee, op. cit., pp. 104-5.
47. Ibid., p. 633.

CHAPTER 17

Mythology as a Protest Narrative: A Lepcha Tale

KERRY LITTLE

INTRODUCTION

The multi-modal protest narratives belonging to Lepcha activists in Sikkim incorporate ownership, tradition, culture, religion, and concern for the environment. These themes were the cornerstone messages which were repeated, modified and then codified as a narrative template for a protest movement against several hydro-electric projects slated for, and being built on, the Lepcha Reserve – Dzongu – in north Sikkim.

The Lepchas draw heavily on their folklore and mythology to establish their position as protectors of a sacred place. They talk frequently about the environment, biodiversity, their culture, their traditions, and their 'sacred' relationship with their land.

My work involves recording traditional and contemporary Lepcha stories and examining how modernity and globalization has impacted on Lepchas' connection to their traditions. I am recording stories over two periods of time – the traditional narratives of the distant past, told to me by Lepcha elders, and contemporary narratives that relate to a Lepcha protest against mega hydro-electric projects which are at different stages of development in the Lepcha reserve – and motherland – Dzongu in North Sikkim.[1]

Many of the Lepcha narratives I record are environment narratives for

- The traditional narratives are concerned with the worship of nature, for Lepchas call themselves the Children of Mother Nature and say their creation began with Mount Kanchenjunga, which they call their mother mountain.
- The contemporary narratives are concerned with the loss of nature and how the dams will destroy their physical environment

> and spiritual environment, for when Lepchas refer to 'sacred land' there is no separation between those words – one does not exist without the other.

This paper looks at the 'sacred' as a form of protest and political narrative in Sikkim as it applies to the current Lepcha protest in north Sikkim. It examines the activists' motivations in deploying their mythology and spiritual beliefs for the purpose of protest. I will discuss the Lepcha sacred protest narratives that are occurring now, but will first relate a similar protest in Sikkim that occurred in the mid-1990s. This protest was also about the sacred and also about a dam. It was a successful protest spearheaded by a small group of Sikkimese elite, widely supported by the Lepcha and Bhutia communities of Sikkim, and carried out by the lamas from every monastery in Sikkim.

First, some background on Sikkim and the ethnic communities that collectively form Sikkimese society.

Before 1975 when Sikkim joined the Indian Union, it was a small Himalayan kingdom, ruled by a Bhutia monarch, known as the Chogyal.[2] The writer Patrick French visited Sikkim in the early 1990s when researching his biography on Francis Younghusband and said:

> This tiny, isolated mountain kingdom had the hopeless glamour of a truly lost cause. Trapped between the competing demands of Nepal, India and Chinese-occupied Tibet, it was swept into history in 1975 when that arch-democrat Indira Gandhi sent in troops to depose the last Chogyal. Since then Sikkim has been the twenty-second state of the Indian Union, a forgotten victim of Superpower politics.[3]

There are many in Sikkim who would agree with French's assessment of their state and possibly an equal number who would not. Sikkim's merger with India thirty-five years ago remains a contemporary narrative for the minority Bhutia-Lepcha people, who fought hard to keep the old laws of Sikkim that protected their land and employment rights. These laws are now enshrined in the Indian constitution[4] and are frequently quoted in political discourse in the state. While the official message is one of communal harmony, the status and special concessions for various tribes is a running thread through Sikkim's political and social narrative. Sikkim's ethnic majority (around 80 per cent of the population) are Nepali-Sikkimese who are mostly Hindu; the second largest ethnic group are the Bhutia-Sikkimese (around 12 per cent) who were the early settlers in Sikkim, and the smallest ethnic group are the Lepcha (almost 8 per cent) who are the indigenous people of Sikkim. I mention the ethnic parity of Sikkim not to reinforce the communal impression of Sikkim but because it would be naïve not to. A person's heritage in Sikkim is a very important part of their identity for cultural and social reasons. And the narratives that relate to the two protest movements may have been spoken in a post-merger time but they originate from old Sikkim; a world which permeates new Sikkim like the smoke from the *sang* – or burned conifer leaves – that is wafted into every room of every Buddhist household, each morning as an offering to the gods.

THE BATTLE FOR RATHONG CHU

In July 1995 500 lamas marched through Gangtok to protest the State Government of Sikkim's plans to build a 30 MW hydro-electric power station at the Buddhist sacred site, the Rathong River, near Yuksom in West Sikkim. They carried banners pleading 'please protect our sacred land' and were followed by hundreds of Sikkimese women chanting prayers. The anthropologist Anna Balikci who was doing her PhD field work in Sikkim during the Rathong Chu protest said:

> the movement began in earnest when the Dorje Lopen (abbot) of Pemayangte monastery expressed his concern about the hydro-electric project and its consequences for Sikkim to Sonam Paljor Denjongpa, a Sikkimese who had been sent to study anthropology in America by Hope Namgyal, an American and the then Gyalmo or Queen of Sikkim. The Dorje Lopen told him that the project had to be stopped, but that he was now too old, his hands were tied, and it was time for the next generation to take over. When the Dorje Lopen passed away two days later, Sonam Paljor was left with the responsibility to carry out his wishes; he joined forces with Pema Namgyal and Chukie Tobden who together formed CSS – Concerned Citizens of Sikkim.[5]

Therefore, this movement started in a religious place – a monastery, with an old lama entrusting the future of a sacred grove to a young lama. It was fought on the grounds that Yuksom is a sacred place for it is the first capital of Sikkim where the first King of Sikkim was crowned in the seventeenth century. The area is considered by the Buddhist Bhutia and Lepcha communities as the abode of Sikkim's protective deities. It is the site of Sikkim's most sacred monastery, Tashiding and every year, the water from the Rathong River is collected in a vessel and taken to Tashiding monastery for distribution to pilgrims during the annual Bumchu ritual – the holiest of Sikkim's festivals. The river is said to turn white and start singing.

The contents of the vessel are believed to date back to the seventh century when Guru Rinpoche is said to have stored sacred soil, water and precious jewels in it from all the holy places in India. Each year the water level is checked as an indicator of the times ahead.

In 1994 a report by Sikkim's State Ecclesiastical Department stated that the 'entire area of Yuksom is regarded as the "most sacred" area of the State'.[6]

The battle for the Rathong River raged for two years from 1995-7. It was motivated by regard for the sacred and it was fought in the courts on environmental grounds. The protest narratives were on four key themes: history, religion, culture and the environment. The lamas' protest narrative was clearly about the sacred, the government's initial response was divisive. The newly-elected Chief Minister Pawan Chamling, said he would 'not allow a handful of people to misguide the people in the name of environment, culture and religion and that those who oppose the power projects were going against the government'.[7]

Concerned citizens of Sikkim commissioned an artist to draw a 'sacred' map of the Yuksom area which depicted the holy sites in West Sikkim according to the 'Neysol' text – the religious prayer books of Sikkimese Buddhists used for invoking the guardian deities of Sikkim. This map was published by the media and given to people with an interest in the project.[8]

A 28-day hunger strike by Sonam Paljor ended when the government promised a review committee. At one point P.S. Ramakrishnan, who was then head of Environment Studies at Jawaharlal Nehru University in Delhi was commissioned to do an environmental impact statement on the project. He found that the Yuksom area of Sikkim was a unique case where 'ecological considerations cannot be separated from historical, social, cultural and religious dimensions'.[9]

For the next two years, there were many court delays. The view of the Concerned Citizens of Sikkim was that the matter was 'in the lap of the gods'.[10] Balikci writes that there were also many incidents that served to reinforce the view that the deities were displeased with the development and that to destroy the land would bring misfortune to all in Sikkim. She described several including:

- A forest officer who had written a false report on the status of the flora and fauna in Yuksom was badly hurt in a landslide and on his deathbed confessed to his wife that the supernatural beings of Yuksom were angry.

- A bus accident occurred in Yuksom, killing five people.
- A bus fell down a mountain in front of the house of the Secretary of the Department of Power, killing fifteen people.
- A junior engineer from the power department committed suicide.
- A power department accountant died when his jeep ran off the road.
- An army jeep with ten people went off the road.
- A petrol truck fell directly into the Teesta River.
- A temporary dam built to divert the river at the site of another unpopular hydro project below Tashiding was washed away by monsoon rains, taking with it a bulldozer.

And, exactly two years to the day from the start of the hunger strike (which was 8 June 1995), on 8 June 1997 a major landslide hit Gangtok, killing 60 people and destroying many buildings. Lamas and Rinpoches said the landslide was due to the deities' displeasure over the dam.

The project was eventually cancelled for political reasons for the Chief Minister Pawan Chamling, early in his term with a slim majority, needed a popular 'event' to gain the trust of the Bhutia-Lepcha community. He cancelled the project at the Gangtok football stadium in front of 5000 people.

THE BATTLE FOR TEESTA

While the Concerned Citizens of Sikkim fought for Rathong Chu, a 1,200 MW dam was also announced for the Teesta river in Sikkim. It was objected to by the Dzongu Lepcha community, in particular former Sikkim government minister Athup Lepcha who said the project would uproot the people of Dzongu and that Rathong Chu 'has defiled our holy places'. Following the cancellation of Rathong Chu, talk of the Teesta project in Dzongu died down but in 2004, a group of Lepcha youth from Dzongu formed Affected Citizens of Teesta – known as ACT – and approached Athup Lepcha to be its president. There were six projects slated for inside the Dzongu Lepcha reserve in north Sikkim and a seventh – 530 MW on the border of Dzongu at Dikchu which is now completed. In all, there are approximately 30 hydro projects at various stages of development in Sikkim. The flagship protest was a two and a half year relay strike in

Gangtok and two long-term hunger strikes by firstly two, then three Lepcha protestors.

There are many similarities between the Teesta protest and the Rathong River protest a decade earlier. The protest narratives are along similar themes: the sacred, culture and environment, however the political climate is quite different. Pawan Chamling is still chief minister but he is much stronger politically now than he was in 1995. In 1995 he held just 19 seats in the Sikkim Assembly, now he holds all 32 seats. Dzongu's MLA has also changed. The MLA in 1995 was Congress member Sonam Chyoda Lepcha who opposed the Teesta project. The current MLA – Sonam Gyatso Lepcha – is with the ruling SDF party and is also the power minister of Sikkim. He is not only a defender of the projects, but a strong and influential enabler. The current battle is focused on the 280 MW Panan project.

The Lepcha narratives that concern the sacred contain the threat of what will happen if the land is disturbed.

One of these places is inside Kanchenjunga National Park at Tholung in Upper Dzongu. There is a sacred cave above Tholung Gompa where the Guru Rinpoche is believed to have spent many days and the stories of Tholung are part of the Lepcha activists' protest narrative.

In a letter to Sikkim's chief minister from Athup Lepcha, the president of ACT, attempted to communicate the spiritual significance of Tholung gompa and the living relationship between the late Sikkimese king Gyurmed Namgyal and the Lepchas of Dzongu.

Another special offering has to be made to the late King, Gyurmed Namgyal, whose mortal remains were embalmed in the gumpa [Tholung gompa] by the Lepchas but later had to be cremated by an eminent lama to exorcize and avert evil spirits which appeared in the forms of a man-eater bear and other predators. The man-eater bear killed and ate two persons at the Lingdong village in Dzongu. The man-eater bear was killed at Lingdong village by two expert hunters sent by the Sikkim government. The other predators disappeared after the completion of the offering puja performed by the eminent lama at the gumpa.

In 1976 some persons instigated the ignorant and innocent residents of Gor in Lower Dzongu to abandon the aforesaid custom and tradition of making offerings to the deities and the late King Gyurmed Namgyal, at the Tholung gumpa on the grounds that the rule of the king had ceased in Sikkim. So the residents of Gor did not participate in the Pang Lhasol function at the Tholung gumpa as prescribed even though it was their turn to make the offerings. After two months there was a plague at Gor which killed nine persons within a week . . . realising their misdeed and disrespect to the deities and the late king, they rushed to the gumpa with offerings . . . instantly the plague disappeared.[11]

In the same letter Athup Lepcha cites Guru Padmasambhava's prophecies to reiterate the danger the government is courting if it goes ahead with the projects.[12] First, he proves Guru Padmasambhava's accuracy by relaying prophecies well known in Sikkim to have come true; the coming of Tibetans to Sikkim to spread Buddhism, how a man born in the year of the mouse would be the first king of Sikkim, how the 11th king would be born in the Dragon year and the warning that if a Tibetan born in the year of the Pig became the 12th king, he would be the last. Then, after more proof of prophecies, and acknowledgement that the chief minister had obtained 'rarest merit' by building a statue of Guru Padmasambhava at Samdrupti which was sanctified and consecrated by His Holiness the Dalai Lama and His Eminence the Dodrupchen Rinpoche, a veiled warning:

. . . in the land blessed by the Guru, [the Chief Minister] may kindly not involve himself in activities to cause destruction of beings which cannot express their sufferings. Let us not forget Guru Padmakara's prophecies relating to Sikkim, Nepal and Tibet. We have a few more prophecies of guru relating to Sikkim, but we reserve the disclosure of them at this point in time.[13]

The public narrative of Dzongu as a sacred site for Lepchas has increased since the advent of the hydro projects. Like the earlier Rathong Chu protest, the protestors involved lamas in their protest. They also consulted and involved the Lepcha shamans – the male bongthing and female mun – who have performed rituals to mother nature to appease the deities. A young female nun has performed many rituals relating to the project. I attended one ritual which she performed in the home of a member of ACT in order to protect the family from harm. She also performed a ritual before the second hunger strike and has frequently called on the Lepcha deities to halt the projects. Like the Rathong River protest there have been incidents relating to the projects:

- The Teesta River flooded and many dam workers died.
- Two dam workers were washed away in a flash flood and machinery belonging to the hydro construction company was washed away.

- At the dam site of one project there was a flood and the drilling machine was washed away.
- A hydro company executive was killed in a car crash.
- When water was released at the Dikchu Dam site several people who were in the dry river bed drowned.

These incidents serve to reinforce the belief of the activists that the deities are angry.[14]

CONCLUSION

The Chief Minister of Sikkim said as recently as 12 February 2010 in a speech to other north-east state leaders:

> All the North Eastern States are rich in natural wealth, rich biodiversity, flora and fauna with all the climatic zones. Now it is necessary that the people of the region in coordination with the Central Government devise some competitive mechanism to transform the North East into the richest zone. The only issue that we must pursue is development of the region.

He then, somewhat incongruously followed this statement with

> We are also the custodian of the Himalayan eco-system . . . more than 30 per cent of all biodiversity reserves of the country perhaps is housed in the North East and also recognised as a biodiversity hot spot. We also have rich reserves to help the nation in terms of overall production of energy in different ways.[15]

In September 2001, the Sikkim government published a notification documenting all sacred places of worship and institutions in Sikkim which are 100 years old or more. The notification concerns sacred peaks, sacred caves, sacred rocks, chortens and *stupas* and hotsprings. Interesting, there are no rivers on the list even though the Teesta River is a well-known sacred river to the Lepchas. The second most sacred monastery in Sikkim, Tholung is also not on the list. But putting that aside, there are 48 sacred places on the list and the notification states that the state government do hereby ban the scaling of the sacred peak and also the defilement of the sacred caves, sacred rocks, sacred lakes, Chortens and sacred hot-springs as notified. It is signed by the Chief Secretary.[16]

If I were to take the list and mark the sacred places on a map of Sikkim there would be several official sacred sites in every state. If I was then to overlay that image with the list of 30 hydro projects there would be projects in every state in the same areas the 'official' sacred places.

Balikci noted:

> When wrong actions are performed against the environment, the agents ritually identified as performing these are often outsiders in competition for natural resources, whether it be land, timber or hydro-power. Through the intervention of the supernatural, these agents are identified as the cause of illness and other misfortunes, and may ultimately be perceived as a threat to the survival of the villagers or even of the Lhopo community as a whole.[17]

The Lepcha activists of Dzongu still hold hope that they will protect their land. They have stopped four of the six projects that were inside the biodiversity hotspot of Kanchenjunga National Park; the same biodiversity hotspot quoted by Sikkim's chief minister when he talks about 'rich reserves' and 'production of energy'. Their most recent glimmer of hope has come with a ruling from the Ministry of Environment and Forests stating that the Panan Hydro project in Dzongu must obtain approval from the National Board of Wildlife before clearing any more of the forest for it is within a 10 km radius of a National Park and Sanctuary. If this rule is strictly adhered to then other projects will have to adhere to this ruling for the Kanchenjunga National Park is within 10 km of many other projects.

The news is not good for the now older warriors of the Rathong River battle. Two dams are in construction on the Rathong River – the disingenuously named 99 MW Ting Ting dam and the 88 MW Tashiding project. The members of the former concerned citizens of Sikkim do not have the same energy or resources that they had fifteen years ago. Pema Namgyal's health has not been good for the past couple of years and Chukie Topden was tragically killed – along with family members – in a car accident a year ago. Sonam Paljor is an advisor to the Lepcha protest movement and remains actively vigilant in his opposition to development that impacts Sikkim's sacred land.

When I was recently in Sikkim I spoke to Chotol Lepcha, a lama and religious painter from the Lingthem monastery in Upper Dzongu, which will have a 10 km tunnel built under it if the Panan project proceeds. Chotol spent more than two years protesting the projects. He moved from Dzongu to ACT headquarters in Gangtok, the site of a relay hunger strike, where he conducted a twice-daily ritual at 7 a.m. and 4 p.m. to the local deities to protect Sikkim from the dams. Chotol believes that once the power developers take all the good land and they become landless they will not be able to do prayers. He said: 'If we can't perform religious puja the deities will get angry and destruction will come to the world'.[18]

The Lepcha protest has some things in common with other Indian protests: government lobbying, grassroots support, rallies, court action and hunger strike. Each of these actions is underpinned by the Lepchas' belief that their land is sacred. ACT secretary Dawa Lepcha (who was twice on hunger strike for 63 and 96 days respectively) pointed out that the Environmental Impact Assessment of the Panan project should have included places of religious importance and structure but that they were not mentioned:

> The hills, mountains, springs, rocks, lakes, rivers are propitiated by the Lepchas of Dzongu, but they have all been utterly disregarded by the people who did the EIA. The Teesta stage IV will be destroying the Tingkyong lake, which is the originating place of two Lepcha clans the Hee-Yongmingmoo and the Turyeomoo. . . . The lake is also the home of a rare fish called Denggnu leek . . . believed to be the living original form of the clans from which they took the human form. Hence, the belief is that should this fish perish the clans will also perish.

Ramakrishnan states that 'sustainable development has to be considered in the context of the ecological framework within which the system operates'. I would add that the ecological framework includes the sacred and agree with his assessment that in Sikkim, the sacred landscape is one where people are truly integrated within the landscape unit itself.

Many would agree that environmental history needs to be engaged with scientists to develop a new paradigm for the future. In company with (or 'taking inspiration from') the Lepcha community of Sikkim, I would like to respectfully ask that culture – and traditional wisdom – also be seen as vital parts of that new paradigm.

NOTES

1. In Sikkim Lepchas make up 7.8 per cent of the state's population of 5,81,500 (*State Socio Economic Census*, 2006: 61) however, in the sparsely populated north, where the Dzongu Lepcha Reserve is located; they are 37.47 per cent – the ethnic majority – of the population. The 7,000 inhabitants of Dzongu are almost all Lepcha.
2. Tibetan word which means king of religion.
3. P. French, *Younghusband: The Last Great Imperial Adventurer*, New York: Harper Perrenial, 2004, p. 169.

4. Article 371F was inserted into the Constitution of India in 1975 when Sikkim became the 22nd state of India. It is designed to protect the old laws of Sikkim and the rights of Sikkimese people. Article 371F also provides that the Government of Sikkim shall have special responsibility for peace and for an equitable arrangement for ensuring the social and economic advancement of different sections of the population of Sikkim and in the discharge of his special responsibility under this clause, the Governor of Sikkim shall, subject to such directions as the President may, from time to time, deem fit to issue, act in his discretion. http://www.answers.com/topic/constitution-of-india-part-xxi.
5. A. Balikci, *Lamas Shamans & Ancestors: Village Religion in Sikkim*, London: Brill, 2008, p. 235.
6. Quoted in 'Sikkim: The Sacred Land', *Himalayan News Magazine, Hill People*, Darjeeling: Hill Media Publications, October 1995, p. 10.
7. J. Kazi, 'Row Over Rathong Chu', *Hill People*, Hill Media Publications, October 1995, p. 6.
8. I received a copy of this map in 2006 from Pema Namgyal, a member of CSS.
9. P.S. Ramakrishnan, *Ecology and Traditional Wisdom: The Cultural Dimension of Ecology*, http://ignca.nic.in/cd_07010.htm (accessed on 27 June 2010).
10. A. Balikci, *Lamas Shamans & Ancestors: Village Religion in Sikkim*, London: Brill, 2008, p. 239.
11. Letter from Athup Lepcha, President ACT to the Chief Minister of Sikkim, 16 August 2007, pp. 3-4.
12. Guru Padmasambhava is also known as Guru Rinpoche and Guru Padmakara.
13. Letter from Athup Lepcha, President ACT to the Chief Minister of Sikkim, 16 August 2007, pp. 6-7.
14. These events were reported in Sikkim media. Another reference is www.weepingsikkim.blogspot.com.
15. Keynote Address delivered by the Chief Minister Pawan Chamling at the Summit of the North East MP Forum, Gangtok, 12 February 2010. Full text was published in *Sikkim Express*, 13 February 2010, p. 4.
16. *Sikkim Government Gazette*, Saturday, 29 September 2001, No. 355 Notification dated 20 September 2001.
17. Balikci, *Lamas Shamans & Ancestors*, p. 239.
18. Interview with Kerry Little in Gangtok on 25 November 2009.

Contributors

S. VICTOR BABU is Professor in History in Babasaheb Ambedkar Central University, Lucknow.

SHYMANANDA BHATTACHARJEE is a Ph.D. in History from Assam University, Silchar.

SRIJANI BHATTACHARJEE is pursuing her Ph.D. in Jawaharlal Nehru University, New Delhi.

BIPUL CHAUDHURY is Assistant Professor in History in Dibrugarh University, Assam.

DEBOJYOTI DAS is in Birkbeck College, London.

BINAYAK DUTTA is Assistant Professor in History in North Eastern Hill University, Shillong.

BASHABI GUPTA is Assistant Professor in Geography in Lady Sriram College, New Delhi.

RAJIB HANDIQUE is Professor in History in Gauhati University, Assam.

BAZLUR RAHMAN KHAN is Assistant Professor in History in Nabin Chandra College, Badarpur, Assam.

KERRY LITTLE is with the University of Technology, Sydney, Australia.

MONISANKAR MISRA is Assistant Professor in History in Tripura University, Agartala.

RILA MUKHERJEE is Professor of History in Hyderabad Central University.

SAJAL NAG is Professor in History in Assam University, Silchar, Assam.

SURYASIKHA PATHAK is Associate Professor, Centre for Tribal Studies, Assam University, Diphu Campus.

BIRENDRA NATH PRASAD is Assistant Professor in History in Babasaheb Ambedkar Central University, Lucknow.

KAUSHIK ROY is Guru Nanak Dev Professor of History in Jadavpur University, Kolkata.

GEETASHREE SINGH has completed her Ph.D. from Assam University, Silchar.

Index

For Product Safety Concerns and Information please contact our EU
representative GPSR@taylorandfrancis.com
Taylor & Francis Verlag GmbH, Kaufingerstraße 24, 80331 München, Germany

www.ingramcontent.com/pod-product-compliance
Ingram Content Group UK Ltd.
Pitfield, Milton Keynes, MK11 3LW, UK
UKHW022111190926
475702UK00013B/1383
9781032652474